The Christian God

Augustine Shutte

Edited by
Patrick Giddy

Dominican Scholars Collection

The volumes in this Collection aim to celebrate the quality of work by Dominican men and women scholars whose reputation has been established through a substantial career. They bring together essays, articles from journals and chapters in publications, often showing a development or progression in thinking over time. ATF Press is pleased to celebrate the series that highlights an author's significant contribution within biblical studies, ethics, history, philosophy, theology, the arts or social sciences. The purpose of the Dominican Scholars Collection is to provide a valuable resource for current and future generations by those who have contributed at an international level in their respected field.

1. *From Aberdeen to Oxford: Collected Essays*, Fergus Kerr OP, 2023.

The Christian God

Collected Essays

By
Augustine Shutte

Edited by
Patrick Giddy

ATF AFRICA

Adelaide
2024

ISBN:

978-1-923206-36-6	Softcover
978-1-923206-37-3	Hardcover
978-1-923206-38-0	Epub
978-1-923206-39-7	PDF

SCAN ME

Published by:

ATF AFRICA

Making a lasting impact
An imprint of the ATF Press Publishing Group
owned by ATF (Australia) Ltd.
PO Box 234
Brompton, SA 5007
Australia
ABN 90 116 359 963
www.atfpress.com

Table of Contents

Acknowledgments

Chapter 8, 'Salvation as "Oop Gesprek"', and Chapter 15, 'Seeing Life as the Creation of Character', first appeared in *New Blackfriars* 51 (1970) and 65 (1982) respectively. Chapter 10, 'Religious Laws: the Christian Problem', Chapter 14, 'A Philosophy of the Human Person for Contemporary Theology', Chapter 19, 'How Jesus Saves Us', Chapter 24, 'The Possibility of Faith Today', and Chapter 25, 'Euthanasia and the Theology of Death' appeared first in the *Journal of Theology for Southern* Africa 15 (1976), 41 (1982), 55 (1986), 80 (1992) and 102 (1998) respectively. Chapter 13, 'Indwelling, Intersubjectivity and God', first appeared in the *Scottish Journal of Theology* 32 (1979). Chapter 17, 'What Makes Us Persons' and Chapter 20, 'A New Argument for the Existence of God' appeared first in *Modern Theology* 1 (1984) and 3 (1987) respectively. Chapter 22, 'Community, Apartheid, and the Metaphysics of Humanity in Genesis 1–11' and Chapter 29, 'Evolution and Emergence: A Paradigm Shift for Theology', first appeared in *Philosophy and Theology* 2 (1987) and 22 (2010) respectively. Chapter 28, 'Telling the Christian Story–by Karl Rahner and me', was published first in *Scriptura* 98 (2008). Chapter 27, 'Evil and the Christian Response' was published first in C du Toit (editor), *Can Nature be Evil or Evil Natural?* (Research Institute for Theology and Religion, 2006).

Preface

Augustine Shutte, who died in 2016, was a South African philosopher and theologian, who taught for forty years in the Department of Philosophy at the University of Cape Town. He is most known—through his books *Philosophy for Africa* (1993) and *Ubuntu. An Ethic for a New South Africa* (2001)—as someone who saw and was able to articulate how the African traditional understanding of humanity, expressed through the term '*ubuntu*', could well be a useful corrective to the materialism and dualism that has characterized modern Western philosophical thinking. For the positive intersubjective transactions enabling personal growth and community—core of the African cultural outlook—may also, he saw, be a way of unpacking religious faith in a non-mythological way suited to a contemporary scientific thought-world.

Augustine was formerly a member of the Dominican Order of Preachers in the Catholic Church. The slogan of the Dominican Friars, *Contemplata alliis tradere*, pass on to others the fruits of your reflection, could very well be applied to his own life. In Cape Town his most recognizable image was that of the teacher. Listeners picked up, even when their intellectual background was too thin to allow them to grasp everything, that here was something of profound value. This was not only in the lecture halls of the university, but in the many popular extramural lectures series he gave to the public, often on philosophical aspects of religious faith and its relation to our scientific knowledge. And in the School of Theology at the university chaplaincy which he co-founded, and that fed the minds of generations of catholic students. Or talks to any number of different groups, high-schools in the Cape Town area, Quakers, University of the Third Age,

Dominican Sisters, the university medical ethics research group, or the Seminary where he began his teaching. The collection of essays presented in this book records a theology maturing over a period of fifty years, from an orthodox, but progressive, understanding to a version of the Christian faith in a secular and scientific age open to all religious traditions. As an introduction to the essays, Augustine Shutte has added his own narrative of this development. In a final chapter, written by myself, I trace further developments in Shutte's thinking, drawing on his notebooks and his religious poetry.

Augustine Shutte's other books are *Philosophy for Africa* (1993), *The Mystery of Humanity* (1994), *Ubuntu. An Ethic for a New South Africa* (2001), and a collection he edited with the help of a Templeton Foundation grant, *The Quest for Humanity in Science and Religion* (2005). A book of his poems, *The Way Home. Poems for the Human Spirit* (2017), was published posthumously. His novel, *Conversion*, set largely in the Dominican priory in Stellenbosch in the later 1960s, is available in a Kindle version under his 'secular' name, Michael Neale-Shutte.

A short account of the Dominican Priory in Stellenbosch, where Augustine studied theology, and the various influences the Dominicans had on the intellectual movements in this heart of Afrikaner establishment during the Apartheid years, is given by Andrew Prior in the book of tributes to Augustine's long-time colleague and fellow South African Dominican, Albert Nolan, *Reluctant Prophet*, ed. M. Deeb, P. Denis and M. James (ATF Press, 2023).

Patrick Giddy
School of Religion, Philosophy and Classics,
University of Kwazulu-Natal
South Africa

Bio of editor

Patrick Giddy studied philosophy at the University of Cape Town graduating with a PhD (1994), with a thesis, supervised by Augustine Shutte, on the neo-Thomist ethical approaches of Alasdair MacIntyre and Bernard Lonergan. He lectured in philosophy for some years at the University of Lesotho before moving to University of KwaZulu-Natal, Durban, where he is currently a Senior Research Associate. Recent publications include: 'A Theological Response to Secular

Public Policy', *Irish Theological Quarterly* (2023); 'Basic Intuitions in African Ethics', in Chimakonam and Rodrigues (eds) *African Ethics. A Guide to Key Ideas* (Bloomsbury Academic, 2023); 'Traditional African Philosophy of Mind: Facilitating a Dialogue,' in Attoe et al (eds) *Conversations on African Philosophy of Mind, Consciousness and AI.* (Springer, 2023).

Chapter One
An Autobiographical Introduction to the Papers

I studied philosophy before I studied theology. And I developed my own philosophy before I developed my own theology. In fact it was philosophy that brought me to religion. In my second year at university I started to think my own thoughts and very soon stepped out of the Anglican Christianity I had been brought up in. For a year or so I was a questing atheist. I say 'questing' because my atheism was not a settled system but rather a rejection of all established religion. Towards the end of my first year at university I had read a book that changed my life, Colin Wilson's *The Outsider*. From then on I saw myself as an Outsider, outside all settled systems of thought and faith, but driven to find, or better, create one of my own. I was an atheist in quest of a god I considered worthy of the name.

In my third year at university I decided to take the Ethics course taught by Martin Versfeld. And there I began to find what I was looking for. In the first place I was forced to think, really think, in a systematic and self-critical way. And to think with passion, as though my life depended on it, as Versfeld did. Martin Versfeld was a mixture of Socrates and Kierkegaard. And what is more he was, to my amazement, a Roman Catholic Christian. After one year with him I took another. And step by step my study of philosophy (Versfeld's course's name was a misnomer; it was about ethics certainly, but equally about metaphysics and philosophy of mind, not to mention political philosophy and philosophy of religion.) took me closer to what I was looking for. It was St Augustine however (in whom I recognized a spirit kindred to both my own and that of my professor), and in particular his *Confessions*, that finally seduced me into a (still very abstract) form of religious faith.

I had a girlfriend then who was a devout Anglican so it seemed quite natural (though in fact it was quite illogical) for me to practice my new faith at her side. I still knew virtually nothing of Christianity and certainly nothing to revise my negative view of the Church. Nevertheless I was now nothing if not a whole-hearted believer and aspired to a whole-hearted practice of my faith. Guided by the counsels of clergy I eventually sailed for England and the Oxford seminary of Cuddesdon to train for the Anglican priesthood. There for the first time I had to come to terms with the fact that Christianity was embodied in the Church, a historical institution with a history of its own.

For the following three years I wrestled with this history, and with the actual present reality of the Church in its Anglican form. As a philosopher I required clarity and universality, or in a word absoluteness, in what I believed and the actual Church I was experiencing fell short of that. The Roman Catholic Church however was not afraid to make such absolute claims, and gradually I fell in love with it. When in 1963 I joined the Catholic Church it was precisely its claim to absolute authority and historical continuity that were the deciding factors. While still an Anglican I had decided to try my vocation to the religious life. And so after a couple of years as a Catholic I entered the novitiate at St Nicholas Priory, the Dominican House of Studies in Stellenbosch, where I spent the next six years studying philosophy and theology.

Theology at St Nicholas Priory was very different from theology at Cuddesdon. It was thoroughly philosophical, in the classical European tradition of Plato, Aristotle, Augustine and Aquinas, with special emphasis on the last since Aquinas, apart from the virtual canonization of his thought by the Catholic Church, was one of the first Dominicans. And at the priory, now secure in what I believed to be the authoritative tradition of Christianity, I began to exercise my critical powers on my faith. This was indeed encouraged by the Order, which had a repetition not only for orthodoxy but also increasingly at the time of the Second Vatican Council then in session, for prophetic criticism of the Church. *Aggiornamento* was in the air we breathed during the sixties in the Catholic Church.

These two principles, that of a certain infallibility of the Christian tradition in essential matters of faith and morals, and of the possibility of finding good reasons for what the Church taught, were the foundation of my theology as a Dominican. The first the theological papers I wrote as a Dominican was on a topic given me by the then prior, Fr Guy Braithwaite, who was my tutor, and which I entitled 'Jesus Now'. Fr Guy wanted me to explain how a person who lived and died two thousand years ago could be present to and influence people now. I have kept my youthful title. In this early paper, written with a certain passion, I am already wrestling with the doctrine of the Incarnation, especially that of the divinity of Christ, since if he were just a man his presence and influence would be no different from any other heroic and saintly figure form the past. And I try and solve the problem by means of the notion of love. Jesus, I say, lived a life of perfect love and since according to the first letter of John 'God is love', there is a sense in which Jesus, though a man, is divine. Not very satisfactory, but at least I recognize that there is a problem. The link between the person in the past and people now is his continuing presence in the Church. This too is a matter of love, a spirit present in lives and communities, but articulated in the Church's moral teaching—which I insist is really just an application of the idea of love to every aspect of life.

The next paper, 'The Prayer of Jesus', is also concerned with Jesus' relationship to God. I had read Rahner's article '*Theos* in the New Testament' and so had no trouble identifying the one Jesus referred to as Father (Abba) as God. But with Jesus himself it was not so easy. The paper is all about Jesus' human consciousness of his intimate relationship to God and of his mission to humanity. I explicitly reject what I call the 'conjuring up the God-in-a-human-skin spectre of the hypostatic union'. But I feel obliged to claim that Jesus' death was both the full realization of his humanity as well as 'a realization of himself as the Word and so of his transcendent relation to the father.' I chose this formulation in order to avoid claiming that Jesus knew he was the second person of the Trinity; I nevertheless assume that he was.

This concern to connect the belief in Christ as God with his death also appears in the next paper, 'The Motive of the Incarnation'. Though here it has the additional function of avoiding the idolatry of worshipping a merely human saviour, since death is the negation of all purely human power. My main aim in this paper is however to argue for a version of the Scotist view that sin was not the ultimate reason for the Incarnation, as Aquinas thought, but the personal union between God and man achieved in Jesus. My reason for thinking this is that this is the appropriate fulfillment of a positive desire for God in human beings which is deeper that the negative reality of sin. God's main purpose in the Incarnation is to inspire faith in Jesus as God's personal presence among us, which faith as a comprehensive human attitude would also undo the effects of sin.

In 1968 the courses taught, both philosophical and theological, centred on the person and work of Jesus, traditionally known as Christology and soteriology. And at the end of the year, as a form of examination, we were required to compose a synthesis that included all the elements taught. This was to show that we had seen how the different bits all hung together and were able to make them our own. 'Christology Now' is my synthesis. This paper is the first of these early theological essays to include an idea that became a permanent part of my theology, that of the human predicament. If Jesus is the saviour of everyone then there must be something common in the situation of everyone that requires this, namely a predicament we all share but are unable to overcome. Further, it must be possible to give an account of this in ordinary non-religious terms that even unbelievers can understand. From the point of view of Christian faith the general form of this predicament is that human beings have natural desires that only a transcendent power can fulfill. Our own attempts to fulfill these desires by means of powers under our control result in a negative situation from which we need to be saved. In this paper I do not actually identify these desires but speak in a general way of a desire for identity or self-possession. Aquinas spoke of a natural desire for the vision of God and for eternal life, but I am concerned to find secular forms that such basic desires take. In general they amount to a comprehensive desire for an unlimited good that we mistakenly and futilely attempt to satisfy with goods that are limited, such as health or wealth, prestige or power.

The second part of the paper deals with Jesus as our saviour. And here again I am trying (unsuccessfully) to find a credible interpretation of the Christology of Chalcedon. I introduce the idea of the relationality of personhood and try to see whether that is capable of giving a coherent account of Jesus' relation to the Word of God. It doesn't, and the paper ends with an admission of defeat. At the same time however I raise the possibility that Jesus' human uniqueness might be the thing to concentrate on in any future development.

The next two papers focus on the theology of the Church and sacraments. The first, 'Sign, Symbol and Sacrament' deals with the very notion of a sacrament as developed in the history of Christian theology. This has two sides to it: it is a kind of sign or symbol and it is a cause of grace in us. At the end of a long development Aquinas puts the two together in his idea that the sacraments 'cause by signifying'. In my paper I point out that this is just what words do in human speech. A good example is a marriage vow; when the couple say 'I do' the marriage comes into existence. The Christian sacraments cause those who receive them to be united to Christ since what they signify are the *mysteria carnis Christi* the acts by which Jesus revealed and fulfilled the saving purpose of God. The effect of this paper is to 'personalize' the sacraments, depicting them as a personal communication with Jesus in which the meaning of his life is communicated to empower the recipient with his spirit.

The second of these two papers, 'The Church and the Sacraments' was written as the synthesis of that year's (1969) study. In it I put forward an interpretation of the Christian notion of a sacrament that is based on distinguishing different forms of Jesus' presence to us: his presence to his disciples before his death, his presence in the resurrection 'appearances', his presence in the members of the Church, his presence in the eucharist and finally his presence to us in 'the Second Coming' or in heaven.

Applying the idea of presence to that of a sacrament I make use of the work of both Schillebeeckx and Rahner, current at the time and which I had studied. Schillebeeckx's famous book *Christ the Sacrament* was required reading then. In it he developed the idea that Jesus himself was the primal sacrament, the manifestation of God's presence in human persons. And to this Rahner added the idea that just as Jesus was the sacrament of God so the Church was the sacrament of Christ; just as God was present and revealed in the human life and person of Jesus, so was Jesus present and revealed in the total concrete historical life of the Church. The sacraments traditionally so called were simply particular expressions of this. The eucharist however, because it was the act in which the Church gave complete expression to its nature, was the fundamental sacrament of Jesus' 'real presence' and our 'holy communion' with him and God. Finally, the Church as the primal sacrament was also to be seen as both the sign and cause of the 'unity of humanity in union with God' that the Second Vatican Council speaks of as the goal of Christ's saving work.

An interesting point made in this paper is that Aquinas' explanation of how sacraments cause grace (precisely by signifying it) represents 'the final stage in the secularization of the idea of mystery in sacramental theology.' The sacraments are no longer to be thought of as 'supernatural' actions, a kind of 'white magic'. This is in tune with his teaching regarding the incommensurability of God and creatures; God is not a 'supernatural' addition to natural things but in everything as their transcendent cause. You cannot add God and the universe and make two!

With that we come to the end of the papers I wrote as a Dominican student but which were never published. At the same time however I wrote another article towards the end of 1970 that was. The journal it appeared in was *New Blackfriars*, a Dominican periodical edited by Herbert McCabe of the Oxford priory. The article was called 'Salvation as *Oop Gesprek*'. I need to say a bit more about it, not because of any particular merit it has but because it reflects very well the intellectual situation of South Africa at that time and the position we Dominicans occupied within it. In fact I first gave it as a paper at a Dominican conference at La Verna, a retreat centre on the Vaal River, where we met to review our life and mission in the light of Vatican II.

My paper, and the article stemming from it, was based on my reading of a book that had recently appeared in South Africa entitled *Beweging Uitwaarts* (The movement outwards), causing quite a stir in Afrikaner circles. It was a collection of critical essays by three well-known Afrikaner intellectuals: Stellenbosch philosopher Johan Degenaar, my old professor Martin Versfeld, and the historical novelist W A de Klerk. The notion of *Oop Gesprek* (Open Dialogue) comes from the Introduction by Degenaar, and the whole collection was an attempt to break out of the closed circle (the *laager*) of Afrikaner culture and politics. *Oop gesprek* connotes both 'dialogue' and 'free speech' and, as Degenaar explained, 'The *oop gesprek* is *oop gesprek* precisely because in it the relational character of meanings, the provisionality of premises, the continual discussableness of standpoints hold pride of place.' In my article I use this idea to define the political role of the Church and within it the prophetic function of Dominicans to break the hold of its ossified tradition. I found an article by WA de Klerk 'Inflasie van die Woord' (Inflation of Language) particularly helpful in this regard. He focuses on the political rhetoric of Afrikaner nationalism as a prime example of what he calls 'lying language', language that lies because of inflation. I produced even better, even more extreme, examples of such 'lying language' from papal encyclicals. And then I comment on them: 'Here it is again: the same lying language, the same concern for self-maintenance and hence for unity, obedience above all. And here too the lying language both conceals and reveals the same myth, that of identity: the one true Church, against which the gates of hell shall not prevail; infallibility that consists in pronouncements that are irreformable; tradition that enshrines unchanging truths; a philosophy that is perennial with which to understand them, and even a language that is immutable in which to express them. Surely the myth of identity has never found a more perfect embodiment.' One can see why that arch-rebel Herbert McCabe would lick his lips at this.

I wrote another paper that year that has never been published. It was called 'The Problem of Communicating Religion in a Secular Society' and was given as part of a series of public lectures at the UCT Summer School of 1971. It carries a personal interest for me because it contains many of the ideas I was dealing with in my as yet unfinished thesis with Degenaar. His influence on it is easy to see. The problem was the same problem I was grappling with in my thesis: religious doctrines (certainly Christian ones) were formulated in terms of a pre-modern sacral world-view whereas contemporary believers naturally expressed themselves in terms of a secular one. After describing in some detail the differences between these two world-views I focus on what I regarded at the major flaw in the contemporary outlook—the fact that it tends to forget the fact that a human being is a *subject* who creates and judges science as well as an *object* that science can study. I then went on to explain our subjectivity as living in a world of meanings as well as things, so that one's identity as a subject consisted in the meaning one gave to one's life as a whole. And central to the truth and authenticity of this meaning was the meaning we gave to the last event of one's life, the event in which it finally existed as a whole, namely one's death. This was so, I felt, whether one was thinking of the meaning of an individual's life or of human history as such. And this was precisely what Christians were doing when they claimed Jesus' death as the climax of our salvation. Rightly understood Jesus' resurrection was not a distinct event that in some way undid his death but the salvific meaning (and power) of his death as such, as an offering of love.

This focus on human subjectivity, by which I meant our unique capacity for self-consciousness and self-determination, was to be a permanent part of my personal philosophy. And the idea that it found its fullest expression in an act of self-giving love was eventually to bear fruit in the detailed analysis of intersubjectivity of my doctoral thesis. But that lay ten years in the future. In 1971 I was assigned to the Dominican community at Hammanskraal that ran the seminary for Black students for the priesthood there, to teach philosophy. My career as a full-time lecturer was beginning and, as a consequence, my literary production ceased for the time being. I was simply too busy preparing lectures to compose articles for publication. The only exception was one entitled 'Man's Search for Meaning' which I wrote at Hammanskraal as the first chapter of the Theology By Extension Course the Dominicans were then mounting.

During 1971 I ended my membership of the Dominicans in order to marry and at the beginning of 1972 I took up a position in the Department of Philosophy at UCT where I stayed for the rest of my academic career until the end of 2009. For the first few years at UCT my intellectual energies were almost wholly taken up in preparing courses so very little of mine appeared in print. Although my lectures at UCT were devoted to philosophical topics I was still just as interested in theological ones as I had been in the Order. In addition to my lectures in the Philosophy Department I gave evening courses in the Department of Extramural Studies. I also became involved in the newly-founded Kolbe School of Theology in Cape Town. This had in fact been started by the Stellenbosch Dominicans when they decided to move their House of Studies from Stellenbosch to Cedara in Natal, as a way of continuing their work in the Cape. Albert Nolan was the director and when he moved away from the Cape I was asked to take over. The Kolbe School of Theology answered a real need, among both lay people and religious. It was also ambitious, attempting to cover (albeit at only a certain depth) the whole field of Christian theology in three years. And with an ever-dwindling staff! When I first became involved there were four or five of us; within a couple of years there was only me! Distinct from the basic course in theology, the school also put on each Lent a series of public lectures on current topics of theological interest. These were extremely popular with attendance averaging between two and three hundred. Needless to say they were organized, and often given, by the director. Two of the talks I gave are included in this collection, the first given early on, the second a few years later.

'Religious Laws: The Christian Problem' was given in 1976. The problem I was thinking of was the way many (if not most) religious people think of religion in terms of obedience to some religious authority whose commands or laws have some divine sanction. And I was able to use the work I had done in my Master's thesis on Kant and Hegel to criticize this in view of the value of the freedom which those authors stress. On the other hand I try to offer an alternative to a radically individualistic notion of freedom as autonomy by stressing the relational character of truly personal life. Accepting the moral authority of a person (Jesus for instance) need not necessarily be destructive of one's freedom; it could even be an enhancement of it. However in the case of the authority of an institution or a religious official, human freedom required the participation of all those bound by religious laws in their formulation and promulgation. This might seem an obvious requirement of social justice, and indeed is one of the pillars of Catholic Social Teaching as far as civil society is concerned, though not (alas) when it comes to the Church.

The other talk, given some years later, 'Do Lay People Have a Vocation?' unlike most of the papers and articles in this collection is full of a certain wry humour. As an ex-religious and priest I was in an unusually good position to be aware of the shortcomings of those with 'vocations'. The talk is thus very critical of the institutional arrangements in the Church, especially of the bureaucracy of the hierarchy. But the positive evaluation of secularity is the animating spirit of the final section where I suggest the necessity of a new 'lay' spirituality for the whole Church. I distinguish three 'ages' of the spiritual life in Christianity: the first age is that of the *fuga mundi* (flight from the world), exemplified by monasticism, the second is that of the apostolic life, exemplified by the mendicant Orders such as the Franciscans and the Dominicans as well as by more modern ones such as the Jesuits, the spirituality being based on the distinction between the sacred and the secular and the aim being to be *in* the world but not *of* it, and now a secular spirituality that sees the world as its home and seeks to make it homely. I think this is the only really original idea in the talk. It certainly caused a stir at the time.

Early in 1979 I presented the paper 'Love of Persons: Unselfish Love as Manifestation of Spirituality' at the annual conference of the Philosophy Society of South Africa and it was later published in their Proceedings. In this paper I deal with my favourite theological theme of love in a thoroughly philosophical way, basing my treatment on that of Aquinas. And certain ideas that would become central to both my philosophy and my theology make their first appearance.

There is first of all the notion that persons are spiritual beings. This was something I was to expound and defend again and again in various ways since the philosophical climate at English-speaking universities was, and is, so overwhelmingly materialist. UCT was no exception to this: Versfeld had retired and the new appointments were all from the anglo-American analytical school, physicalists to a man.

Then there is an analysis of interpersonal relationships in terms of the Aristotelian notion of friendship. This is extended, with the help of Aquinas and Augustine, to the relationship between us and God. I attempt to show that unselfishness is as natural, indeed even more so, than self-seeking love.

I even use my analysis of interpersonal relations to outline the basis for a new kind of natural theology, arguing that our experience of unselfish love, whether given or received, is in fact an experience of God's creative action in our lives.

The rest of 1979 I was on sabbatical in England, mainly in Oxford but also in London. Alan Ryan, the New College political philosopher, had been a visiting professor at UCT several times in recent years and we had become friends. And as luck would have it he was also on sabbatical, spending the year at Princeton. So he very kindly lent me his New College flat, his house in Camden and his little Renault car! So I was able to work both in Oxford and in London with a simple connection between them. In Oxford I worked mainly at Blackfriars with Herbert McCabe and Fergus Kerr, using their excellent philosophical library. In London I worked at Heythrop with Gerry Hughes and used their even better philosophical library. For most of the year I was working out in greater detail my philosophical anthropology, in dialogue with kindred spirits instead of critical physicalists. The results of this appear in later articles in this collection. The major influence on me in this endeavour was the work of Karl Rahner in the philosophy of persons. Towards the end of the year I came up against another aspect of Rahner's thought in a surprising manner. I was in the library at Heythrop (in its former situation in Cavendish Square) when the front cover of the current number of *The Thomist* caught my eye. The whole number was devoted to a monograph by Andrew Tallon of Marquette University on Rahner's understanding of persons and the relationships between persons! I read it from cover to cover at a sitting scarcely able to believe my eyes; it was as though I had written it myself! In many ways Rahner's conception (as described by Tallon) was similar to Macmurray's. But the difference in depth and philosophical scope was huge. I immediately wrote a long letter to Tallon, telling him how close our thinking on this topic was. And he at once wrote back inviting me to Marquette. I cut short my stay in England and spent a month at Marquette, talking to Tallon and reading two papers to his department. One was the paper on unselfish love I have just described, the other was 'Indwelling, Intersubjectivity and God' which later appeared in the *Scottish Journal of Theology*.

In this article I am concerned to show how a philosophical understanding of intersubjectivity can help one to make sense of a pervasive feature of Christian theology, namely the notion of indwelling that characterizes the relationship of Christians to Jesus and to God as well as their relationship to one another in the Church. What is expressed in the metaphorical and mythical terminology of the New Testament can be understood in the precise philosophical terminology of philosophical anthropology. The article is constructed on a foundation of Macmurray's work but builds on that with insights from Rahner and others, the French personalists in particular. The references show the wide range of reading I had been doing in the latter part of my sabbatical.

In 1981 I completed a doctoral thesis entitled 'Spirituality and Intersubjectivity' in which I tried to show that what is traditionally known as the spiritual dimension of human persons reveals itself especially in certain peculiar characteristics of intersubjective relations between persons. The most striking characteristic, and that which my thesis was especially concerned to illuminate, is that whereby our capacity for freedom of choice and action is enabled to be exercised and to develop the *more* and not the *less* we are influenced by *certain kinds of relationship* with other persons.

'A Philosophy of the Human Person for Contemporary Theology' which appeared in the *Journal of Theology for Southern Africa* in 1982 is an attempt to show the relevance of the philosophy of my thesis for formulating the fundamentals of Christian faith in a scientific and secular age. In it I identify the chief problem facing faith in the dominant culture as materialism, both theoretical and practical. There are two versions of this the individualistic version of the capitalist West and the collectivist version of Communism. And there are two inauthentic Christian responses corresponding to these: dualistic fundamentalism and a baptized communism. In their place I put forward my own version of existentialist Thomism, following Rahner and the authors I had used for my thesis. In conclusion I insist that a *secular* (that is, philosophical) understanding of human persons is essential if one is to make human sense of *sacred* realities such as grace and sacraments and, in general, religion as such.

My thesis also lies behind the article 'Seeing Life as the Creation of Character' that appeared in *New Blackfriars* in 1982. There it has an explanatory sub-title: 'A Talk Given in South Africa'. I think I gave it as a talk at another of the annual conferences of the Catholic Theological Society of Southern Africa. In it I am concerned to distinguish the way God acts in human life to save and sanctify us both from the 'supernatural' influences and interventions of the traditionalists and from the purely secular forms of institutional and political change of some of the liberationists. I am trying to reveal something in our ordinary interactions with one another that is genuinely *mysterious* because transcendent but not at all *unusual*. And in this attempt I have in mind two groups in particular whom I am addressing, my Christian students and my atheist colleagues.

Quite different in both topic and tone is a paper I wrote in 1982 for a conference of the Catholic Theological Society of Southern Africa, of which I had recently been made chairman: 'Ecumenism Today'. It is quite a 'progressive' piece in a Catholic context in that it extends the ecumenical interest of the Church far beyond specifically Christian denominations to include other religions and those with no religion at all. The basis for the Church's role as a 'focus and facilitator' of integral human development (which I take as the secular equivalent of salvation) is its belief in God's presence in the human nature of everyone and in human history in Jesus and the Church as his 'sacrament'. The Church thus has it in her to be 'an expert in humanity' (Pope Paul VI's phrase) and to exercise this expertise in the service of development and peace. I am however highly critical of actual Catholic practice in this regard, and especially of the way it understands and exercises authority which I accuse of being 'deeply unChristian'. I also affirm the uniqueness of God's presence in Jesus, and thus in the Church, in a way I no longer would. I now see this as a matter of degree rather than of kind. Personal presence is a relational concept and depends on both members of the relationship: from God's side, as it were, there is no difference between God's presence in Jesus and his presence in me, the difference is all from our side. Jesus' uniqueness consists of his insight into his unity with God and the inspiration with which he lived it. Both insight and inspiration (Word and Spirit) are of course the work of God and hence it is true to say that God is more fully present in his life than elsewhere.

The next article in chronological sequence, 'What Makes Us Persons?', is even more directly derived from my thesis. In it I am concerned to offer my own phenomenological account of the necessary intersubjective conditions for the exercise, growth and fulfillment of our specifically personal capacities to overcome what I judged to be the inadequacies of Macmurray's account. And I am doing this so as to expose the errors of a physicalist understanding of persons and in the process providing a foundation for an argument for the existence of God, on the lines of that given by CS Lewis in *Miracles*. As far as theology is concerned I also argue that my account of interpersonal relations provides a better analogy for the relationship between Creator and creature than any traditional one. I had just spent a month of study leave in Oxford where I met Ken Surin, who was editing a new journal published by Blackwell's *Modern Theology*. We spent many happy hours in discussion in a variety of Oxford pubs and found a lot of intellectual common ground. He invited me to send him something for his journal. I did so, and 'What Makes Us Persons' appeared in the very first number. Three years later he published the sequel to this article, 'A New Argument for the Existence of God', in which I attempt to fulfill the promises I had made in it.

Before that however come two other articles, one for my physicalist colleagues in the Philosophy Department, the other for Christian theologians of whatever kind. In 'Persons are Transcendent' I bring together all my arguments for the spiritual nature of persons. I then go on to explain why human persons, although material as well as spiritual beings, must not for that reason be seen in a dualistic way. Instead we are possessed of a radical unity of being, but a unity that is constituted by a duality of relationships. There is an inner relationship to oneself as a spiritual being that makes us self-conscious and self-determining. And there is a relationship to what is other than oneself as material, to other members of one's own species primarily but to the rest of the non-personal world as well. And being a human person means that we cannot realize the internal relation to self without engaging in the external relation to what is other than oneself. A paradox, I argue, but not a contradiction.

The other, theological, article, is 'How Jesus Saves Us', and is a *tour de force* of my own 'secularised' version of the essentials of the Christian faith. There are a lot of biblical references but the article is focused on the famous seventh chapter of Paul's letter to the Romans with its brilliant account of Paul's own experience of the need for 'salvation'. It attracted a lot of interest from non-Catholic theologians for the unusual way in which I explain the notion of 'justification by faith'.

The article 'A New Argument for the Existence of God' is, in my own mind, the most important in this collection. Together with 'What Makes Us Persons?' it provides a succinct summary of the thought of my doctoral thesis, which in turn is the foundation of my system of theology. And because of its special phenomenological character, the fact that it is intended to be empirically (though subjectively) verifiable, it brings the spheres of philosophy and theology closer together. So I am especially glad that it is reappearing in this collection. Over the years I have had some scholarly responses to it. One in particular has made me glad, that of Sebastian Moore. He wrote me a long letter saying that it presents in an explicit way a line of thinking that is implicit in all his work but which he had never been able to formulate to his satisfaction. Still I hope that its reappearance will provoke further thought in such kindred spirits, both philosophical and theological.

The article 'Understanding Forgiveness' has never been published. It is in fact a detailed examination of the real-life situation in which the interpersonal causality that produces personal integration and growth (which I describe in my thesis and refer to in so many of my writings) actually occurs, namely that of conflict between and within human persons. This is a situation characterized by ill-will and suffering, and forgiveness, both given and received, is the mechanism whereby personal growth and community are achieved. I reveal in my analysis an unlimited dimension to such an interpersonal transaction which indicates the presence of a transcendent power. This account of forgiveness is in fact a purely philosophical description of the New Testament account of Jesus' ability to forgive sins and so to 'change the hearts' of sinners and of what is known in theology as the 'working of grace'.

'Community, Apartheid and the Metaphysics of Humanity in Genesis 1-11' outlines what I believe is a novel exegesis of one of the most (justifiably) famous texts in the history of religion. I say the exegesis is novel—though it has much in common with those of well-known biblical scholars—because it is my attempt to relate very traditional ideas about sin and salvation to contemporary science and philosophy and even to the socio-political context of the twentieth century. It is certainly a work of demythologization but I hope a constructive rather than a merely destructive one.

For the next five years I was engaged in producing two books, one philosophical, the other theological. The philosophical one grew out of my experience in both the University of Cape Town and the Catholic parish of St Mary's in the Nyanga African township to which I and my family belonged. It represents my first philosophical engagement with African culture and traditional thought. UCT was at last able to admit students with an African cultural background, and many of them were keen to study philosophy. And in order to communicate with them at a more than superficial level I had to move beyond my purely European background. At the same time my involvement in parish affairs brought me face to face with a wholly different ethos and outlook on life. Here too I had to open my mind to Africa and learn something from it. And this after having lived there for my whole fifty-year old life! My book, *Philosophy for Africa* grew out of these experiences.

The other, theological, book *The Mystery of Humanity*, was a case of me following my own advice, the recommendation I had made in the article 'A Philosophy of the Human Person for Contemporary Theology', that one use a viable philosophical conception of human persons as a foundation and framework for formulating the fundamental doctrines of Christianity in a way that was appropriate for our time. Aquinas had done it, Rahner had done it; this was my attempt. It was thus in the nature of things a *tour de force*. I intended to cover all the essentials of Christian faith in language that would be meaningful to twentieth-century believer and unbeliever alike.

As with *Philosophy for Africa*, *The Mystery of Humanity* grew out of an interaction with groups, in this case primarily a group of teachers of religion in Catholic schools that I had called together, but also with my classes in the Kolbe School of Theology and in Extra-Mural Studies at UCT. As I composed each chapter I tested it on the group of teachers. The test took the form of answers to three questions: Is it intellectually satisfying? Is it orthodox? Is it teachable? In general I got affirmative answers to the first two questions, in spite of the novelty of my formulations. The third however failed the test: my version of Christianity was *too different* from what the children got from home and church. And it was too intellectual even for children in the matric class.

I was encouraged by the positive personal response of the teachers to my material but disappointed by the problem they faced of getting their own new understanding across to the children. If only they had a more appropriate text. That was the answer! I thus set myself to produce one, the same material that formed the book but now presented not in discursive but in narrative form. I called it *The Great Story*, though its original title was *For Jonathan at Sixteen*, after my eldest son whom I was preparing for confirmation. Thanks to the vision of Else Strivens, the editor of the excellent Catholic periodical *The Trefoil*, it was serialized in that publication virtually as I wrote it. The first chapter, dealing with the creation of the universe and humanity and the origin of religion, appears here. As can be seen I am trying to replace the myths of Genesis with modern ones to convey the same important truths. Since composing that text I have learnt a great deal more about contemporary cosmology but I have left the story as I wrote it then. Though it was written for schoolchildren most adults seem to find it more illuminating than *The Mystery of Humanity* itself!

'The Possibility of Faith Today' is in fact the last chapter of *The Mystery of Humanity*. Because it sums up the basic argument of the book I also published it separately in *The Journal of Theology for Southern Africa*. In it I identify the barriers to religious faith thrown up by our secular culture. In particular they make it difficult for people to believe in the reality of a transcendent creator and in a life beyond death. But I also make the point that faith in the Christian sense is not simply a matter of believing that these things—and others—are true. It is not a purely mental attitude but an attitude of the whole person, of the will and the emotions as well as the intellect. Thus in a secular culture such as ours where the public understanding and symbols of faith has been marginalized it is perfectly possible for people to have this attitude of 'saving faith' and not know it!

I then go on to describe the attitude of faith in greater detail to show how this could be true. Finally I speak of explicitly Christian faith where the attitude is directed towards the person of Jesus in the first instance, and secondly to the personal tradition of faithful persons we call the Church.

The article on Euthanasia is one that grew out of discussions of the Anglican Theological Commission (on which I was a Catholic 'observer'). Parliament was preparing to discuss a Bill on euthanasia and the Anglican bishops wanted to present their view on the matter. I had for many years been part of a seminar on medical ethics at Groote Schuur, UCT's teaching hospital, organized by the Head of the Department of Medicine, Solly Benatar. This, in addition to my background in ethics and theology, led to the commission asking me to write a theological introduction to the bishops' statement. 'Euthanasia and the Theology of Death' is the result. In it I point out that one's answer to the question 'What happens when a person dies?' depends on one's idea of what a human person is. I then contrast the Christian view of persons as 'the image of God' with the two dominant but inadequate views current in our scientific and secular culture: a materialist 'scientific' view that sees death as annihilation, and a dualist 'religious' view that sees death as the liberation of our true immortal self. For Christian faith death is our final transformation and completion by God's creative power. It is thus not something to fear, least of all by the medical profession. Their job is to deal with the things that can cause sickness and death so that ultimately we can die conscious and pain-free. In this context it is a mistake to contrast God's power over our lives with what medical personnel can do. Thus euthanasia in certain circumstances can be a profoundly Christian option.

'Dialogue Between Religions' appeared in 1999 as part of a pamphlet, the first in a series entitled (nostalgically) 'Tracts for the Times' organised by the Goedgedacht Forum for Social Reflection. The Goedgedacht Forum was an autonomous initiative in the Catholic Church set up to foster free discussion of the important issues of the day. I had been its chairman and subsequently its research officer, and it was my idea to host a series of seminars to prepare the organizers of the huge (there were some 8000 participants) Parliament of the World's Religions convention in Cape Town in 1999. A variety of religious traditions were represented at the series: African traditional, Bahai, Unitarian, various Hindu traditions, Buddist, Jewish, Muslim, new age movements and various Christian denominations.

'Dialogue Between Religions' is my opening address at our first seminar. In it I describe the present state of the 'global village' as one of perpetual conflict, conflict caused also by religion. A scientific and secular culture seems inherently opposed to a traditional religious one. In particular the value of self-determination that is the heart of secularity seems incompatible with the solidarity and authority stressed by religion. I argue that it need not be, that genuine human freedom is only possible through authentic solidarity, and refer to my pet African motto (*umuntu ngumuntu ngabantu*) in support. It is this feature of our humanity that in fact makes genuine religious dialogue possible. For although the different religious traditions have developed in different cultures with differing rituals and customs and conceptions of their gods, all are products of and aim at the fulfilment of humanity itself. It is this then that provides both a basis for dialogue and a standard for judging religion, especially one's own, in terms of its truth and value.

Except for the following article 'Evil and the Christian Response: Science, Philosophy and Theology' there is a chronological gap between this and the final articles in this collection of almost ten years. Early in the New Millennium I was appointed the director of a UCT research project on science and religion in a South African context. This was an ambitious affair funded by the John Templeton Foundation and involved a lot of travel and networking as well as thinking and writing. Eventually the research issued in a book *The Quest for Humanity in Science and Religion: The South African Experience* which appeared in 2006. After that I was able to return to purely theological matters.

The article on evil was produced during this period for the annual conference of the South African Science and Religion Forum since it had turned its attention to this topic, following the lead of the celebrated international collaboration of the Centre for Theology and the Natural Sciences at Berkeley and the Vatican Observatory that had chosen the topic after the completion of their twenty year-long research project *Scientific Perspectives on Divine Action*. Thus it was produced out of my involvement in the science-and-religion field. This fact is evident in the article though rather less so in the purely theological section, as a comparison with the final articles in this collection will show. In these it is clear that my reading and reflection in the science-and-religion field has had an influence on my theology.

The most recent articles in this collection, 'Telling the Christian Story–By Karl Rahner and Me' (2007) and 'Evolution and Emergence: A Paradigm-Shift for Theology' (2009), were both produced for conferences. The first was one organized by Ernst Conradie of the University of the Western Cape for an invited group of South African theologians. Its theme was 'Telling the Christian Story'. We were given the brief to write about the influence on us in this connection of some well-known theologian, and I chose Rahner. The second was a conference organized by the Ian Ramsey Centre in Oxford to celebrate the bi-centenary year of Darwin's birth; its title was 'Religious Responses to Darwin'. A cursory glance at both articles will show that there is almost as much of Rahner in the second as in the first. This is not surprising in view of my admission in the first article to the degree to which I have been influenced by Rahner's thought. There is however a significant difference between them that reveals a development in my own thought, a development that I think goes beyond what Rahner would allow. It concerns the way I understand the Incarnation.

In the first article I associate myself with Rahner's view that the effect on the human person of Jesus of God's Incarnation in him is no different in kind from the effect of God's grace in us. The uniqueness of Jesus lies in the position he occupies in the history of salvation, the belief in his 'sinlessness' notwithstanding. Rahner nevertheless still seems to hold that this is because of a 'special' self-communication of God (from God's side as it were) that is different in kind from the self-communication that occurs throughout human, and salvation, history. This certainly seems to be the traditional view, that God is present 'in person' in Jesus in a way that is true of no-one else. But it doesn't seem to fit in with Rahner's view of God's creative and saving presence throughout human history and whose creative and saving acts are incommensurable with those of human persons.

In any case in my study in the field of science-and-religion I had come across the work of the Scientific Perspectives on Divine Action research project mentioned above. In the final 'capstone' volume of this twenty-year-long project the acronym NIODA (non-interventionist objective divine action) was devised to identify a kind of consensus reached by at least a majority of the participants. According to this even God's 'special' acts in salvation history (such as the Incarnation), as distinct from his 'general' activity in creating and sustaining world-process and bringing really new things into being, could be understood in this non-interventionist way. This is explained by Stoeger in the article, and summarized by me in mine so I won't elaborate it here. But if this is indeed possible then Jesus' uniqueness consists in certain human qualities rather than a unique kind of divine presence. I am thinking of such things (things that Rahner also mentions) as an experience of closeness to (and hence personal knowledge of and insight into) God which he was able to communicate to his disciples. There is also the moral quality of his life and the love the New Testament authors bear witness to. Of course it follows from the conception of God he communicated to his followers that this insight and these qualities were in fact the work of God in him. But so they were in his followers. If there is a difference it is only a matter of degree. In both Jesus and his disciples it is the work of God's Word and Spirit that unites them to the Father. Seeing God's 'special' action in history in the non-interventionist way recommended by the 'capstone' volume makes the uniqueness even less of metaphysical exception to the rule than Rahner himself seems to suggest. And it certainly is a 'development' of the traditional doctrine, a development I agree with—though I don't think Rahner would.

Chapter Two
Jesus Now

Modern scripture scholars seem agreed that the word *theos* in the New Testament refers in nearly every case to the first person of the trinity of traditional theology. Similarly, though for different reasons and with a slightly different sense, Jahweh in the Old Testament can be understood to refer to God the Father of the Trinitarian formula. At any rate in what follows I intend either the first person of the trinity or Jahweh when I use the word God.[1]

The essential and unique and unsurpassable teaching of Jesus about God is summed up in St John's 'God is love'. The synoptic presentation of this truth, though differently expressed, adds up to the same thing. For there we are taught to think of God as our father. And if he is our father we are his sons. That this father/son language is intended to denote a relationship of love is pretty clear, nowhere more so than in Luke's account of the Transfiguration where God refers to Jesus as 'my Son, my Beloved'. The two terms obviously signify the same. It is St John however who draws out the implications of this teaching and suggests the possibility of a whole metaphysic of love and consequently of a doctrine of the Trinity. For love is the essential definitive act of a person. And a person comes to be only in relationship to another. Love therefore implies relation. So God is seen as an utterly original movement of love in a relationship that must needs be both reciprocal and complete. If God is love it is only because he is in love with another. This other, this Beloved, is the Son.

1. See Karl Rahner, '*Theos* in the New Testament' *Theological Investigations*, Volume I (Darton, Longman and Todd, 1963), 79–148.

But Jesus' revelation of the truth about God was not confined to his teaching this truth. His life itself revealed, and was intended to reveal, God far more fully and profoundly. It did this primarily by its attitude to God. This attitude was of course one of unique and total love. To the apostles, loyal worshippers of Jahweh though they may have been, this attitude must have been something new. The degree to which they adopted it was the measure of their faith in and love for their leader, the Jesus who stood amongst them. What in fact they were witnessing, were participating in, was the first and last, unique and complete, response of love to the love of God in the history of the world. That it was this so definitive and absolute act, in spirit of the particularity of the circumstances in which it occurred, is the essential mystery of Jesus.

Like any man Jesus gradually becomes himself, struggling from matter into spirit, spiritualising the matter that he is, uttering himself, evacuating himself in this loving relationship of love into the bottomless abyss of God. He becomes himself, throughout his life til at his death he is who he is. Three days later he is seen to be himself, pure movement towards God, Jesus. The gospels do not only show us Jesus' pure movement, his complete relatedness to God; they also show us the attitude of the apostles to Jesus himself. And in a way for us this is more important. For what we discover there is the record of a commitment that is absolute and total. The process whereby it came about is sketched, especially in the gospel of John. But the end result in each case is the same: an attitude of attachment, of commitment to Jesus that is so absolute as only to be able to find expression in St Thomas' 'My Lord and my God'.

Jesus became Lord and his disciples recognised him as such—that is one way of putting it. Or he became what he was—a pure response of love to the love of God, a Son to a Father. At all events his uniqueness consists in this: that his response was absolute, complete. If God is love so is he.

Throughout this exposition I have tried to avoid using such terms as 'God's nature' or 'man' or 'god' where this refers to a common nature possessed by the three person of the Trinity. In other words I have tried to deal only with persons and expound my faith in terms of them. God as I use it is a proper name. I could instead say 'Abba, Father'. So of course is Jesus. But these proper names alone can never provide a means of understanding. Hence the use of the idea of love. But here I must explain my use of it more fully.

God is the creator of the world from nothing; hence if God is love each thing that is is a particular act of love or nothing. Each thing is a particular determination of love. Love is what all things, an act of the human will or a pillar of marble, have in common. This is only another way of saying what men such as de Chardin[2] say when they postulate the continuity of spirit and matter and the evolution of the one from the other. The less real is explained by the more real and love is the realest thing that is; it is the term of the evolution of the universe. Indeed if that is so then the universe has already reached its term in Jesus and this is what I believe. He is pure relatedness to God, the true Son of the true Father. Our happiness consists in our relatedness to them. 'I and my Father will come and make our home with you'—this, when we are filled by their Spirit.

The most difficult part of all this to grasp is the apparent clash of opposites: the particularity of Jesus' life in Palestine so long ago and the universality of its effects, one of which is that I can be present to him now.

We come at last to a consideration of Jesus Now. And we must first note this: that since the life of Jesus love has a proper name: Jesus. And this is simply true, without exception—there is no such thing for instance as Christian love. All love just because it is love is that. All love is love for God and love of Jesus. It is this truth that is the basis of our relationships with Jesus now. In the activity of loving we are in most intimate union with him. Our love is aimed ultimately at God. So was his. Thus we stand side by side. Nevertheless this is all too general, we need to discover in our love the particularity of Jesus. After all he is a single person with a unique name. He is neither this one nor that but himself. We cannot reduce him to a Cosmic Christ or a universal essence. We cannot love such things. We can only love a person. For us this particularity is defined by the *moral teaching* of the Church. What is shown forth in the Church's moral teaching is a particular loving face, the face of Jesus. For the moral teaching of the Church is that of Jesus (so we believe) and this in spite of the obviousness it may have for us after 2000 years of Christianity in Western Europe is a particular morality. It is not any amalgam of the 'wisdom of the ages'. The characteristic note of this teaching is love but even this is not inevitable from an a priori point of view. From the point of view

2. See P Teilhard de Chardin, *The Phenomenon of Man* (Collins, 1959) and *Le Milieau Divin* (Collins, 1960).

of history it has been only once and definitively taught. The fact that it has not been superseded, nor ever can be, tells us something about the teacher. It nevertheless remains his own. This 'love' presented for us by the Church's moral laws is further particularised by certain modalities: self-sacrifice, mortification, humility—all these are drawn from a particular life lived in a particular place 2000 years ago. Yet they cannot be superseded. They are at once particular and universal. Love could show no other face. Sometimes this face of Christ revealed to us by the Church takes on a concrete form, is limited and determined by another contemporary of ours. But this, though cause for trumpets of joy, is of secondary importance. The church itself is the true bearer of the character of Jesus.

In Palestine the body of Jesus did not deserve the adoration of the disciples yet it was before it that they bowed the knee. And rightly so for it was the sign of the person whom they could adore, who drew love from them and brought them face to face with God. It is the same for us. For our materiality the presence of Jesus is defined by the outlines of his enduring body the Church. This is not the spiritual Church, nor the mystical Church; this is the most visible and external church defined not by its sacraments or its members but by its hierarchy, by the successors of the apostles, ultimately, definitively by the pope. Here is the THING which we may look upon and touch with our hands and believe in. This is the present particularity of our faith.

All this concerns the outside: Jesus as a phenomenon of 1966. This is the most visible Church with its most unalterable moral law. At times she is as hard to recognize as the vehicle of love, as love incarnate, as was the figure on the cross. Once however she is recognised as that one stands on the inside in the presence of God. Seeing her we see the Father. We no longer face the Church for we are within her, we face God. We face him in the life we live within him. This is Jesus' life, continually being lived. Thus we realise that we are living it side by side, in the same direction, united by the same goal. Side by side is too weak and expression for St Paul. He uses the preposition IN—IN CHRIST. He also says somewhere that the second Adam became a life-giving Spirit and teaches that we live by this spirit in us. So we are involved in a trinity of relations: indwelt by a Spirit, dwelling in Christ, living towards God. This is only the inevitable pattern of love stamping itself upon us. If we love it is the pattern of all our actions but especially in that one action which is our official action as the microcosm of the Church, the Mass.

(1966)

Chapter Three
The Prayer of Jesus

This essay is interested in the prayer of Jesus, as it in presented in the New Testament, chiefly as uniquely important evidence concerning the quality of Jesus' intimate personal relationship with his Father. For the prayer of Jesus would seem to be, in theological language, that structure of his existence in which we are most likely to be able to make out the effect on his human consciousness of its hypostatic union with the Word. In saying this we of course presume a view of prayer, namely that it is that human activity whereby a man most consciously gathers himself together, takes possession of himself, in order to orientate himself totally in a direct and immediate way to the ultimate ground and goal of his existence. We feel justified in this presumption largely on account of the view of prayer that arises from the New Testament itself, especially in Luke and in Jesus' own sayings on prayer.

References in the New Testament to Jesus and prayer fall into three main groups: Jesus' own teaching on prayer; the frequent references to him praying, himself and the few passages in which Jesus actually addresses the Father directly. For our purpose the last group is the most important; we shall therefore summarise very briefly the material in the first two groups by way of introduction to the more revealing material in the third.

In the teaching of Jesus on prayer recorded in the Gospels three themes stand out. Firstly, prayer is seen (in for instance, the Sermon on the Mount) as an absolutely unconditional and total activity in which the one who is praying must find himself in a face to face encounter with God characterised by the most radical sincerity and simplicity. Nothing pseudo- or quasi- or even semi- is at all relevant here. Secondly, prayer is eschatological; it is directed to the bringing in of God's Kingdom. Thirdly, prayer is a fundamental expression of faithfulness and trust.

These themes provide the setting for the 'Our Father' which turns out on analysis to be a very simple prayer. Its structure (according to van den Bussche[1]—and it fits both versions in the New Testament) is that of an invocation followed by two sets of petitions. The first set is the most important and centres on the petition for the coming of the Kingdom. The second set is subsidiary and consists of requests for help in the present situation in which man has to live until the Kingdom comes. Even these requests, especially the last, are related to the coming of the Kingdom and the inevitable trials and judgement that it will involve. Thus the whole prayer could be summed up: 'Father, bring in your Kingdom, and in the meantime help us to prepare for its coming.'

We now turn to the references to Jesus himself praying. And here at the outset we must distinguish between theologically organised and truly historical material. With regard to the latter it seems possible from the references to say at least that it was Jesus' custom to pray alone, and in silence, in deserted places, at great length and with eyes raised to heaven. On the borderline between history and theology it can be noted that Jesus' prayer is orientated towards his disciples. That is to say he either prays with them, for them, or with them in mind. In Luke both Jesus praying and the presence of the disciples are mentioned at the Transfiguration and the Agony, as well as before the giving of the 'Our Father'. Before the beginning of the final trial he prays that Peter's faith may not fail.

This orientation of Jesus' prayer towards the disciples points to another aspect of his prayers: his consciousness of his mission. As we have indicated all the crucial salvific events in Luke are underlined by a mention of prayer. Jesus prays after his Baptism and before his Passion; he prays before beginning his ministry and before choosing. the Twelve. The Transfiguration takes place while he is rapt in prayer. The frequent mention in the descriptions of the presence of the Father (in the case of the Agony it is 'an angel from heaven') serves to emphasize the consciousness of his mission present in the very heart of Jesus' intimate dialogue with his Father. From the Transfiguration

1. H Van den Bussche, *The Lord's Prayer* (Sheed and Ward, 1963).

onwards this consciousness is also that of the inevitable approach of his passion and death.

Hebrews makes this last-mentioned aspect of Jesus' prayer absolutely central, within the context of its general conception of him as a priest 'appointed to act for men in relation to God' (5:1). Jesus is depicted as obtaining salvation by means of his prayer on earth (5:7) and communicating it to men through his continuing intercession for them in heaven (7:25). What made this earthly prayer effective was its quality of godly fear, that is pure piety or religious reverence. But most important of all, this prayer of Jesus is a prayer to him 'who was able to save him from death'. Within the general consciousness of his mission lies a particular awareness of death as the sine qua non of its success as well as the final enemy to be overcome.

The major themes of Jesus' prayer that have emerged from our look at the second group of references are thus: his concern for his disciples, his consciousness of his mission, and a gradually growing awareness of the special character and inevitability of his death.

With these in the back of our mind we can now turn to the most important references of all: those in which Jesus addresses his Father directly. As we should imagine, it is these that in spite of their overwhelmingly theological character, tell us most about the quality of Jesus' personal relation to the Father and the matter of their dialogue.

Apart from the high-priestly prayer itself there are only seven separate occasions when Jesus prays directly to the Father. All except two are associated with the Passion, three of the seven are prayers from the Cross.

The two prayers unconnected with the Passion are the one in Luke after the joyful return of the seventy and the one in John just before the raising of Lazarus. Both are prayers of thanksgiving.

Luke 10:21: 'In that same hour he rejoiced in the Holy Spirit and said, "I thank thee Father, Lord of heaven and earth, that you have hidden these things from the wise and understanding and revealed them to babes; yes, Father, for such is your gracious will. All things have been delivered to me by my Father; and no one knows who the Son is except the Father, or who the Father is except the Son and anyone to whom the Son chooses to reveal him."'

This prayer is basically a thanksgiving for the success of his mission. Jesus sent the seventy out to preach the kingdom. They return joyful at the success of their preaching and he, sharing their joy, turns it into a prayer of gratitude to the Father. A consciousness of his mission is absolutely central to this prayer and it is defined in terms of revealing the Father to men, 'these things' to babes. What are 'these things'? Surely the 'all things' that have been delivered to Jesus by his Father, that is the intimate personal knowledge that they share. It is this that Jesus wishes to share with the 'babes' too.

Who are the 'babes'? The seventy, yes. But also those to whom they successfully preach the coming Kingdom. There is clearly a close link between the matter of their message and Jesus' conscious closeness to the Father, though it is not made explicit here.

John 11:41: 'And Jesus lifted up his eyes and said, "Father, thank you that you have heard me. I know that you hear me always, but I have said this on account of the people standing by, that they may believe that you did send me"'. The chief theological point of this prayer is to emphasize Jesus' absolute confidence in his relation to the Father. For this reason, although it is a thanksgiving, it is placed immediately *before* Lazarus emerges from the tomb. The scene has however a strong historical flavour about it. Let us assume at any rate that Jesus' grief was real. Is it possible then to explain this confidence without conjuring up the God-in-a-human-skin spectre of the hypostatic union. I think one can, provided one is prepared to accept that Jesus experienced his power as a *gift*, a gift moreover that was given only at the moment it was needed and according to the circumstances in which it was needed, without violating the human integrity of the situation that called it forth.

Further, this prayer reveals Jesus' over-riding concern for his mission, but this time in terms of care, care for those standing by. The mission is here defined in terms of winning from men the faith that 'you did send me'. The accent is on 'you'. What form could this concern to reveal his *sentness* by the Father have taken in the human consciousness of Jesus? Surely nothing else but the attempt to reveal his intimate personal consciousness of the Father in all its detail and reality.

All the other prayers of Jesus are centred on his death. The first of these is the prayer of the Agony, versions of which appear in all the gospels and which is also referred to in Hebrews. John's version appears at the end of Chapter 12 immediately prior to the farewell discourses: 'Now is my soul troubled. And what shall I say? 'Father, save me from this hour?' No, for this purpose I have come to this hour. Father, glorify your name'. And the prayer, like Luke's version too, is answered: 'I have glorified it, and I will glorify it again.' The synoptic versions of this prayer are too well-known to need repeating here. It is sufficient to note their parallel to the prayer in John: the distress, the dread of 'the hour', the prayer for release, the final act of faith and hope. I wish though to put a more speculative question: What is the Agony? What is going on here?

For it seems pretty clear to me that, in the contest of the Passion narrative, the account of the Agony has a definite theological function to perform. And in the Gospels, having a theological function usually means having something to say about either the mission or the person of Jesus—or, as is most often the case, about both.

Now it is also pretty clear that it is the death of Jesus that the Agony is centred on. But what is it about his death that the Agony is intended to reveal or underline? I would like to suggest that it is the *saving* character of his death. Even without the evidence of Hebrews 5 there is enough in the actual prayer to bear this out. Our question however remains: Why the Agony? Why is this point made in terms of apparent temptation and dread on the part of Jesus? Let us be clear about this. The point that is being made in that Jesus' death is the consummate salvation event. Thus it is not sufficient to say that it is simply as death that Jesus dreads it, for that would not make the point. One must instead say that it is precisely as a *saving* death that he dreads it. And I interpret this in terms of his human consciousness in the following way. As a man Jesus dreads with an absolute and fundamental dread the act whereby he takes on the form of God, the Saviour. For the whole dynamism of the act implies just this: that he *must save himself*. And that means that he is lost; for no man can save himself. It is for this reason that Jesus dies desolate, in a condition that seems like despair but which is in reality on the far side of hope. Obedient to his Father's will he had trusted in him to achieve the salvation that the consciousness of his mission seemed to imply. And now that death itself emerges as the crux of this salvation it alters the whole meaning of the word. It is a different sort of salvation; it means that he must save himself. But as a man, whose whole mission, whose very life was to fulfill the saving will of God, he must lose God, and himself, in making himself the Saviour. It is for this reason that he is in agony. It is a religious agony, as Hebrews 5 would lead us to expect, caused by the apparent blasphemy that is being forced upon him. It is also an agony of human desolation at the apparent separation from the Father who is his life. Finally, I think, it is the inevitable consequence of the doctrine of the hypostatic union. Jesus' human consciousness, like that of any man, is bound to develop until the last moment of his life. It is only then that it can achieve a full and final presence-to-itself, which is to say, in the case of Jesus, a realisation of himself as the Word and so of his transcendent relation to the Father. But before that it is being moved in that direction, to fulfil a role that implies that relation, yet without the achieved self-consciousness that could explain what was going on. For this reason the death of Jesus, unlike that of many Christians who die trusting in him, is experienced as the ultimate agony of human loss.

According to Van den Bussche[2] John's farewell discourses must be taken as a commentary on the passion narrative, parallel to it and, if it were possible, to be read simultaneously with it. On this scheme the crucifixion occurs at the end of Chapter 16 with Jesus' cry 'I have overcome the world.' His high-priestly prayer that follows immediately, though obviously in some sense a prayer 'from the Cross', is thus identified with the eternal prayer of Hebrews 7:25. It is a summing-up of Jesus' ultimate concern, in relation to his Father and in relation to men. As such it is a strictly theological piece of work; one feels nevertheless throughout this prayer that although its words are more the author's than in any other of the prayers we are given in the Gospels, yet the sentiments and the spirit are probably closest to the actual prayer of Jesus.

The structure of the prayer is simple: it divides into four sections, roughly verses 1–5, 6–19, 20–24, 25–26. The first and last chiefly concern Jesus' relation to the Father, the middle two his relations with men, firstly his disciples and then those who are to believe in him through their preaching.

In verses 1–5 the central theme of Jesus' prayer to the Father is glory. The hour has come and it is the hour for the Father to glorify the Son. Jesus desires this for two reasons. First so that the Father may be glorified in this act, and second, so that this glory of the Father's may be revealed through him for the sake of men. 'Glorify' here has two shades of meaning, the one tending towards 'reveal' the other towards

2. H Van den Bussche, *The Gospel of the Word* (Priory, 1967).

'exalt'. In accomplishing his work on earth Jesus makes the Father 'shine out' for men; in fact making the Father 'shine out', manifesting him, *is* his work on earth. In addition he wishes to 'shine out' with the same glory in the Father's presence for the Father's own sake.

From verse 6 onwards Jesus centres his concern on his disciples. And inevitably the question of his mission is also raised. This is defined in this prayer as manifesting or making known the Father's name, as giving men the words or the glory which the Father has given him, as giving them the Father's word. In these phrases we can see how Jesus sees himself, simply as that which reveals, manifests, shines out in neon lights to men, the Father's name—or, in a word, his Word.

This realisation by Jesus of his relation to his Father is the same thing as his realisation of being *given* to men. He realises he is his Father's Word. And a word is essentially something that is already uttered, expressed, in the matter of the world. So he does not think of his disciples as simply 'his'. 'Yours they were and you gave them to me'. Like his glory. In this prayer Jesus *makes* the disciples his own through his care for them. It is they, primarily, whom he is praying *for*. He has kept and guarded them and now he is praying for them 'that they may have my joy fulfilled in themselves . . .' At this point, almost exactly halfway through the prayer, Jesus' attention turns from the past to the future in a quite dramatic way. Up to now it has been reflective, filled with serene faith; now it becomes urgent, demanding, full of a passionate hope. He reels off his desires for his disciples: that they may have my joy fulfilled in themselves, that you should keep them from the evil one, that they be sanctified in truth, that they be one 'even as we are one', that they may be with me where I am.

This turning of his attention to the future brings Jesus to the section of the prayer—versus 20–24—that expresses his concern for those who are to believe in him through the disciples' preaching. This transition from a concern for his immediate band of followers to a concern for all mankind begins in verse 18 with 'As you sent me into the world, so I have sent them into the world'. This parallel between the work of Jesus and the work of the disciples is striking, but it echoes another even more so. They are to share in *everything* that is his, not only his work but also his joy, his glory, the love which the Father has for him, even the unity with which Jesus and the Father are one. In this prayer Jesus regards himself in relation to his disciples not so much as 'Master and Lord' but rather as 'the first-born of many brothers'.

Ideas peculiar to the second half of the prayer are those of unity and love. Unity comes up first in verse 11 and seems to evolve out of the 'your-my' intimacy so frequently referred to in this prayer. Love is mentioned first in verse 23 where it appears to evolve naturally from the unity idea: 'I in them and you in me so that they may become perfectly one so that the world may know that you have . . . loved them even as you have loved me.' The next verse begins fiercely 'Father, I desire . . .' and love is the dominant theme through the conclusion to the prayer. The phrase 'Father, I desire' has all the terseness and informality of intimate familiarity—and as such has a definite air of authenticity about it.

We are now in a position to sum up what this prayer reveals concerning Jesus' intimate personal relation to his Father. First of all there is the consciousness of intimacy, of closeness and the confidence that stems from that. Nevertheless this confidence appears as always centred on the Father and not in himself. For this reason it reveals unmistakable signs of faith and hope. It also has an intellectual as well as an affective aspect. Jesus knows what is going on. Yet this knowledge too is not something that acquires its certainty from having originated in him. The plan that he is in on and that gives him his confidence is his Father's plan. And it is a plan that is only fully consummated, and that also means *revealed*, on the Cross. Thus it would be a mistake to say that Jesus *possesses* this knowledge in the sense of *comprehending* the plan. His foreknowledge of the plan is of the same order of his knowledge of the Father. It does not exclude the necessity for utter trust and self-surrender.

As far as his disciples are concerned Jesus' chief desire seems to be to share this inner life of his with them. His joy he wishes to be theirs.

The joy he is at such pains to communicate to others stems, as the final section of the prayer makes clear, from the love that is the chief characteristic of his personal intimacy with his Father. The basis of this love is Jesus' consciousness and therefore also the ontological fact, that all he has, his disciples as well as his glory, is from the Father. All he has, has been given him. And surely, so we believe, no one was ever given more.

(1966)

Chapter Four
The Motive of the Incarnation

The primary reference of the title of this essay is to the question of whether or not the Incarnation was caused by the Fall of man. This question comes into the limelight in the history of theology in the controversy between Scotists and Thomists beginning in the thirteenth century. St Thomas had said that if sin had not existed the Incarnation would not have taken place; Scotus contended that even without sin it would.

St Thomas prefaces his consideration of the question with two points: first, that it was entirely fitting for God to become incarnate on account of his goodness. The essence of goodness is to communicate itself to others. Hence the highest possible good should communicate itself in the highest possible way to the creature. Secondly, though a fitting means of man's redemption for many reasons on man's side, the Incarnation is not an absolutely necessary means for redeeming man. God could have chosen other ways.

St Thomas' argument for saying the Incarnation was in fact caused by sin goes like this: human nature does not of itself imply God's communication of himself to it in a hypostatic union; hence the cause of the Incarnation can only be known by revelation. But the Bible always gives the sin of the first man as this cause. So we must say that the Incarnation was ordained by God as a remedy for sin.[1]

Scotus' argument against this seems to be based, as far as I have been able to find out, on a stepping-up of Thomas' point about God's goodness making his incarnation fitting into a matter of necessity. Because God is so good he must will the highest good, and this, in

1. *Cf Summa Theologiae* IIIa, Q.1, art.3

respect of the creation, is the hypostatic union. Now what is highest comes first in the order of final causes. Hence everything else, including the creation of man is willed for the sake of the Incarnation. Hence even if man had not sinned God would have become incarnate.

Scotus' argument is based on a metaphysical analysis of God's will from which he seems to deduce the necessity of a particular, contingent act. For this reason he is criticised by the Thomists. The *Theologische Woordenboek* adds to this a criticism of anthropomorphism which seems to me to be justified.[2] For the real question about the motive of the Incarnation cannot be about a world in which sin has never taken place for such a world has never existed. Rather, it is a question about the relation in this world of sin to the Incarnation; does the Incarnation derive its meaning solely or even chiefly from a situation of human sin? Or is there some other aspect of the human condition that gives it its deepest meaning?

Certainly from the time of Anselm till the time of Thomas the Incarnation was seen almost solely as the remedy for sin. Indeed in the *Cur Deus Homo* Anselm takes sin for granted as the motive of the Incarnation. He is not at all concerned with the Scotist/Thomist question. His question is why was it necessary for God to *become man* in order to redeem man from sin. Why not a simple act of his omnipotent will? Why not in fact simply forgive him? His answer of course is given in the terms of feudal and forensic notions of the relations between vassal and lord, debtor and judge, and does not strictly concern our inquiry. One point however is important: Anselm's stress on the fact that while it is only God who *can*, it is man who *must* pay the satisfaction due. This is the centre of his argument and although it seems to follow from all sorts of medieval scruples about God's honour in fact it proceeds from an awkwardly formulated but none the less real concern for the integrity of human nature and that it be respected even by God.

We no longer share Anselm's scruples. One has in fact to demythologise them. And it seems to me that the other books of the New Testament provide the key to this demythologising. Let us take as starting-point the work of Luke. What has happened between the end of the Gospel and the beginning of Acts? Jesus' preaching in the gospel centres on the idea of the Kingdom; the apostles' preaching

2. H Brink, *et al*, *Theologische Woordenboek* (JJ Roman, 1952)

in Acts scarcely mentions it. It is indeed one of the themes of the *kerygma* but totally subordinate to another. This other, far and away the most important, is simply that concerning the person of Jesus himself. His words and works, his life and death and resurrection, overshadow everything else. What has happened between the end of the Gospel and the beginning of Acts is precisely Jesus' resurrection. And this has had the effect of turning the apostles' attention from the expectation and proclamation of a future kingdom to the recalling and proclamation of a past event. But this past event is of such a nature as to provide the bases for a totally new and *present* experience. Acts is full of the Spirit. The gift of the Spirit forms one of the major themes of the *kerygma*. And its outpouring is inextricably related to Jesus, his resurrection and exaltation.

This same phenomenon, the disappearance of the kingdom, is apparent in the epistles of St Paul (the epistles to the Thessalonians notwithstanding). What takes its place is the doctrine of Jesus' abiding presence in his church.

All this suggests to me that if one wishes to discover the real significance of the terms 'kingdom of God' and salvation, one has to see them in relation to the person of Jesus. After the resurrection a certain identity between the kingdom and the personal presence of Jesus' Spirit reveals itself. Following on in this line of thought I want to suggest that in the expression 'kingdom of God' the really significant word is not kingdom but God. Jesus proclaims and inaugurates the kingdom, but the important thing about it is not any particular characteristic of the kingdom, its peace or safety, but that it is *God's*. What Jesus is saying is that God is coming to reign. This implies that up till now God has *not* been reigning. And this is so—for the reign that Jesus preaches is an immediate and direct one, not simply the lordship of creator over creature. The point about the new kingdom is that it implies the personal, *historical* presence of the king. Now up till then God had not been personally present to man in human history. Jesus is saying that from now on he will be.

But of course he also goes further than that. Word and work combine in Jesus' life to proclaim God's personal presence in history in his own person. 'God is coming' goes Jesus' message during his life. 'God has come' is the message that his death and resurrection convey to the apostles. Surely this understanding comes across in St John's gospel. Jesus has come so that man may believe in him, that

that absolute gift of himself that it is in the power of every man to give, may be given to him and not to some or other idol in the world. The only way the men of the Old Testament could escape idolatry was by hoping in the promise of God; it is to recall them to this that forms the continual effort of the prophets. But in the New Testament men are able to believe in him present among them.

So if we would now reformulate the motive of Jesus' life and work we could say it was to elicit faith from men, faith that would attach itself to him. Or, in terms of salvation, to save men from themselves by providing an object for their absolute desire to give themselves to something beyond themselves. In so doing of course he provides a true focus for the unity of mankind in union with God that so many of the parables of the kingdom illustrate.

Having come this far we have now to ask only how sin is related to this intention. And at once we can see that forgiveness of sin is not the end towards which Jesus' life and work is directed, but the means to that end. The absolute end is faith in him as God personally present to man in human history. And all forms of sin impede this commitment. So repentance is a preliminary for entering the kingdom: 'Repent for the kingdom of heaven is at hand'. Repentance is to clear the way for faith: 'Repent and believe in the gospel'.

In spite of this it could be said that salvation from sin is not meant in this limited individualistic sense but as salvation from the devil, cosmic evil. And there is no doubt that Jesus saw this as the motive of his life and work. But one must also see that it was achieved by going farther than sin as such could have required. It is to answer a positive God-given desire in man that Jesus dies and rises again, so announcing God's personal, historical presence—not to set right a wrong state of affairs. True, it is precisely man's desire for God that, unable to find any appropriate object in human history and attaching itself to a variety of idols, that has brought history to the brink of disaster. But man's desire is created for fulfilment and it is this fulfilment that provides Jesus' ultimate motive. The creation and the incarnation form two strands in the mysterious relation between God and man.

But what of Jesus' death then? What special significance does it have on this view of the incarnation? It is the high-point of his redemptive work certainly but it is only this because it is also the ultimate proclamation of the *transcendence* of his person. Death here is seen not simply as a punishment for sin but the boundary between man and God. Hence death is the ultimate form that his proclamation of identity with God must take. Because human commitment to Jesus must take into account his death it is a commitment to a transcendent person. Short of that, it too could be idolatry. A Jesus who had not died would not be in the position of meeting the ultimate demand of man and so fulfilling the longings of human history.

To sum up then: we have come out on what appears to be the Scotist side of the controversy, but we have arrived there from a different starting-point. Our starting-point is twofold:

1. The New Testament evidence which shows Jesus' revelation of himself as God as the deepest, though not perhaps the most obvious, theme of his life and work.
2. A view of human nature which sees the created desire for God as a more fundamental fact of human history even than sin. It is as an answer to this fundamental call that the Incarnation can best be understood.

(1967)

Chapter Five
Christology Now

Christology (and I use the word to include what is usually called soteriology) is the very heart of Christian theology. Hence the history of Christology is really the history of theology. In different ages different problems predominate and these reflect the basic theological, and therefore cultural, problems of the times. Thus in the first age of Christian theology, where the general cultural background was that of the Greek mystery religions and a belief in the supernatural was part of the zeitgeist, the divinity of Christ was virtually taken for granted. This however raised acute problems for Hebrew monotheism which were finally resolved in the Trinitarian definition at Nicea and, later, at Constantinople. Between Nicaea and Chalcedon the Christological development can be seen as the attempt to assert the unity of Christ in such a way as to preserve the distinct properties of his divine and human natures. The starting point for this development is the recognition of his divinity, involving a too exclusive stress on his unity: he is God incarnate, pure and simple. This issues in a neglect of the reality of his human nature and its properties, especially the possession of a true, spiritual soul. To all intents and purposes the human soul is obliterated by the presence of the divine Word. At any rate it is not seen as having any theological function. Chalcedon, in vindicating the distinct properties of the two natures in Christ, thus emerges as stressing the reality of Christ's manhood. Its extreme formal categories however were no proof against continuing monophysite tendencies and it is not until after the reformation that the manhood of Christ once again occupies the centre of the picture. Such development as does take place in the scholastic period is largely soteriological.

The scholastic development begins with Anselm, whose systematic *Cur Deus Homo?* virtually puts an end to the earlier 'Christus Victor' theory of the atonement. Anselm's theory centres on sin and the satisfaction that is due to God because of it; the incarnation is seen as necessary because, while it is only God who can, it is man who must, pay the satisfaction due. Christ's saving work is elaborated in forensic and feudal concepts that depict the relation of man to God as that of vassal to lord or criminal to judge. The inadequacy and anthropomorphism of such an account was one of the chief things against which the reformers protested.

The question of the motive of the incarnation remained an important one throughout the middle ages, resulting finally in the unresolved controversy between the scotists and the thomists. In this the point at issue was whether the incarnation should be seen primarily as a remedy for sin or rather as the perfection and completion of God's creative work. In modern theology the latter view has tended to predominate.

With the reformation the theological norm shifts from the idea of salvation from sin by the sacrificial death of the God-man, to the figure of Jesus as the representative of the personal and social ideal of human existence. So, at least, Tillich asserts. At any rate there is a shift from the God-centred 'objective' view of the Latin theory to the man-centred 'subjective' view of the reformers.

In the classical theology of the reformers soteriology took predominance over Christology. The biblical idea of the covenant provided a background to a view of Christ in his three roles relative to man as prophet, priest and king. With the growth of secularism and rationalism Christ is seen predominantly as a religious genius, our example (as for Schleiermacher and the nineteenth century) or a symbol of the ideal religion (as for Hegel and other idealist philosophers). A comparative study of religion takes the place of natural theology and the divinity of Christ is either denied or simply not considered.

This brief sketch of the development of Christology should prepare us for the special problems of our contemporary situation. As has been borne out by this year's course the chief problem is that raised by the phenomenon of secularisation that has issued in recent times in such theological movements as 'the death of God' and 'religionless Christianity'. The problem is illustrated in the Creed of so-called Christian Atheism: 'I believe that there is no God and that Jesus is his Son.' And also in Bishop Robinson's *Honest to God*.[1] It is nothing other than the problem of God. The direct relevance of the problem of God for Christology should be obvious. If 'God' is a meaningless term then it is equally meaningless to predicate it of Jesus. That it is an actual problem for us here has been demonstrated ad infinitum during the year. It also shows itself as a problem in the various attempts made by current theology to dispense with natural theology (in the Catholic tradition) or the phenomenology of religion (in the Protestant).

This problem has another side to it. The contemporary evolutionary view of the world with its emphasis on human historicity together with the new perspectives opened up in anthropology by existential philosophy and psychology have created a climate in which the humanity of Jesus has to be taken more seriously than ever before. Chalcedon did not go far enough in the question of Jesus' human psychology and this development must take place now.

These two problems provide the framework, as I see it, for Christology now. The other source is of course the Bible and the tradition of its interpretation in the history of the Church. In what follows I shall attempt to give due weight to all these elements.

Unless 'God' has meaning apart from Jesus it is meaningless to predicate it of him. The most logical of the 'death of God' theologians appreciate this and attempt to ascribe significance to Jesus which does not involve the use of the term 'God'. In short they attempt to describe his unique significance as an event in human history that has consequences for that history as a whole. Salvation history is transformed into a radically secular history, theology becomes anthropology.

Such a secular Christology must proceed from an analysis of the human situation from which it can elicit categories in terms of which the figure presented in the New Testament can be seen to have a unique and saving role to play. The basic pattern of such attempts at a secular Christology is as follows: the analysis of the human situation reveals it as a predicament. Man is revealed as in a state of need, of

1. J Robinson, *Honest to God* (SCM, 1963). See also T Altizer, *The Gospel of Christian Atheism* (Westminster, 1966).

non-salvation, from which he cannot save himself. (The Bible itself presents just such an analysis.) Man needs a saviour. Attention is then turned to the New Testament which reveals Jesus as the answer to this need, either by a point for point correlation of human need and gospel promise or as an overall promise that would answer any conceivable need, save from every possible situation of non-salvation. From such an analysis it would appear that one could bypass the problem of God, simply referring one's situation of non-salvation directly to the historical figure of the saviour and his saving promise.

But such a solution is facile and open to criticism for two reasons. The first is this: however clearly the New Testament may represent Jesus as the saviour from the human predicament the fact is that men appear to remain unsaved. The predicament remains a predicament. Nor is it to the point to say that the salvation that Jesus offers is a matter of promise. For, as far as human history is concerned, my own and that of the whole secular world, all hopes in the future of this promise are cut short at my death. It is not to the point either to object that this is an excessively individualistic way of regarding the promise. The promise is not to individuals, it is the promise of community to mankind as a whole. To this one must answer that any community from which I am excluded, and excluded simply by the fact of my death, is simply not a community of *mankind*.

The centre of this first criticism is this: that one of the elements in the human predicament is death. And although a purely secular saviour may inspire in me sufficient courage and hope in his promises to go smiling to my death, the fact of death remains as the negation of those promises and that courage. A secular saviour could remove the sting from death but there is nothing he could do about death itself.

With this we come to the second criticism of the attempt at a purely secular Christology. It ignores the most fundamental element of the human situation. This element has been variously named; I shall call it 'unconditional desire'. It reveals itself in dissatisfaction or boredom with any particular fulfilment and for this reason I call it unconditional. It is the desire for no particular thing or goal but always goes beyond each possible fulfilment. Finally it reveals its unconditional nature in that it goes beyond death. It is the desire to transcend death. And even this is not to specify it for it is not simply death as a physical event that it desires to transcend. Various accounts have been given of this desire. The one I find most helpful is that given by Dorothee Soelle.[2] She calls it the desire for identity. Rob van der Hart (our lecturer on philosophical anthropology) seemed in basic agreement with this when he spoke of it in terms of the desire to transcend the subject/object structure of human existence. At all events it is not difficult to see what is being got at: man is a being who partially possesses himself and who has it in him to make himself. And the desire to achieve himself in perfect self-possession is one that is built into this fundamental structure of his being. It is in fact nothing but the conscious experience of what it is to have such a structure. Identity seems a good word to specify this totally unspecifiable desire. For identity suggests at once a relation and a union of the two things related. And this is just the case with human reality. I achieve myself only by self-transcendence into what is other than myself. And the meaning of the unconditional desire is that this achievement should be possible through an identification with another that will render my identity final. This identification would only be possible if the other with whom I identify were in fact unconditional.

Thus unconditional desire raises the question of the unconditional as such, of the Other who would make my achievement of identity possible. This is the question of God. As Tillich says: 'An awareness of the infinite is included in man's awareness of finitude. Man knows that he is finite, that he is excluded from an infinity which nevertheless belongs to him. He is aware of his potential infinity while being aware of his actual finitude. This shows the presence of something unconditional within the self and the world.' And 'unless such an element were present, the question of God could never have been asked, nor could an answer, even the answer of revelation, have been received.' (*Systematic Theology* Volume I [Chicago, 1951], 228–229)

A more concrete way of making the same point is to draw attention to the category of mystery. The human situation is not adequately analysed unless the analysis reveals the element of mystery in our experience. Mystery as such is not a question, rather it is the basic condition for questionableness. The question about identity arises out of the experience of mystery. This is based on the fact that experience transcends the subject/object structure of human consciousness. Man's fundamental experience is real but it is mysterious. He can call

2. D Soelle, *Christ the Representative. An Essay in Theology after the 'Death of God'.* (SCM, 1967).

it an experience of himself—but this 'self' is not a self that is distinct from the Other as subject from object. Or he can call it an experience of an Other—but this Other is not distinct from himself as object is from subject. So, in truth, neither 'self' nor Other is an adequate description of the reality experienced. So we need another category altogether, a non-objective and a non-ideal category, which is to say a non-historical, non-secular category, namely God.

This is the reason that the being of God is so often misconceived: the reality of mystery is not recognized. As real mysteries God and the self are not distinct objects. In reality there are not two mysteries; the mystery of God and the mystery of man are identical. As Rahner[3] finely says: 'Our whole existence is the acceptance or rejection of the mystery which we are, as we find our poverty referred to the mystery of the fullness. The pre-existent object of our acceptance or refusal, of the decision which is the deed of our life, is the mystery which we are. And this mystery is our nature, because the transcendence which we are and which we accomplish brings our existence and God's existence together: and both as mystery.' (*Theological Investigations* Volume IV: 108)

Thus any analysis of the human situation which does not reveal it as mystery falls short in neglecting its fundamental structure. But in revealing it as mysterious it also reveals it, in its very humanness, as transcendent, as orientated beyond history and the world. This mystery in philosophy since Kant is described in terms of God, freedom and immortality. But it is truly grasped at the reflective level as question rather than statement. Freedom, immortality and God are three elements of the fundamental question asked by human existence. This is the question that the gospel must answer if it is to be an answer that genuinely saves.

The same must be said of the unconditional desire for identity. It is really this desire that constitutes the human situation as predicament for it is through it alone that each particular aspect of the human situation can acquire the character of horror and loss or at the least boredom and dissatisfaction. Because it is unconditional the salvation it demands must be an absolute salvation; because it is the desire for identity this salvation must consist in the achievement of union with

3. 'On the Theology of the Incarnation', in K Rahner, *Theological Investigations*. Volume IV (Helicon Press, 1966), 105–120.

the Other of our mysterious transcendence. Thus one can say that unless God is present in the human situation as its most fundamental and inescapable question, the question of salvation is not even raised and anything the gospel may have to say is irrelevant. Conversely, if the gospel is interpreted as the answer to a question which is anything less than the question of God it is again irrelevant.

So much then for our criticism of the 'death of God' analysis of the human situation. It has this reference to Christology: Jesus must be seen as the answer to a question that already includes the notion of God. God is not imported by the gospel. He appears as the unconditional, the mysterious, in the human situation. If Jesus is to be our saviour it is primarily in a situation dominated by mystery and unconditional desire. Although I have criticised the attempt of modern theology to avoid the problem of God by making straight for Jesus and his gospel as the answer to the human predicament, I don't wish to imply that beginning with an analysis of the human situation is as such a mistake. On the contrary I think that one must begin in this way. There are certain fundamental structures to human reality in terms of which alone it is possible for the gospel message to have meaning, and it is obviously a good thing to be made more conscious of them, for they will in any case determine our approach to the gospel. That this is not only a legitimate but also the inevitable approach to Christ is borne out by the structure of the Bible itself. There the question is posed in the Old Testament and answered in the New.

The question grows out of Israel's interpretation of its history as a story of the nation's relations with Yahweh. The basic structure of this story is that of a promise made by Yahweh of a glorious future for his people, a 'day of Yahweh' when the history of the nation will be consummated in the inauguration of Yahweh's kingly rule over them by his representative, the Messiah. The history of this promise in the chosen people is seen as a dialectic of rebelliousness and unfaithfulness on the part of Israel and steadfast loyalty on the part of Yahweh. Yahweh's faithfulness to this covenant sometimes shows itself in the punishment of Israel's sins but it always issues in a renewal of his promise to them. For Israel too, in spite of continual unfaithfulness, there always remains an element who are ready to repent, to return to Yahweh and to an expectant looking-forward to the fulfilment of his promises in the coming of the Messiah-King. This expectation is answered in the New Testament with the identification of Jesus as the Messiah-King. As such he is accorded the titles of Lord and Christ and the Son of Man.

So it is true to say that the Bible itself has this structure of a question posed by a view of the human situation and answered by an understanding of Jesus. And such a structure is basically soteriological: Jesus has meaning first and foremost as our saviour. Logically the Christological question, that of the special relation of the saviour to Yahweh, is secondary. Jesus must be identified as the Messiah before his relation to Yahweh can be of interest. What actually seems to happen in the New Testament is this: Jesus is identified as the Messiah but his actual presence and life makes necessary a new view of what the Messiah is. The reality exceeds the expectation. To mention just two ways in which this shows itself, there are the fact that he takes the form of a suffering servant whose saving act par excellence is death on a cross, and the extraordinary absoluteness and universality of his claims. Things like this constitute the more radical question of who or what he actually *is*—and this is the question of Christology.

In the past there has been, I feel, too sharp a distinction made between Christology and soteriology. The one has been seen as a matter of history, the other a matter of metaphysics. We would like to bring them together again in the way in which modern biblically-oriented 'functional Christologies' attempt to do.

In our criticism of the secularising analysis of the human situation we gave as the fundamental characteristic determining our need for salvation our unconditional desire for identity, where identity is only conceivable through an identification of ourselves with the Other of our mysterious transcendence, namely God. Salvation, if it is to be the salvation we desire, must also have this unconditional character. It must be salvation for identity and that means that it must consist in nothing less than the self-communication of God to us, the realisation of the union implicit in the mystery of our transcendence. This last follows from the fact that of ourselves we are unable to achieve identity; it can only come from the Other. And only from an Other who already has it. Whether this project is truth or illusion is ultimately only made clear by the actual achievement of identity. At any rate this, and nothing less, is the task of the saviour if he is really to save us.

For this reason every description of the saving work of Christ that leaves out of account this unconditional, supra-historical element fails to do justice to the demands of our situation. Because of the apparent contradiction between such an idea of salvation and a superficial understanding of the human situation all sorts of problems arise. False solutions can be sought in the sphere of eschatology, where in order to escape the issue of unconditionality and mystery, salvation is pushed into the future, a future which remains nevertheless fully historical and therefore not absolute. Another false account of the saving work of Christ is that which would make it a purely psychological affair. He is the perfect man, the man who overcomes all life's problems, and as such can be our model and inspiration. There is also the possibility of a retreat into the realm of collectivity, of politics. Jesus is seen simply as providing a revolutionary doctrine for the transformation of any and every society by the radical nature of its criticism.

Granted then that all such accounts fall short of the salvation that is required how are we to understand Jesus correctly as the true saviour. And because of what we have seen a correct notion of salvation to imply this question is really the fundamental question of Christology.

Put very simply: we shall have to demonstrate that our concept of salvation implies that of hypostatic union. Salvation can be nothing less than God's communication of himself to man. If we recognise Jesus as the saviour of mankind we shall have to say that in him this self-communication of God to man is achieved, that what in all men is only a potentiality in him is historically present. The resurrected Jesus has achieved identity through a real identification with the Other of his human transcendence. Or, put another way, he has been given identity through his union with the source of identity, God.

We can define this union of God and man in Jesus as hypostatic in two ways, metaphysically or in terms of the salvation for the sake of which it takes place. Because of what I have already said about the relation between Christology and soteriology I intend to do the latter.

If God's communicating of himself to man is to be a communication to man as he is in his fullness, his concrete historical bodiliness as well as his transcendent selfhood, it must be fully historical and concrete, no merely ideal or spiritual reality. If it were not this it could never be the object of a free response of man's either. Further, if it were not this it could never be the means of uniting men in their salvation; it would be a salvation *out* of the world, a destruction of natural structures of community. All this points to the pattern of this self-communication taking the form the Bible says it does: that of an initial communication to an individual as a *pledge* and means of a final communication to all men. The saviour is the individual in whom the communication first occurs and through whom it becomes available for all. His uniqueness is primarily a uniqueness of position but, precisely because of the nature of what is being communicated, as we shall see this also implies a uniqueness of nature. For it is of the very nature of such a pledge that it be *irrevocable* and *unsurpassable*. It is God, the transcendent as such, that is being communicated and he communicates himself *absolutely*. There is identity—nothing less. And as long as the pledge of this self-communication were not, in the strictest sense, *a divine reality itself*, it would be basically transitory and surpassable since it is finite, historical. Hence if Jesus is the pledge of our salvation, and our salvation consists in the communication of himself to us by God, it follows that Jesus himself must be God, a source and not only a receiver of identity. How this is possible for a truly historical man is the question that the Christological development from Nicea and Chalcedon attempts to answer. Though answer is the wrong word—rather this is the mystery it is grappling with. Nevertheless, if what we have said above is true, soteriology and Christology have been reconciled insofar as it will be seen that once one has accepted Jesus as the true and only saviour, the irrevocable and unsurpassable pledge of God's self-communication, one will have by that very fact assented to the doctrine of the hypostatic union.

We have finally formulated our demand for a saviour in an adequate way. For Jesus to be truly saviour it is necessary for the acts of his life whereby he strives towards identity, the total act that is his life, to be the act of God. We must now put our question to the New Testament. Does it present us with such a saviour?

The New Testament contains different accounts of the salvation that Jesus offers and different descriptions of him as the saviour. Basically there are three different accounts, the Synoptic, the Pauline and the Johannine, with Hebrews as a possible fourth. Here I shall simply choose one to illustrate the substantial truth of the hypothesis suggested above.

For St John it is *eternal life* that man stands in need of and which God offers him in Jesus: 'God gave us eternal life, and this life is in his Son. He who has the Son has life . . .' (1 Jn 5:11) This eternal life

John defines as consisting in the knowledge of God: 'this is eternal life, that they know thee the only true God, and Jesus Christ whom thou hast sent.' (Jn 17:3) This knowledge must not be thought of as objective knowledge; John does not mean that for 'By this we may be sure that we know him, if we keep his commandments' (1 Jn 2:3), and the only Johannine commandment, the new commandment, is love: 'He who does not love does not know God' (1 Jn 4:8). Thus eternal life consists in a truly personal knowledge of God such as is suggested by the Old Testament use of the word 'know' to signify the intimate union of the lover with the beloved. That the ultimate character of this eternal life consists in personal union with God is indicated by such expressions as 'by this we know that we abide in Him and He in us . . . God abides in him and he in God . . . he who abides in love abides in God and God in him' (1 Jn 4 passim). It is moreover only in *Jesus* that man can attain to this knowledge of God: 'He who has seen me has seen the Father' (Jn 14:9). There is the question here of a real though mysterious identity: 'I and the Father are one' (Jn 10:30). Jesus is described by John as both Life and Word of God: the significance of this description, in the light of the above, is that Jesus' very being consists in God's communication of himself to men. Life, as we have shown above, signifies man's participation in God for St John. And Word connotes the most intimate possible identity with God together with the function of communicating the reality of this identity with all that is not God. Word stands for both thought and expression, thus it is the ideal term for this double purpose.

From this brief sketch of a New Testament Christology it can clearly be seen that the figure of the Saviour it enshrined is adequate to our demands. The only question that remains is how the salvation that has become actual in Jesus can be salvation *for us*. Our demand is not simply that there be salvation but that *we* should be saved.

Salvation can only be wholly the work of God; it is he who communicates himself to man. Yet for this self-communication to be truly historical, to be truly a communication to *man*, it must be accepted by man's own response to it, by Jesus first and then by each man. The question of Jesus' human response to God's initiative is part of the second problem we intend to deal with, that of the reality of his humanity in the face of the hypostatic union, so we shall leave it out here. But in structure it is no different from ours so a consideration of our appropriation will do just as well. And the first thing that must be said is that we participate in salvation by identifying ourselves with Jesus as saviour. This identification is that act commonly called *faith* in theology. It is absolutely central in St. John's account of salvation; one could in fact say that it *was* salvation, considered from the point of view of the human situation: 'For God so loved the world that he gave his only Son, that whoever believes in him should not perish but have eternal life' (Jn 3: 16). More properly though *faith* describes this act of identification with Jesus insofar as it is an identification with a *past* historical event, namely the life, death and resurrection of the saviour. Insofar as it is identification with the personal *future* of which he is the pledge and promise, it is called *hope*. And insofar as it is a *present* act it consists in that identification with others on the basis of our common community with Jesus that is called *charity*. Together the three words define the totality of man's response to God's saving act.

But in describing salvation from man's side one must not forget that it remains something wholly transcendent. Faith, hope and charity do not describe primarily psychological attitudes; they retain the element of transcendence. For this reason they are called 'theological' virtues. They are only ultimately specified by God. Even in the heart of the human situation salvation never becomes something *simply human*. One must not appear to translate *God* into *faith, hope and charity* as though one were translating the sacred into the secular, the transcendent into the simply human. The simply human is a myth in the worst sense of the word and has no existence except perhaps in a test-tube.

Nevertheless salvation for all its transcendence does make a difference to our experience of the human situation (Jesus' humanity was real after all). It alters the nature of our predicament.

Faith describes an absolute commitment to a past event, the historical life of Jesus. But that life is also present to us in the form of a unique and concrete social organism—the Church. Faith as a fully concrete historical option consists in our participation in this life through membership of the Church. This act of membership of a particular social tradition gives history a shape and direction for us. We look at the world from a particular context and point of view, from a milieu that is more far-reaching than any particular set of doctrines, laws or programmes. So by faith we choose a particular version of history, in the sense that we commit ourselves to a particular social tradition, become part of a movement that is in the process of *making* history.

Hope describes the putting of all our value in the absolute future. We hope in Jesus and his promise of the coming Kingdom. We hope in him alone as having the power of bringing in the Kingdom. In spite of this absolute character of our hope it does not lead to quietism. Indeed precisely because our hope is a hope in the absolute future we are freed from an enslavement to any particular present state of affairs. No status quo can be adequate and hope urges us forward to what is new. This forward movement provides the necessary basis for a radical criticism of any and every status quo. Any suggestion of finality or absoluteness about any institution or authority is seen by hope as idolatry. In this way hope frees us from the 'powers of this world'.

Finally, charity describes an absolute identification of ourselves in the present. This is certainly a paradoxical conception but none the less real for that. It is an identification with others but on the basis of our common community with the Saviour. This is the meaning of the age-old Christian injunction to 'see Christ in others'. We identify with them *as with him*. Hence the form this identification must take is that of *death*. For no other *present* reality could be the means of an *absolute* identification. In Jesus' life too it took this form; it had to. Death, as the negation of all finitude, is the only symbol available to communicate the unconditional. This is the reason that Christian love must take the form of an annihilating death to self. This death to self is however the one thing that can give meaning to our eventual death. It is a death-in-life that communicates life to others for we now see, on the basis of our faith, in the mystery of our fellowman the saving mystery of God's self-communication. We identify ourselves with him *as saved* and so incorporate him too in the salvation which the unconditional desire of his own heart demands.

We have tried to show how Christology grows out of the human situation and also returns to it to alter it. Christology approached in this way is at the same time soteriology. But because of the nature of salvation a problem inevitably remains about the humanity of the Saviour. It is not the hypostatic union itself that is problematical; that must remain mysterious. The problem consists in how we are to understand the consequences of this union for the human nature of Jesus. And this problem is rendered especially acute by modern insights into the structure of human consciousness and the essential temporality of human existence.

In the past protestant theology has not felt the problem of Jesus' humanity, but only because it had virtually dispensed with the doctrine of his divinity. Catholic theology on the other hand has shown a marked monophysite tendency in its exclusive stress on the divinity of the Saviour and neglect of his humanity. Since the reformation however the burgeoning cult of Mary has witnessed to a felt lack on the part of Catholics to an understanding of Jesus' humanity. The significance of Mary in theology has always been this: to stress the reality of Christ's humanity. Even the title *theotokos* has this effect, the point being that Mary, an ordinary woman, is *really* Christ's mother. A person who really has a human mother even though he is the Son of God must be fully human after all. But although the Marian movement in theology indicated the problem it could not solve it. What was needed was a renewal of interest in Christology as such. And just such a renewal has been evident since the appearance of Galtier's book in 1939.[4]

The subject of this book was the knowledge and self-consciousness of Christ. The scholastic treatment of this theme has been conceived of as a defence of Christ's human knowledge against its reality being undermined by the divine. Three modes of human cognition were distinguished, acquired and infused knowledge and beatific vision or the direct knowledge of God. But these categories make little sense to a modern understanding of human personality and consciousness. And they appear to split up Jesus' human consciousness into separate compartments. A further difficulty is raised by the idea of Jesus' having beatific vision from the first moment of his existence. Apart from the fact that such an idea would seem to contradict a great deal of the evidence of the gospels it seems incompatible with a true idea of human reality. For man is a being who achieves himself only through an essential self-transcendence that is never complete but always reaching beyond itself. And if the beatific vision is the name we give to the final goal of this development it is simply contradictory to imagine it as already present at any stage prior to that in any *human* life, Jesus' included. Perhaps this problem is best solved, as a number of theologians have chosen to in recent times, in the following way: in normal human consciousness one can distinguish between the knowledge of objects and a pre-conceptual awareness that is

4. P Galtier, *L'Unité de Christ: Être, Personne, Conscience* (Beauchesne, 1939).

its ground. This awareness is totally unspecified and general yet it is the most concrete form of human consciousness. It is simply the consequence of man's being a conscious being. And in it the reality that underlies the distinction of subject and object is directly present. We have spoken of this reality already and equated it with God. But in the case of Jesus his consciousness at this level is unique. For he *is* the Word of God. For him this basic self-awareness is an awareness of the Word. Yet because of its basic character this awareness need not be explicated in conceptual knowledge at all, or only gradually throughout his life. Indeed in human reality the clear and certain knowledge of 'who one is', is what one understands by the achievement of identity and is only possible in the transcendence of one's death. Could this have been possible for Jesus before that moment? It is not excluded that he may have had a clear conception of his role in God's plan and the closest possible intimacy of adoration and personal union with his Father at each moment of his life, yet because of the very nature of human life such intimacy is only fulfilled in death.

This problem is closely related to another: Because of its possession by the Word the human nature of Christ is traditionally said to be without human personality. What is meant of course is that Christ is only one individual, the Word of God, and not two. Yet for the modern notion of personality as conscious presence-to-self to say that Christ is not a human person or that the self of his conscious self-presence is not a human self but that of the Word is to detract from the reality and dignity of human personality. A lot of the difficulty lies in a confusion of terms, between the modern and the medieval use of the term 'person'. But a genuine Christological advance may be possible through the modern insight into the relational character of human reality. In normal human existence selfhood is only fully and finally achieved through man's conscious self-surrender to God in love and adoration. The hypostatic union must simply be seen as the perfect and therefore unique example of such self-surrender. The humanity of Jesus is thus supremely personal not in spite of its possession by God but because of it. A rider to this is that the term and goal of Jesus' self-transcendence is not the Word but the Father. To imagine him as man adoring himself as the Word of God is to make of him two individuals. He is related only to God the Father. It is precisely because of the absoluteness of this relation that he is the Word. This relation is given by the Father as his own self-communication and hence Jesus, as the Word, is said to proceed from the Father or, as Son, to be begotten by him. His uniqueness consists in being 'the first-born of many brethren'.

In conclusion we should just like to indicate a possible future of development for Christology now. The idea of Jesus' *uniqueness*, as Saviour, would seem to be one particularly open to a renewal of understanding of the Christian mystery. The idea of uniqueness has inevitable consequences for our view of history and as I have suggested, the more we can speak of the hypostatic union in historical terms the better. Such a theory of history would have to be elaborated within the framework of transcendence and mystery I have suggested if it is to do justice to the Christian phenomenon. At the moment neither existential nor historical theology seem capable of it.

(1968)

Chapter Six
Sign, Symbol and Sacrament

The aim of this essay is to situate the Christian sacrament in the sphere of signs and symbols, with a view to gaining, perhaps, a better understanding of it and, perhaps, a solution to some of the theological problems that swarm so thickly about this particular aspect of our faith.

Our point of departure will be to put ourselves, in the most general way, the question: what is a sacrament? To put this question is at once to posit another, the question of the actual phenomena we are questioning and define as 'sacrament'. And certainly the answer to this second question is, for a faithful Catholic, perfectly clear: the sacraments are the seven ritual actions of the church defined as such by the Council of Trent. This answer however though true, is insufficient. We know very well that each of the seven has a history, and we are sufficiently well acquainted with that history to know that not all of them have always been called sacraments, and that they have been called sacraments in different senses.

It is necessary, therefore, in the briefest possible way, to return to the origin of this history, to the primitive Church and the writings of the early Fathers, to see what is there referred to by the word, 'sacrament'. For once one has done that one will be in a better position to unveil the essential notion of the Christian sacrament.

When one does return to the origins of the Christian sacraments, what one finds being referred to by the word *sacrament* is rather the totality of the Church's cult than a number of distinct ritual acts. The content of this cult is basically the same for patristic and new testament periods. In his *Early Christian Worship* Cullman lists the elements of the Church's cult in the New Testament times as baptism, a Word service consisting of preaching and prayers, and 'the Breaking of Bread'. As for the Fathers, Schillebeecx, in his monumental *De Sacramentele Heilseconomie* (1952), gives their view of a single whole formed by Baptism, Confirmation and the Eucharist. It is this composite whole that Tertullian, following the common usage of the time, refers to as '*totum salutis sacramentum*'.

Having thus sketchily designated our object of enquiry, we are now in a position to ask what primitive theology intended by referring to it as *sacrament*.

In fact the first word used to designate the fundamental act of the Church's cult, was not the Latin *sacramentum* but the Greek *mysterion*. This word gets its original pre-Christian meaning from the Greek mystery religions. Here it signifies, according to Schillebeecx, a consecration to a deity by means of participation in symbolic ritual acts. Because of this prime meaning, *mysterion* also gains the meaning of secret knowledge or *gnosis* that is gained as a result of participation in the deity by means of the rite. Important aspects of this pagan use of *mysterion* are (a) that is usually refers back to some event in a mythical past *in illo tempore*, and (b) that it is considered to make this past event present for participants in the rite.

In the New Testament the word is used, and especially by St Paul, to refer to God's secret plan kept hidden form the beginning and now revealed in Christ (Col 1:27, Rom 16:25, Eph 1:9, 3:2, 5:32, 1 Cor 2:7, 1 Tim 3:9). Jesus himself, as the embodiment and fulfilment of God's saving plan, is referred to as the *mysterion* of the Father. Hence there is this in common between the pagan and the Biblical usage of *mysterion*: both include the notions of a divine secret that is hidden from human eyes but which is revealed in particular human acts.

It is precisely these notions that are made much of by the Fathers. Christ is the primal *mysterion* because it is he who, par excellence, reveals in his human life, in all his acts but especially in his death and resurrection, the saving will of God. The Christian *mysterion* is thus nothing other than a making present by means of symbolic ritual acts the '*mysteria carnis Christi*', the saving acts of the Word-made-flesh, the primal *Mysterion* himself. And of course precisely this that the original Christian cult, centred as it was on Baptism and the Eucharist, did so economically and effectively.

The Latin Fathers enjoyed the same basic conception of the Christian liturgy as the Greeks; *sacramentum* is used as a synonym for *mysterion.* Yet it is probably true that the secular meaning of *sacramentum* had not a little to do with the distinctively Latin development in the theology of the sacraments during the time of the scholastics. In secular use *sacramentum* had two basic and distinct meanings. In military parlance it carried the sense of a binding oath or devotedness; in the language of the courts it referred to the monetary pledge that the contestants had to stake on the success of their suit. Then too there was the etymological meaning of making holy (*sacramentum*). None of these meanings however, would seem to account for why the word was used as the equivalent of *mysterion.* According to Schillebeecx, no scholar has yet offered conclusive evidence as to why this occurred. My own conjecture, for what it is worth, is that the move can be explained by the fact that the verb *sacrare* has its root in *secernere,* a verb meaning to hide or secrete. Hence, for instance, the notion, implicit in that of sanctifying or making holy, of being *set aside.* The connection between secrete and secret is obvious. And we have already seen that the term *mysterion* in Christian usage, referred primarily to God's secret, his hidden plan for man's salvation finally revealed for faith in the human life of Christ.

Be that as it may, these different meanings of *sacramentum,* served to distinguish and make explicit notions implicit in *mysterion.* The notions, pre-eminently, of cause, of sign, of pledge, and even of character.

Enough has now been said to give a general idea of the patristic understanding of sacrament. The key notions in this are (a) that Jesus himself is the primal sacrament, (b) that in the Church's cult his saving acts are made present, (c) that they are made present by symbolic liturgical acts, (d) that by means of the rite the faithful are able to participate in the re-presented acts of Christ, (e) that by doing so they share in the salvation Christ achieved.

When one looks at the scholastic development of these notions one finds a persistent attempt at definition and systematisation. Certain aspects of the earlier inclusive notion are highlighted by controversy. From Isadore of Seville, 647, onwards, the predominant interest is in the idea that sacraments *cause* grace. There is however another train of thought, actually begun by Augustine, but emphasized and made famous by Berengarius, which is centred on the idea of a sacrament as a *sign.* Of course it is an efficacious sign; but it is efficacious precisely because of the similarity between the sign and what it signifies.

Both streams of thought meet in St Thomas. In his early works the causal aspect is predominant, and even in the *Summa* a sacrament is primarily something that makes holy—sacra-mentum. Yet he uncompromisingly places sacrament in the category of sign. He does however make use of an expression which suggests the possibility of a synthesis of the two traditions. For it is not simply (so he argues) that sacraments cause what they signify. They actually cause by signifying—*significando efficient* (IIIa Q.62, art.1 ad.1).

For the purposes of this essay this is all we need to know of the scholastic treatment of the theology of sacrament. It was assumed without question by the Council of Trent in its canons on the sacraments. Here the chief points of interest for us are the assertions that the sacraments *contain* grace, *confer* it, and do so *ex opere operato* and not because of the faith of the recipient. Thus Canon 8:

> Si quis dixerit, per ipsa novae Legis sacramenta ex opera operato non conferri gratiam, sed solam fidem divinae promissionis ad gratiam consequendam sufficere: a.s. (If anyone should say that grace is not conferred by the sacrament of the New Law *ex opera operato* (by the mere performance of the rite); but that they only express faith in the divine promise to confer grace, let them be anathema.)

To which Antonius Solisius comments:

> Omnes theologi concordant quod sacramenta conferunt gratiam ex opera operato; sed in *modo* conferendi discordant, et ex utraque parte sunt multi theologi. (All theologians agree that sacraments cause grace *ex opera operato*; but differ as to how this is conferred, and in many different ways.)

St Thomas' answer to this is 'significando'. We will take this as our point of entry into the enquiry of what sort of signs sacraments are, and what it means to say that they cause what they signify.

The general theology of the sacraments since Trent has developed in roughly two different directions. On the one hand it is said that the Christian sacrament causes what it signifies because God has pledged his gift of grace to the performance of this particular external rite. Because the promise is God's it is infallible. At bottom this notion of sacramental causality is thoroughly juridical. God could just as well have attached his promise to grace to quite other signs (say, for instance, the solemn utterance by the Christian minister of the appropriate number from 1 to 7!) There is no intrinsic connection between the signs *as signs* and the causing of grace. More accurately, the sort of signification attributed by this view to the Christian sacrament is that commonly experienced in the use of money. A coin is a sign of the government's promise to give its owners so much gold in exchange for it. The coin as a sign is arbitrary, there is no intrinsic connection between it and what it signifies.

Against this view one can set the attitude of the modern 'sacrament-as-mystery' school associated with the name of Dom Odo Casel, and the whole movement for liturgical reform in the modern Church.[1] For this school sacraments are symbolic actions that must be appropriate to the sacred realities that they signify. Because our salvation is gained through the death and resurrection of Jesus, a ritual action of plunging down into water and then emerging again is possible as a Christian sacrament. Further, so this view goes, it is precisely because they appeal to certain fundamental religious archetypes in man that the Christian sacrament is effective. The historic events of Christ's life actually are a realisation of man's universal religious aspirations. Hence it is that the symbolic ritual expression of those events can be so supremely effective. Because they are composed of the absolutely basic symbols of man's religious nature (and here there is reference to and comparison with primitive and, more especially, Hebrew, religion) they are able to involve him in this way, by taking him out of himself and plunging him in the supremely moving symbols of the rite, they transform him, give him a new vision and new possibilities of expressing it—in short, they communicate grace.

Clearly there is truth in both of these positions. It is *grace* that the Christian sacrament causes, only because it is *God* who, in his perfect freedom has elected to attach his offer of himself to certain human acts. Then too, God's saving self-communication can only be offered to *humanity* if it is articulated in a fully human and historical way. We now have to ask ourselves the question of what precisely this involves.

1. O Casel, *The Mystery of Christian Worship* (Darton, Longman and Todd, [1932] 1962)

Let us say at once, following St Thomas, that sacraments cause by signifying. What else that we can think of in our ordinary human experience does precisely this? Words, surely. Words are signs. And when a word is uttered it communicates to the mind of the hearer (provided he knows the language) the meaning that it signifies. That is to say, it causes the meaning to be present to the person. It causes meaning simply by signifying it.

One can put this in a slightly different way. A word is a special sort of sign; it is a symbol. That is to say, it is a sign of a sign. For it is a sign of a concept which is the sign of a thing. A word is said to *connote* a meaning or concept, but to *denote* a thing. It is the concept that is caused to be in the mind of the hearer when the word is spoken. It is caused simply by the signification of the word. The concept *is* the signification of the word.

Let us now apply this to the Christian sacrament. This is like a word in that it too is a sign, and a sign of a sign. It is a sign of Christ's incarnate acts which in turn are signs of God's saving self-communication to man. There is a further resemblance too. For in the case of a word one can distinguish between its physical and its intellectual reality, between the word as sound and the word as meaning. This is the same distinction that must be maintained between any spatio-temporal human act and its truly personal significance. It is also true of the Christian sacrament. For it too is a particular historically conditioned human act and it too has a meaning, that is conventionally determined by the authority of the Church's traditions and ultimately by its institution by Christ.

Let us now take the sort of causality we have discovered in words and apply it to the Christian sacrament, in the hope that it may help us to understand their action more profoundly and, perhaps, solve some of the problems that contemporary theology has faced us with.

The fact that a sacrament is said to cause in precisely the same way as a word, should prepare us for this truth: a sacrament is a word. The Christian sacrament is a word with a meaning, and it confers grace on the recipient by presenting him with its meaning. One is of course prepared for this insight by the scholastic distinction between a verbal form and a material action in the Christian sacrament. And certainly it has always been the verbal form that constituted the decisive element of the sacrament. But in addition to this one must take account of the fact that the *matter* of the Christian sacrament is also largely symbolic, meaningful; in some sacraments the matter is actually made up of words. Hence the element of *word*, and therefore of meaning, in the Christian sacrament is much larger than might at first appear. In fact it so dominates the sacrament as almost entirely to exhaust its very essence. All that remains in the sacramental act once meaning has been subtracted is just the fact of the act itself. The Christian sacrament is a word; it causes by meaning; it causes grace by meaning, ultimately, God's offer of himself to man in Christ.

To say that the sacraments cause grace in us by presenting us with a meaning might at first appear paradoxical. How is it that we are transformed, saved that is, by a spoken word—and *ex opera operato* at that? We must be clear here where the real difficulty lies. It is precisely God's Word that saves us, his historical self-communication to us in the human acts of Jesus. It is the same Word that communicates itself to us in the authoritative acts of the Church. This immediacy is ensured by the material element of the sacrament: God really offers himself here and now, his offer of himself is really present. For God to speak is to utter himself. The Christian sacrament is essentially the proclamation of the Gospel.

This last statement might sound a bit strange to Catholic ears. One is seldom taught to think of listening to preaching or the reading of the bible as an infallible means of grace. Yet it is, just as surely as the sacraments themselves. One might object: but here it depends solely on the hearer's response. So it does too in the sacraments. We are often inclined to think of the causality of the sacraments as obviating the need for a response. After all, if it all depends on me, what is the point of *ex opera operato*. At this point, in order to conclude what I feel is a rather more than usually opaque paragraph, it will be instructive to quote a passage from Karl Rahner's *The Church and the Sacraments*:

> Someone repents of his sins with genuine contrition and conversion, in his own conscience. If he does this, he knows with absolute certainty, by reason of the faithful and irrevocable words of the divine promise, that God truly forgives him his guilt. What happens then is an actual instance of grace being conferred, not a merely 'subjective' desire for it to happen. Another man confesses his sins contritely in

> the sacrament of penance. He knows that God forgives him his guilt by the Church's power of the keys, if he is truly and genuinely repentant. In neither case is there absolute certainty about the fulfilment of the condition. In both cases, over and above what the man does and experiences, he must also trust in God and his inscrutable judgment, seeing that in both cases he is obliged to trust firmly and unshakenly (not to know), with simple and childlike hope, (for God is greater than our hearts), that God will truly have produced by his grace the necessary condition, our 'good will'. In the first case we speak of *opus operantis*, in the second of *opus operatum*. What is the difference between the two? (1966: 7)

Rahner's answer is 'none' so far as grace or causality is concerned. The difference is only in the sign. In the case of the Christian sacrament the sign is a sure and certain offer of grace in which the offer is really and historically present to the believer's faith. Other signs, personal and private, though equally efficacious, are essentially fragile and indeterminate, without the guarantee of the Church.

We are now in a position to draw some conclusions about the meaning of the Christian sacrament as an efficacious sign. Comparing it to a word has put us in the position of being able to conceive its causality in a nowise physical way. Defining the Christian sacrament as the Word of God communicating itself to men has made it all the more clear that sacramental efficacy cannot be explained as a one-way process in which grace flows from the sacrament and into the recipient. Nor is the question of the disposition of the recipient to be solved by appealing to the profoundly evocative and moving character of certain fundamental symbols and rites. One is forced rather to posit another grace-bestowing act of God, reciprocal to that embodied in the sacrament and responsive to it, that works immediately in the will of the recipient making it a 'good will' and prompting its free and whole-hearted response. Only thus could the will respond in terms of the recipient's understanding of the divine meaning of the sacrament. And this is to say that in a fruitful sacrament God moves the will of the recipient by means of the meaning the sacramental word causes in this intellect. But because a natural faculty could not respond of itself to a supernatural solicitation, the will too is elevated by a secret action of God's Spirit. Thus, in the sacramental encounter, man is taken up into the life of God. He is presented with the Word and moved by the Spirit. And the occasion of this encounter is the material reality of the Christian sacrament.[2]

(1969)

2. Works consulted for this essay: For the historical account of the practice and understanding of the sacraments: H Bettenson, *The Early Christian Fathers* (Oxford, 1956); O Cullmann, *Early Christian Worship* (SCM, 1959); Dom G Dix *The Shape of the Liturgy*; (Dacre Press, 1945); J Jungmann, *Mass of the Roman Rite* (Benziger, 1951); H Rahner, *Greek Myths and Christian Mysteries* (Biblo-Moser, 1963); the *Didache* is in A Louth, *Early Christian Writings* (Penguin, 1987).

   For the philosophical background: M Eliade, *Myths Dreams and Mysteries* (Harvill, 1960) and *Patterns in Comparative Religion* (Sheed and Ward, 1958); K Jung, *Man and his Symbols* (Picador, 1964) and *Psychology and Religion* (Yale, 1960); Langer, S. *Philosophy in a New Key* (Harvard, 1984); H McCabe, *Law Love and Language*, esp. Ch 5 (Sheed and Ward, 1968); M Merleau-Ponty, *Signs* (Northwestern, 1964).

   For the theological analysis: St Thomas Aquinas, *Summa Theologiae* IIIa, Sacraments; N Lash, *His Presence in the World*, esp. Ch 5 (Sheed and Ward, 1968); X Léon-Dufour, 'Mystery', in Léon-Dufour (ed.) *Dictionary of Biblical Theology* (Geoffrey Chapman, 1982); H McCabe, *The New Creation* (Sheed and Ward, 1963); J MacQuarrie, *God-Talk* (SCM, 1970); J Powers, *Eucharistic* Theology (Seabury, 1974); K Rahner, *The Church and the Sacraments* (Burns and Oates, 1970) and his essays 'Theology of the Symbol' and 'The Word and the Eucharist' in *Theological Investigations IV* (Helicon Press, 1966); E Schillebeecx, *De Sacramentele Heilseconomie* (Nelissen, 1952) and *Christ the Sacrament of Encounter with God* (Sheed and Ward, 1963); the article 'Sacrament' in *Theologische Woordenboek* (edited by Brink *et al*) (JJ Roman, 1952).

Chapter Seven
The Church and the Sacraments

Any theological synthesis or overview of the subject-matter designated by our title must if it is to be fully founded on Christian faith, be derived from—or at least adequately linked by logical ties to—an understanding of the person and the work of Jesus.

For our present purposes (that is, the outlining of a theological synthesis of Christian teaching on the Church and sacraments) this understanding can, to my way of thinking, most conveniently be based on the doctrines of the Resurrection and the Second Coming of Jesus. Hence in what follows it will be these two doctrines especially that will form the basis for our synthesis. In order to derive from them theological conclusions relevant to our subject-matter I will make use of the notion of *presence.*

I choose this notion for a number of reasons. Firstly, and most obviously, because of its connection with 'real presence', a fundamental notion in the traditional theology of the sacraments. Secondly, and perhaps more importantly, *presence* refers to a whole range of ideas current in contemporary personalist philosophy. Presence is a relational concept, implying at least two terms, each of which is connected in some way with the other. In human existence it implies a conscious presence to the other (based on a presence-to-self) which could be called *community* and which is in fact the basis for all forms of social communication. In this regard common idiom has phrases such as 'in the presence of so-and-so', referring to an action not directly involving so-and-so but in which he nevertheless has a definite role, this role being fulfilled by the simple fact of his being present.

There are, I think, other reasons why *presence* is a useful word for our purposes, but these will appear in the course of our treatment.

We have mentioned conscious self-presence or the presence of persons to one another in human society. Clearly Jesus was present to his followers in this way. The Resurrection, however, raises the question of another way of being present, and the Second Coming of yet a third. We do not doubt that at the Second Coming we shall, for the first time, 'see him as he is'. We shall only then see 'face to face' and, in the countenance of the man Christ Jesus, the glory of God. Whatever the precise nature of this transforming vision, one can surely safely claim for it the fulness of personal self-communication, that is to say, the full presence of one person to another in mutual self-achievement. This way of being present (to the Saviour first, but then of course, because of him, to all men) forms the substance of the Christian hope, the beatific vision as it is called. It surpasses, therefore, all other modes of personal presence which, for that very reason, must never be thought of as more than provisional. It surpasses, for instance, in intimacy and reality, the presence of the risen Jesus to his followers during the forty days that followed the crucifixion.

A fortiori it also far exceeds the presence of Jesus to his followers in the days before his death. The presence of one person to another, even the most intense solidarity of spirit, is at best a flickering and a fluctuating flame in the days of our 'exile'. There are moments, it is true, 'hints followed by guesses', moments of transfiguration, but what is after all our ultimate concern retains its ultimacy.

The truth of this last, in the case of Jesus, is important for our thinking about the sacraments. If our model for personal presence is simply physical presence, then we may very well wonder in what sense sacramental presence can be 'real'. It is enough at this stage to note that the central dogmas of the faith imply modes of personal presence that far transcend that—even if one hadn't, as a corrective to one's thought, the common experience of human love.

That the presence of the risen Jesus to his followers goes beyond this common mode of presence must be the case. Not only is their experience of the resurrected Jesus the historical basis of his followers, hopes for the future. There is also the consideration that if the meaning of the resurrection is at least that the death of Jesus is not only the end but also the consummation of his life, the definitive and irrevocable achievement of his human identity, then the mode of his presence to his followers—if it occurs at all—must be correspondingly more complete.

This is not the whole truth though. Although Jesus is in the glory of the Father his followers certainly are not. And the mode of presence (presence being a relational concept) depends on both terms of a relation. Hence the oddness of the resurrection appearances. There is an imbalance. The presence is even more fluctuating and flickering than before. But there is on the other hand a greater symbolic depth.

Having qualified the presence of the risen Jesus to his followers in this way one must nevertheless go on to stress that it is the supreme historical basis for the Christian hope in the Second Coming of Jesus. It is the 'same Jesus' who died, who rose, and who will come again. No question of three incarnations or even of three 'manifestations'. His personal identity is preserved.

Here perhaps it is helpful to introduce Moltmann's point[1] that although the resurrection of Jesus from the dead implies the full achievement of his personality and the end and consummation of his human life, nevertheless Jesus has a 'future'. Not only a future in the sense that his human individuality is not annihilated in his death, but also a future in the sense that a *further* consummation still lies ahead of him. The Second Coming will be an event for Jesus as well as for his followers.

This certainly does not mean that Jesus' risen existence is a sort of prolongation of his earthly one and that, for instance, he continues to merit. But it certainly does point to a certain 'excess of glory' that is to be the Saviour's in his final communion with the saved. When our joy is full his will overflow.

Perhaps this consideration points to the deepest significance of the doctrine of the Assumption in Catholic theology: The perfection of the Saviour implies another with whom to share it—another human person. Personal perfection implies personal presence; hence a lonely soul in glory is unthinkable. However this may be, the precise extent to which the ultimate fulfilment of Jesus' manhood is bound up with ours does not matter. That there is a connection must be admitted, even if it is only that of our participating in a glory that is already his though even now shared by his human mother.

At all events, now that we have distinguished between the different modes of Jesus' presence to his followers, one can put the question that directly concerns our understanding of the Church and sacraments.

How is he present to us now?

1. See J Moltmann, *Theology of Hope* (SCM, 1967).

Sacramental Presence

An answer to this question must take into account what has already been said. Jesus will be fully and properly present to his followers only at the Second Coming. Hence the 'real presence' that we speak of in connection with the sacraments cannot be really 'real' in the sense of being unsurpassable. Sacraments are surpassable; we will not adore *for ever* 'the most holy sacrament'. But Jesus was certainly and powerfully present to his followers in the days before his death. Between these two modes of presence, his presence in the 'flesh', and his presence at the Second Coming, we must seek an answer that does justice to both, an answer that maintains the tension between them. Such an answer is bound to be dialectical, paradoxical.

First of all it must be said that to us now Jesus is not present, he is absent. He was present in the 'flesh', now he is absent in the 'flesh'. But we cannot stop there. He will be present at his Second Coming, not in the 'flesh' but in the glory of achievement. So this ache of absence has an echo in it of a note that has not yet sounded. Not yet? That is not wholly true. The Resurrection itself is both the pledge of what is to come and of a piece with it. The threefold doctrine of resurrection-ascension-pentecost (in other words, the glorification of Jesus) implies another mode of presence. Insofar as Jesus has ascended into heaven he is really absent from us; insofar as the Spirit is present in the Church he is also really present.

Two things must be said about Jesus' presence in the Church as a 'life-giving Spirit' (1 Cor 15:45). First, the spirit of the Church is always the spirit of 'him who died upon the cross'—it is a fully human spirit. Secondly, the Spirit of the Church is the Spirit of 'him who is to come'—it is the Holy Spirit.

It is the history of this Spirit that one is dealing with in discussing the Church and sacraments, for the Church is nothing other than the historical embodiment of this Spirit, and the sacraments its historical expression. In investigating the Church's traditional understanding of itself and the sacraments one is attempting to touch more closely our experience of Jesus' presence to us now, his presence in the persons of our fellow-men, and this is nothing other than our experience of everyday human society.

In the New Testament itself Jesus is sometimes *referred* to as the 'mystery' of God, where mystery is the Greek word later translated by the Latin 'sacrament'. As God's 'mystery', Jesus is the revelation of something that has been kept secret, the manifestation of something hidden, since the beginning of time—God's plan of a saving communication of himself to man within the course of human history.

In the Greek Fathers this idea of Jesus as the manifestation or revelation of God's saving self-communication is elaborated to include the idea of re-presentation or *anamnesis*, whereby Jesus himself as the primal 'mystery' is once again made *present* to his followers through the liturgical celebration of the saving events of his life, the *mysteria carnis Christi*. Thus the Church's cult, the *mysteries* as it was called, is seen primarily as a form of presence of the risen Christ to his worshippers and of his worshippers to him.

This original notion of Christian worship is not denied by the Latin Fathers. The inclusive idea of 'mystery' (together with that of re-presentation that is so closely bound up with it) is however broken down into a number of more precise subsidiary concepts, those of 'sign' and 'cause' and, to a lesser extent, that of 'pledge'.

The concept of sign as developed in the Latin theology underlines the fact that the actions of Christian worship which 're-present' the acts of the Saviour, nevertheless make these present in only a provisional and intermediate way. Sacramental reality is symbolic reality. The concept of cause as applied to the sacraments balances that of sign. Christian sacraments really do cause what they signify because of the reality of Jesus' resurrection. Symbols point beyond themselves, and the sacraments in their very function of re-presentation, point beyond themselves to the real 'real presence' at the Second Coming.

The pledge of the Second Coming has in fact (for faith) been made, and because it is God's pledge it cannot fail of fulfilment. Hence the sacraments are effective; they are not only expressive, they are creative too, of the communication that they signify.

In St Thomas these two lines of thought are carefully synthesised.

His formula is *significando efficiunt*; the sacraments effect by signifying, their signification is their effect. This means that though the sacraments do really constitute a mode of Jesus' presence, this mode is symbolic. It is not simply physical and fluctuating, nor is it glorious and achieved; it is in tension between the two opposing terms, *cultural* rather than physical or final.

St. Thomas' synthesis represents the final stage in the secularisation of the idea of mystery. It therefore opens up the way for the modern anthropological interpretation of the meaning of the Christian sacraments.

The Church as Sacrament

This investigation of the human dimensions and significance of the sacramental idea goes hand in glove with the advance of modern philosophy. It becomes associated therefore in ever-greater degree with the theology of the reformers. It is only in fairly recent times however that it seems to have borne fruit in a real renewal of appreciation of the sacramental idea—in Protestant and Catholic alike.

The Protestant emphasis on the primacy of faith—and therefore of the word (whether in scripture or in preaching), opened up in the understanding of Christian worship and spirituality the areas of 'dialogue', 'encounter' and 'response'. Together with this discovery of the specifically personal dimension of Christian worship (and of Christian life) goes an emphasis on the congregation, the gathering of Christians and the fellowship (*koinonia*) that characterises it. In other words, once the personal note has been sounded, the way is open for the idea of community to be taken seriously. And this is precisely what both modern Catholic and Protestant theology attempts to do in their re-evaluation of the sacraments.

Accordingly sacraments are seen as means of communication, the whole sacramental system as communications media, if you like, between the followers of Jesus. They constitute a language that has its roots in a Word of God uttered in a historical past but which will only reveal its full significance in a future that transcends all determinations of the present. The Christian sacramental system is a very spare and simple language game, but in common with all languages it has the property of not only expressing a community that already exists—and that is rooted in a tradition stemming from the past, but also of creating a community that does not yet exist but which has the possibility of gathering up into an ever-more-comprehensive newness all that the past has brought to fruition. It is the Christian hope, based on a faith in a promise from the past, that this possibility will be realised.

The emphasis on the sacraments as means of communication between members of a community has led to a realisation of the Church, the actual social entity itself, as the primordial sacrament. It is the socially definable, hierarchically structured Church and its concrete existence in human history that, first and foremost, makes Jesus present to mankind. The particular sacraments are seen accordingly as various actualisations of this basic property possessed by the Church; they are the gestures which alone *fully* express the true nature and mission of the Christian group.

In view of this, it is not difficult to see why there is in fact only one sacrament in which Jesus is said to be 'really present'. There is in fact *only one sacrament.* Only the Eucharist is the full actualisation of all that the Church has it in her to be. The other sacraments are derivations or particular expressions in certain fundamental human situations of this basic actuality. Thus the Eucharist itself is the sacrament of Jesus' *real presence* in the Church, the sacrament of that *holy communion* which is the Christian's hope for mankind. The sacrament of order expresses the relation of this communion to an historically real society. (Thus bishops are at one and the same time the structural principle of the Church's social existence and the ordinary ministers of the Eucharist.) Baptism is the sacrament of reception into the saving community, and confirmation of the mission to others that membership implies. Anointing and penance are the sacraments of reparation and healing, both biological and cultural, of a unity that in the process of construction suffers continual violence and disintegration at the hands of men. Marriage, finally, is the sacrament of a truly human community which, because it is rooted in the concrete stuff of the world is embodied and therefore sexual too.

Having said all this of the seven sacraments one must not leave out of account the other ways in which the Church represents the Saviour to mankind: To name a few, there is prayer, and preaching, the reading of Scripture and the promulgation of dogma. The seven sacraments, explicitly so called, centred as they are on the Eucharist, are the supremely representative actions, authoritatively recognised, and defined as such, which actualise the Church's nature as the presence in the world, in mission to mankind, of grace.

Seeing the actual Christian group as the sign and realisation of Jesus' presence in the world reminds the theologian that the subject of salvation is mankind and not the Church. The Church exists for the world; the Christian group for other men. The Christian vocation, that the sacraments and the whole preaching of the Church proclaim, is to be the effective sign for mankind of true community. Here as before it must be stressed that the primary datum is the community of believers with *one another*—that is the sign, there is no other. The primary datum that constitutes the human reality of the Church is the spirit of faith, hope and love that animates the followers of Jesus.

Of course, as we have already mentioned, this spirit is nothing other than the human spirit of Jesus. Fundamentally it is a spirit of love, love that is universal and non-exclusive; but this love, because it is a fully human love has notes in it of faith and hope, of trust in an origin and a past tradition that is particular and historical and timebound, and of openness to a future that will be unimaginably new.

I have said that this spirit is the inner reality of the Church. It is more than that. It is the inner dynamic of mankind. But in the Church, in the sacramental language, it is revealed for what it is.

And also in the Church (and Christian faith commits us to this too) it is triumphant, revealed in the actual holiness of its members. Sacraments effect what they signify because of the divine pledge they translate. The human spirit of the Church which is the spirit of Jesus, is also the Holy Spirit. Which is to say that it is the presence of God among us, the dynamics of the divine self-communication which moves history to its fulfilment in that kingdom where:

> 'All shall be well, and all manner of thing shall be well
> When the tongues of flames are infolded
> Into the crowned knot of fire
> And the fire and the rose are one.' ('Four Quartets'—TS Eliot)

(1969)

Chapter Eight
Salvation as Oop Gesprek

The logic of the word 'salvation' involves the idea of a person or situation *from* which the subject of salvation is saved. There are a variety of models used in the Bible for describing such a situation or person; I choose to use that of *slavery*. Apart from other considerations, this model is useful in that it connects the idea of situation to that of person: slavery is always slavery *to*. Salvation is thus the setting-free of someone from slavery to someone else. In the Bible the paradigm case of salvation is the setting-free of the Israelites from their slavery to the Pharaoh. Ultimately, however, in the Gospel, salvation becomes the setting-free of man from his slavery to the Devil.

So much by way of defining how I intend to use the word 'salvation'. I wish now to question our contemporary experience as to how far it contains anything which this model of salvation can help us to interpret. Do we experience a need which could be called the need for salvation? And if so, how does it show itself? What are the characteristic forms of the need for salvation today? Where, in our multi-storeyed modern society, does it show itself most clearly? To indicate at the outset the way in which I intend to deal with this question, let me say that it is in the sphere of language, or more generally that of communications, that I discern the clearest evidence of this need.

Consider the following. They are passages quoted in an article by WA de Klerk (a well-known Afrikaner novelist and playwright) in the recently published *Beweging Uitwaarts* (The Movement Outwards), a collection of critical essays by de Klerk, Johan Degenaar and Martin

Versfeld, that is at present causing quite a stir in Afrikaner cultural circles.[1]

> 'Our ultimate destiny demands of the leaders of the Volk a purposeful and effective fulfilment. Shoulder to shoulder we shall have to wage war against a tidal wave of liberalism, internationalism, Communism. There is a lurking danger and powers that are working against us. We must continually withdraw ourselves from influences that run counter to our cause. Our survival as white civilization must be assured. We are concerned here with the fulfilment of a commission: the urge to survival; to realize here a dispensation in which, together with the peoples that surround us, we may live in peace and progress.' And finally: 'Let every one of us, man and mouse, now pledge ourselves to the Mother of the Volk, to support her through thick and thin for the realization of the destiny which is hers—and therefore also ours.' (My translation from the Afrikaans rather blunts, I am afraid, the rhetorical force of the original.)

The title of the article is 'Inflasie van die Woord'—inflation of the word. It is an analysis of the language of Nationalist politics, of which the above quotations are all examples. But the phenomenon of *lying* language is not peculiar to Afrikaner nationalism; the English-language newspapers are just as full of it. Nor is it peculiar to political speeches; you find it in sermons and in schools, in advertisements and in songs. Wherever you look in our media-manipulated society you will find yourself confronted by, and in fact responding to, the powerful presence of lies.

Isn't it significant how many of the excerpts—from separate sources in fact but too easily able to be strung together as above—are concerned with self-maintenance, the preservation of identity. The language of nationalism is full of such terms as 'voortbestaan', 'self-behoud' (self-maintenance), 'handhawing' (preservation) and 'volksidentiteit'. This idea of racial or 'volks' identity is the basic premise on which South African society is being built. And I am quite

1. WA De Klerk, JJ Degenaar, and M Versfeld, *Beweging Uitwaarts* (John Malherbe, 1969). Martin Versfeld is Professor of Philosophy at the University of Cape Town, Johan Degenaar is Professor of Political Philosophy at the University of Stellenbosch.

sure that it is no accident that the language in which this concern finds articulation is a fundamentally lying language. To establish the connection between the myth of identity and a language of lies, and to make it quite clear that it is not simply an accidental concomitant of White South African nationalism, let me quote here something else:

> 'If we are not to be deceived by the angel of darkness who is wont to 'transform himself into the angel of light', our supreme standard must be to love the Bride of Christ such as Christ willed her to be, such as he purchased her with his own blood. Therefore we must love not only the Sacraments with which our loving Mother Church nourishes us; not only the solemn feasts which she celebrates for our solace and joy, and the sacred canticles and liturgical functions with which she raises up our minds to heavenly things—but we must also hold dear the sacramentals and the various practices of piety by which she fills the hearts of the faithful with the Spirit of Christ and with consolation. Nor is our duty confined to reciprocating with filial devotion her motherly love towards us; we must also reverence her Christ-given authority which brings 'into captivity every understanding into the obedience of Christ'. We are therefore bound to obey . . .' And so on. (Pius XII, *Mystici Corporis*)

Here it is again; the same lying language, the same concern for self-maintenance and hence for unity, obedience above all. And here too the lying language both conceals and reveals the same myth, that of identity: the one true Church, against which the gates of hell shall not prevail; infallibility that consists in pronouncements that are irreformable; tradition that enshrines unchanging truths; a philosophy that is perennial with which to understand them, and even a language that is immutable in which to express them. Surely the myth of identity has never found a more perfect embodiment.

In order to grasp the intrinsic connection between lying language and the myth of identity I proposed to make use of a view of man which sees human existence primarily in terms of language, of expression and communication. This is a view which gives a definite primacy to the word, as the seminal characteristic of human reality. In the beginning is the word. That is to say, that man only comes to be in the utterance, the expression of himself. Human nature is the product, the creation, of men. It has its roots in biological nature but it grows and flowers in a cultural world, a world of products, art and institutions, a world above all of language. The individual can only become human by sharing in this common product, only find himself in words that are uttered and heard. Put another way: man defines himself in his word. Who he is, his identity, is determined by the word.

If this view is a true one—and it certainly has much in common with fundamental biblical notions—then the consequences that follow from it are important. For if it is true that man only comes to himself in his word, then it follows that the definition of himself can never be final or complete. For utterance is never complete; each new word adds to the definition. Hence the concept of a final word is simply contradictory. Because his existence is determined by his word, man is essentially open-ended, undefined. It is precisely this fundamental characteristic of human existence that is denied by the myth of identity and the concern for preservation and self-maintenance in which it finds expression. A word is torn loose from its historical setting and enthroned in finality and abstraction. In an absolute identification with this final word life loses contact with reality and wanders in a world of lies. In finding his identity in a final word man makes himself its slave.

Who is the devil? For the Bible there is no doubt about the answer to this question. He is 'the father of lies'. As John describes him: 'he was a murderer from the beginning, and has nothing to do with the truth, because there is no truth in him. When he lies, he speaks according to his own nature, for he is a liar and the father of lies.' (John 8, 44) And from the beginning his lie consists in the promise of power. Adam and Eve shall be 'as gods'. Again, he is 'the ruler of this world' and he offers all his power to Jesus if he will but worship him.

It is the 'father of lies', then, a fundamental lie, who has the world in his power, and to whom we are enslaved. It is thus from a slavery of this kind that the saviour must set us free. Paul has, in Galatians, a formulation of the dynamics of salvation which I find particularly evocative: 'Formerly, when you did not know God, you were in bondage to beings that by nature are no gods; but now that you have come to know God, or rather to be known by God, how can you turn back again to the weak and beggarly elemental spirits whose slaves you want to be once more?' (Gal 4:8) Here salvation is seen as a process of being set free from slavery to 'elemental spirits' who appeared as 'gods'. What spirits these were we can guess at, or we could look about us with a would-be discerning eye. Salvation from them involves a change in 'knowledge'. We come to know God—with a capital G, the true God. But this 'knowledge' is not simply a product of our own activity; it has a passive element as well. It is rather we who are 'known by God'. The 'knowledge' does not originate in us. For Paul it is the light of the proclamation of the Gospel that exposes the elemental spirits as weak and beggarly, and beings that by nature are not gods. For in the proclamation of the coming Kingdom, which is the Gospel's centre, the reign of the true God is characterized by its futurity and its reality over against the present and abstract character of the rule of the Devil and his powers. Thus it is the preaching of 'the eternal gospel' as such that effects salvation; in its moment of truth the slaves who served and worshipped the lying spirits are set free.

The salvation achieved for us by the saviour must correspond to the conditions of our slavery. And so if our fundamental enslavement is to the father of lies it is only the truth that can make us free. It is thus in the battleground of language that the war is to be fought. Eliot spoke of the true poet's concern to 'purify the language of the tribe'. What the saviour has to do must have something at least in common with this. It must also have something in common with another, distinct but related, literary activity, that of criticism. The new, original word of the saviour must judge the precious verbal structures we have erected, the ideologies we produce to justify our lives. So it is that Jesus comes to us as a Word, proclaiming a Gospel. He is the one 'Who spoke up as a witness for the truth in front of Pontius Pilate' (1 Tim 6:13). And in Luke he defines his work in terms of speech, of proclamation: 'to bring the good news to the poor, to proclaim liberty to captives, and to the blind new sight, to set the downtrodden free, to proclaim the Lord's year of favour' (Lk 4:18). To proclaim, to free. The proclamation of the gospel *is* salvation. With the word of truth the reign of lies is destroyed.

This is a way in which I find it possible to fill out my basic model of salvation, trying all the while to be true to the New Testament material. If it is acceptable then surely it is appropriate to the way in which I have outlined the problem of our need for salvation today. Having made use of a view of human existence as essentially a matter of utterance and word, it is surely very useful to be able to conceive of salvation in terms of *proclamation* and of *truth*.

We have a need for some discipline by means of which we can guard ourselves against the insidious influence of the rule of lies in the communication systems in which we are involved. I want to suggest one possible way of achieving this. It is the way of the '*oop gesprek*'. I get both the idea and the phrase from Johan Degenaar's introduction to the collection of essays mentioned above. I use the Afrikaans expression (which, roughly translated, means 'open discussion') because it says more than any English expression I can think of. It is also the centre of a widely ranging debate between 'verligte' (enlightened) and '*verkrampte*' (reactionary) elements in White South African society.

The '*oop gesprek*' connotes both 'dialogue' and 'free speech'. It can be seen as an on-going conversation with persons and opinions that tries to remain open to whatever person or opinion that might seek to enter it. As Degenaar points out, an essential pre-condition for the '*oop gesprek*' is that no word or standpoint can be regarded as absolute or beyond all possibility of criticism. For words and meanings, and therefore truths, are relational through and through: 'The "*oop gesprek*" is "*oop gesprek*" precisely because in it the relational character of meanings, the provisionality of premises, the continual discussableness of standpoints hold pride of place.' (*Beweging Uitwaarts*, 10) It is this attitude to truth that can make the '*oop gesprek*' an effective though demanding discipline for communication in an age when it is increasingly difficult to discriminate between the phoney and the true. For when truth is seen as a function of a conversation rather than a private possession, one is opened up to 'horizons of understanding' other than one's own. And it is precisely then that the creative exchange which has the power of making new possibilities can come about.

The sphere of our relation to ecclesiastical and dogmatic traditions is one which seems to me to demand the discipline of the '*oop gesprek*'. If we think of tradition as a sacred *objet d'art* which has to be handed on 'essentially undamaged' (Pope Paul's phrase) then it will be difficult if not impossible to live truly in it. Rather we should think of it as a dialogue with the past in which, as in a successful conversation, truth emerges in forms that are new and able to provide us with a critical and creative grasp of our contemporary situation. An example of 'oop gesprek' already initiated within Christian circles is the dialogue between the Christian Faith and Communism. In South Africa two areas in which '*oop gesprek*' is to my mind sadly needed as far as we are concerned, are those of Afrikaner Calvinism and the as yet chiefly latent African Nationalism.

The effect of this attempt to come to grips with the question of our need for salvation today has been, for me, to highlight the importance for a Christian believer of language and the whole sphere of words and their power. Christianity is a religion of the Word; the proclamation of the gospel *is* the process of salvation. We are lucky to live in an age when Catholic theology is seeing a real renewal of the theology of the word. Preaching, in all its forms, is beginning to be returned to its rightful place; the Christian priesthood is once again seen as essentially prophetic.

In view of this emphasis it might be felt that the sacraments will lose their importance in the Christian life. But this surely need not be so. In the light of personalist and existential philosophy we are able to see what the scholastic philosophy of nature tends to obscure: the Christian sacraments as a communications-system in which all of life receives its Christian interpretation. In this perspective we are able to make more sense of St Augustine's description of a sacrament as '*verbum visibile*', a visible word. The Christian sacrament is nothing other than the definitive, and therefore effective, proclamation of the Word. It is this word of judgment and promise which, because it is God's word and not man's, is the only answer to the need for salvation today.

(1970)

Chapter Nine
The Problem of Communicating Religion in a Secular Society

This paper has a very ambiguous title. I don't know what it suggests to you, but I hope you are not expecting to hear some helpful hints on how to 'get it across' or 'put it over'! For that would imply that 'it' is something that we have and that other people need, and that our chief problem is that of getting it to them. That in turn implies that we have a clear understanding of what 'it' is. And it is precisely there, I think, that the real problem lies. It is not primarily a practical problem of how to communicate something that we have to others, something we refer to loosely as religion. Rather it is a personal problem of one's own understanding of *oneself*. It is the problem of understanding oneself as a religious person and at the same time a member of a secular society. For the religious man in a secular society *can* have a double consciousness; he appears to be two selves—a religious and also a secular self. And the primary problem of communication is between these two selves. This problem will underlie any others we might have in making sense of our religion for the sake of others. Hence my concern in this paper is chiefly with the problem of the religious person's self-understanding in terms that are consistent with his involvement in a secular society. A theoretical problem in other words, rather than a practical one. But, as I hope to show, it is a fundamental characteristic of a true understanding of oneself as a religious being that it moves one to purposeful activity in the world. Further, a true understanding of religion will reveal, in my opinion, that the fundamental structure of such activity is communication.

So much by way of indicating the problem I intend to tackle. But the ambiguities in our title remain. They cluster most thickly about the words 'religion' and 'secular'. Whatever precise meaning or set of meanings we decide to give to the word 'secular' I take it as signifying that sort of society of which contemporary Western Europe and the United States are the classical examples. And it is a fact that this sort of society has developed side by side with Christianity. I do not think this connection is pure chance, but that there is some sort of causal link between Christianity and secularisation is not a point I am interested in making now. The point is instead the more obvious one, that when people in this sort of society use the word 'religion' they usually mean Christianity. So I want to make it quite clear at the outset of this investigation that when I use the word 'religion' I do not mean Christianity. In contrasting a religious with a secular view of the world I understand religion in a very general way as the relation of man to God, where the word 'God' is given its meaning by the particular religion used as an example. For 'God' means something different in each different religion—Christianity, Judaism or Islam. Actual religion only exists in particular different religions, so a general definition of religion is an abstraction. It is a very common one however, encouraged by such disciplines as comparative religion, sociology of religion, psychology of religion and so on. Hence one is forced to take it into account; people do distinguish between a religious and a secular view of the world and if one is trying to describe this distinction one must accept it as one finds it. And in this context religious means a world-view in which man is related or relates himself to God. What is meant by God is not of prime importance; the important thing is the structure man/God. It is a dualistic structure: there is the world of man and a beyond that is God. By contrast a secular view of the world implies a radically unitary structure. There is man-in-the-world (hyphenated!) and that is all there is. It is the content of these two differently structured world-views that I wish to describe and compare with a view of getting a better grasp of what it means to be a religious person in a secular society. And in attempting to give such a description I must refer what I say to historical realities. I have already indicated what I mean by secular: the sort of world-view that exists at present in Western European and United States society, a world-view in which we in South Africa share though in a way that is all our own. By religious I mean the world-view implicit in the classical formulations of the Christian faith which still exist today as the criteria of orthodoxy in the various Christian denominations. As I have already said I do not equate Christianity with religion; I take it as my example however both because I understand it best and because of its intimate relation to the whole phenomenon of secularisation. It is not Christianity that I intend to contrast with secular society but the understanding of it as a religion and therefore the way it is traditionally formulated and practised. I could just as well have chosen Hinduism or Islam. Insofar as they are brought into contact with secular world-views similar problems will arise. The ambiguities that I have pointed out are not only ambiguities in the title of this paper. They are, I believe, real ambiguities in our contemporary experience. I offer the analysis that follows as my own attempt to come to terms with them. Needless to say it is both experimental and incomplete.

The structure of what I want to say will be as follows: first I will describe in concrete terms the difference between a secular world-view and a religious one. In terms of our central problem, that of understanding ourselves as religious persons in a secular society, this description will present us with a problem of *translation*. There are, as we shall see, two languages: that in which we naturally come to grips with our contemporary experience and that in which we articulate our faith: secular language and a religious one. In the interest of true communication we must therefore see the problem as one of translation. If we are truly to make our faith our own, to be at home in it, we must grasp it in the same language in which we live and experience and understand ourselves. This in turn raises the problem of whether such a translation is possible. For it will involve, among other things, the translation of statements about God into statements about man. And will not this destroy the meaning of our faith?

In order to tackle this problem I will outline a view of man which at the same time being articulated in the language of contemporary experience also attempts to do justice to a traditional understanding of religion. This view will be based on the phenomenon of man's self-consciousness and his use of language. It will conclude with a definition of religion in anthropological terms that provides a context for the understanding of God.

I will then apply this understanding of religion firstly to the sphere of specific religious activity or worship and then to life in the sense in which it is said to be lived in a religious spirit, in order to understand better what is going on in religious worship and what place religion has in human life. At this stage it should become clear, at least in terms of my definition of religion, to what extent religion is communicated in worship and in ordinary life and what demands this makes on the would-be-believer.

Finally I will apply my understanding of religion to contemporary experience in an effort to see what aspects of secular society are important for religious communication and how best to put our theory into practice.

Let us begin then with a concrete description of the situation that presents us with the problem of translation. We are confronted by two languages, that of our twentieth century experience of the world and that in which the Christian faith is formulated, which in all Christian traditions goes back to medieval times and beyond. One can be even more specific: the classical formulations that determine our understanding of the Christian faith even now are those of the Council of Trent in the sixteenth century and the various Reformation catechisms of the same period. And this is precisely the period from which most writers on the subject date the phenomenon of secularisation. To put it mildly, a lot has happened to Western Europe since then. From the point of view of the believer who is compelled both by natural necessity and his own faith to be a man of his time, three classes of events seem of special significance for the way in which they have changed the Western European world, and so too the world-view, the language, of the would-be believer, since the time when the Christian faith took on a fairly fixed and final formulation at the dawn of the modern era.

Firstly there are the 'discoveries', chiefly—as with Copernicus and Newton and Darwin—those of the scientific investigation of nature. The earth is not the centre of the cosmos; mathematics is the key to the so-called laws of nature; man has evolved out of sub-human species. But other types of discovery too: the discovery of new countries and of old cultures—the discovery of history.

Then there is the phenomenon of social change, change in the economic and political structures of Western Europe. From emperor and feudal system to autonomous nations under kings. From monarchies to republics. From laissez-faire capitalism to ever increasing socialisation, to communist- and welfare-state. Not only the fact of social change but also the ever-increasing tempo of the process.

Finally there is the new and artificial environment created by technology—a snowballing product of industrialisation and urbanisation. From the manufacture of gunpowder and the first printing-press via that of pre-stressed concrete and nuclear power to artificial organs of the human body and man-made satellites—a development in which man has partially refashioned the features of nature's face.

Taken together these three areas of change constitute the foundation of events on which the thought-world, the language, in which we live has grown. I now propose to give a summary description of this world contrasting it with the thought-world embodied and expressed in say scholastic or even classical reformation theology. As I have already indicated the two periods in question I will simply refer to the two languages, the two worlds-of-thought, as 'then' and 'now'.

Then men thought of the universe as a basically changeless totality. It was composed of definite different substances that had permanent and unchanging essences. Creation was an event that occurred at the beginning; thus the important time, the time of value, was the past. Somewhere in the past was the golden age, the state of original innocence. On a stage that is adequately fitted with properties at the start, all change is change for the worse. Within a fixed frame of reference man experiences himself as having fallen away from some original perfection. Something somewhere on the perfect picture has been altered destroying the harmony of the whole. With this attitude to the past, the paradigm for all valid thinking is memory. The traditional is the true. If the tradition has become sullied it can be purified only by a return to its source. In this atmosphere of reverence for tradition, social changes, when they do occur, will tend to be based on models from the past. But there is a general resistance to change, a basic conservatism that is opposed to anything really new.

Now the world is evolving, changing itself, developing out of itself. There are no stable essences—*species* change. The world *itself* is a process. So is creation—a present movement directed towards the future, continually in act. It is the future, the goal, that is the focus for man's images of value. The valuable is the new—the newest drug is usually the best. Invention is the ideal of knowledge, the hypothesis never before conceived. In society too the new is the true; the dynamism of social change is revolution. Man has torn himself free from brute nature and progresses by means of a dialectic of conflict, a series of revolutions, towards a classless, conflict-free utopia. The blue-print has replaced the golden age!

Then man's moral norms were given him—by legitimate authority and ultimately by God. They were absolute and universal, binding on all men for all time. They were as changeless as human nature itself. Authority was the principle of morality and of all of life. It manifested itself in an ordered hierarchy of government in both church and state. Obedience was the supreme social virtue.

Now moral values are chosen. In a pluralistic world one is forced to choose. We are aware of the variety and therefore of the relativity of all moral codes. Values, like men, are conditioned by time and place and circumstance. The word 'law' hasn't the prime connotation of a statute promulgated by legitimately constituted authority; first and foremost it suggests to the modern mind the prediction of a probability based on a statistical analysis of data. The one and only principle of morality is self-determination, freedom. It is embodied in the democratic ideal of society in which social responsibility is the cardinal virtue. One man, one vote—and he must use it!

Then nature was the origin and image of power. Confronted by nature man was dominated, subject. His natural attitudes to the uncontrollable powers that ruled his life were those of fear and awe and reverence. Underlying these was an even more fundamental attitude towards the world—a contemplative passivity that found its natural expression in a speculative metaphysic of nature in which man was merely an integrated part. Philosophy was first and foremost cosmology, 'What is reality?' its basic question. And reality was seen in terms of substance. In viewing reality as a system of things (*res*) thought was naturally realist in the technical sense.

Now the centre and the source of power is man. He has mastered nature which has become mere matter for his use or at the most a tool for his creativity. Man, having created an artificial second nature regards his environment with familiarity and confidence. As he wonders what he can make of it hope replaces awe as a typical mood. His basic attitude is one of productive creativity. It is in fact more act than attitude; it expresses itself in art and technology rather than in speculation. Yet one can speak of an attitude to the world that is scientific in a broad sense, full of interest in detail and coherence, and asking a basic question 'What is its use?' Philosophy as such however is not concerned with the world but with man. Cosmology has made way for anthropology, for epistemology, linguistic analysis and existential phenomenology. And here the fundamental category is that of meaning. We are instinctively idealist in the technical sense. The 'really real' is the meaning the world has for man.

These then are the two thought-worlds that to a greater or lesser extent contradict each other in our lives. From the point of view of the would-be believer the significant difference between them is that the world of 'then' has a place in it (or rather, alongside it) for God, and the world of 'now' does not (because it has no 'outside'). Now I am going to argue that *the reason that God does not exist for our contemporary consciousness is ultimately because man does not exist either*. All of us suffer from a false consciousness (at least that is how it seems to me) which I am going to try briefly to describe by way of introduction to a view of man which would include the experience of God.

The scientific approach to the world and to knowledge, as expressed in the various special sciences, has proved enormously effective. Proof of its power is present all about us in its products. It has incredibly extended our environment and at the same time increased our capacities to exploit the new possibilities opened up to us. Precisely because of this, and because of the prestige that is inseparable from success of this kind, scientific method has tended to universalize itself as a form of thought. And in doing so it has also tended to become the paradigm and model of *all knowledge* that would claim to be valid or true.

Nothing I say here must be interpreted as a criticism of scientific method. It works—that is its justification. But it is of the essence of the scientific approach that it be limited to a particular and strictly defined field. The true scientist would be the first to object to its extension to the whole of reality and to claims on its behalf to establish universal criteria for truth. The fact remains however that this happens and that a false consciousness is created in which the archetype of the true is the empirically verifiable and the standard of the real is the measurable. And this leads to what CS Lewis has referred to as 'the abolition of man'.

For the essence of the scientific approach is its *objectivity* and its *abstraction*. It is *objective* in the sense that its objects of study must be precisely defined, clearly delimited from other objects and carefully isolated from influence by the scientist himself. The ideal observer must not interfere in any way with what he is observing; if data can be recorded electronically so much the better. It is best suited to the investigation of material objects as in chemistry and in physics. Its starting-point is the construction of a hypothesis or abstract model which is then tested by means of experiment. Thus it is the abstract model or hypothesis that determines what is looked for and therefore also what can be found.

It is this objectification and abstraction inherent in the scientific method that rules out the possibility that it could ever be adequately applied to man. For man can never be simply an object to himself. He is always at the same time a *subject*. To know himself then as he truly is he must grasp this subjectivity. And this cannot be done by attempting, to separate himself, as the knowing subject, from himself as the object known. To do this is to exclude the possibility of grasping the very thing that makes him man, the personal unity of subject and object. The technique appropriate to gaining knowledge of this reality is thus the very opposite of abstraction. It is a matter of involvement rather than separation; it is dialectical rather than univocal, the truth arrived at does not appear as an isolated unit of information but consists in an alteration of consciousness. It is for this reason that the behavioural sciences that deal with man, such as psychology, economics, sociology, linguistics and so on, can never give a complete account of human reality, and stand in need of a complementary discipline to integrate the results of their investigations into a true understanding of man as a personal being. Philosophical anthropology (or existential phenomenology as it is usually and polysyllabically called) is the attempt to do just that. Hence it is to such a phenomenological or descriptive analysis of human existence that we must turn if we are to correct the image of ourselves that scientistic rationalism has left us with. In doing so we shall be restoring man to existence as a truly personal being. And it is my conviction that if we can do that we will be in a better position to understand him as a religious being and to approach the mystery in human existence that we call God.

The depersonalisation or dehumanisation of man in a world that is increasingly the product of a scientific cast of mind is not a matter of concern only for the organized religions. The whole philosophy of Marx is an expression of this concern. And it is a central theme in the writings of existentialist philosophers such as Sartre, Camus and Marcel. But perhaps the most striking presentation of this theme in any medium is that contained in the films of Antonioni. In a sequence of films reaching from *L'avventura* to *Zabriskie Point* he has depicted contemporary man as lost in a modern maze of his own construction. Antonioni's man is a searcher who is not sure what he is searching for. He has time on his hands. He is dying of boredom. The secular city has produced him but he does not feel at home there. Stable and satisfying relationships with others seem impossible in an environment that grows more and more like a machine. So he wanders away into the wilderness, to waste and desert places, waiting for a sign that never comes, half-hoping for a revelation that will restore meaning to existence and bring the hollow men back to life.

As a response to this challenge I will now attempt to sketch a view of man which will do justice to the mysterious personal characteristic of human existence that science cannot cope with. As a foundation on which to base our philosophical anthropology I am going to take the human phenomena of self-consciousness and language.

Man is a self-conscious being. That is to say, every act I perform, every word I utter, is accompanied by the consciousness that it is *my* act, that it is *I* who speak. To what do these pronouns refer? To the physical body, the crude materialist would say. But surely that isn't so. I experience my body as *mine*, that is to say I refer it to what I feel to be me, my *self*. The self is not the body. Is it perhaps another sort of object, a spiritual rather than a material one, a soul? This is the view of the crude idealist. The ghost in the machine. But it won't do either because it would mean that my body was simply a sort of instrument wielded by my soul-self. And that is not the way we experience our bodies. We know where our hand ends and the hammer begins. The connection of self to body is much closer than the idea of a separate soul will allow. The self of human self-consciousness has an element of mystery to it which no amount of reflection can remove. Yet I think it in possible to discover what sort of mystery it is, not to explain it away but to locate it in the total field of our experience.

We have a clue, I think, to the mystery of the self in the instinctive way in which we define a man by what he does whereas in the ease of a dog we don't. Both men and dogs are bodily beings, but if one was asked to describe a particular man, the most significant details of our description would refer to the sort of life he led, the things he had said and his job. In the case of the dog the important thing would be to know whether it was a dobermann-pinscher or a pekingese.

In existentialist philosophy man is actually defined as 'existence'. The word is used in a special sense to mean 'to stand out from' (*ex-sistere*), the implication being that man only comes to be in his projects, his activities in the world. Man only exists in his activity; even his body, as a human body, must be seen rather as a sequence of actions rather than an object. If then we then ask the question 'What is man?' the answer will be in terms of *a particular series of events*. If we ask the question of an individual, 'Who or what are you?' his answer will be his autobiography. If we ask it of mankind the answer will be a universal history. Man is what he has done. *Man is history*.

If we define man as history we open up a new way of talking about the mystery of the human self. For history is a sequence of events and as a human phenomenon it is a self-conscious sequence. That is to say each event is accompanies by the consciousness of 'I' or 'we'. And now if we ask to what the pronoun refers we can answer that it refers to nothing other than the series of events itself but experienced as a *unified whole*. I am my life, and I experience my life not simply as a series of unrelated events but as a unified whole. I identify myself with each act I perform, each word I speak, by relating it to this whole. Each event is me, though not in quite the same way as the whole of my life is me. Clearly the mysteriousness of the self has not been lost; it has simply been transferred to the idea of man's life or history considered as a unified whole. What sort of a whole is it that we are concerned with here and what is the principle of its unity?

The first and most obvious thing we must say about the whole to which a man refers each particular moment of his life in his experience of himself as a self-conscious being is that it does not yet exist. Throughout the course of a man's life it is in a state of coming-to-be. It is only at the end that it can be thought of as complete. Hence man's consciousness of self, because it involves seeing his life as a whole, is the reference of what he already is to what he will finally be. It is the present reference of a past series of events (which constitute what he already is) to the future, and not to just any intermediate future but to the absolute future, the end, when the series of events that constitutes his true identity will be complete.

The whole that constitutes the human self has thus the character of an ideal or a project. We experience our life as a whole at each moment in spite of the fact that it does not yet exist as such. And thus we experience our life as intrinsically referred to the future, to the final event, the absolute future when the whole will cease to be merely ideal and be real.

The other thing that we must say about the whole that constitutes the human self is that it is not simply a completed series of events in the sense of an aggregate of unconnected happenings. In idea at any rate it is a unity, a unified sequence. The question thus arises as to what sort of unity this could be. In order to answer this question I will take language as the phenomenon that defines man and use it to throw light on the problem of the self.

Human language exists primarily as speech. It is made up of an infinite series of spoken words. One must distinguish between a word as a sound and as a meaning. Words are meaningful sounds. There is a particular sound-event, and a particular meaning is expressed. Nor is there any necessary connection between a certain sort of sound and a certain type of meaning. The connection between sound and meaning is determined by the rules of the language that is being spoken. In fact physical movements can take the place of sound, as in the case of meaningful gestures, or marks on paper, as in the case of writing. It doesn't matter what kind of event contains and expresses the meaning; what matters is the meaning. It is meaning that makes language language.

And now I am in a position to make this point: that every event in a human life expresses a meaning. Not only sound-events or the making of marks on paper. The expression of meaning is the distinctive characteristic of human reality. Meaning is man's basic product as it were. Thus a human life is not only a series of events, it is a series of meaningful events, a series of meanings. So if we raise the question as to the unity of the series we are in fact asking about its meaningfulness. If a human life is to constitute a unified whole its unity will be a unity of meaning. We can now ask the question: What sort of meaning could a series of events have? Clearly a sentence has a unity that is a unity of meaning. Each word in it has its own meaning but the unity that is the meaning of the sentence depends on the order and position of the words in it and the way in which they are connected with one another. This then is the sort of unity which is implied in the ideal of the self, a unity of meaning, which is to say, a meaningful series of events.

The phenomenon of language points us to another feature of the human self seen as a unity of meaning. It is not a private possession but only exists in relation to others. As words have a meaning only in terms of their relation to the total system of the language of which they are parts, so the self only exists in relation to the whole of human reality. The meaning which is its reality is a shared meaning, a public meaning. Thus the meaning-giving event is the same for all and this establishes one aspect of the actual content of the meaning—that is to say, community or existential interdependence. Truly human life is a conversation.

Now as we have seen the idea of the self implies the orientation of all the events of a man's life to its end. Thus, if this series of events is to be a meaningful one, as it must be if it is to constitute a unified whole, it will derive its meaning from this end, the final event in which the whole series is present and complete. All this is the formulation of a fairly common experience. We do ask questions about 'the *meaning* of life' and when we do so we think of our life as a whole. It is this complex of truths about man, that he is able to conceive his life as a whole, that in doing so he instinctively refers himself to the end of it, the absolute future, and that in doing so he raises the question of the meaningfulness of his life taken as a whole, that constitutes him as a religious being. In defining man as history I wish to stress that man only exists as a series of events and that such a series if it is to be a meaningful whole can only derive its meaning from an *event*—which must be the final event of the series. More important, we instinctively refer this whole to its end. 'Where is it all going?' we wonder. 'What will it all add up to?'

Religion then is possible because of man's capacity to see his life as a whole and to raise the question of its meaningfulness. Religion thus consists in man relating himself at each moment of his life to its final event as the meaning-giving event for his life as a whole. And if we take the traditional definition of religion as the relation of man to God we are now in a position to apply the word God to a clearly designated area of human reality. In our anthropological perspective when we speak of God we will be referring to the *event* that gives meaning to the series of events that makes up man and establishes the self as a unified whole. And this event is the last in the series, the absolute future, the end. This is our formal definition of God in terms of human existence. I have tried to show how the concept arises naturally out of a phenomenological analysis of man's self-consciousness and his distinctive use of language to create meaning.

We have thus come to the end of our anthropological sketch. But this is only the beginning of a truly existential grasp of our actual religious life and the reality of God. For the final event that is so crucial for man's self-definition, the absolute future to which he relates himself in religion is nothing other than death. And it is this that gives the truly 'religious' character to all religion and makes the reality of God a mysterious reality. For death has a natural meaning of its own for a bodily being such as man; it has the character of annihilation, of the annihilation of meaning. And if it is precisely this event which is singled out as that, which, if any, is to give meaning to human existence, then man is faced with a truly crucial opposition. It is this opposition which in fact is a sort of summary of the human situation. All religions can be seen simply as various ways of responding to it. And in doing so what they are in fact doing, each in a different way, is giving priority to the demand for meaning, inseparable from human existence, over the natural character that death has for bodily beings, which is the annihilation of meaning.

I want now briefly to give you some idea of how this could take place, first with regard to what we think of as specifically religious activity: worship, prayer and membership of a religious organisation, and then with regard to our real life in the world in the sense in which it can be said to be lived religiously.

It is in worship and conscious membership of a specifically religious group that the communication of religion actually takes place. Worship is thus the conscious making present of death as the meaning-giving event of human life. Because the event that is represented is one that gives meaning and point to existence worship takes the form of celebration. It is the expression of *joy*. But because the event represented in worship is the absolute future, worship is the expression of *hope* as an absolutely fundamental human attitude. Because the event is death in all its mysterious ambiguity, worship will inevitably contain an element of awe. Most important of all death has the character of annihilation; this is the real deadliness of death at the level of meaning. Worship is thus the expression of the most radical self-surrender or abandonment. This is why worship naturally contains the element of sacrifice. This whole complex of attitudes is what makes up the most fundamental religious attitude, so often so sadly misdefined. I mean the attitude of charity or love. This open-hearted attitude which is characteristic of the authentic acceptance of death is the source of the communal character of the meaning which derives from death. Death unites individuals in their free recognition of their powerlessness to construct and possess a meaning for themselves that justifies their existence as individuals. The attitude of the worshipper who celebrates death as the giver of meaning is that of one about to receive a gift. And the gift is precisely the communal character of the meaning that death contains, the actual creation of community on the basis of a gift. Death naturally divides, separates man from man. Hence if death is to give meaning to life it must be the contradiction of this—the creation of community through the open-hearted offering of oneself. Hence if worship is adequately to express the social character of the meaning expressed by death it must itself have a social form. It must not only created community; it must be the expression of a community which recognizes itself as such. Finally worship must have a symbolic or sign character to it. For it is only a means to an end. The end of worship is life. Worship symbolically represents the meaning-giving event; life must achieve it. The meaning that is expressed in worship is the meaning of *life*. Nevertheless as man's being consists in meaning so worship as this meaning's expression actually has power to give life the meaning that can only be realized in death, in the form of a certain consistent style of life. If death is the unifying principle, the moral law as it were, of human life, then this is expressed in life as a certain spirit whose fundamental characteristics are those of hope and charity and love, as we have sketched them above.

We now finally have to consider the character of a religious life. We have already defined its spirit as a love whose distinctive characteristic is that of hope. We have to show how such a spirit will express itself in action. As we have stressed a religious life is one that is oriented to an absolute future, an event that is to come. In the notion of love we already have a partial indication of the character of the event and also of its social character. In hope however man has a dynamic principle which is a means of bringing it about. The secret of hope's creativity is its negativity. It is by no means the visualising of pie in the sky. On the contrary it is an essentially critical attitude that takes effect only in opposition to the false futures, the gods, the ideologies that man inevitably sets up to give meaning to his life. A secular world-view is a closed world-view; death is an unambiguous event. And yet as we have shown, man is unable to live without creating meaning.

And the truth is that any meaning he constructs for himself that fails to take account of death is ultimately a meaning that imprisons him in privacy, alienating him from any possible community of man. He has closed the future and builds his life on a particular aspect of human life, turning it into a total justification of his existence. Hope liberates man from these closed systems by daring to see the future as an open one, even a future that ends in death. Thus it is not religion's task to set goals for man but to liberate him from goals that tend to dominate and so dehumanise him. The fact that man's life ends in death means that there is a continual pressure on him to make absolutes that provide a false sense of security or else to opt out of the attempt to create meaning completely in a private world where that question is simply shelved. At all events the fact remains that any human status quo is an inauthentic one and the effect of religion is to disrupt it. On the one hand one has ideologies such as communism and nationalism; on the other the drop-out world of the hippie and the affluent suburban family. Each however contains an element of truth which an authentic religious life must try to synthesise.

Communism in addition to being an ideology is also a revolutionary force for change: its aim is the destruction of the world of bourgeois affluence. As such it is an expression of true religion. Similarly the hippie drop-out is an expression of protest against the idols of the secular society. Its emphasis on prayer and mystical experience is a result of its sense of the inadequacy of society's goals. Religious life has to mediate between the contemplative character of hippie-dom and the world-building activism of the communist. It can only do this if it remains true to its fundamental principles of hope and community-creating love.

I have now reached the end of what I set out to do in this paper. And I am left with a sense of dissatisfaction. It probably stems from a sense of being a little dishonest. Perhaps some of you have noticed the absence from the scene of the third member of that well known triad, faith, hope and charity. I have spoken about hope and charity but not of faith. The reason for my doing this was a resolution not to let my own Christian faith colour my presentation of the human phenomenon of religion. But in fact it has done so. I have attempted to formulate a philosophical anthropology which would at least be compatible with Christian faith. Though I would not expect anyone to accept it on those grounds. But the question of faith must be raised in a paper concerned with the communication of religion. Because faith is the cognitive element in man's religious experience it is the point at which different religions differ. Faith is the actual meaning ascribed to the meaning-giving event at the end of human life. For Christian faith this is resurrection. Other religions deal with it in other ways. But it is important I think to point out that the language in which this ultimate meaning-giving event is described is a special sort of language. If it is thought to contain knowledge of a special sort then religion has been reduced to ideology. Rather it is the expression of a particular way of being open to whatever the absolute future may be. The Christian bases his faith on a past event, also a death, but a death which is seen as an event of promise for all men, and this promise he describes as resurrection. This is not to say that the Christian has grasped the event that is God. That is still to come. And the only image his love can cling to in faith and hope is the dead man on the cross.

(1970)

Chapter Ten
Religious Laws: the Christian Problem

When we think of religion as the recognition and observance of religious laws we are, I would suggest, thinking primarily of two kinds of laws. The first kind of law is believed to have been made or revealed by God, or at least promulgated on his authority. The second are the laws of a particular religion or church which are made by and are binding on its followers or members. The first kind concerns the relation of a man with God whereas the second apply to the relations between the members of a particular religious organization. Examples of the first could be the ten commandments of the Old Testament; examples of the second could be such laws as that of the celibacy of the clergy in the Catholic Church or the regulations governing the celebration of mass or the election of a pope. The distinction between the two kinds is fairly clear. We Catholics at any rate are well aware that the expressions 'a man of God' and 'a good Catholic' do not really mean the same thing.

In this article then I am going to explore the concept of religion from these two points of view. That is to say I am going to look at religion as obedience to the laws of God and as obedience to the laws of a particular religious organization.

This article will be divided into four sections. The first section will deal with different ideas about God's laws and man's religious response to them. The important distinction between positive law and natural law will be made and the notion of divine positive law will be introduced. The second section will deal with the various types of laws in any religious organization; let us call them ecclesiastical laws. In this context I shall also have to touch on the relation between ecclesiastical laws and the laws of the state. The conflicting claims of the various laws will bring us to the question of 'positivity' in religious laws and the post-Renaissance, post-Reformation critique of positivity in religion. This critique is based on a view of man as a free, self-determining being and so in the third section I will examine briefly the question whether a religion that claims to be 'revealed', and so also authoritative is compatible with human freedom. Finally in the fourth section I will suggest conditions that submission to religious laws of both kinds must fulfill if it is to be worthy of a responsible and faithful man

The first section will follow a roughly historical sequence beginning with very primitive forms of religion and ending up with what seem to me central problems of our contemporary religious experience.

1. The Development of Religious Law

In primitive societies the powers of nature that influence human life are thought of as divine. The ancient Greek thinker Thales expresses this outlook when he says that 'all things are full of gods.' Thunder and lightning, trees and sea, the seasons and the sun. Human happenings too: birth and death, sleep and luck—there is no distinction between ordinary events and the workings of the gods. Even human decisions and actions are determined by the gods. As Pindar says, 'From the gods come all the means of mortal exploits; thanks to the gods are men wise and brave and eloquent.'[1] Even the customs and conventions of human society are instituted and sanctioned by the gods. And this is still the case when these customs and conventions are codified and recognised as laws.

With law however a new stage of society and religion is reached. No longer are our lives governed by blind chance or fate. Laws create a certain order in our lives. And with law men's attitude to their gods also undergoes a change. No longer do the gods play with our lives according to their own whims or fancies, or at least they do not do so all the time. Because the laws that regulate our lives are ultimately promulgated and sanctioned by them, and because the laws have something unchanging or permanent about them, we now enjoy a rather more stable and sensible relationship with the divine powers that rule us. Admittedly in the sphere of nature the god can still

1. The quotations are from E Gilson, *God and Philosophy* (Yale, 1941) Chapter 2

surprise us with an unexpected hailstorm or drought. But in our social life we now know more where we are with them. Because the laws are promulgated and sanctioned by the gods they reveal to us a certain amount about how they want us to behave and also precisely what they will do to us if we do not. With law men's relationship with the gods becomes more personal, more of a two-way process. No longer a matter of naked power, at least there is a contract which can be kept or broken by men according to their choice. Where in the most primitive societies religion was often merely a matter of trying to persuade or bribe or even, by magic, force the gods to do what you wanted them to, now one can at least appeal to the god's own laws. A religious man, we could say, is one who binds himself to these laws, trusts the gods to keep them and tries to obey them himself.

There comes a point however when laws are not simply handed down from generation to generation in unchanging codes, but new laws are made. And these new laws are seen to be made by men, by kings or priests or councils. And with this a new stage of men's social and religious awareness is reached. It was reached dramatically in the city-states of ancient Greece. Being now aware that many of the laws had been made by men it was natural for Socrates to question their necessary and god-given character. Was it necessary now for a religious man to obey the laws, even the ones that men and not the god had made. There could be no question that it was right to obey the laws of the gods. But it is another matter where man-made laws are concerned. With slightly different sets of laws in neighbouring states it even becomes possible to ask the question as to which set is the best. And if one does ask this question, how does one decide?

Arising out of this new awareness a distinction came to be made, the distinction between what is called 'positive law' and what is called 'natural law'. It was a distinction made by philosophers but it has important consequences for religion. 'Positive' laws are the laws made by men in society. In this sense the Suppression of Communism Act is a 'positive' law made by a particular group of men in a particular society at a particular time. 'Natural law' means something very different. Perhaps it is necessary to say at once that 'natural' laws are not the 'laws' of nature that science discovers. 'Natural' laws in this special sense are really not laws at all in the usual sense; they are instead the natural tendencies of human nature. The tendency to preserve one's life, for instance, or the life of one's offspring. Or the tendency to procreate and educate offspring. Or the tendency to live in society or to acquire knowledge. Natural laws in this sense mean roughly the same thing as 'instincts' in our common speech. Natural laws in the sense of tendencies or instincts in human nature are only thought of as laws when men think of human nature as created by God. God creates man for a certain purpose and so creates him with certain tendencies towards it. These tendencies of human nature thus reflect God's intention and reveal his will for man. They can thus be expressed as laws. For instance, the tendency to preserve life, can be expressed in the form of a commandment or law: 'Thou shalt not kill'.

The consequence of this is that natural laws have divine authority. They are the laws of God, in a similar sense to that in which the laws of primitive societies were thought of as the laws of the gods. But there is this important difference, the natural laws are not the laws of society, they have not been made by men, they are simply there in human nature. And so they can conflict with the laws that men make in society, the positive laws. A certain society might for instance make a law saying that female children must be put to death at birth. In such a case the religious man who has bound himself to obey the law of God is bound to disobey the positive law of society. The natural law, because it is the law of God, has greater authority than and can act as judge over society's positive laws. This being the case it becomes of first importance to determine what laws actually are natural laws, laws of human nature. Not only so that we shall be able to judge which positive laws of society are good laws but especially, for the religious man, so that we shall know what it is that God wishes us to do. How do we discover these natural laws?

The obvious answer to this question is that we discover these innate tendencies of human nature by observing the behaviour of others and reflecting on our own. When we do this however we realise that it is by no means easy to determine which tendencies shall count as natural. Is the tendency to selfishness, for instance, that I might discover in myself natural in this sense? Is it more natural than the tendency to consider the needs of others? How does one decide? One can spend a great deal of time weighing up the pros and cons but it will certainly be a very difficult and taxing process. And one will never be certain that one has thought the matter through properly.

The other answer to this question that has been given in the history of European thought is that God himself reveals these laws to us.

Although in theory these laws can be discovered by us (they are after all the laws of our own nature, and part of our nature as human beings is to be able to consciously direct our natural tendencies towards their proper fulfillment.)—although this is true in theory it is very difficult in practice and if God himself reveals the truth about the nature he has created so much the better. The main religions of European history, Christianity, Judaism end Islam, believe that he has in fact done so. This revelation of the natural law consequently exists quite independently of the systems of positive law in different societies, and because it is God's law it has the highest possible authority for the religious man. The religious man has now a split allegiance, his duty to the positive laws of society and his duty to the revealed laws of God. Where there is a conflict he is bound to choose the latter. The conflict between positive law and natural law is actually intensified when men believe that the natural law has been revealed by God. If religious behaviour is defined as submission to religious laws this now means submission to God's revelation of the natural law. The positive laws of society have lost their 'religious' character.

2. Religious Law and its Secular Critics

The idea that God reveals the law he wishes men to follow leads at once to the question of the laws of particular religious organizations. For unless one holds that God reveals his laws from moment to moment to every individual one must believe that the revelation once given is preserved in a more or less public and social form. All the religions I have mentioned do in fact believe this. God's initial revelation is to an individual, Jesus or Moses or Mohammed, but the revelation is then preserved by his followers. They may interpret it or make deductions from it to meet changing circumstances but they may not add to it. The revealed laws become the foundation laws of a particular religious organization.

Now in each of the religious traditions it is not the case that the revealed law is simply a particular formulation of the natural law. The ten commandments of the Old Testament can reasonably be understood as a divinely given summary of the natural law. Other laws such as the necessity of faith in Jesus for salvation, the necessity of Mass for the proper worship of God and the indissolubility of marriage cannot be seen as such. Men could *never* have discovered them if God had not revealed them. They are not laws of human nature strictly speaking at all. The truth is that in all revealed religions God is believed to have revealed more than just what is contained in the natural law. Some theologians call this bit extra 'divine positive law'. The laws of religious organizations, or ecclesiastical laws, therefore include the following distinct types: natural laws revealed by God, divine positive laws, other laws based on them or deduced from them and finally laws made by the organisation itself to regulate its worship, its doctrine and its internal discipline. All these laws can claim to count as religious laws. And under the heading 'laws' one can include not only laws about how you are to behave but also laws about what you are to believe and how God is to be worshipped. Religious laws in religions of this sort are very comprehensive indeed. Unlike the positive laws of society they cover every aspect of human life, inner as well as outer.

Now it is an interesting feature of religious behaviour in this kind of religious organization that believers tend to be much more rigorous in their observance of the divine positive law, and the purely ecclesiastical laws than the natural law itself. This may be because the natural law demands a different type of effort on our part to obey. In many ways it is easier to fast than to be honest. At all events obedience to divine positive laws and ecclesiastical regulations can raise real problems when it involves disobedience to the positive laws of society. Think of the conscientious objection of Jehovah's Witnesses for example. The difficulty is this: if our obedience to the natural law as revealed by God causes us to fall foul of the laws of society we can reasonably object that it is because the laws of society are not in accordance with the laws of human nature and should be changed. But if it is our obedience to divine positive laws or ecclesiastical regulations that lands us in trouble we cannot object that the laws of society should be altered so as to include them too. Because they have been revealed and cannot be known in any other way. It is unfair to expect a society that has not received this revelation to include it in its laws. And of course this applies to all societies whatever. Revelations do not come to societies but only to individuals.

This is one difficulty that obedience to religious laws can cause when these laws are not simply identical with the natural law. But there is another and much more serious one. We have seen that ecclesiastical laws include a whole spectrum of laws ranging from ad hoc ritual regulations or rubrics to the divine revelation of the natural law and truths of the faith. And clearly the submission of the believer to these different grades of law will be of differing degrees. He will not consider himself bound to the same extent by rubrics as by the natural law or, if you like, formulations of faith contained in creeds. Nevertheless he will regard his obedience as unconditional to at least those aspects of ecclesiastical laws he believes to have been directly revealed by God, that is to say, the natural law and divine positive law. It is precisely here that the problem lies. For in obeying God's revelation of the natural law a man is only obeying the true laws of his own nature. These are laws which he is in principle able to discover for himself. And now that they have been revealed he is able to understand them, to see their point and to see them as the true expressions of his deepest desires. So in obeying them he is able to act from his own conviction of their validity. In the case of the divine positive laws however it is quite otherwise. For by definition man could not have discovered these laws by his own efforts. For him to know them they had to be revealed. They are not laws of human nature and so cannot be seen by men to be true and valid for all men. Instead they simply have to be believed in because God has revealed them and God would not reveal unnecessary truths or demand obedience to unnecessary laws. They are submitted to thus not on the believer's own insight and conviction but on the authority of God. I obey them not because I see them to be true but because God has told me to. Any religion which, like the Christian religion, claims to be revealed must for this very reason also be a religion of authority. The question can now be put whether it is right for a man to bind himself to believe and do things that he does not know to be true or right. And remember that such obedience cannot be conditional for the religious man. He cannot say that he will obey God's laws unless they seem to him to be wrong. For by definition they cannot be wrong; they are the laws of God. If he feels in his deepest heart that they are wrong he must nevertheless believe that in fact it is he who is wrong and still obey them. And the question can be put: Can such an attitude be right? Is it not a surrender of moral responsibility? Will it not lead to a loss of integrity on the part of the believer? Will he not even eventually become cynical about all religious laws? 'Just obey, don't ask why' is quite a common religious attitude. But it is also an attitude encouraged by every sort of totalitarian system.

After the Renaissance and the Reformation this was precisely the criticism directed by thinkers of the Enlightenment at all forms of religious positive law but especially at the idea of divine positive law.[2] They felt that unconditional obedience to this kind of religious law violated the moral integrity of the believer, and in fact prevented him from becoming fully responsible. Their objections to this form of religious obedience led them eventually to deny the authenticity of any divine revelation other than that of the natural law. If God were good, they argued, and had created man with free will so as to direct himself responsibly according to the God-implanted tendencies of his nature, then God could not possibly ask him to submit blindly to apparently arbitrary extra laws issued from above. Kant even wrote a book called 'Religion within the bounds of reason alone' in which he showed that it was actually our moral duty to judge revealed laws by the ordinary standards of the natural law that we had discovered on our own.

Now it seems to me that these criticisms have a certain weight. It also seems to me that it is criticisms of this sort that underlie a lot of our present controversy about obedience to religious laws and to religious authorities. It seems to me therefore worthwhile to dig a little deeper into their foundations to try and discover their roots. And when we do so we discover that they are rooted in a certain view of man, a view of man that burst on the European scene at the time of the Enlightenment and is still with us, but which can claim to have *its* roots in the very Christian revelation that it seems so hostile to. According to this view the very essence of human nature is a power of freedom. Because of this power man is a self-determining being. Unlike other animals he is not more or less forced to be what his instincts make him. It is within his own power to choose what sort of man he is to be. And this power is not something as it were added to his human nature. Without it he would not be a man, and if he were prevented from exercising it he would cease to be a proper man.

With this power of freedom is bound up the notion of responsibility. Because man is free to choose what sort of a man he is to be, he is responsible for what he becomes. To deprive him of this responsibility

2. The idea of 'positivity' in religion, as elaborated by such thinkers as Kant and Hegel, is the forerunner of later Marxist and Existentialist critiques of Christianity as a form of 'alienation' or 'bad faith'. The critique considered in this article is substantially the same.

either by brainwashing or by insisting on uncomprehending submission to laws he doesn't understand is to undermine the very thing that makes him human. Kant's criticism of religious positivity was that it prevented men from exercising precisely that capacity that made them human. This then in brief is the view of man on which his criticism was based. One of the reasons it took such firm root in Europe at the time of the enlightenment was the new sense of power and freedom that the development of science and technology had given men. Men were no longer so dominated by forces of nature that they neither understood nor were able to control. Protestantism had emphasized the responsibility of the individual before God and this had led to a reaction against all forms of authority in religion. This new vision also had far-reaching effects in the economic and political fields. 'Free trade' and 'free enterprise' were the slogans of the burgeoning capitalist economy. And 'freedom' was the motto of the new political leaders. Much has changed since then but in broad outline the view of man itself is still with us. And the criticisms of religion based on it are as strongly felt as ever. To counter them we shall have to offer a more adequate view of man than that on which they are based. This is especially incumbent on us as Christians in view of the claim often made that this view of man is simply the Christian one shorn of its 'religious' trappings.

3. The Christian View of Man

It seems to me that the view of man I have outlined is, as far as it goes, a true one. It is our Christian faith that man is 'the image of God'. And in what does this likeness to God in man consist? What if not that power of freedom, of self-determination, that the thinkers of the Enlightenment valued so highly. It is because he has this power that man can be creative in a similar sort of way to God; because he has this power man is responsible not only for what he makes of the world but also for what he makes of himself. In the book of Genesis where this view of man as the image of God is expounded a view of God is also presented. God appears as a creator. He makes man in his own image with the express intention of making man responsible for his creation and for what he himself is to become. Each time the word 'image' is mentioned the notion of responsibility is immediately added: 'God said, "Let us make man in our own image, in the likeness of ourselves, and let them be masters . . ." and again "God created man in the image of himself, in the image of God he created him, male and female he created them. God blessed them saying to them, "Be fruitful, multiply, fill the earth and conquer it. Be masters . . ."" And the whole story of the two trees and the snake is a parable of man's responsibility for what he himself shall be.

So far, so good. Man as the image of God possesses a power of freedom or self-determination that is his highest gift. But the notion of image has another side to it, one that would not have been so popular with Kant. An image is a reflection. That is to say it only exists as the reflection of something else. Take a pace backwards from the mirror and your image ceases to be. This simple truth is a pointer to the other aspect of the view of man presented in Genesis. Man is absolutely dependent, dependent for his very being, on God. God is his *creator* and this relationship of absolute dependence is what is meant by creation. That being the case this relationship must be seen as the source of all man's powers including that of his power of freedom, indeed especially that since it is his highest, most godlike power. And doesn't this appear contradictory? Surely freedom is incompatible with dependence, all the more with the total dependence involved in creation. Kant seemed to think so and certainly the climate of thought that stems from the time of the Enlightenment equates freedom with independence. In contemporary political thought, especially in the emergent nations of Africa and other parts of the third world, the terms are practically synonymous. Let us nevertheless ask ourselves whether a view of man in which freedom and dependence are not mutually exclusive is a possible one or not. Notice firstly that according to Genesis it is only in relation to God that man is dependent. As far as the powers of nature are concerned he really is independent in a very important sense. Although he is part of nature man is not totally determined by it but is free to determine himself according to his own decisions and choices. In relation to God however this freedom seems actually to grow out of his dependence. Now I think that such a paradox even if it doesn't appear to us as nonsense must remain mysterious. Christians at any rate cannot think that they can comprehend what is referred to by the word 'creation'. Yet I do think we have enough evidence to prevent us from at once dismissing this whole idea as nonsense. Consider after all relationships between human persons. Is it not true that at least in the higher, more spiritual, relations between people personal freedom seems to increase with increasing dependence? Think of the elements of freedom and dependence in such relations as loyalty, love or forgiveness for instance. Perhaps in the case of such personal relationships one should use the word 'interdependence' to make clear the mutuality involved. In these cases interdependence seems not so much to destroy the free response of the persons involved but actually to create it. Might it not be that the relationship between God and man is a radical case of such freedom-in-dependence, and the very condition for such relationships between men. If this is so then it would not be nonsense to see freedom and dependence as compatible, at least as far as relationships between persons are concerned. Here I think we come to the root of the trouble with the view of man that equates freedom with independence. It is an insufficiently *personal* view. Relationships between men are thought of according to a model that is only adequate to deal with relations between things, or perhaps with relations between men that are only functional and not personal in the strict sense. It is a highly individualistic view that sees persons rather in the same way as a scientist would regard the universe as being made up of a countless number of separate atoms. Now it may be useful to think of the physical universe in that way but it is simply inadequate to think in that way of the world of persons. have we got to now? We have uncovered in Genesis a view of man as a free being whose freedom is only realized in personal dependence on others, on God in the first instance but also on other men. Now such a view of man is impossible if man is not created by God. Relationships with other men may actualize man's power of freedom, but they cannot actually create it. Men can only realize their freedom in personal interdependence because it comes to them in their creating relationship with God. Further, such a view of man is impossible if the relationship between creator and created is not seen in properly personal terms. And this I think is where such thinkers as Kant made their mistake. He saw God simply as a law-giver whose relationship with man was dominated by the demands of the moral law. The moral law inherent in human nature was quite simply the voice of God and there was no other way in which he spoke. So relationships between man and God were purely a matter of law. Such relationships, though not the same as relations between impersonal things are nevertheless not the highest relations possible to personal beings. We have come full circle back to the subject of law.

4. Freedom and Authority in the Church

I have suggested a view of man that seems to me more adequate to the personal character of human beings. It involves a view of God as a properly personal being. What consequences does this have for our understanding of religious behavior as submission to religious laws, and does it help us to answer the criticisms of the Enlightenment?

Firstly, a properly personal view of God implies that we cannot simply oppose God's power and initiative to man's freedom and responsibility. It cannot be the case that the greater God's authority, the greater man's submission must be. Hence it is inadequate to think of religion simply as the submission to religious laws. God, if he is truly personal, demands more than this from man, a greater submission if you like but one that stimulates and expresses his freedom. As Aquinas put it 'God does not make laws, he makes men', or words to that effect. Aquinas points out that laws are always general whereas God's will is always particular. Of course he wills that you follow the tendencies of your nature. That is why he made you that way. But he does not will that you formulate these tendencies in some more or less abstract, more or less general scheme (such as the ten commandments, or the creeds or even canon law) and then confuse this with his personal will for you. God wants friends not subjects.

Well, on a view such as this what would be the religious function of the natural law whether revealed or not? That of a teacher I suppose. Like a good teacher such laws should stimulate us to reflect on the tendencies of our nature in whatever situation they reveal themselves so that we grow in wisdom and responsibility by making them consciously our own. They introduce us to the facts of the situation in which we must make our religious response to God. So much for the natural laws. What of the divine positive laws? They are after all the centre of Kant's criticism. Once again I think it is necessary to remember that God does not make laws. He makes men and men make laws. This is not to say that some laws to not have God's authority. It seems to me that as Christians we are committed to such a view. But they have authority *as laws*—and we have seen what that is. But I would like to make a further point, though one I cannot elaborate on now. I am inclined to think that at least as far as the Christian religion is concerned, all positive revelation by God whether expressed as laws or as dogmas or as ways of worship amounts to just one thing—the revelation of Jesus as God-among-us encouraging our complete submission and promising us total freedom. And it is on this one point that I would like to answer Kant. Because he cannot conceive of freedom in dependence he cannot admit that man can centre his religion on the personal authority of another. And because I have another view of man I think he can.

In conclusion I want to suggest two conditions that submission to religious laws must fulfill if it is to be compatible with the view of man that I consider Christian faith implies. Firstly with regard to laws that have the authority of God. These can only function properly in a person's religious life if they are fallowed in the context of faith in Jesus and the desire to discover or to work out God's particular will for oneself. If that response is lacking the observance of the laws can only have a deadening effect on our moral sensitivity. Thus far Kant is right. Secondly, with regard to all ecclesiastical laws including those formulations that are held to be *de fide*. Unless all members of the religious organization recognize their responsibility for these formulations and, what is more, actually participate in some way in their formulation and administration, but instead leave this to a self-perpetuating sacred caste, their religion will lose its personal character and tend to become the inauthentic, self-alienating thing that the thinkers of the Enlightenment and the Marxists of our own day describe. In religion in general and specifically in religious organizations authority must be personal or else it is inhuman, unworthy of human beings and destructive of true religion. In our day, and thanks perhaps to the labours of such thinkers as Kant, we see the condition for this more clearly—it must be shared.

(1976)

Chapter Eleven

Do Lay People Have a Vocation?

The subject of this series of lectures (the Kolbe Lenten Lectures at UCT in 1978) is the laity, namely those members of the Church (99.9 percent actually) who are not clergy. In spite of that we will be spending a good deal of our time—perhaps most of it—thinking about and discussing the clergy. And that is inevitable. Why?

Because in spite of the fact that virtually all normal Christians are lay people next to nothing has been written about the nature and function of lay people as such. In fact it probably comes as a surprise to many of you to hear that they are supposed to have a special function at all. But more of that later. Up till fairly recently it was only the clergy whose nature and function attracted the interest of theologians—and of course they were all clergymen too. And vast seas of ink have been spilt on that topic. The nature and function of the clergy has been exhaustingly analysed and defined. And since Vatican II just as much if not more than before. Already the College of Bishops has devoted one of its annual Synods in Rome to it. And now they have turned their attention to the laity. The result of this is that we all (more or less) have a fairly clear idea of what the clergy are and what they are supposed to do but only very vague ideas about 'the vocation and mission of the laity in the Church and in the World' (which is the official title of the theme of the Synod). Even if this is so, it ought not to be too difficult, one might suppose, to work out the function of lay-people. After one has got clear the function of the clergy one simply looks to see what is left over—and that is what is to be done by the laity. Even if all we find for lay-people to do is 'to obey and support' the clergy, well, at least that is something. And the method of discovering it seems both obvious and perfectly sound.

Perhaps it is. But it has its dangers. If our conception of the laity and their function is so dependent on our conception of the clergy and their function, then our conception of the clergy had better be beyond reproach.

I don't think it is. And for two reasons. Firstly, because of the way in which our understanding of the Church itself and its mission has been so exclusively focused on the clergy, the distinction between the powers and duties that belong to them as Christians and those that belong to them purely as clerics has been obscured. Many powers that are commonly thought to belong only to them are, in fact, powers that are possessed by every Christian. We shall be considering some of these presently. Secondly, the status and function of the clergy has had a social and cultural development in the history of the Church. And this development also affects our conception of the clergy, of the sort of work they ought to do, the sort of people they ought to be and the way they ought to live. Many of the forms of life and responsibilities that we assume to be essential to the clergy are in fact only social and cultural developments that stand in need of theological justification.

In order to remind you of your own assumptions about these things I am going to sketch two different conceptions of the clergy. Each of these will suggest its own conception of the laity. We will then be able to address the question of how to find out which is right.

Let me start with what I shall call the 'received' conception. And let me start with the received conception of the most senior members of the clergy, namely the bishops. According to this conception, bishops are rather like generals in an army, or branch managers in a multi-national corporation with its head-quarters in Rome. Each is, in a sense, his own boss. But above them all is the 'big boss', the pope. He it is who in the last resort, hires and fires, or if you like, commissions and court-marshals. This popular conception is closely bound up with very strong feelings about the size and number of each bishop's area of influence, the diocese. The size of the average modern diocese entails that the amount of resources the bishop is responsible for and the number of people he is expected to serve, is far too great for him to cope with. He is virtually doomed to become an office-bound bureaucrat, always behind his desk or in an aeroplane, unable to keep in close personal touch with his people, or even with his clergy.

Because dioceses are so big there are as a consequence very few bishops in the Church, a bare 3,000 or so for the whole world-wide

Church. This, of course, makes centralised organisation and control comparatively easy. But that, of course, also has the tendency of undermining regional vitality and solidarity. 3,000 may seem a large number but isn't that because we assume that that also means 3,000 large chanceries, 3,000 large houses and 3,000 large cars. It's all part of the received conception of a bishop and the sort of job he ought to do and the sort of person he ought to be.

Consider the alternative conception. Each diocese is as large as the average parish. Like it was in the early Church, about 500 families let us say. Now instead of 3,000 bishops there are 300,000. Clearly each of these will control far less resources and have far less to be responsible for than at present. Even more significantly, it will be simply impossible to control so many bishops by a centralised government. Regional councils of bishops will acquire real autonomy to develop their own local customs, liturgies and laws. African bishops, for instance, might decide to make celibacy optional for the clergy, whereas Japanese bishops could make it compulsory.

Of course the Church's unity of doctrine and moral discipline and sacramental life must be maintained. It would be impossible to fit 300,000 bishops into St. Peter's for a General Council like at Vatican II. Instead regional bishops' councils would elect delegates and these, under the chairmanship of the pope, would constitute a permanent Roman Synod. Of course this would not need to be always in session; modern communications media make that unnecessary. It would have a permanent secretariat that would replace the present Roman curia.

A final touch to our alternative picture of a bishop. He would, of course, be elected by the people of his diocese. A local synod of clergy and lay representatives would choose a person, who would then be ordained by at least three other bishops from the region. The synod in Rome would, of course, be informed of the election, but there would be no question of his being appointed by Rome.

We turn now to the junior clergy, the ones popularly known as 'priests'. Let us consider, first, the received conception of them. Part of this conception, as with that of the bishop, has to do with the amount of resources and the number of people each priest is responsible for. And what has been said of bishops applies equally to priests. But there are other things too. In this conception a priest is unmarried, he doesn't have an ordinary job by means of which he earns his living, he has had a special sort of theological education—at least five or six years—and so is a specialist, a professional, of a sort.

Because of these requirements for being a priest according to the received conception, there are—understandably—very few priests around. Not nearly enough to do all the things which, on the received conception, priests are responsible for. In many parts of the world, for instance, participation in the eucharist is no longer seen as a basic requirement of Christian life but a rather rare luxury. There can be no doubt that this is one of the main reasons why there is so much interest in the role of the laity at present on the part of those who want to maintain the received conception of the clergy.

According to the received conception a priest is responsible for a very wide variety of different things: he must of course be something of a leader and organiser, able to delegate duties and handle personnel; he must be able to apply church law and discipline; he must be able to celebrate the sacraments and maintain a place of worship; he must be experienced at prayer and able to give spiritual direction; he must be able to cope with psychological and social problems; he is responsible for the financial administration of the parish; he is supposed to be something of a theologian, or at least to keep up with biblical and theological reading and thinking. Above all, he is supposed to be in close contact with the people of his parish so that they can recognise him as the centre and focus of their local Christian community. Of course no person can do all that. It is just as well that priests who feel they ought to, are unmarried and without ordinary jobs. At least they have time to have nervous breakdowns!

The alternative conception of a priest is very different. Instead of insisting on certain requirements, such as six years special education, full-time work and celibacy, which ensure that there will always be only a very few 'professional' priests, it starts from the assumption that every Christian community (every parish) needs a eucharistic minister (a priest) and the proper size for such a community is 100-150 people, say 30–40 families at the most. In other words according to this conception there is a real shortage of priests. We don't need just more priests, we need ten times as many priests as we now have. At least we need that number of people ordained to say mass.

Let me paint a picture of the alternative parish of the future. Sunday mass will consist of a gathering of 100–150 people. The priest will be a local person, elected by the parish (the 30 or 40 families that constitute the parish) and approved by the local bishop (who will know him personally as a committed Christian of reasonable intelligence and emotional stability). He will probably be married; he will certainly have an ordinary job.

All very well, you may say, but how will such a person even begin to do all the things that priests are expected to do. The answer, of course, is that he won't. The different things that have to be done, the things I have listed, will be done by different people. In a parish community of 40 families some of them will hardly need to be done at all. In other words in the place of one omnicompetent professional, we will have a more or less variously competent team. The priest will be one Christian minister among others, others who (in the terminology we are using) are all lay-people.

I have presented these two sketches of alternative conceptions of the clergy in order to make you aware of your own assumptions about what sort of people the clergy ought to be and what sort of work they ought to do.

I am sure it is clear which of the two conceptions I favour. But I haven't tried to give good reasons why everyone should think as I do. This is not the place for that. Our main concern is with the nature and function of lay-people in the Church. And I think you will argue that one's conception of the laity and their function will be very different depending on which of the two conceptions of the clergy one adopts. Our conceptions of the laity are still very vague; our conceptions of the clergy are not. But they will determine the way we think about the laity.

If we want to make up our minds what lay-people ought to be and do in the Church—and what clergy (and religious and any other group or class) ought to be and do, we have to clarify our ideas about what any member of the Church, any Christian, ought to be and do simply because of being a member. Once we have done that we can see what, if anything, is necessary for different categories of people—clergy, laity and religious to do and be over and above this basic job of being a Christian.

In the past in fact, we have concentrated so much on the nature and vocation of the clergy that we have come to see them as the model of a fully active Christian. And this has led us to think of some things which are, in fact, powers and duties of any Christian, simply as a member of the Church, as special powers or duties of the clergy and therefore as things that don't belong to the laity. There are many examples of this but here are some important ones: We think of the clergy as priests, but Vatican II tells us that all Christians are priests in the primary and most important sense of the word; we realise that we are not really clear about what it is to be a priest. We think of the clergy as having a vocation, a mission to spread the Gospel, and Vatican II tells us that all Christians have the same vocation and mission to do this. We think of the clergy as having special powers, as being sources of grace for the rest of us. Vatican II tries to persuade us that we are all sources of grace for each other simply because of our being included in the Church, by being baptised.

To sum all this up I suppose it is true to say that the big mistake that Christians, and especially Catholics, have made in the past is to think of the clergy as the active and the laity as the passive members of the Church. Within the Church the clergy are the givers and the laity the receivers; as far as the Church's outward activity is concerned, its mission to the world or whatever, well that is the responsibility of the clergy, and the job of the laity is to keep them fit and happy so that they can do it properly.

To put this mistake right some people now insist that the laity should become active members of the Church, like the clergy. There should be no passive members, passengers, in the Church. But that is also a mistake I think. To think of being a Christian simply in active terms, as being a certain job to be done, a mission to the world, is inadequate—whether one is a lay person or clergy. Being a Christian is always being passive, a receiver, as well as active, a giver and doer. All Christians, clergy as well as laity, are always passive, receivers, as far as God is concerned of his influence and inspiration. And we are all also active, or should be, transmitters of this influence and inspiration to others. Put like this it is easy to see that the passive side of our life is primary—we can't give anything that we have not already received. In concentrating on the role of the laity in the Church one must never lose sight of this important truth.

If we want to clarify our ideas about what any member of the Church, simply as a member of the Church, whether clerical or lay, is supposed to be and do, and do this in a way that is relevant to the contemporary situation in the Church and in the world, then we must consider what Vatican II has had to say on the topic. Vatican II was the scene of royal doctrinal battles between progressives and conservatives, and its decrees reflect this. Often two adjacent paragraphs are written in entirely different language reflecting the fact that they were included as a compromise to express the views of opposing factions. But there are certain themes that are dominant in all the documents and certain emphases that attracted an overwhelming majority of votes.

Those of you who attend these Lenten lectures regularly will perhaps have noticed that whatever topic I am talking on I always end up by quoting one particular sentence from the documents of Vatican II, namely its own special definition of the Church. To my mind even if the only thing all those bishops and theologians meeting over such a long time did was to formulate and promulgate that single sentence, the whole council would have been worthwhile. So I don't apologise for quoting it again. If you end up knowing it off by heart, it will be all to the good.

'By her relationship with Christ, the Church is a kind of sacrament or sign of intimate union with God and of the unity of all mankind.' It is this definition of the Church that can provide a foundation for the sort of insight we are looking for. It is a new definition, constructed during the Council. And the novelty, and strength, is contained primarily in two terms: 'unity of mankind' and 'sacrament'.

The expression 'unity of mankind' is the Council's term for the goal of God's plan, of Jesus' saving work. It is, of course, a unity of mankind in 'intimate union with God' as the definition puts it. That is taken for granted. The novel idea is that the creation of true human unity is the work of God and moreover the ultimate goal of history and salvation. As the decree on the missionary activity of the Church puts it: 'it pleased God to call men and women to share in his life and not merely singly, without any bond between them, but he formed them into a people in which his children who had been scattered were gathered together' (*Ad Gentes*, 2). Of course salvation consists primarily in being united to God. But here the idea is that we are united to God by being united to one another and indeed to all mankind in some way or other.

The union with God and the unity of humanity are not achieved separately. The one is the sign and expression of the other. The degree to which true human community is achieved is the sign of how far we are influenced and inspired by God and united to him. Of course this is not really a new idea. It is the same idea as the one we get in the first letter of St John: 'if we love one another, God abides in us' (4:12). But the language is new and importantly so. In speaking of the unity of mankind the emphasis is not so much on our internal dispositions but on an actual state of affairs in society and one moreover that involves the whole of humanity. The Church's nature and function, and so that of all its members, must be understood in relation to that. And this is expressed in the definition by the term 'sacrament'. In technical language a sacrament is a sign of something that also causes what it signifies to happen and does so precisely by signifying it. That's rather a mouthful so let's apply it to the Church and see what is being said. Here the Church is seen as the community of Christians and it is this community that is to be both a sign of the unity of mankind and also a real cause of that unity. As the consultation document for this year's Synod on the laity in Rome puts it: 'The Church is the universal sacrament of salvation, it is the People of God who welcome the gift of salvation and at the same time it is the People of God who proclaim, announce and communicate the gift of salvation to people in every age. At one and the same time it is the saved community and the saving community' (*Ex ecclesia coetibus*, 14). The 'unity of mankind in union with God' is what salvation is and if the Church is the sacrament of that, then it is because it is able to cause it to happen. But it can do so only as a sacrament does, that is by signifying that unity in itself. In other words it is only insofar as the Church really does express in its community life the 'unity of mankind in union with God' we are talking about that it can be an effective cause of the growth and fulfilment of this, in the lives of its members, and in the whole world wherever Christians make their presence felt. This is the way that God's spirit works in the world; revealing in the Church the community he is planning for the whole of humanity, and by revealing it there, actually helping to bring it about.

So the work of Christians as Christians is not something different from simply being members of the Church. Insofar as they make their common life in the Church more complete, so they are causing it to spread beyond the limits of the Church.

In view of all this it can be seen that the quality of the community life of the Church is of absolute importance. And it is something for which every Christian as a Christian is responsible since it is an expression of that union with God that is salvation. There is no distinction, as far as this fundamental vocation and mission is concerned, between clergy and lay-persons. 'There is a common dignity of members deriving from their re-birth in Christ, a common grace as children, a common vocation to perfection . . . . (and) just as baptism forms the basis of the common vocation and Christian dignity, so also it lies at the origin of the common mission entrusted to each and every baptised person in the Church and in the world' (*Ex ecclesia coetibus*, 16). Neither priests, nor bishops, nor even the pope are more responsible for the Church's mission. We are all equally to be active, givers or transmitters of Jesus' influence and inspiration. And we all have equal dignity as those who have received it. This is important to remember; our practice so often contradicts it—the courtly manners, the false modesty we affect towards bishops and priests, make it difficult (especially for them) to behave towards each other as real brothers and sisters in the family of God. There can be no leaders in the Church as there are leaders in other organisations; our leaders must be our servants. That means that they must think of themselves as servants and we must treat them as servants should be treated.

If the work of Christians as Christians is to create genuine human community both in the Church and in the world it is important to be aware of the forces that actually work against this in our age and culture. We will thus have a more concrete picture of what the creation of community entails and be in a better position to decide what the different parts to be played by clergy and laity are to be.

Our age and culture is dominated by science and technology. In principle humanity is now able to control the material environment it depends on and overcome the material deprivation suffered by so many. We can therefore clearly see that underdevelopment in all its forms—the lack of the means to a full and flourishing human life—is not merely a sad fact; it is our fault, the result of our failure to mobilise our resources properly, a failure that is in the last resort caused by a sinful lack of concern and effort. This culpable under-development of the environment is the most powerful barrier to the unity of humanity in the world today. It is not only that severe deprivation prevents even the most simple and essential forms of human community such as family life, to flourish. But the opposition between undeveloped and developed peoples creates inter-group conflict that threatens to become a global war. All over the world this opposition is producing actual armed struggle. When resources are scarce the competition for them is pretty fierce; when there is actually enough for all but it is not shared then anger and fear know no limits.

The global state of conflict is paralleled by a conflict of ideologies, conflicting systems of thought each with its own conception of the ideal society and how to achieve it, each with its own conception of humanity and human values. On the one hand are collectivist ideologies emphasizing equality at the expense of freedom and issuing in various forms of totalitarian state-control. On the other hand are various forms of individualism, valuing freedom above justice, making it possible for unprincipled multinational organisations to exploit vast numbers of people for their own profit. Both kinds of ideology are based on false conceptions of humanity and true human community: they are incapable of producing that 'unity of humanity in union with God' that the Church is concerned to create.

This is not the place to show in detail how such false systems of ideas actually prevent the realisation of human community in a society dominated by science and technology. One particularly clear example where this happens is in the sphere of sex and family life. At one end of the scale is the threat to family life presented by migrant labour all over the world; at the other end is the threat to marriage posed by the 'playboy' attitude to sex. The loneliness of urban life, the soaring divorce rate, are both manifestations of the breakdown of community life in a society dominated by both theoretical and practical materialism.

Last but not least there is apartheid, our own home-grown form of alienation, which we all claim to hate but which nevertheless we seem unable to say goodbye to.

All these forces that work against the creation of true human community in the various realms of life—social, political, cultural, sexual—make themselves felt in the Church as well as in the world at large. Each of us after all is a citizen both of the city of the world as well as of the City of God. So these forces also pervert our attempts to form Christian communities that are the sacrament of 'the unity of humanity' that God wants. The opposition between those who have and those who do not have power, resources, authority exists in the Church as well as in the world. And so does the opposition between totalitarian ideas and individualism, between different conceptions of sex and the roles of men and women. And last but not least, apartheid. We feel these forces too.

One of the things we need to do in this Lenten series is try and get clear in our minds those permanent powers in the Church emanating from Jesus himself that can overcome such forces, and how best to institutionalise them in the day to day life of Christian communities. If, for instance, the Eucharist is a permanent source of power in the Church, then perhaps we can find ways of celebrating it that actually do counter-act the forces I have mentioned above. And the same may be true of such things as prayer and religious life, and confession, and the way we share our material resources in the Church. And perhaps different categories of ministers that have not even been thought of before are necessary in our age if the gospel is to be lived and spread.

In recent years the social sciences have taught us the crucial role played by institutions in human life. So to see the Church as an institution is not to de-value it. It is a very special kind of institution in a world of institutions. It may be that it is precisely in the sphere of institutions, social, political, cultural, ecclesial that one can find a way of distinguishing between clergy and lay people, in terms of which institutions they are primarily responsible for. But that is not my concern in this introductory lecture so I will say no more on that head. Whatever the special role of the laity turns out to be I have tried to argue that it must be derived from that vocation and mission to the creation of true human community which is basic to all Christians, clergy and laity alike.

I want to make one more point before I end. According to Vatican II the defining characteristic of the laity, that characteristic that distinguishes them in a positive and not merely a negative way from clergy and religious, is their *secularity.* As the Constitution on the Church puts it 'A secular character is proper and special to laymen' and it explains this as follows: 'By reason of their special vocation it belongs to the laity to seek the kingdom of God by engaging in temporal affairs and directing them according to God's will. They live in the world, that is, they are engaged in each and every work and business of the earth and in the ordinary circumstances of social and family life which, as it were, constitute their very existence' (*Lumen Gentium*, 31).[1] This idea appears throughout the Council documents and is repeated in all official documents on the topic since then, including the Consultation document for this year's Synod. It is closely bound up with what might be called *the* dominant theme of Vatican II: namely that the Church has a mission to transform and

1. See Flannery, A (editor) *The Documents of Vatican II* (Pillar Books, 1975)

renew the whole social and material environment in which human life is lived and the salvation of humanity is achieved. 'The work of Christ's redemption concerns essentially the salvation of humanity; it takes in also, however, the renewal of the whole temporal order. The mission of the Church, consequently, is not only to bring people the message and grace of Christ but also to permeate and improve the whole range of the temporal order' (*Decree on the apostolate of the laity*, 5). And this job is the special job of the laity because of their *secular* condition, as opposed to the *sacred* vocation and mission of the clergy. Paul VI, in his Apostolic Exhortation *Evangelii Nuntiandi*, describes the laity's job as follows:

> Their own field of evangelizing activity is the vast and complicated world of politics, society and economics, but also the world of culture, of the sciences and the arts, of international life, of the mass media. It also includes other realities which are open to evangelization, such as human love, the family, the education of children and adolescents, professional work, suffering. The more Gospel-inspired lay people there are engaged in these realities, clearly involved in them, competent to promote them and conscious that they must exercise to the full their Christian powers which are often buried and suffocated, the more these realities will be at the service of the kingdom of God and therefore of salvation in Jesus Christ, without in any way losing or sacrificing their human content but rather pointing to a transcendent dimension which is often disregarded (*Ev.Nunt.*, 70),

What strikes me most forcibly about all this, especially the last quotation, is that what is being described is *not* the special character and vocation of the laity, but the character and vocation of every Christian. No clergyman or religious that I know would like to feel that they were excluded from the missionary task I have just described; that they were relegated to some strange *sacred* function that was not concerned with the secular world. In fact I find the weight that is still attached to the distinction between the sacred and the secular somewhat anachronistic. Isn't it after all supposed to be one of the great achievements of Christianity to overcome this distinction. The whole of God's creation is supposed to be sacred, especially such things as 'human love, the family, the education of children and adolescents, professional work and suffering.'

At all events, I think the emphasis on the secular character of the Christian vocation and mission, especially when it is seen as a characteristic of the whole Church, not just the laity, is of the utmost importance. With it, our conception of evangelisation and mission really has gained a new dimension that fits in to a scientific age where we do have the power to control and organise the 'temporal order', to make the world a home for the human family.

This vision of a world transformed to provide the milieu in which humanity can reach its full development could be the foundation of a new spirituality better fitted to release God's power in our hearts. Perhaps this is the 'lay spirituality' that people so often speak about. In different ages different forms of spirituality are dominant in the Church. For the Middle Ages monastic spirituality was dominant. It set the tone for every one in the Church. Its emphasis on *fuga mundi*, the flight from the world, was perhaps especially appropriate for those times. Since the time of the renaissance however, monastic spirituality has lost its influence in the Church. Gradually a new clerical spirituality came to predominate, so much so that even monastic spirituality became clericalised. This was an apostolic spirituality based on a 'hunger for souls'. But it was intimately bound up with the distinction between the secular and the sacred. Clergy, and to a certain extent, all Christians were encouraged to see themselves as foreigners on earth, pilgrims, travellers to their true heavenly home. Now it seems we have another option. *This world* is our home. But it is still in process of construction. As we grow up in it we are to make it a suitable place to live in. We must make it beautiful enough for God himself to live in. He has promised that he will come and make his home with us. And this is where he will do it, this world he made, this truly human place, not some other heavenly one we go to when we die. The only thing that can exclude us from this world is sin, not death. This is the faith that believes in resurrection, our own and that of the whole temporal order.

A spirituality based on this vision could, I suppose, be called 'lay', as opposed to 'clerical' or 'monastic'. But, like the earlier spiritualities, it could provide a dominant model for all spirituality, that of clergy and religious included. Perhaps it should. A provocative idea I'd like you to think about. If lay people do have a special vocation in the Church today it could be this: to be masters of the spiritual life in a secular age.

(1978)

Chapter Twelve
Love of Persons:
Unselfish Love as Manifestation of Spirituality

I wish in this article to investigate what is involved in unselfish love, the love of someone for his own sake. I want to discover the conditions for the possibility of such a love and what is necessary for this possibility to be realized. It is my belief that unselfish love is possible only because of the spirituality of human persons. And I hope to show too that the actual occurrence of acts of unselfish love implies the creative activity within human relationships of a personal God.

That acts of apparently unselfish love occur I take as a fact. There are different kinds of such love and, within each kind, differences of degree. And there would seem to be a great deal of agreement among writers on the subject of love as to the most common forms. Mother-love is perhaps the most common, though usually considered the most lowly, form. Then there is sexual love, covering a whole spectrum of varieties from a wholly self-centred lust to a genuinely unselfish adoration of the beloved. Associated with, but not to be confused with, sexual love is the strange and much-discussed phenomenon of romantic and courtly love. What is common to all these forms of love is their possible one-sidedness. Sexual love indeed is not usually one-sided but it can be. Friendship however cannot. For that reason it is usually reckoned as a higher, more typically personal, form of love. Of course friendship admits of degree, from trivial forms of companionship or camaraderie to a heroic readiness to make one's friend's happiness a condition for one's own. Finally, Christian teaching on the subject of charity recognizes the possibility of friendship with God, a love of him for his own sake beyond all thought of recompense. A peculiar feature of genuinely selfless love seems to be the ease with which it can be transferred from one object to another, even to the lover's enemies.

I propose to develop my account of unselfish love through a consideration of Thomas Aquinas' teaching on love. Not only is it the most detailed and systematic analysis that I know of; it is also thoroughly philosophical. At the same time it lacks nothing of psychological richness. Some of his detailed analyses rank with the best of modern phenomenological descriptions of various aspects of love. Above all, however, it is Aquinas' metaphysics of being, which makes its presence felt in everything he has to say about love, that provides, so it seems to me, the 'one thing needful' for a full understanding of unselfish love. I do not intend simply to repeat what Aquinas has said but to offer my own interpretation of the truth he has uncovered. So I will not attempt an exhaustive presentation of his doctrine of love but concentrate rather on those aspects of his theory that have reference to the topic of unselfish love. The unity of his theory is such that this is a difficult enough task. I must give enough to demonstrate the coherence of his doctrine to those who are not familiar with it. I hope I shall not give so much as to bore those who are. I am uncomfortably aware that to most contemporary philosophers Aquinas is a closed book while at the same time there are at large experts on this thought who, because of the special place the study of Aquinas has in the Catholic Church, are very expert experts indeed.[1]

Aquinas' theory of human love depends for its basic categories on a philosophical psychology that is a development of Aristotle's. Fundamental to this is a distinction within the psyche of apprehensive and appetitive powers or capacities. 'Since whatever operates must in some way be united to the object about which it operates, it follows of necessity that this something extrinsic, which is the object of the soul's operation, must be related to the soul in a twofold manner. First, inasmuch as this something extrinsic has a natural aptitude to be united to the soul, and to be by its likeness in the soul . . . Secondly, forasmuch as the soul itself has an inclination and tendency to the something extrinsic.' Within the first, the apprehensive powers, a

1. Among those I wish to make special mention of Professor R Johann. Those who have read his brilliant little book, *The Meaning of Love* (Paulist Press, 1954) will realize how indebted the present article is to that work. Indeed it can be regarded as merely drawing out some implications of his original and scholarly analysis. The only reason I do not refer explicitly to this work is that reference would be so continuous as to be burdensome.

distinction is made between sensitive and intellectual powers, the distinction once again resting on a distinction between the objects of their acts or operations. 'In this way there are two kinds of powers—namely, the sensitive in regard to the less common object—the sensible body; and the intellectual in regard to the most common object—universal being' (*Summa Theologiae*, Ia, Q.78, art.1). Within the second, the appetitive powers, a corresponding distinction is made between the passions and the will. It is the orientation of the distinctively human powers, intellect and will, to being as such or universal being that constitutes human spirituality for Aquinas.

The most general name given to the operation of the apprehensive powers is knowledge, to that of the appetitive, love. The difference of character between the apprehensive and appetitive powers is revealing as regards Aquinas' notion of love. By means of his apprehensive powers man is open to being; by knowledge he is able to include what he knows in his own being albeit in the manner peculiar to knowledge. Aquinas makes use of Aristotle's dictum that 'the soul of man is, in a way, all things by sense and intellect' (*Summa*, Ia, Q.80, art.1). In this regard, the reality known is really present in the knower but after the manner of the knower's own being. In the case of love however, the union between subject and object is quite other. Here the subject is assimilated to the object rather than vice versa.

What is aimed at is a union with the object as it exists in distinction from the subject. The result of love is a relationship between two real things, a sort of communion that depends for its character on the nature of the thing loved.

By associating love with the appetitive powers we see it as a sort of 'inclination' or 'tendency' (in Aquinas' words) towards reality. Contrary to common notions this tendency must not be understood principally as desire. Desire, for Aquinas, is love for something not yet possessed; joy is love for something possessed already. Love itself is neither of these. The words he uses to describe it are, variously, *aptitudo, proportio, complacentia, inclinatio, coaptatio, connaturalitas.* Etienne Gilson[2] sums up the idea thus: 'Fundamentally love is a modification of the human appetite by some desirable object. This modification consists in the fact that the appetite takes pleasure in the object. Such pleasure or complacency is, so to speak, an immediate

2. E Gilson, *The Christian Philosophy of St Thomas Aquinas* (Gollancz, 1957).

experiencing of natural *affinity*, of the fact that the living being and the object it is meeting are somehow complementary' (1957: 272). Such affinity is the essential characteristic of love, the condition for its possibility. Desire and joy are simply its conscious expression. As affinity, love is not limited to human beings. Aquinas even speaks, in an especially medieval moment, of the love of stones! In examining human love, however, this doctrine of affinity must never be forgotten. Without it as a foundation the rest of the theory would be incomprehensible.

The most common definition that Aquinas gives of love is Aristotle's 'to love is to wish good to someone' (*Rhet.* 2.4). This definition is the perfect locus for distinguishing the two fundamental, and fundamentally different, types of love. These are *amor amicitiae* and *amor concupiscentiae*, and are usually called in English love of friendship and love of desire. Since however *amor concupiscentiae,* as a *type* of love, has nothing in common with desire, as a *part* of love, and *amor amicitiae* is something quite different from friendship, I will follow R Johann's usage and call *amor amicitiae* direct love and *amor concupiscentiae* simply desire. The expression 'direct love' for *amor amicitiae* is amply justified since, as is clear from the definition, the act of love terminates in the person for whom whatever is desired is desired. 'Desire' on the other hand need not cause confusion since I shall not be talking about the *parts* of love at all, and anyway this is what we commonly call the sort of love that Aquinas is talking about as *amor concupiscentiae.* Not of course anything to do with sex!

Let us consider now the two types of love. I have stressed their difference. Yet usually they go together. We desire the goods we desire for the sake of the one whose good we have at heart, whether oneself or another. To forestall confusion, the distinction between desire and direct love is not that between love of things and love of persons. Persons can be desired (though wrongly so, Aquinas would maintain) for the sake of other persons. Nor is the distinction that between egoism and altruism, or selfish and unselfish love. Direct love can be either for oneself or another.

Desire is a subordinate type of love as it is always referred to the good of a person. Its character as a deficient form of love is seen in the fact that it does not extend to the thing itself of which it is desire. This needs explanation. Something is desired because it is felt to contribute to the happiness or well-being of a person. It is seen in relation to a person's needs and desired because it is the *sort* of thing that will meet them. It is not desired in its very particularity as a separately existing thing. This is not to say that it may not be desired for qualities which it and it only does possess. But one must distinguish between such qualities and its actuality as a separately existing being. Thus I am able to desire salami and especially perhaps the sort containing whole peppercorns. What I am not able to desire is that it exist quite apart from any relation to the needs of a person, myself or others. If I do will its being thus, simply, then it is by virtue of direct love and not desire. Whether Aquinas, as a Neapolitan, would have admitted to the possibility of direct love for salami is doubtful. He would probably have put salamies in the class of *irrationalia* for whom direct love is only possible in a metaphorical sense! The point however is that the object of desire, even if it is the only one of its kind, is not desired for its own sake. It is not the sheer fact of its existence that is loved but the fact that it is a being of such and such a type or even, in addition, that it has such and such unique qualities of its own.

Direct love on the contrary does will the being and the well-being of the beloved. Thus direct love and desire differ both as regards their relation to the lover and as regards that aspect of the beloved that is loved. In desire the lover is concerned with his or someone else's needs and their satisfaction. In direct love he is affirming someone's worth, though not with regard to any virtue they might have or anything else that distinguishes them from other men. Nor even in regard to their human nature. It is simply the fact of their existence that is celebrated. Direct love affirms that it is a good thing that they exist. It wills the good of the beloved, not in the sense of desiring something additional for them (though of course it does that too because it wills their good) but in the sense of willing their full development or perfection, the complete flowering of what they have it in them to be. It is difficult to catch in non-scholastic language the sense of Aquinas' 'act of being', which, beyond all essential character and accidental quality, is the term of direct love.

More insight into the nature of direct love is gained when it is seen why only persons can be loved directly. This conclusion follows from the fact that only persons can directly love. As only persons are conscious of themselves as distinct individual beings it is only persons who can love themselves directly. The important point in all this is that for Aquinas it is this direct love of *self* that is the source and foundation for all love, both desire and direct love, for others. It is something natural to a being possessed of a will to will its own good and hence to desire what it conceives this good to be. How this natural love of self comes to be extended to others is the very heart of Aquinas' metaphysics of love. I shall at this point simply expound his explanation, deferring comment till later.

As we have seen Aquinas considers human nature, by virtue of its spirituality, to be open to being as such, or universal being as he puts it. A consequence of this is that he is able to apprehend that unity in a particular complex of sense experience that constitutes an actually existing thing. It is just because he has the notion of being as such that he is able to recognize the individuality of a particular existent thing. The animal's consciousness is so swamped, as it were, by particular things that it is unable to recognize either their or its own distinct particularity. Because man's mind has this universality of scope and penetration he is able to distinguish particulars against that background. And in becoming present to a universe of particular beings he becomes conscious of his own distinctness from them, conscious of himself. For Aquinas man is present to himself because he is present to being as such. Thus he loves himself, because he *is*, not just because he is himself. The object of will, as with the intellect, is being itself. 'Being' in the way that Aquinas uses the term does not refer to a merely ideal notion but to the actual intrinsic ground of the reality of any existing thing. Nothing can be without being something, but actually being is something really distinct from actually being human or actually being white. The best way to conceptualise it, though only analogically, since by definition it is beyond the reach of concepts, is as activity or action. Every individual being of whatever form is actively being itself. So in every form of being and in every individual being it is being as such that is known as true and loved as good. In this sense it is because I am present to being that I am present to myself and because I love being that I love myself. But is it also because I am present to being that I can be present to others similarly present, and because I love being that I can love the being of others. That act of being I love in myself I love not because it is mine nor because it is human, but simply for its own sake. I am able to transfer this love to other human beings not because I love human beings but because being human they too are present to being as such. So in gaining properly personal knowledge of another human being

I become present to an act of being which has nothing to distinguish it from my own except that it is not mine. Hence the tendency or affinity in me that issues in direct love of self produces the same love for another. What makes me capable of direct love for myself, also makes me capable of direct love for others.

It is because it is love of being that direct love can extend to the very being of another rather than stopping short at qualities of his being that make him an object of my desire. Because his being is incommunicable it is irrelevant as a term of desire for the lover. Instead he can only love it, if he loves it at all, as he loves himself—directly. 'When a man loves another with the love of friendship, he wills good to him, just as he wills good to himself; wherefore he apprehends him as his other self, in so far, to wit, as he wills good to him as to himself' (*Summa*, IaIIae Q.28, art.1). Thus direct love for another, on Aquinas' understanding of the notion, goes beyond simple goodwill, whether general or particular. It also goes beyond that respect for the dignity of the other person as a human (that is, a rational) being that Kant was so concerned to vindicate. Seeing another as another myself and willing good to him as I will good to myself also implies an affective union with him whereby I cherish and promote his being in its uniqueness as I do my own: Direct love, says Aquinas, 'differs from goodwill, because it denotes a certain union of affections between the lover and the beloved, in as much as the lover deems the beloved as somewhat united to him, or belonging to him, and so tends towards him. On the other hand, goodwill is a simple act of will, whereby we wish a person well, even without presupposing the aforesaid union of the affections with him' (*Summa*, IIa IIae, Q.27 art. 2).

We now have sufficient of Aquinas' teaching on love to turn to an explicit treatment of unselfish love, namely direct love of another in Aquinas' terminology. I have tried to give some idea of the conditions for its possibility according to Aquinas but have as yet said nothing to indicate what could motivate such an act. Direct love for self would seem so natural as hardly to need explanation (though something more needs to be said on that head too, as will be seen.) Direct love of others, and perhaps to the point of self-sacrifice, seems to contradict such natural self-centredness. We have seen that even Aquinas who believed firmly in its possibility had to account for it in terms of an extension of our love for ourselves. What moves us to such an extension? If we are all capable of it why is it that we do not all achieve it? Or do we not, at least in some measure? In that case is it not natural? If on the other hand we decide it is a natural tendency what good does it do us? A natural tendency that can lead even to the sacrifice of the one subject to it is something of a paradox. We shall have to attempt some explanation of unselfish love that does justice to it as a personal, which is to say a rational, activity and not simply a sort of herd instinct making itself felt in opposition to our conscious intention or, on the other hand, explain it away as a fiction, an illusion with possibly pathological roots. Finally, assuming we are able to give a satisfactory account of it, so that it does appear a real possibility and a value, we shall have to ask about the conditions necessary for the possibility to become reality.

[In passing it is perhaps necessary to explain the apparent oddness of retaining the term 'unselfish' love for a love that is indeed directed at the self. My reason for this is partly because the sort of love I have in mind (and as I have analysed it) is in fact denoted thus in common usage. And also the most striking evidence of its existence in a person is a sort of self-forgetfulness, a willingness to sacrifice one's own particular goods for the sake of others.]

Aquinas' definition of love certainly seems apt as long as one considers only the subject's love of himself. Clearly I desire whatever I desire only because I will good to myself. But this self-love is more complete than at first appears. Clearly if I love myself only because I am myself there is no way in which this love can be extended to another. Since he is simply not myself. If this is all there is to it, then I can only love another person for my sake, that is with a love of desire. If however we take seriously the insight embodied in Aquinas' distinctive notion of being another possibility becomes apparent. By virtue of my spirituality I am open to being in its unlimited scope. It is precisely this lack of limitation which as far as my intellectual powers are concerned enables me to be conscious of myself *as* a self, a real individual subject distinct from every object I experience or conceive. It is equally this lack of limitation in my powers of volition that establishes me as a self-determining origin of acts of judgment and of choice. This is not the place to expound this connection fully. We simply take it as a fact and refer those interested to the detailed elaboration of it by Karl Rahner.[3] The importance for our purpose of

3. Especially the extended treatment in *Spirit in the World* (Herder and Herder, 1968) passim, and more compendiously *Hearers of the Word* (Sheed and Ward, 1969), 51–70.

such unlimited openness to being is that it makes possible another dimension to our direct love of self. In loving myself directly it is also possible that it is this individual 'act' of unlimited openness to being that I love. To say this is not to suggest that I come to realise explicitly what sort of being I am and love myself because I am that sort of being—and hence am able to extend this love to others because they too are beings of that sort. That would be to retreat from the depth of interiority to which Aquinas has guided us. It is of course because I am that sort of being (that is, spiritual) that I am able to love myself in this way, and indeed that there is that in myself that can be thus loved. It is myself that I love and it is only by virtue of my spirituality that I have such access to the self that I am. But what I love is an individual being open to being in its unlimited scope. It is because the ultimate term of this sort of self-love is unlimited that it can be the foundation of a direct love of others. Of course both self and others are actually limited, needy beings. To that extent the love of self and the love of others is not and cannot ever be identical. As a spiritual being however I have a potentiality or capacity for being that is not so limited. And it is as such that self and other appear to coincide. What this means is made clearer by Aquinas' teaching on *friendship*. It is here too that the rightful place of desire in the love of person is indicated. We have been speaking almost exclusively of direct love as the model for unselfish love; but as we shall see desire must not be excluded as something inevitably selfish. Desire and direct love can never be separated in fact as we have separated them in theory. They are different aspects of the love of person as is evident in Aristotle's definition. Persons however can always be understood from two different viewpoints. From the point of view of their nature, human beings have a determinate set of capacities or powers able to be realized and developed in the course of their lives. From this point of view they will tend to desire their fulfillment, to desire the things their capacities require, including the things that only another person can give them. As we have seen however it is part of human nature to be present to being in its unlimited scope. And as such a person can be the object of direct love. But we have also seen that the real object of direct love is not limited to the particular self I happen to be but is in principle extendable to all other persons. We have spoken of this extension, that made possible by unselfish love of oneself, as a value. But in what sense can it be a value if it is unconcerned with the perfection of the individual's nature? It may seem natural to love oneself unselfishly but in fact it is not, as has been shown; it is perfectly possible simply to love the satisfaction of one's natural needs and particular wishes. There seems in fact to be something gratuitous, even *de trop*, about direct love as we have defined it. How can we include the two types of love within the same person? Aquinas' answer to this would seem to be as follow: to the extent that we do realize our specifically human, that is spiritual, capacities we will find ourselves actually involved in unselfish love. Unselfish love is as it were the product of a properly developed human being. It is unconcerned with the perfection of the individual as such because it is concerned with the realization of a greater value that is external to him but which he is capable of establishing and in which he for that very reason participates. This value is in the most general terms that of *community*. At every level of being it reveals itself: at the organic in the way that parts of a plant contribute to the welfare of the whole, at the animal in the way that individuals exist for the preservation of the species. At the human level it shows in all societies as a natural concern for the common good. Indeed human beings ought to be more concerned for the common good than for their own individual good. As persons however human beings may not subordinate their own development to that of others, though the impulse to community still remains. A new form of community is indicated, a community of persons that does not contradict the value of personality but which is built on the perfection of human nature. This is *friendship*. Friendship is a good that transcends the good of the individual. But true friendship can only be based on the perfection of the individual's capacities. It is in this way that desire for self-realisation and direct love combine, or are capable of combining. One desires one's own perfection to be sure, but for the sake of friendship. And similarly one desires the perfection of one's friend. True friendship does not contradict unselfish love because it is based on a direct love of one's friend. This is not quite the whole truth though, since friendship must be *mutual* to be friendship. Hence included in the desire for friendship is the desire that my friend should love me directly, not for my sake but for his, that he may help to create the community of friendship and participate in it himself. And this is only possible insofar as he tends towards the perfection of his natural capacities. Friendship thus does not exist for the sake of the perfection of the friends but as an expression of it. It is in a way capable of being desired for its own sake but not in such a way as to contradict the unselfish love which alone can bring it about. Perhaps it is more accurate to see friendship as the term of a direct love rather than desire. True friendship is a communion of persons made possible by the perfection in each of their spiritual powers. It is primarily a unity of life, of being, in which each participates. There is a sense in which the distinction between self and other is secondary to this unity, so that the direct love of the unity is simultaneously a love of self and other. The friendship thus exists as a concrete expression of the lack of limitation towards which the spiritual powers of persons tend.

In what precise sense the friendship of persons can be an unlimited form of being is indicated by the reflection that the perfection of man's spiritual powers, on which alone it can be based, can only be realized by the activity of an *actually* unlimited being. As the scholastic dictum has it, a being that is in potency as regards some perfection cannot itself bring that potency to act. And if the potency in question is a capacity for unlimited being then the only agent capable of actualizing it to perfection would be an actually unlimited one. No human person is actually unlimited. Hence the agent in question must be God. Certainly for Aquinas, God is not to be seen as external to his creatures. In fact he expressly teaches that God is more internal to the creature than is the creature to itself. The perfection of man's spiritual powers is simply the highest case of God's activity in creation, the created expression of his own self-knowledge and self-love.

The perspective opened up by such a natural theology does moreover suggest possible solutions to the paradox of unselfish love for others and the friendship at which it aims. The paradox is at once that of a desire that goes beyond the satisfaction of our needs and the realization of our human capacities, and that of the apparent lack of motivation, the gratuitousness, of unselfish love. If God is both source and term of direct love and his love the inner dynamism of unselfish love, then it is indeed God who is loved, both by desire and direct love. The notion of desiring God raises no problems, since he alone, in the doctrine of Aquinas, can bring us to perfection. We desire, that is, what he alone can give us. Aquinas does however go further and teaches a direct love of God that is unselfish. In his treatise on charity, which in scholastic doctrine is reckoned as one of the three 'theological' virtues of the soul brought about by grace, he defines charity first and foremost not as a virtue but in terms of friendship. 'Since there is a communication between man and God, inasmuch as he communicated his happiness to us, some kind of friendship must needs be based on this same communication . . . The love which is based on this communication, is charity; wherefore it is evident that charity is the friendship of man for God' (*Summa*, IaIIae, Q.23, art.1). Virtue is the perfection of the human powers and such perfection is happiness. Now although for both Aquinas and Aristotle happiness is what is ultimately aimed at by all men, and Aquinas ordinarily always speaks of our love for God simply as the provider of our happiness, here he suggests an end beyond happiness. It is the fulfillment of our powers that make this end possible to be sure, yet the end itself is friendship, a personal communion between man and God that man participates in *for God's sake* and not his own. This will not surprise the theologian who holds that charity is in fact a participation in God's own love, which of course ultimately has himself for its term. But this doctrine of friendship with God does seem to imply that common teaching about the ultimate goal of human life being the beatific vision is inadequate. As far as the perfection of man's nature is concerned that might well be the case—the full exercise of his highest powers on their truly adequate object, as is commonly said. But this having been achieved, surely more is possible. Since it is only achieved by God's communication of himself in friendship it would seem to call for some answering self-donation on the part of man, a culmination, as it were, of those acts of unselfish love that marked the road to happiness. The intellect and will are the highest powers of human beings but ultimately they are oriented, even metaphysically, to action that is external since God is always also external to his creation in the sense of transcending it. What shall we name this activity consequent on the beatific vision? Why not 'worship'? The self-donation of the creature to God which is the centre of all earthly religion surely will not cease in heaven. Augustine appears to get the order exactly right when he writes in *The City of God* 'we shall rest and we shall see; we shall see and we shall love; we shall love and we shall praise. Behold what shall be in the end and shall not end' (*City of God*, Bk 22, Chap 30).

Theology apart however it does seem as if those common experiences of unselfish love referred to at the beginning of this paper do require a view of man as naturally capable of, and in some sense naturally 'drawn to', the exercise of such a love. The fact that the actual realization of this love implies the operation of an unlimited and independent person should not be allowed to obscure this requirement. It must not on the other hand be supposed that assent to such a view of man is assent to a strict proof of God's existence. Unselfish love as we have defined it is not strictly a necessity of nature and cannot therefore be the basis for a metaphysical proof of God's existence or even of human spirituality. Aquinas certainly believed that such proof existed. These proofs do not however take the place of what I have suggested in this paper. They are preliminaries and the assent to them is of a partial kind, in fact being included in the sort of assent to the necessity of the conditions presupposed by unselfish love. This on the other hand is more like the assent of faith, albeit of an implicit sort. It is based on an understanding of personal life in its total situation and not merely on an abstract analysis of capacities. Unlike Aquinas' proof of the spirituality of the soul as a component of human nature it is an analysis of its exercise within the whole dynamism of the person, one which moreover presupposes that it meets with *success*. To recognize success is to make a judgment of value. Thus though there is no question of explicit faith being required to recognize unselfish love and the consequences it entails, such a recognition does appear to be an act of implicit faith, requiring in addition to insight into one's own nature and its capacities a certain act of the will.

Recognition of human spirituality and its effects would seem to be a half-way house to recognition of the operation of a personal God. The one is a condition for the possibility for unselfish love, the other the condition for its realization. The link between them is the awareness of and movement towards the unlimited mode of being implied by unselfish love and the common familiar sign of this is the direct love of other persons.

(1979)

Chapter Thirteen
Indwelling, Intersubjectivity and God

I suspect that at its close this article will be judged to have fallen between two stools, that of the theologian and that of the philosopher. Not being in a position to remedy the defects of either quarter makes me the keener to communicate to others something that has recently struck me and given me pause for thought, namely an apparent parallel between a certain aspect of contemporary philosophy and another of traditional theology. It is to these that the expressions 'intersubjectivity' and 'indwelling' in my title refer. It is my hope that an examination of the parallel between them will prove fruitful for the contemporary pursuit of the perennial occupation of *fides quaerens intellectum.*

For surely there is, now as always, a problem of the understanding of Christian faith, a problem for believer and unbeliever alike. If for the one it is necessary to believe in order to understand whereas for the other some degree of understanding is a prerequisite for authentic faith, yet both are required to seek understanding, that common human insight that is nevertheless inseparable from well-formed faith.

The understanding of faith as both a necessary prerequisite for faith and the natural intellectual expression of it, is inevitably dependent on the categories available in the culture of the day. It is this that gives a peculiar twist to the problem of understanding Christian faith today. Simply put, there is an embarrassment of riches. We have to choose between traditional and contemporary, between western and eastern, between categories that are definitely religious and those that are definitely not. Other religions provide new categories and so do the special sciences.

In choosing categories with which to formulate an understanding of Christian faith one has to have an at least preliminary notion of what it is what one wishes to understand. One has to have some way of identifying the Christian faith as an historical phenomenon distinct from other religious and secular systems of thought, before seeking that deeper understanding that leads either to conversion or to the vision of God. It is not enough to produce some Creed or Catechism, however authoritative, and say 'There it is'. Because the various doctrines are expressed in theological language, the 'translation' of which is part of the problem we are concerned with, they don't identify the faith, at least intellectually, in an ordinary 'secular' way. One needs some intellectual handle or token, one that is both more comprehensive than any specific doctrine—in order to be able to represent them all—and capable of being articulated in fairly ordinary language. Is something of the sort even a possibility?

When one considers the classical Christian creeds or the authoritative catechisms that have appeared at different times in the Church's history, and especially if one pages through a collection such as Denzinger, one is apt to be struck by the number, the variety and the richness of the doctrines of the faith. Eventually however, as one's familiarity with such documents increases, a second impression, that of a marked and persuasive unity of style or flavour, succeeds the first. It is not that each doctrine is related by an encompassing system to all the rest (that would be more the mark of theological work, than of lists or collections of formulas of the faith); it is more that each different doctrine seems in the end to be saying very much the same thing. Of course it could not be the case that each formula was intended to express literally the same fact or truth. The common import, if such there is, would be of a more general and possibly less easily expressible kind. It seems to me that there is something of the sort that is common to at least the central doctrines of the faith and I shall try to describe it clearly.

Ultimately, I suppose, the unity of Christian doctrines derives from the fact that they have all a common function, namely to define the significance of Jesus himself for those who believe in him. 'The person and work of Christ'—this is the ultimate source of even the most seemingly insignificant and obscure doctrines of the faith, at least if they are genuinely such. The common style is the style of his life, the common flavour is the flavour of his teaching; this much at least all Christians will believe. My interest now is to catch this common spirit conceptually. Not that one should expect or even desire to produce a sort of superdogma that would contain all the others in itself. But rather that one should be able to formulate a verbal sign or symbol that would express in a summary way what differentiates Christianity from other religions and provide a simple portmanteau with which to carry one's faith. Both are desiderata in a situation of cultural pluralism. If one is to enter into intelligent dialogue with other faiths one must know what is one's own, and if one is not to be put off by only apparent conflicts of belief one had better travel light. What follows is my attempt.

I propose to consider here only the most obviously fundamental Christian doctrines. Most of the Creeds have a more or less Trinitarian structure and it is certainly traditional to distinguish three broad aspects of God's activity in relation to us, namely creation, redemption and sanctification, and to appropriate each to one of the three divine 'persons'. The distinction is I think intended to be comprehensive. I will examine each aspect in turn.

That there is something other than God—though God is the sum of all perfections—is the first half of the doctrine of creation; and it is mysterious enough that there could be anything in addition, as it were, to the positive fullness of all possible types of being. But the second half of the doctrine is equally mysterious: that every aspect of the being of created reality derives from God and from no other source at all. The otherness itself of the created world is God's creation. A succinct formulation of this particular mysteriousness is that you cannot add Creator and creature together and make two. Hegel makes the same sort of point in another way: the 'bad' (the false notion of the) Infinite is simply opposed to the finite as its contrary, the 'true' Infinite contains the finite within itself. For if there is anything 'outside' the infinite, in opposition to it in any real (as opposed to notional) way, then the 'infinite' is as finite as its opposite.

There is thus a sense in which created reality is *in* God, though not a part of him since he has no parts. The sense of *in* will be made clearer in what follows. Here one need simply notice that the relation between Creator and created reality is most clearly exemplified in the creation of persons. That beings with a power of free choice are created poses the paradox inherent in the doctrine of creation at its sharpest. Especially when one reflects that there is a sense in which the creation of persons is the most typical and complete example of creation, since every level of created being is represented in humankind and here alone is the image and likeness of the Creator properly achieved. It is precisely because persons participate most fully in the being of God that they are most free of, and to that degree distinct from, him. The more a creature is like God, the more he possesses his own being.

This brief exposition of the doctrine of creation is intended to emphasise just this, the way in which Creator and creature are shown to 'coinhere' (to adapt Charles Williams' expressive term) in one another. They are distinct to the degree that the creature participates in the fullness of being that is God's, not in spite or because of it.

In the case of the doctrine of redemption it is on the notion of the hypostatic union, of two natures in one person as it is commonly expressed, that I wish to concentrate. That this notion effectively sums up the Christian faith regarding the person and work of the Redeemer is the burden of the famous patristic dictum that 'what is not assumed is not redeemed'. If Christ is not wholly human then it is not mankind that is redeemed—if he is not truly God then it is not redemption that is achieved. Hence the redeemer is both God and man. At the same time he is one person. The words translated by 'person' in the ancient creeds all have the express function of defining a unity of the most absolute kind. What can we learn from this? What if not, and once again, that a union of being between God and man establishes rather than obliterates distinction? Indeed the incarnation can be seen as a special, perhaps even as the archetypal, case of creation. Christ's human nature is not first created and then united to the Word. Its union with the Word is precisely its creation. In fact if one views the incarnation in a Scotist rather than a Thomist perspective, one can see the incarnation as the culmination of creation, the moment in which the Creator communicates himself, and so the creature's own being, to the creature. Moreover it is precisely because the divine nature is fully communicated, so that the Word is present in person, that the human nature that is brought into being is the realisation of all that humankind can be. Just as there are two distinct natures in Christ so too are there two distinct wills. Yet whatever the divine will wills is willed also by the human will, and so by a human will that is fully formed and free.

The doctrine of the hypostatic union is perhaps the sharpest example in Christian theology of distinction increasing in direct proportion to union, where one of the persons in the relation is God. But it should not be assumed that this sort of union is so entirely peculiar to the case of Christ that it has no parallel or analogy in the general case of personal union between God and human persons. Rather the opposite is the case, so that whatever is held to be true of the human nature of Christ is held to be possible for all other human beings too, with this one proviso—that he is its cause. What he is by nature, we may be by grace and glory. This is held to be true with regard at least to the deep essential consequences of union with God. To believe anything less would be to reduce the doctrine of redemption to the status of myth.

We have come to the third part of our summary examination of the fundamental doctrines of the faith, that dealing with God the sanctifier. And here I will take a quick look at the doctrine of grace. In this case the paradox can be simply put: the more we are moved by God's grace the more the action is our own. If grace is really the activity of God's Spirit in our lives then it is not the case that one aspect of our acts originates in God whereas another is due to us alone. The only place where a case could be made for acts performed independently of God's grace is in the case of sin. Yet it is precisely here that the weight of Christian tradition has judged sin to be really a failure to act, a sort of nonbeing in the realm of action. There is not space to discuss this problem here, but if the sphere of moral action can be seen as the final expression and working out of creation—the creation by God of complete human persons in a spatial and temporal setting—then it is free centres or origins of action themselves that are in process of construction and insofar as each successive stage of this construction is a *success*, just so far is it equally the act of the grace of God and of the progressively cohering centre of the human person. A failure on the other hand is a lack of God's action and at the same time an interruption or dissipation of the building of a centre. I have allowed myself the use of a mechanical or organic model to try and express an essentially personal relation and it is inadequate. The mysteriousness of sin at any rate is not going to be adequately delineated in that way. Let me rather leave the question of sin on one side. Whether or not it can be accommodated by a properly personal account of the creative relation between God and man might even appear in what is to follow. For our present purpose it is enough to remark that as far as successful (in the moral sense) human development is concerned, the doctrine of grace exhibits the same 'coinherence' between what is of God and what is of man that we have noted in the doctrines of creation and redemption.

What I have called coinherence could also be designated by the term 'indwelling', and this, I think, is a term that does in fact, in the history of theology, refer more or less to the feature I have been discussing. Although I have examined only three fundamental doctrines I want to claim that this feature is far more generalised than that. In fact I want to suggest that there is good reason to regard Christianity as a religion of indwellings. In the New Testament itself there are indwellings of various sorts, of God in man and man in God, of God in Christ and Christ in God, of Christ in us and us in Christ, of the Spirit in us and us in the Spirit. Nor is the indwelling normally one-sided; if we are in Christ, then Christ is in us, and so on. The interpenetration is mutual. Various other metaphors of union are used though none quite so strong. An exception perhaps is the notion in Genesis that when they marry man and woman become one body. This metaphor of the body, and the way in which the head is not simply joined to but present in all the members, is the typical New Testament way of stressing the peculiarly intimate interconnections possible between persons. 'Just as all men die in Adam, so all men will be brought to life in Christ' (1 Cor 15:22). Possibly the background to this sort of language is primitive notions of the corporate personality of groups. That should not obscure however what seems quite clear, that in the New Testament and even more in the later development of doctrine, the idea of the mutual indwelling of persons, human and divine, is used consciously and carefully both to define and to explain the Christian faith.

Theologians may feel by now that I have lumped together too many altogether disparate items under one heading. Be that as it may, I hope I have said enough to have shown that the notion of 'indwelling' is a fairly pervasive one in the corpus of Christian doctrine. That it is *the* typical or defining feature of the central Christian doctrines would require more labour of demonstration than I can expend here. But even to suggest the possibility raises the question as to what sort of feature it is that I think I have disclosed. My reply to this will show the sort of status I think it has. The notion of 'indwelling' as I have described it is a metaphysical consequence of the distinctively Christian idea of God, namely that he is a properly personal being.

There is no space in this article for a full development of this idea. The notion of 'indwelling' is, however, one that would express a fundamental characteristic of the creature who is the image and likeness of a properly personal God, and of God's relations with it.

Having explained what sort of notion I take that of 'indwelling' to be it should be apparent that certain alternatives are excluded. One cannot, in the case of divinehuman indwellings, either piously or with a skeptical shrug, consign it to the realm of mystery. Nor can one, with regard to the indwellings of human persons with one another, make of it merely a metaphor. On the other hand if one believes it to have metaphysical status then one is bound to justify that belief. Justification of this sort must be philosophical and I shall seek it in the place promised at the beginning of this article, namely in one field of contemporary philosophy, which is concerned with what I have called 'intersubjectivity'. It is my hope that the philosophical treatment of the one notion will throw the light of rational insight into the theological depths of the other. But there is also the possibility that the theological notion will provide something that a purely philosophical analysis of this feature of experience lacks and reveals itself as lacking. After all if our faith is true we should expect it to complement and augment what human reason can discover of a nature that God has made. There is, however, another reason why I feel bound to attempt some philosophical justification of the notion of 'indwelling'. This is because on the face of it such a notion goes against received notions of personality, freedom and responsibility considered inseparable from a Christian view of man. I am thinking especially of Kant's account of human autonomy and the enormous influence it has had in Christian thought in spite of its original rationalist setting. If our notion of 'indwelling' is coherent then the absolute status of the autonomy of the will is overthrown. Nor would such a reversal affect only Kant. His insistence on autonomy made it impossible for him to admit any genuinely redemptive influence on one person by another, divine as well as human. But the doctrine that grace is imputed and not imparted has the same effect and would suffer the same fate if the theory of indwelling were true. Still, it could only possibly be true if first of all it were coherent. Let us now try to make up our minds on that.

By the term 'intersubjectivity' I wish to refer to the notion that persons are uniquely dependent on other persons for the acquisition, development and perfection of their distinctively human capacities. More concretely, it is by virtue of a peculiarly intimate influence of other persons that a person is enabled to acquire selfconsciousness, the power of conceptual thought and deliberate choice and so, ultimately, the freedom of selfdetermination.

This notion or some variant of it is not the special discovery of a particular school. It is a typical feature of the writings of the French personalists and of the many varieties of existentialism and phenomenology. It is also found among the transcendental Thomists.[1] In the Englishspeaking world it occupies a central position in the work of the Scots philosopher John Macmurray In particular it is the major theme of his Gifford lectures of 1953–1954, 'The Form of the Personal'.[2] His purpose as he puts it is 'to show how the personal relation of persons is constitutive of personal existence; that there can be no man until there are at least two men in communication' (1961: 12). Or, even more strongly, 'Persons, therefore, are constituted by their mutual relation to one another' (1961: 24). I propose now to show fairly briefly how Macmurray attempts to justify this thesis. There is a clear parallel between the notions of intersubjectivity and indwelling and it may be that a philosophical justification of the one will also justify the other.

1. Books I have found especially useful are:
   (a) Of the personalists: Maurice Nedoncelle, *Love and the Person* (Sheed and Ward, 1968) and *La Réciprocité des Consciences* (Aubier, 1942); also Maurice Blondel, *L'Action* (Paris, 1893); and an extensive paraphrase and commentary on this in English, JM Sommerville, *Total Commitment: Blondel's 'L'Action'* (Corpus Books, 1968).
   (b) Of the existentialists: All the classical writers deal with intersubjectivity but a lucid and fairly synoptic account in English is WA Luijpen, *Existential Phenomenology* (Duquesne University Press, 1960).
   (c) Of the Thomists: Karl Rahner, *Hearers of the Word* (Sheed and Ward, 1969); and 'Reflections on the Unity of the Love of Neighbour and the Love of God' in *Theological Investigations*, Vol. 6 (Darton, Longman and Todd, 1967): 231–49. Also R Johann, *The Meaning of Love* (Paulist Press, 1954).

   Useful periodical articles in English are: K Gallagher, 'Self and Other: the Radical A Priori', in *International Philosophical Quarterly*, 12 (1972): 5–18; and John Heron, 'The Phenomenology of Social Encounter: the Gaze', in *Philosophy and Phenomenological Research*, 31 (1971): 243–64.
2. Published in two volumes, *The Self as Agent* and *Persons in Relation* (London: Faber and Faber, 1956 and 1961).

For Macmurray the defining characteristic of a person is the ability to act. Action he defines as conscious and intentional self-movement in relation to another. He holds moreover that agency of this sort is indubitable and does not require proof. Still he himself offers a proof of a sort by showing that any attempt to negate agency will of necessity affirm it.

If our agency is a fact what are the necessary conditions for its possibility? There are two. The first is a minimal condition for action in the common or conventional sense of the term; the second, one that is required for action in the strict and proper sense of the term. The first condition is the existence and presence of persons other than the agent. The second is that the agent and the others be related by an intention that is mutual and positive (in a sense that will be made clear). Let us examine the first condition first.

Action involves both movement and conscious intention. Movement itself involves two elements—energy or effort and resistance or support, an element that is initiating and another that is receptive. In the case of animal behaviour the relationship between organism and environment is such that the environment is not a 'resistance' to the 'initiation' of behaviour: it makes it possible by 'supporting' it. The same applies to human action: there is a distinction of two elements in the unity of the act. These can be called in the broadest sense 'self' and 'other'. But it must not be thought that the action 'belongs' to the self in a special way. Both self and other are equally necessary for action, are essential elements in the actual occurrence and process of the act, and are only recognised as distinct by subsequent reflection. 'The resistance of the Other is not merely a negation of the act of the Self, it is necessary to the possibility of the act, and so constitutive of it' (1956: 110). Thus, to give a purely formal description of action (or behaviour or movement), it is a unity containing and constituted by two opposing elements—called by Macmurray, quite abstractly at first, positive and negative. In the case of action, the movement is consciously intended. Thus both elements that make up the act must have this character. (Whether one is considering simple movement, animal behaviour or human action, the distinguishing characteristic that defines each specific stage applies to both elements in it.) In other words both effort and resistance are constituted by a conscious intention. So Macmurray concludes, 'The possibility of action depends upon the Other being also agent, and so upon a plurality of agents in one field of action. The resistance to the Self through which the Self can exist as agent must be the resistance of another Self' (1956: 145).

To bring this abstract analysis of action closer to intuition Macmurray presents a developmental model in which the elements of the analysis appear as moments in a process. The model is that of the relationship between a mother and a child, but ideally conceived so that the mother represents an agent in the strict and full sense of the term whereas the child represents the bare capacity for agency. Thus the distinct elements that go to make up action as we commonly experience it are sketched in as stages or interactions in a process of maturation.

Some readers might be tempted to object to such a model. It is surely true that children require the presence and initiative of other persons if they are to realise their distinctively human capacities—for conceptual thought, deliberate choice and hence for action proper. The cases of 'wild' children would seem to prove this if proof were needed.[3] But it can hardly be true of adults, who surely often act quite on their own in total isolation from other persons.

Such an objection misunderstands Macmurray's purpose. He is not out to provide a detailed description of what empirical psychology could discover from the observation of human behaviour, nor just to analyse our ordinary understanding of the word 'action'. He is concerned to set out the conditions for the *possibility* of action as the agent himself experiences them prior to all reflection. And he does want to claim that the presence and initiative of another person is implied by the very notion of action that he holds to be inevitably corroborated by such experience. Of course if he is right then his analysis has a factual implication that is perhaps surprising. Before any act at all can be performed a person other than the agent must exist already.

This however is not the only paradox that Macmurray's model presents one with. There is another, and it has two sides. If to be a person is to be an agent and agency is only achieved at the end of a process of development then there must be degrees of agency and hence of freedom. This means that talk of freedom of choice, of intention and agency, at any stage but the last is metaphorical and

---

3. *Vide* Suzanne Langer's analysis of these cases in *Philosophy in a New Key* (Harvard, 1984), Chapter 5.

conventional. Guarded consent may be given to that (though when is the final stage reached?). But here is the poser: how can freedom admit of degree? One is not talking here of freedom from constraint of whatever sort, but freedom of choice. And isn't that something that one is thought either to have completely or not at all? I remark on this paradox not as a sign that Macmurray's analysis of action is at fault but because it suggests a line of thought to which I shall later return.

We come now to the second condition for action. Though relation to another is necessary it is not enough; to constitute a sufficient condition for action in the full and proper sense of the word the relation between self and other must be positive and mutually so. So far Macmurray's analysis of action has involved the notion of positive and negative elements in a purely formal way, really simply as elements in opposition. In the mother and child model however he introduces a properly personal sense of these terms. In the process of maturation in terms of which the model is worked out he discerns what he calls a 'rhythm of withdrawal and return'. This is that aspect of the process whereby the mother brings the child to do for itself what previously she had to do for it. In general terms it is the complex personal transaction whereby a person (in this case 'fullyfledged') enables another to achieve full exercise of his own power of agency or personhood. In the case of the mother and child, the mother deliberately and for the child's sake alone, so that it will realize its own capacity for action, refrains from satisfying one or other of its needs. On the one level, the practical, she withdraws. On this level and from the child's point of view her action is negative, contrary to its wellbeing, a simple lack of care. On another level, the properly personal, and from the mother's point of view, the action of withdrawal is completely positive, an expression of her love for the child, her will that he be a person in his own right. And however perfect her motivation, it costs her suffering; there is the appearance of neglect and the possibility that the child will misinterpret her act. The child will either respond positively, recognising and accepting the withdrawal as a sign of the love that prompts it, or negatively, itself withdrawing in anger or in hate. A positive response is coherent since it both answers its strictly personal need for personal love and realises its own capacity to act on the basis of the intention of another. A negative response is incoherent and indeed contradictory for it is an annulment, albeit symbolic, of a relationship on which the child absolutely depends.

A positive intention is one that wills the being and the agency of the Other. This is illustrated by the model. What the model also shows is that if the agent's environment, that which is actually modified by and thus constitutive of his action, is a world of persons, then making their intentions his own is a *sine qua non* of his intentions being realised at all. For his intentions are not realised (that is his acts are not completed) in some neutral or impersonal medium between him and others—they are realised precisely in the effect they have on the persons who constitute his environment, that is on their intentions. Hence if the effect intended is to be realised it must be the one willed by the Other. Therefore mutuality is a necessary condition for action. Moreover the mutuality must be positive. For a positive intention is one that assents to and wills the being and agency of the Other. Hence a mutuality of anger or hatred is incoherent. Because the Other is necessary to my own agency a negative attitude towards him is one that simultaneously accepts and rejects him. Of course such conflicting states of mind occur but they occur precisely because we are not properly personal or agents in the full sense of the term.

This analysis might appear fanciful if one forgets Macmurray's purpose is not to give a realistic depiction of the actual setting of our acts, but in this case to define a condition which he admits is only ever present as an ideal. If proper personhood is to be achieved then the ideal of positive mutuality must condition all our actions. This ideal and its relation to the various actual forms of human society, Macmurray describes in a second theoretical model that he calls 'community'.

The community which is the necessary and sufficient condition for action in the full sense of the term consists of two persons in fully reciprocal and positive relationship to one another. That which makes each person an agent in the full sense is the same factor that makes the relationship fully positive—a totally heterocentric attitude on the part of each. Each lives wholly for the other, making their will the ultimate condition of his own. Because of this complete mutuality there is perfect freedom, both in the sense that there is no constraint between the two and in the sense that there is no division in the will of either. Macmurray notes that this freedom is conditional on the inclusiveness and universality of the heterocentric regard. In the model there are only two; potentially however all persons in the universe are included in the selfforgetful will of each. Let me conclude this all too sketchy account of Macmurray's analysis of the second condition of action by quoting his own description of the community model.

> 'If, then, we isolate one pair, as the unit of personal community, we can discover the basic structure of community as such. The relation between them is positively motivated in each. Each, then, is heterocentric; the centre of interest and attention is in the other, not in himself. For each, therefore, it is the other who is important, not himself. The other is the centre of value. For himself he has no value in himself but only for the other; consequently he cares for himself only for the sake of the other. But this is mutual; the other cares for him disinterestedly in return. Each, that is to say, acts, and therefore thinks and feels for the other, and not for himself. But because the positive motive contains and subordinates its negative, their unity is no fusion of selves, neither is it a functional unity of differences—neither an organic nor a mechanical unity—it is a unity of persons. Each remains a distinct individual; the other remains really other. Each realises himself in and through the other' (1961: 158).

Before we finally leave Macmurray I want to point out that his second model too presents us with a paradox. If to be a person is to be an agent in the strict sense, an irreducible and independent origin of intentional acts, how can the acquisition and perfection of such a character be dependent on the activity and attitude of another? There is no doubt of it in Macmurray's mind: it is the efficacy of the other member of the community model that enables me to realise my free agency to the full. Yet how can what is most intimately one's own, the very secret substance of one's spontaneity as it were, lie in the gift of another?

Whatever we may think of Macmurray's attempt to justify the notion of intersubjectivity philosophically—and my sketchy account of it certainly does not do justice to either its immense suggestiveness or its persuasiveness—it would appear at the least that persons do rely on other persons for the development of those capacities that make them persons, and that a growth in personal self-sufficiency, self-possession or freedom (or whatever it is that establishes a person as a distinct and creative origin of action) depends on a growth in intimate personal union with others. And this is enough to establish the parallel we were seeking with the theologically derived notion of indwelling. An investigation of intersubjectivity reveals the personal relation of persons to be mutually creative in some sense.

Might it not be, as the notion of indwelling suggests, that God's relation to his creature is simply the limiting and perfect case of such 'intersubjectivity'? In other words, a relation of strict analogy obtains between them.

In conclusion I would like to make a few further remarks on the significance of such a parallel and the possible uses to which it could be put. They arise out of the two paradoxes concerning freedom that Macmurray's analysis of action seems to produce. We seem to be forced to accept, first, the idea of a freedom that develops or increases and, second, that for each agent this freedom is the gift of another. Now it seems to me that there is something about both these paradoxes that is relevant to our topic. To take the first one first: the problem of how a person can become progressively freer is a similar one to that of the origin of such a capacity in the first place. The one problem reduces to that of how more freedom can emerge from less, the other to how the capacity for free action can arise at all, in the history of either the universe or the individual. Could it not be that the cause necessary for originating the capacity would be sufficient for its development? And if it is the case (as surely it is) that the cause of a personal effect could not be less than personal itself, then the analogy between this paradox and the Christian doctrine of creation is clear. Only an infinite personal being could account for the production of a being that was free from matter that was not.[4]

The second paradox, that of freedom being the gift of another, is closely connected to the notion of a positive intention as Macmurray expounds it. According to him it is the positive intention of the Other that enables the agent to develop his own power of free action. The problem about being given freedom can thus be seen to be related to the question of the acquisition of a positive intention. How does one in fact acquire a positive intention? From another who already has it of course. And from whom does he acquire it? If positive intentions are to exist at all then someone somewhere, at some time must have a positive intention that was not acquired but, as it were, self-generated. Such a notion is that of a person who does not depend on others for his personhood. A totally independent person is an infinite one. Thus the second paradox too exhibits an analogy with the Christian doctrine of God.

---

4. For the traditional 'proof' of this *vide* Thomas Aquinas, *Summa Theologiae*, Ia, Q.90, Art.2. cf. also Ia, Q.118, Art.2.

Both paradoxes in effect pose problems that are solved if the Christian account of the relation between man and God is true. They are, in other words, what a Christian would expect to find in an accurate account of the relations between human persons. In Macmurray's account we have a philosophical justification for a sort of personal interdependence that closely parallels the notion of indwelling that seems to be a keynote of Christian faith. On the other hand, as the paradoxes show, his account requires a final factual condition if it is to stand, and this the Christian faith supplies in the infinite personal being of God. Could this final condition be supplied by purely philosophic means? That would depend on the grounds for either of two judgments: 'Yes, I do have the capacity for being an agent in the strict sense of the term' and 'Yes, I can identify a genuine increase in personal freedom'. Possibly the second judgment represents the only adequate evidence for the first. If one could make it solely on the basis of reflection upon and analysis of one's experience of other persons (the experience of forgiveness would seem to me to offer special promise—both Hegel and Charles Williams recognise its importance but Macmurray appears to overlook it)[5] then one would be in a position to complete Macmurray's account of the conditions for action. One would also have sufficient grounds for believing in the existence of a moreorlessChristian God.

I hope I have said enough to establish the parallel between the notions of indwelling and intersubjectivity. As I have already suggested, I believe that each side of the parallel is able to illuminate the other. For between the theologically derived notion and the philosophically justified one there exists a *tertium quid* to which both refer, namely our actual experience of ourselves as persons in relation to others. This is the common ground in which both faith and understanding have their roots and where alone they can meet. The believer is bound to ask himself whether his faith is actually an illumination of that, the unbeliever equally whether an unbiased understanding of it does not imply the presence and the creativity of God.

(1979)

5. Vide Hegel, *Early Theological Writings* (Chicago University Press, 1970) and Charles Williams, *The Forgiveness of Sins* (Eerdmans, 1942).

Chapter Fourteen

A Philosophy of the Human Person for Contemporary Theology

The following remarks concerning the need for a philosophical understanding of the human person in contemporary theology are offered as an invitation to a further discussion of the subject. They will also show why I think such a discussion an important one and what theoretical and practical problems it would be directed towards solving. Whether the problems are those of a contemporary Catholic theology, or even any Christian theology, throughout the world or whether they are more especially felt in South Africa and other similar societies, is an issue that would be part of any such discussion. The only claim I am in a position to make is that they are felt among Catholic students in an 'open' South African university; the more general of the remarks that follow must be seen as extrapolations from this limited experience.

I am going to argue that there is a conflict within the Church between those who see religion primarily as a matter of 'prayer and those who see it as primarily a matter of 'politics'. These positions result from contrary but equally inadequate reactions to one or other form of contemporary materialism. And a truly theological reconciliation of these positions is only possible on the basis of a renewed philosophical understanding of the spirituality of human persons. This renewed notion of the spiritual is derived from contemporary work done in the philosophy of persons in the tradition of 'transcendental Thomism'. Further study of this work would, in my opinion, have fruitful consequences (both theoretical and practical) one of which could be the rescuing of the sacrament of penance from its present limbo-like position. In any case, too great a pluralism of views, or even broad conceptual models, on something that is so fundamental to a coherent theology as the nature of the human person is not a good thing, and a broad consensus on this topic would also be a desirable goal for our discussion. Let me begin it without more ado by setting out my thesis.

The Division: Prayer or Politics

There is a division in the Church between two groups of Catholics. The first group is dutiful about private prayer and reception of the sacraments. It practices various devotions, is interested in the saints and our Lady, and in miracles. This group includes both those who hark back to before Vatican II, are keen on the Latin mass and benediction and also those influenced by the charismatic renewal. They are all agreed, whatever their precise spirituality might be, that Christianity is primarily concerned with God and the supernatural, getting to heaven and avoiding hell.

The second group is engrossed by matters of social and political life. It is interested in one or other form of welfare work or in matters of political justice, particularly with regard to those deprived of political rights or economically disadvantaged. It sees Christianity as primarily directed towards overcoming the sufferings of humanity. So the religious life of a Christian is one of practical action in the world to establish justice and political freedom. This group finds it difficult to see the relevance of prayer and the sacraments.

Though both the concern to worship God and the desire to be of service to others are essential elements of Christianity the way in which these are understood and practised by these two groups is seriously inauthentic. It is not only that each group tends to reject the concern of the other as 'irrelevant' or 'unchristian', and is therefore one-sided. There is even inauthenticity in the way they live the aspect that they do value. So the prayer-life and sacramentality of the first group will be fanciful and escapist. The interest in miracles will obscure the reality and beauty of God's presence in the normal course of events. And the political or social activism of the second group will often be the expression of egoism, the desire for power, prestige or popularity, or even simple agressiveness or rebellion against the notion of authority. In some cases it can even condone the use of terrorist violence to gain legitimate political goals.

These two tendencies characterise both groups and organisations in the church. But they can both be felt within a particular individual who, as a result, feels that different aspects of his Christian life are irreconcilable. The partiality and inauthenticity of each is however the expression of a real perversion of Christian sensibility brought about by two different reactions by the Church to different aspects of contemporary Western technological and secular culture.

The underlying feature in our contemporary culture that provokes both reactions and whose powerful influence is manifested in the beliefs and behaviour of both the groups I have described, can be called, in a general way, *materialism*. Materialism is a feature, first of all, of capitalist individualism in the affluent, highly developed societies of Europe and America. It shows itself in such phenomena as consumerism, hedonism and money worship, but also in popular programmes for health and beauty and 'self-realisation'—whether of a psychological or recreational kind. All these phenomena are expressive of a concern for material security, well-being and success at both the individual and family level.

Materialism is also a feature of socialist collectivism in Marxist states. Here the official ideology is strictly materialist and the whole state-machine is organised for the purposes of material production, of arms for increasing political power, and commodities to continue to improve the material standard of living. There is an obsession with security at the collective level, security of the state and of world-communism, and individuals are readily sacrificed to totalitarian social control.

The influence of both those types of materialism is present in our society. Although they are connected with incompatible political ideologies they are present side by side in our cultural environment, in the media, in books and magazines, in public institutions such as state education and health care, as well as in the general ethos of commerce and recreation.

Dualism or Materialism?

Just as no-one can escape the spirit of the age he lives in, so are we, without necessarily being aware of this materialism, influenced and educated by it. The two groups I have described represent two different ways of reacting to it within the Church.

Those who stress the importance of prayer are, on the face of it, opposed to the materialist ethos. And yet this stress often goes hand in glove with an apparently contradictory over-reliance on embodiments of that ethos, including the use of the most materialist commercial practices and institutions. Because this side of life is considered irrelevant to the true interests of Christians, there is a lack of serious critical reflection on it. This lack extends to the political sphere as well so that an insensitivity to certain forms of suffering can result. In short, for this group life can become divided into two, a private sphere in which religion is at home, and a public sphere which is religiously irrelevant. Inauthentic other-worldliness leads to a practical dualism.

Those who stress the importance of social justice and political freedom and equality often come to consider material values like health and standard of living as the most important human values. They can come to sacrifice individual interests for social goods. Above all, in their work for social and political ends they can come to forget God and the specifically religious response to God altogether. They become, in short, as materialist in practice and ethos as Marxists themselves.

The Need for a New Theology

If one is to overcome the opposition between these two groups in the Church, or the conflict of these two tendencies in individual Catholics, it is not enough simply to recognise the element of truth in each position and exhort people to remember the one without forgetting the other. There are of course many Catholics who do just that. Their prayer-life and their involvement in social action are integrated, feeding and feeding off each other. But one will not be able to foster this integrity of Christian life in the whole Church without having a real understanding of how the apparently opposed tendencies really do hang together. If one is to mount an educational system that is opposed to the influence of the secular environment in this respect—and I think that nothing less will do—then such a programme must be based on an understanding that integrates the opposing tendencies *theologically*. Otherwise it will remain inadequate to express the real unity of the Christian vision in every sphere of a person's life, the imaginative and emotional, as well as in his choices, beliefs and actions.

Now as it happens Catholic theology is, I believe, well placed to perform this task. Catholic theology has always been thoroughly philosophical. By this I mean that the Church has always recognised the necessity for understanding, systematising and communicating the truths of faith in rational or 'secular' terms. This recognition is, I think, a fruit of the conviction that there can be no ultimate contradiction between the genuine insights of human reason and the truths of faith. It is the same God, after all, who both creates our rational nature and who reveals himself in Jesus. Hence the persistent opposition of the teaching authority in the Church to the Biblical positivism and fundamentalism of certain Christian groups as well as to the 'modernists' who went to see the Christian faith as one among many 'philosophies' or ideologies.

It is because of this attitude that there has not occurred in the Catholic Church that division between secular and sacred sciences that is such a feature of the post-Enlightenment process of secularization which has affected Christianity so profoundly. And it is precisely this division that has encouraged Christians to opt for one of the two inauthentic reactions to materialism I have described above. Either one opts for an other-worldly fideism and fundamentalism and rejects the secular out of hand, or else one adopts a secular 'version' of Christianity such as humanism or socialism or even one or other form of nationalism.

Admittedly, as some critics have, with justice, pointed out, this preservation by the teaching authority in the Church of a philosophically formulated and systematised theology has been part and parcel of a thoroughly suspicious and defensive attitude towards modern movements of thought. Catholic theology and official teaching has too often been content to repeat philosophical formulations of faith that go hack to the time of the great scholastic synthesis.

But oddly enough, in the contemporary climate of thought even this appears to be to our advantage. The philosophical foundations of scientific rationality that underly the process of secularization are to be found in the thought of Descartes. He is the philosophical progenitor of both contemporary materialism and the dualistic reaction. The philosophical foundations of Catholic theology however are Thomist. And the thought of Aquinas not only ante-dates Descartes but, more importantly, is radically opposed to both dualism and materialism.

This is especially true of his philosophical understanding of persons, which is from a theological point of view the most relevant, and sensitive, area.

So, if it is granted that a new theological synthesis is required to reconcile the opposing tendencies in the life of the Church at present, and it is recognised that such a synthesis must be genuinely philosophical, then it would appear that we have an ideal philosophical tool at hand with which we can perform the task.

A New Form of Thomism

I am not suggesting, for one moment, that we once again attempt to breathe new life into long-dead formulas. Nor that we re-write the dreary manuals of all the Thomist revivals of the past. Apart from anything else there is no need. Thomism, at least in its philosophical form, is alive and well and living in the works of such contemporary philosophers as Bernard Lonergan and Karl Rahner and many others.

Since the beginning of this century those (exclusively Catholic) writers known collectively now as 'transcendental Thomists' have in a genuinely philosophical way been developing a philosophical system based on the metaphysics of Aquinas which attempts to integrate on that basis the important insights of philosophers since Descartes.

This development does, it seems to me, provide an alternative to the other most influential contemporary philosophical approaches to the human person. There are two of these, that of analytical philosophy which originates in Anglo-American circles but whose influence extends far beyond that, and Marxist philosophy which originates in continental Europe but whose influence extends far beyond that. Both of these philosophical approaches are materialist and entail materialist conceptions of the human person. Analytical philosophy issues either in one or other form of physicalism or mind/brain identity theory or else in a reductionistic behaviourism. Marxist philosophy sees humanity as the product of a social process the ultimate determinants of which are material.

These two philosophical movements can, without any special pleading, be seen as the expression at the philosophical level of the two types of materialism I have already described. And the two types of Christian reaction to contemporary materialism can also have their philosophic expression: a radical soul/body dualism in reaction to the physicalism of the mind/brain identity theorist and, on the other hand, various attempts to baptise Marxist materialism. But neither is capable for various reasons of providing the philosophical understanding of the human person that is needed for Christian theology. Dualism won't do in the face of such Christian doctrines as the resurrection of the body, and materialism is incompatible with the notion of eternal life. In any case I think there are strictly philosophical objections to both dualism and materialism. And it is just this that makes me hopeful about the understanding of the human person that contemporary transcendental Thomism has developed. It avoids materialism but without falling into dualism.

Persons are Spiritual

The notion of the human person developed by transcendental Thomism is based on a re-interpretation of the traditional Christian notion that persons are spiritual beings. The spirituality of persons is understood as their possessing the capacity for *self*-enactment of the radical kind that shows itself in distinctively human self-consciousness and self-determination. A radically self-enacting being can't be material. All material things have parts and a being that, in the strict sense, enacts itself must be simple. Further, all material things are dependent on external causality for their operation whereas to be self-enacting entails being free from external causality. *Human* persons on the other hand are material as well as being persons. So if one holds that persons are spiritual beings it would seem one is doomed to dualism. Transcendental Thomism however understands materiality as dependence-on-another (a notion for which there is ample Thomist justification) and thus human materiality can be seen as our undeniable dependence on and orientation towards other human persons for the exercise, growth and fulfilment of our specifically human powers. In other words substantial dualism is avoided by saying that we human persons realise our (spiritual) power of *self*-enactment in a radical (material) dependence on *other* persons. Although that appears on the face of it to be a contradictory formulation, the actual experience of personal relations would seem to justify the formula at the phenomenological level at least. (I am thinking of the way in which the personal autonomy of a child is developed rather than diminished by the influence of a loving parent, or how personal growth in an adult increases in *direct* and not *inverse* proportion to the influence on him of understanding and unselfish friends). But transcendental Thomism offers a metaphysical solution to the apparent contradiction as well. It stems from the fact that the necessary condition of our being capable of self-enactment in the strict sense is the presence to us and causal influence on us of a strictly infinite being. And this for two reasons: we would not be able to know our own finite reality were we not at the same time (however implicitly) also aware of something infinite; we would not be able to transcend the causal influence of our worldly environment were we not at the same time open to the causal influence of an infinite being. Thus the contradiction we have referred to above is only apparent. Self-enactment and other dependence are not contradictory when the relation is between finite and infinite. And it is this relation which for human persons is mediated through their relations with other human persons. Thus insofar as human persons are persons (that is, spiritual beings) and so capable of self-enactment they are open to the presence and influence of an absolutely infinite being; insofar as they are human (that is, material beings) their capacity for self-enactment can only be realised by the presence and influence of an infinite being within the relationship in which they stand to other human persons.

Such a formulation may seem horrifically tortuous. Nevertheless it is nothing more than the expression in philosophical terminology of the familiar Christian vision of man as 'the image of God' and our teaching about the relation of identity between the love of God and the love of neighbour. Of course I have presented it in as summary a form as possible and this must add to the apparent obscurity. I cannot, needless to say, present the philosophical justification for it here. But insofar as it is philosophically coherent it does represent a real alternative to both dualism and materialism, and (so it seems to me) one that is well suited to a philosophical articulation of Christian faith.

A 'Psychology of Grace'

Basing our theology on such an understanding of the human person (presuming it were worked out in detail) would have certain consequences for the sort of problems I have described above.

It is clearly opposed to materialism of both a theoretical and a practical sort. If persons are capable of self-enactment then they cannot be subject, nor ought they be subjected, to the determinism of their natural or social environment. Insofar as human beings are spiritual they have needs that no technology or social organisation can meet.

It is also opposed to the dualistic reaction to materialism. If the openness to infinite being that constitutes human spirituality can only be developed within and through relations with human persons, then there is no possibility of seeing the spiritual life, prayer and the sacraments as an alternative to life in society. Closeness and sensitivity to God is as much a possibility of our public, active life as of our private, reflective life.

Above all, however, understanding human persons as spiritual beings in the sense outlined above does make it possible to understand and express the truths of faith without, on the one hand, using language that is incomprehensibly 'other-worldly' or 'supernatural' and, on the other, 'translating' what we believe into the terminology of a secular world-view that is inadequate to express the fullness of the faith. The object of faith is God, so theology must be about God. But theology, as *fides quaerens intellectum*, is concerned above all with understanding, and so must be expressed in terms that have meaning in themselves, outside the special reference to God. And this is why our notion of the human person is so important. If man is 'the image of God' then our understanding of man will, and ought to, influence our understanding of God. As Aquinas himself said, 'an error concerning the creature ends as false thinking about God' (*Contra Gentiles* 2, 3).

It is thus, essential to base our theological articulation of our faith on a philosophically justified notion of the human person. And in view of the problems I have outlined in this paper it is especially necessary at this time to refer all our theology to a notion of the human person that does justice to our spiritual nature.

As far as our attitude to prayer and the sacraments, to miracles and all the strictly 'supernatural' elements of faith is concerned, it is most important to be able to describe the workings of grace and the various stages of the spiritual life in terms that express the actual constitution of human beings and the way in which they can either develop or fail to develop as persons. It is a common enough notion that all the practices and institutions of religion in the Church are to be understood as 'means of grace'. What I am urging is that an account be given of how these means work in building up and fulfilling our natures as spiritual beings. What is required for an understanding of the sacramental and spiritual life that is not merely 'mythical' or 'miraculous' is what has been aptly described as a 'psychology of grace'.[1] And it is precisely such a philosophical psychology that the notion of person sketched above could provide. Psychology of that sort would moreover provide that so-necessary bridge between moral and ascetical theology that seems to have been blown up some time in the sixteenth century and never to have been properly repaired since. If both the norms governing the celebration of the sacraments and the technique of prayer, as well as the principles and precepts of morality can be seen as deriving from an actual understanding of human nature and its requirements for growth and fulfilment, then not only will the 'relevance' of these laws became clear, but there will also be an end to the sort of legalism, the apparently arbitrary divine positivism, that has given the Catholic Church such a bad name.

As far as our attitude to our social and political lives is concerned the notion of human persons I have outlined ought to make it clear why the Christian life must of necessity be expressed in inter-personal relations. First of all we can only grow towards the fulfilment of our nature as persons in relation to other persons. And secondly, it is only in communion with other human persons that we can develop our communion with God. The progress of the human sciences has made it increasingly clear how we depend on other persons for our own personal development. The notion of the human person sketched above which incorporates an openness to God as a constitutive element in our nature as spiritual beings, is also able to give an account of how our growth in union with God depends on our relations with other human persons too. For these reasons the nature of our social and political attitudes becomes of crucial import for our relation to God. But because they are seen as expressions of our spiritual nature, they will always be referred back to and judged by the needs of that nature. Any question of a political programme devoted to merely material ends will be ruled out. And our social criticism will be based on self-criticism; the motivation of our political involvement being as important as our policies.

---

1. Meissner, W, SJ, *Foundations for a Psychology of Grace* (Paulist Press, 1966)

A Concrete Example: Penance

A concrete example of these considerations can be made of the sacrament of penance. Of all the sacraments it is the most clearly connected with our personal growth. If our theology is rooted in a notion of the human person such as transcendental Thomism offers then the drama of personal growth will occupy the centre of the stage in our Christian lives. The 'gamelike' symbolic quality of sacramental celebrations will gain in seriousness by virtue of being seen in relation to the building up of Christian character in individuals. If prayer and sacraments really are seen as essential ways of changing and perfecting our characters then they will be more highly valued and frequently used—on one condition. That the building up and perfecting of our characters are seen in relation to the goal of communion with other persons and with God. This is the necessary condition for preventing, say, our interest in the sacrament of penance as a means to greater self knowledge and personal integrity, from becoming self-centred and narcissistic. We want to become like that in order to be more capable of communion with others and with God. But it is precisely this interest in our own qualities of character and their development, expressed in the regular life-long celebration of a sacrament like penance, that will ensure the Christian quality of our involvement in social and political matters. A self-critical spirit based on insight into the true needs of our personal nature will prevent our promoting inhuman institutions or subordinating spiritual to material values. It will also prevent our adopting inhuman means to perfectly human ends.

(1982)

Chapter Fifteen
Seeing Life as the Creation of Character

I suppose each of us has his or her own way of making sense of his or her faith. By that I mean that underlying the various things we believe and value are some fundamental, often unexamined, notions and attitudes that give coherence to what we believe and do. It is these notions, and the attitudes that are dependent on them, that make for us the connection between the public historic dogmas of the Church and our own intimate, immediate lives. They are not themselves dogmas or articles of faith—but much vaguer, more ordinary-seeming but also more all-pervasive, notions. Their origins are, and will always remain, obscure, though in part of course we have acquired them through the history of our involvement with the Christian 'thing' itself.

Various things have prompted me recently to do a bit of digging in my own hidden conceptual foundations and I want to share the results of this mental archaeology with others. Inevitably one's presuppositions are partial and the language in which one holds them muddy and obscuring. So I want your detached, less biased assessment of notions that I hold too closely to me to see as clearly as I could. In the process of looking at what I have to show, you will probably become aware of how different, or differently expressed—which is after all a real difference too—my insights are from your own. And so you may become more aware of the notions that do the same work for you.

It is mainly reaction to the ideas of others that prompted my examination of my own. Amongst the university students I teach I come up against two very different ways of understanding the Christian faith. The one is, I suppose, a version of liberation theology.

Everything is seen against the background of the imperative of changing the political institutions of our society. The other is more recognisably mythical: our faith has primarily to do with God's battle against the devil and his angels; miracles are always happening, and we have detailed knowledge of what happens after we die.

My colleagues typify yet a third set of assumptions about reality, one which I reckon many students and others share as well. It could be called the outlook of secularism. There is no God, or any overall purpose or direction to evolution, history or an individual life. Reality is matter in motion, more or less highly organised. Death is the total destruction, beyond repair, of the human personality. This set of assumptions about the world seems peculiarly at home in the environment created by western technology, medicines, motor cars and telephones.

Finally, I have recently been confronted vividly by various forms of suffering. There is the suffering of the poverty-stricken squatters around Cape Town. Then there was a newspaper story that horrified my wife: it told of a little boy in an English mental home who had to be tied to a pole because his need for emotional re-assurance was so great that he would otherwise spend all his waking hours simply clinging to anybody he could find. And I myself saw a friend dying of cancer in such continuous pain that he couldn't even concentrate on the answers to questions he asked me and couldn't prevent a small involuntary sound coming from his throat each time he breathed.

I'm not sure why these four things seem especially significant. Perhaps it is that between them they both present one with a vision of what the real problems of life are and of a variety of ways of responding to them. And surely it is true that the Christian faith, or any faith, does at least see itself as the answer to a problem. That, at any rate, is an assumption in what I am going to say.

The notion I want to explain to you—which seems to me to be the central, co-ordinating notion in my grasp of faith—is that of *the creation of character*. It seems to me that the ultimate aim of everything that God does in the universe, in the evolution of nature and the history of persons, can best be described as *the creation of character*.

'Creation' is certainly a very orthodox word. Usually it is distinguished from 'salvation' or 'sanctification', or something like that, and used to denote the initial bringing into being of human beings in their natural setting rather than the development of persons in history. I want to use it to refer to both processes in order to stress the unity between them, and also to counteract the idea that we are created (in the old sense) finished or complete. The truth is rather that what is initially brought into being in the case of each of us is the mere *capacity* for personal development, rather than fully developed human persons. This capacity, or system of capacities, is what constitutes our human nature. It is equally part of Christian faith as I understand it that the development of this capacity is as much the work of God as its initial bringing into being. It certainly cannot be the case that the process of 'salvation' or 'sanctification' or whatever, is less wholly God's work because it is one in which we also are personally involved.

This brings me to my second word. It has a decidedly old-fashioned, almost Victorian ring—Character: It is what enlightened headmasters of English public schools used to hope that rough games would produce in their pupils. I have deliberately chosen it because I think that none of you will be tempted to like it without thinking about it. It is certainly not a 'favourite' word of mine. One can get at what I want to mean by it by thinking of what is referred to by the word 'character' in a novel or a play. Characters in plays and novels don't really exist, but they are known as sets or systems of insight and choice, of feeling and action. Certain ideas or emotions or ways of behaving are typical of them, and these diverse elements form a more or less integrated system that we refer to as the character so-and-so. I would think that central to the notion of a person's character, whether fictional or real, is the notion of value. It seems to me that a person's character is determined by what he judges to be truly valuable, whether and to what degree he consents to this insight and lives by it, and how far his convictions enter into and organise his emotional life. I could go on a great deal longer about the notion of character but it is not necessary for our present purpose. I hope I have said enough to indicate the sort of notion that it is. It is a notion rather like that of 'nature', as in 'he has a generous nature'. It is a 'sort-of' word in that it tells you what sort of person a person is. And it tells you this by giving you, what is most uniquely theirs, what has been most personally appropriated by them, and made their own.

Having said all this I hope it won't surprise you when I say that I think that what God is most concerned to create in the whole of the universe is precisely characters. Everything else is either the necessary means to this end or else it provides the conditions under which character can be expressed. Having now said what my notion is I must say why I think it is so important.

I believe, on Jesus' authority, that God wants me to be happy by sharing in his life. I find it easiest to envisage transactions between myself and God by using the metaphor of marriage. If a husband and wife are to be happy in their marriage to each other they must both develop certain qualities of character (humour, patience, generosity, imagination). It is fatuous to expect to be happy without such qualities of character. Similarly, to be happy sharing in God's life certain qualities of character are required. What, one may ask, could they be? Well I don't think they are entirely different from those that make for a happy marriage. But in this case I think that one can describe them in such a way as to make it clearer where they come from and how they work.

If God is infinite then so is his life, and the qualities of character required to live it must have something of infinity about them. If God wants me to share his life he will have to develop such qualities of character in me. I must therefore have at least the capacity for acquiring such qualities from the very start. That is, I must have that sort of nature. In fact I think that having the capacity to share God's life is a very good definition of human nature. It is the scholastic equivalent of being 'the image of God'.

How does the possession of such a natural capacity for infinite life show itself in people? In two ways chiefly, I think: in being self-conscious in such a way that we are capable of self-possession, and in being self-determining to the extent that we are capable of self-donation. These self-referring capacities of human nature do have a sort of infinity about them. Being present to ourselves in the radical way of which we are capable enables us to have real knowledge, to enter into the being of others and so transcend our own limitations. Being self-determining means being free of, that is unlimited by, the influence of others and so able to respond freely to them, to love them for themselves.

This infinite side to human nature is not at all a matter of faith. It is a matter of common experience, or rather of reflection on common experience. It could be given the most thorough-going philosophical foundation. It is in fact the source of all the astonishing creativity, and perceptiveness and selflessness that humankind is capable of, it is present to the same degree and in the same way in every child born of human stock in whatever circumstances or whatever society and no matter what genetic endowment.

This capacity for self-possession, or alternatively, for self-transcendence, is what makes us, in traditional terminology, spiritual beings. Because spiritual beings possess a certain sort of infinity they cannot be wholly explained as the result of finite causes. Nor can their spiritual capacities be developed in an environment of merely finite beings. Hence, if they do develop then it must be as the result of the influence of a properly infinite being. That such an influence is exercised and realised in the lives of human persons, and indeed in the life of everyone without exception, is not something that science or philosophy can demonstrate. It could only be a matter of faith; but for Christians it is at least that. We do believe that as a matter of fact God shares his life with everyone from the first moment of their existence and whether they know it or not. There is no such thing as a human nature without grace. And this without prejudice to the possibility of an ultimate refusal of grace on our part.

If it is true then that God is actually at work in the lives of all persons, no matter what their origins or cultural tradition, bringing into being in them those qualities of character that will enable them to be happy sharing in his life, then it is a legitimate question as to how this actually occurs. On the one hand the development of character in spiritual beings cannot be reduced to the working of natural or social forces in us. On the other hand we do not want to resort to merely mythical explanations that involve all sorts of divine interventions and miracles. There can be subtle forms of these myths. One such is the doctrine that grace is imputed and not imparted to us in this life. That is we do not undergo a fundamental change in character this side of the grave. All the real transformation, since it must be done, is done on 'the other side'. Against this, for the sake of sanity, one must hold that this life, and just because it is *real* life, is the place where the fundamental change must take place. How then does it occur, in actual fact?

It occurs, it seems to me, of necessity, in our relations with other human persons and as a result of their agency. We cannot realize our distinctively personal capacities except in relation to other human persons. It is a nice question as to whether God could have created a finite person who stood in no need of others of his species in order to realize himself. This is in fact the medieval notion of an angel. But angels are purely spiritual beings, whereas we are certainly material as well. The meaning of materiality in the philosophy of St. Thomas is that of being *incompletely* actual (and therefore as existing in time) and depending essentially on what is *other* than oneself for one's self-actualisation (and so existing in space as well). As material beings therefore we must always be more than one of a kind, and this plurality is essential to our being the sort of beings that we are. So my relations with other human persons are as much me as my qualities of character. They are, if you like, both the causes and the expression of those qualities. And also, being essentially incomplete and so existing essentially in time, my completion is essentially bound up with the peculiar event known familiarly to us as death. Death is the event in which our materiality, and hence the finiteness of our persons, is most manifest. Death is the negation of all material power, the ultimate test for finite persons who are material. As persons we are spiritual and possessors of a different sort of power, and having an infinite capacity for a life that is not finite at all. Our attitude to our death will express which aspect of our composite nature we have really identified with. And this identification will in turn grown from and define our relationships with other human persons. Our attitudes to death and to other persons will mutually condition one another.

So, if God wants to create character in the universe he can only do it to the extent that he does it simultaneously in a number of finite persons, and by working through the natural capacity they have for infinite, that is to say, self-possessing and self-transcending life. And he is bound to do it by what one could call either a spiritualizing of the material (without obliterating the material) or better, an expressing of the spiritual in the material. The infinite is to be expressed in the finite, and this cannot occur without a conscious turning from what is familiar and controllable and a growing alienation from a selfhood that is merely exclusive, valued simply because it is one's own.

There is no space here to spell out the way in which the notion of creating character can be applied to the various aspects of Christian faith. But I can relate it briefly to the problems with which I began this reflection.

Seeing the drama of evolution, of history and of individual lives as the creation of character is a useful antidote to what has become the dominant myth of our time, namely the development of persons through the transformation of social institutions. That persons only exist in relationships with others is something I have already stressed. That these relationships gain their character not only from the individuals involved in them but from the institutional structure of society is a further insight in the same direction, and one which has become more and more influential since the time of Hegel and Marx. This is but another consequence of our materiality however, and it is therefore important for a Christian to stress the essential transcendence of institutions of human persons. We cannot exist without them, just as we cannot exist without food. But 'man does not live by bread alone'.

Grasping the reality of character as it exists in us liberates one simultaneously from on one hand the myth-making and miracles of the fundamentalist and on the other the impersonal universe of the secularist. There is mystery enough in our own familiar persons without requiring more. And if our faith is right, we have to do with and wield a power in our everyday lives that is genuinely 'supernatural' and yet expresses itself through faculties common to the whole of human kind. And so is mysterious without being *unusual*. Grasping this depth in ordinary human persons seems to me to be an inseparable accompaniment of a mature faith. A world-view that denies it must make it difficult to conceive of the sort of being Christians worship in calling Father.

Finally my notion helps me with suffering, other people's and my own. As St. Paul says, 'suffering produces character'. Suffering is not however what God ultimately wants for us; happiness is. So insofar as we share in his life that will be our attitude too. Yet suffering of a certain kind is the necessary means to this for material beings. And because suffering produces character, even the other kind of suffering, the sort that comes from sin, can be turned to good account.

Well, there's my notion. And now that I have expounded it, it occurs to me that it is probably an expression of my present preoccupations as a parent. Being a parent is such a super-human task and fraught with such frightening responsibilities that it is good to be able to think of oneself as only an instrument in God's hands in the truly divine task of creating character.

(1982)

Chapter Sixteen
Ecumenism Today

The context of ecumenism has changed dramatically in the last 50 years. It now takes place beyond the boundaries of traditional European culture. Christian faith so shaped and was so shaped by European culture that this embodiment of it became its classical form. And it was in this form that it spread out from Europe in the colonial period, taking with it the well-known denominations.

Since then quite new Christian bodies have sprung up outside Europe, either variants of the original denominations or else mixtures of Christianity and the indigenous cultures and religions.

In the post-colonial context all forms of Christianity exist in close contact with the other world-religions, often as a minority.

In the meantime the traditional culture of Europe has also changed. It is secularised. Christianity has ceased to be the folk-religion of Europe. And the secular culture that began in Europe has spread across the globe wherever science and technology have gone.

It must be remembered that Christianity is not primarily a culture or a world-view or way of life, but an event, namely the interaction between Jesus and his followers, an interaction that continued after his death. The Catholic understanding of the Church is that it is what makes this interaction a possibility even for those who did not know Jesus before he died. Of course the meaning of such an event is culturally conditioned and expressed. The original and subsequent interactions of people with Jesus is what constitutes the Church, which thus forms a continuing tradition of interpersonal life and thought and feeling, embodied in practices, artifacts and institutions, which grows through time and spreads through space.

The meaning of this interaction with Jesus, and so too of the Church, is expressed in this tradition by such a term as 'salvation'. Such a term is of course also culturally and linguistically conditioned, but it provides a good example in the context of ecumenism. The expression 'extra ecclesiam nulla salus' certainly is familiar to all Catholic ecumenists.

The term 'salvation' has however a rather special meaning in Catholic theology. This can be brought out by the following quotations from official documents from different Christian traditions.

> 'No-one remaining outside the Catholic Church, not just pagans, but also Jews or heretics or schismatics, can become partakers of eternal life; but they will go to the everlasting fire which was prepared for the devils and his angels, unless before the end of life they are joined to the church.' (Denzinger, 714)

This is the Council of Florence.

> 'In the years since the war, more than one billion souls have passed into eternity and more than half of these went to the torment of hell fire without even hearing of Jesus Christ, who He was, or why He died on the cross of Calvary.'

This is the Congress on World Mission of Protestant Churches in Chicago in 1960.

Even as learned a Christian scholar as John Hick, from whose book *God has Many Names* (John Knox Press, 1982) I have taken these quotes, sees them as saying the same thing. And so would most unsophisticated non-Catholics. But they would be wrong.

The quotation from the decrees of the Council of Florence is typical of the way in which the Catholic doctrine is expressed, from Popes Innocent III and Boniface VIII up to Pius XII, and can be fairly taken to represent the tradition. Pius XI, for instance, was merely repeating what was taken for granted when he declared 'By faith it is to be firmly held that outside the Apostolic Roman Church none can achieve salvation. This is the only ark of salvation. He who does not enter into it, will perish in the flood.' (Denz.1647) Yet in his next sentence he goes on to say, 'Nevertheless equally certainly is it to be held that those who suffer from invincible ignorance of the true religion, are not for that reason guilty in the eyes of the Lord.' And this is equally expressive of traditional doctrine.

How the traditional doctrine has in fact been understood in the Catholic Church can be gauged by the following excerpt from a standard reference manual *Fundamentals of Catholic Dogma*, by Ludwig Ott (Mercier, 1952). Ott, lest the contrary be suspected, was not by any stretch of the imagination a 'progressive' or 'liberal' theologian.

> 'The necessity of belonging to the Church is not merely a necessity of precept, but also a necessity of means, as the comparison with the Ark, the means of salvation from the biblical flood, plainly shows. The necessity of means is, however, not an absolute necessity, but a hypothetical one. In special circumstances, namely, in the case of invincible ignorance or of incapability, actual membership of the Church can be replaced by the desire for the same. This need not be expressly present, but can also be included in the moral readiness faithfully to fulfill the will of God. In this manner also those who are in fact outside the Catholic Church can achieve salvation.' (1952: 312)

Anyone could be forgiven for failing to discern that such traditional theological terminology means almost exactly the opposite of what it appears to mean. The traditional formulations give rhetorical support to the idea, very similar to that expressed by the Protestant document, that very few people are saved and those who are, are all members in good standing of the Roman Catholic Church. Whereas in fact the Catholic doctrine is far more lenient than the Protestant. Almost anyone at all can be saved, whatever their religious affiliation happens to be.

That this is the true import of the doctrine 'extra ecclesiam nulla salus' is borne out by the authoritative treatment of the topic by the Second Vatican Council. In its fundamental document on the Church, the Dogmatic Constitution on the Church *Lumen Gentium*, it explains the term to mean that not only non-Catholic Christians can be saved but also faithful Jews and Muslims, those with other religions or none.

This passage, however, also makes clear what most official statements do not, that it is only objectively that Jesus and the Church are necessary for salvation. Subjectively all that is necessary is a good conscience and trying to live a good life: 'Nor does divine Providence deny the help necessary for salvation to those who, without blame on their part, have not yet arrived at an explicit knowledge of God, but who strive to live a good life . . .' (*Lumen Gentium*, 16).[1]

There is an important point to be grasped hidden beneath this web of detailed and often dubious distinctions. The theological basis for this teaching is this: Salvation consists in our personal union with God. In order for this to happen God must be personally present to us. At least that. For if God is not personally present to us in our world then no personal union with him is even possible for us. And this is what Catholics believe is the case in the person of Jesus and, continuing through history, in the Church. But this personal presence of God in the world, though necessary, is not sufficient, for salvation. For that something more is required, namely the development of a quality of life and character in us that enables us to enter and enjoy such a union with God. The development of this quality in us is of course the work of God but it happens in all sorts of ways depending on our circumstances. It was going on in John the Baptist even before he met Jesus. It is going on in Russian Marxists who think Christianity is a lot of capitalist ideology.

So Jesus, and the Church, have two functions. They make God present in a historical way so that we can enter into a personal relationship with him. They also empower us to do this. This double function is well expressed in the novel definition of the Church provided by Vatican II: 'By her relationship with Christ, the Church is a kind of sacrament or sign of intimate union with God, and of the unity of all mankind. She is also an instrument for the achievement of such union and unity' (*Lumen Gentium*, 1).

Jesus empowered his original followers to become more able to enjoy a personal relationship with God. But they were empowered to do this in all sorts of other ways as well, in all the ordinary circumstances of their lives. He was not their exclusive means of grace. But he also embodied God's personal presence to them. Nowhere else could they find that. The same is true, mutatis mutandis, of the Church. It is the one place in the world where God is present in this particular historical way. And it is also only one among many sources of grace for people to enable them to cope with this presence.

1. Flannery, A (editor) *The Documents of Vatican II* (Pillar Books, 1975).

I have laboured this point because I think it is the foundation of a Catholic approach to ecumenism. If it is salvation we are interested in, then we will not imagine that it is necessary for us to be Roman Catholics in order to be saved. Of course if we are right about Jesus and the Church then, other things being equal, it is an advantage to be a Roman Catholic. We know what is really going on. And so we are in a better position to enter into it, to consciously engage and co-operate with what God is doing. But we also have a special responsibility, for the rest of humanity.

The secular culture that is now the dominant culture in the world is in part a product of Christianity. Its fundamental characteristics are the abolition of the supernatural and the centrality of human freedom, both as a fact about human nature and as a value for human life. The Christian recognition of God's absolute transcendence abolished the distinction between a natural and a supernatural realm within the created order. There is only one world and God is not a part or dimension of it. This is the death of pagan idolatry, of the gods who, in the words of St Paul, 'are not gods' (Gal 4:8). Furthermore, in this one world humanity occupies the central place. Humanity, as 'the image of God', is also a transcendent creator. We transcend the causal determinisms of the world and thus are free to exercise our creativity in ordering and directing it.

A secular culture and world-view is thus in no way an alien environment for living the Christian life. On the contrary, the Christian insight into God's absolute transcendence, his incommensurability with his creation, entails his immanence in every part of it as its creator. He is present in it all as the singer in the song.

Understanding the secular world-view in this Christian way can make a huge difference to the way in which one relates to people in respect of salvation, and therefore to ecumenism.

One will see in all efforts at personal growth, all attempts to create community, however conditioned and stunted by inhuman societies, the creativity of grace. And in all systems of thought, especially but not only religious ones, one will see the variously adequate, variously culture-bound understandings of this. In ordinary life salvation is going on, and in the various cultural traditions of humanity there are different understandings of this. Our role is to help people explore what is going on so as to understand it better. But we have to start where they are and with the ideas that mean the most to them. And that means that we must be familiar with the way they live and understand the ideas that they live by.

The role of the Church, in the widest sphere of ecumenism, is that of being a focus and facilitator. Pope Paul VI coined the phrase 'expert in humanity' to define the Church's competence in the social sphere. I think it applies in the sphere of ecumenism too. In a secular world, because we recognise the workings of God in everything, we can engage with the human struggle at the human level in whatever way it shows itself, offering this expertise. This will be primarily in the sphere of understanding, of interpreting what is taking place. This is the form that 'preaching the gospel' can best take in a secular world. Actually telling people about Jesus, and what he means to us, if it is to be authentically done and so salvific, can only grow out of this. In any case they meet him, to a greater or lesser degree, in us. So we have no need to worry that he is being left out. Our most important concern is that we are acting in his spirit.

In relation to other, non-Christian, religions the Church also has the responsibility of being focus and facilitator. And here too the key to co-operation and dialogue is our common humanity. But we must recognise that here we Catholics, or at least some of us, are in the vanguard when it comes to the assimilation of secularisation. We have already crossed the 'brook of fire' (Feuerbach) that Marx spoke of. And some of the others have not reached it yet. Fundamentalisms of various kinds are the greatest enemy of genuine dialogue and co-operation between believers. Fundamentalism, of whatever kind (Catholic included), is indeed the greatest threat to genuine faith, being everything that Marx and Freud and Sartre have accused religion of being. One can only fight fundamentalism by appealing to the humanity it denies. It is only insofar as believers come to value the common humanity that they will make contact with the real God who is alive in everyone.

Because of their unique position in world religions, Christians are able to recognise a solidarity with other believers that other religions cannot. We are able to recognise them as 'anonymous Christians' and so as fellow-faithful, whereas they are unable to recognise us as 'anonymous' Jews or Muslims. This is because we believe that Jesus identifies the God to whom all religions point, Christianity included.

This uniqueness is what enables us to engage with other religious traditions deeply, at their heart, seeking in them what we have found in our own. It is after all those who have most deeply and authentically appropriated their own religious life who are closest to each other in spirit. The realistic aim of Christian engagement with other religions is not a universal common religion but the development in each tradition of the insights and values they possess. In all traditions, including of course our own, there are special inadequacies and aberrations that have to be grown out of or abandoned. So the obverse of our openness and appreciation of other religions must be an honest self-critical attitude towards our own. If we are all to become more in touch with the humanity that lies at our heart then there are a lot of historically acquired impediments that will have to be jettisoned. Our motto for the next millennium should be 'Travel light!'

When it comes to ecumenism within the Christian sphere the same principles should apply as in the sphere of world religions. Just as it is not the function of the Church to make faithful followers of all religions Christians, because they are already that—as anonymous ones, so it is not the function of the Church to make all faithful Christians Roman Catholics, because they are already members of the one and only Church there is. They might think they are members of a different church from us. They might want to be members of a different church from us. We Roman Catholics believe otherwise.

According to the Catholic doctrine of the Church sketched above it is an absolute necessity that the Church exist as a specific historical institution if it is to identify God's personal presence in the way that Jesus did. It must be this one, not that one, here and not there, just as Jesus was not Peter or John the Baptist.

So the Church, which (as Vatican II puts it) 'subsists in' and is identified by the Roman Catholic Church (though it is certainly not co-extensive with it), is not a competitor with all the various Christian organisations for their members' loyalty. Insofar as they are animated by faith, hope and charity they are members already.

In our ecumenical conversation with fellow Christians the aim is to enter into communion with them at the deepest possible level of Christian life. In order to do this we also need to practise two special disciplines I have already mentioned. We need to be wholeheartedly committed to understanding and appreciating the deepest springs of other traditions. And we need to be as wholeheartedly self-critical of our own. If everyone does this we are bound to grow closer and closer together, as we each discover new depths of Christian life and discard old impediments to communion.

In the spirit of this discipline we Catholics have to recognise that the papacy and its exercise has become a scandal to Christianity, to other Christian traditions but also to our own. The exercise of authority in the Catholic Church takes its tone from the papacy and is so deeply un-Christian that it undermines genuine respect for the real sacramental authority of the Church and the proper role of the papacy. One does not have to rehearse a list of examples of the abuse of papal authority. There are so many and they are so well known: teachers dismissed without any attempt at fair procedures, discussion of various points forbidden, new rules applied, new oaths to be taken, political interference in episcopal appointments.

These are particular instances, but they reveal an attitude to authority and especially to papal authority and its exercise that will always be an impediment to ecumenism. It is a holistic, all-pervasive spirit. It animates the procedures of the Roman curia and the tone of their documents. It is evident between every line of Canon Law. It is a quite distinctive thing that any sensitive social or literary critic can identify. All those of us who are theologically educated are familiar with it. And it is quite alien to Christianity.

We must of course also be self-critical about what is actually taught in the name of the Catholic Church, about birth-control and sexual ethics, about women priests and clerical celibacy. But the medium of this teaching is more important, and more dangerous, than the message. And we Catholics, especially those of us in positions of authority, must take responsibility for it. Power comes from the bottom up. And it is our attitude to the papacy that has allowed it to develop in this way. Even if we were to replace the Roman curia with a permanent episcopal synod, disband the college of cardinals, abolish the Vatican diplomatic corps, discontinue the papal appointment of bishops there would be the alien spirit of authority to deal with. It is the chief enemy of ecumenism because it is alien to Christianity itself.

On the other hand the discipline of self-criticism can also make us more aware of our strengths. We have a lot to offer: our tradition of natural theology and natural law, our social teaching of the last hundred years, our mystical and ascetical and sacramental life. Ecumenism is only one aspect of the Christian life, or rather it is a special dimension of that life as a whole. It is living that life that should take up most of our time and energy. Ecumenism, because it involves seeing ourselves through the eyes of others, can help us do this better.

(1982)

Chapter Seventeen
What Makes Us Persons?

John Macmurray, in his Gifford Lectures of 1953–1954, 'The Form of the Personal',[1] presents an extended argument to show that 'the personal relation of persons is constitutive of personal existence; that there can be no man until there are at least two men in communication' (1961: 12). Summarily put, his thesis is that 'Persons . . . are constituted by their mutual relation to one another' (1961: 24).

'The Form of the Personal' is a largely programmatic work and there is much that one can find fault with in Macmurray's argument.[2] In particular it is often difficult to tell whether his descriptions of the intersubjective relations of persons are intended to be scientific or philosophical. Nevertheless he presents a picture of personal interdependence, and so of persons too, that is both rich in detailed perceptions and possessed of a remarkably comprehensive and simple overall structure. It is a picture attractive enough to invite one to find reasons for supposing it to be true.

In this present article I propose to do just this. I shall follow Macmurray in trying to show that persons depend on the presence and personal activity of other persons for the exercise of their distinctively personal powers. I shall also follow Macmurray to a certain extent in his descriptive method since it seems to me peculiarly appropriate to an investigation of the nature of personal existence. But I must

1. 'The Form of the Personal' is published in two volumes, *The Self as Agent*, 1957, and *Persons in Relation*, 1961, London: Faber.
2. I have analysed this critically elsewhere and as it is unnecessary for my present purpose will not do so again here. For those interested, see my 'Indwelling, Intersubjectivity and God' in *The Scottish Journal of Theology*, 32 (1979): 201–216 (Chapter 13 of this volume).

emphasize at the outset that I intend my descriptions to be genuinely philosophical and in no way scientific. That is to say, I am concerned in them to reveal the *necessary* conditions for the exercise of our specifically personal powers.

My ultimate purpose in trying to fulfill the programme that Macmurray set up is twofold. It is also theological. As we shall see from the description that follows, the dependence and the influence of one person on another is of a quite peculiar kind; I shall call this 'personal causality' to distinguish it from any kind of physical causality. Insofar as persons are capable of exercising such a causality they transcend any system of physical causes and are thus, as such, immaterial.

Of course more needs to be said about *human* persons (since they are also undeniably material), but the immateriality of persons (of whatever kind) has important theological consequences. It undermines the possibility of any radical materialism, in the sense of a view of reality as being in the last resort physical or, even, such as could adequately be described by any conceivable set of the special sciences. And if our developed technological culture has a blind spot surely it is here. To refute the possibility of any radical materialism has an intrinsic apologetic value in respect of the Christian faith, since if materialism were true and human beings simply parts of a material universe it is difficult to see how they could be *capax Dei* in the way that Christian faith entails.

CS Lewis[3] (1947: 23–31) has used the fact of our transcendence of any system of impersonal causality of whatever kind as the starting-point for an argument for the existence and the historical causality of God. Our descriptions of personal interdependence do, if true, provide an even more comprehensive and familiar support for such a purpose.

Finally, the account given in the following pages of personal relations between persons could also serve as a useful and, I think, illuminating analogy for our relations with God. In particular, the notion of personal causality could, I think, help to solve some of the problems concerning the relations between Creator and free creature, and between nature and grace. Discussion of these topics has often suffered from a conception of causality too closely wedded to the physical.

3. CS Lewis, *Miracles* (London: Bles, 1947).

Those acquainted with Macmurray's work will realise my indebtedness to him, both for the overall structure of the project and for the method itself. His descriptions focus chiefly on two models of interpersonal relations, that of the relation between a mother and child, and a special mutual relation between two adults which he calls 'community'. The first is intended to display the necessary conditions for the bare exercise of our personal powers, the second those that enable their full development. In this article I will confine myself to the first, that of the relationship between mother and child. This relationship is intended as an abstract model of a purely 'potential' person in relation to a fully 'actual' one, vet my descriptions are intended to have reference to the actual experience of personal activity though only to those activities that are unavoidable if one is a person in any sense of the word. Thus there is a standard of 'realism' implied, though it is not that of the scientific study of child behaviour, it is rather that of an imaginative reflection on his own experience by a mature adult. To isolate a pair of persons from the rest of human society is not realistic in the scientific sense of the term. But it is essential if one is to discern with any real insight what is required, from whomsoever or however many, for our personal capacities to be realised in human life.

The 'mother' thus stands for the personal milieu of persons, the 'child' for the natural possibility of personal existence. And it would seem to be a fact in the most obvious meaning of the word that persons cannot realise their distinctively personal characteristics in a wholly impersonal environment. Suzanne Langer's account[4] of 'wild children' and the attempts to teach them the human use of language confirms the *prima facie* plausibility of this thesis (Langer, 1942: 103–143). On the other hand, the Kelloggs' experiment of bringing an ape up from birth with their own baby shows that it is not simply communication with persons at a crucial ('Lalling') stage of infancy that is sufficient to introduce the child to language proper (Kellogg, 1933[5]). The little chimp for all its precociousness and in spite of its far greater practical intelligence never learnt to speak. Thus a natural capacity is necessary as well as a personal environment. If it is true that persons depend on other persons for the exercise and

4. S Langer, *Philosophy in a New Key* (Harvard University Press, 1942).
5. W Kellogg, and L Kellogg, *The Ape and the Child* (McGraw-Hill, 1933).

development of those powers that make them persons then it is in the relations between persons that one would expect those powers, and hence the nature of persons, to be most fully revealed. Nevertheless in order have some principle of selection for our description we do need to have at least a preliminary notion of what it is that entitles us to be called persons. For Macmurray it is our capacity for agency, in a specially strong sense of the word that is exhaustively adumbrated in *The Self as Agent*. That seems as good a starting-point as any and so I shall extend my discipleship of Macmurray by making it my own as well.

By calling a person an agent one does not mean merely that he is capable of movement or of behaviour. To act implies at least that one is aware of oneself as the cause of certain happenings in the world. Thus it involves self-consciousness of a practical as well as a theoretical sort. By practical self-consciousness I mean that one is conscious of having power, or alternatively (since in the way in which I am using the term it amounts to the same thing), of being a cause. By theoretical self-consciouness I mean simply one's consciousness of existing as a real being distinct from others.

To bring out this self-referring character of personal agency we can take as an example of an agent a person singing a song. The singer is a cause because the existence of the song depends on her own. Various elements are involved in this dependence. She knows she is singing the song. She wants to sing the song. Her wanting to sing the song is a 'cause' of its being sung. And in addition she wants her wanting to sing the song to be a 'cause' of its being sung. Wanting to sing the song knowing that she is singing it are unproblematic. The third condition is perhaps less so. It means first of all that if the existence of the song did not depend in any way on her wanting to sing it, then the singing could not be seen as an action of hers. It also entails that this dependence be not merely a fact; she must want it as well as the mere existence of the song. Perhaps this distinction is difficult to grasp in the case of singing a song. Consider instead the case of a mountain climber who wishes to extricate his partner on the rope from a fissure where he has stuck. In the course of his attempts to dislodge his partner he loses his footing and falls, thus jerking the rope and successfully dislodging his partner. As the partner comes out of the fissure his falling friend would not be unaware that he was the cause of setting him free. He would certainly want him to be free. But in this case his wanting to free his friend was not a cause of freeing him since his fall was a mistake. And in comparing his former attitude with his present the falling climber would be able to see that in addition to wanting to free his friend he also wanted his wanting this to play a 'causal' part in setting him free.

The reason that I have put all reference to causality in inverted commas in the above paragraph, is because it seems to suggest that the wanting and the singing, or the saving, are two distinct events that are causally linked. This is of course untrue. They are instead two distinct elements in the all-embracing unity of agency. They are of course not merely logical elements; they could be called distinct acts to establish their reality, but this must not be taken to mean that they are 'little' actions within the principal action we are concerned with. They have no existence except as parts of a whole.

The concept of action certainly does include that of being a cause, as appears from our example. In addition however there are the elements of knowledge and what I have called 'wanting'. The first wanting is simply wishing or desiring and is directed towards the object of the act. The second is what I shall call 'consent' and is directed not at the object but at the subject of the action. It has two degrees, the first being the consent of the wanting what the action achieves, the second the consent to the action and its achievement being partially caused by the very wanting itself. This self-directed affective act corresponds in the realm of the affections to the self-knowledge that is the inevitable concomitant of a judgement of value and thus an inevitable ingredient in any action.

One could say in fact that the distinction between the two types of wanting is that between wishing and willing. However one wants to put it, the crucial point is that the second type is referred to the self and not to the object of the act as its primary term. And so in addition to the realisation of events in the world an action modifies the agent. And this not only in the obvious sense that it involves perceptions, judgements of fact and value, wishes and movements, all of which are of course new events in the history of the agent. The more important way in which an agent is affected by his action is that it involves a minimum of self-knowledge of oneself as a single distinct being having causal power, and a minimum of self-determination, both in that one's own mere wish has a causal role in the action and also because in one's consent to what one judges and wishes one actually concerns oneself with oneself in a direct and total way and so affirms, appropriates and enacts what one has become. The first meaning of 'self-determination' is that it is the subject (and not some other) that is the cause of the event, the second is that in addition to causing something in the world to happen the subject deals with and so enacts himself.

The self-knowledge involved, though minimal, is also certainly real and objective. It must of necessity include an awareness of what one desires, what one intends to do to realise the desire, and one's consent. And all this is referred, however implicitly, to oneself and constitutes a concrete notion of oneself. If, after the act, one was questioned one could tell the truth about oneself under each of these heads.

Self-consciousness and self-determination thus represents two aspects of self-enactment in the performance of any act. So all action is self-referential in this way and it is this that we shall take as its distinctively personal character. I hope that the description of intersubjective relations between persons will throw fuller light on this self-enacting character of persons.

Clearly a human child is not self-conscious in either a theoretical or practical sense from the start. We must now try to see what is necessary for it to become conscious in both. Certainly from the start it is both conscious and a cause. To say that it is conscious is to point to a certain effect that its environment has on it. There is experience. In addition to the world of things there is also experience. If one wants a word to characterise the simplest type of consciousness 'feeling' seems a natural choice, particularly as 'feeling' can refer both to the experience of being touched or affected by one's environment (I feel the warmth of the sun) and to one's response to one's environment (I feel desire). One's sensations as well as one's emotions can be called feelings. And the ambiguity of the term preserves the fact that at this stage there is no distinction felt between subject and object within experience. Consciousness also always has a subject in the sense that it is always somebody's consciousness but it need not have this subject as a distinct object, whether vague or specific. I should not for instance be seen as possessing initially a vague sense of self which then becomes stronger and clearer. This could never be verified by direct experience and it is difficult to see how it could even be inferred. In its simplest form consciousness should rather be seen as the capacity a person has for experience, a real 'psychological' capacity for being present to the world, rather than merely being in causal contact with it. At the start, in itself (if one wishes to forget the model), it is wholly non-specific and hence able to be specified by whatever contacts do occur. At the same time it is a particular capacity of this particular person.

What must occur for this consciousness to become self-conscious in the sense entailed by agency? The answer to this question is that the child must be present to another person. The reason given by Karl Rahner for this necessity is that only another person is sufficiently 'other' for the distinction between self and other to appear as an object for consciousness. Mere things can always be simply subsumed into the domain of the self as elements in its self-constituting activity. Their otherness is the mere passive otherness of space and time, their simple physical existence; the otherness of persons however is the otherness of autonomy and originality, a real opposition of intention and effort to our own. According to Rahner (1969: 138):

> '. . . it is only in that (man) always already enters into the concretely determined other of *materia* and experiences its determination (*forma*) as his own reality, that he is truly 'with the other' in his own existingness (without this being again, simply, the pure negativity of his being-with-himself). This concrete otherness precisely because it is always executed as one's own determination from the basis (*forma*) of one's own being (*Motus* as *actus moti*), can only be experienced as the one not in our hands, as the 'truly' other, when it (this otherness) is understood as coming from a *free* other basis (*forma non mere materialis, sed subsistens*). This in turn again implies, from another point of view, the transcendental deduction of a plurality of the co-world of free persons as regards man.'[6]

Without metaphor, the self of self-consciousness can only be found where consciousness discovers all its objects—in its environment. Now the only place where a trace of it could be found is, not in things since they are limited to being simply what they are, but in another consciousness. Before we clarify this it is as well to note that the 'self' in question is no purely logical entity. We are not investigating the dawn of the realisation that consciousness as such implies the distinction

6. K Rahner, *Hearers of the Word* (Sheed and Ward, 1969).

between subject and object. We are instead considering the origin of a person's knowledge that he is a separately existing real being. We are in other words talking about a real item of knowledge (although it need not be explicit) rather than a purely logical condition for all knowledge. The self-consciousness that is a necessary requirement for action in the strict sense of the term is a real though very general item of knowledge. If it were not so the agent could not be held responsible for his acts; it would be as though they all proceeded from an 'invincible ignorance' of a peculiarly radical sort.

Having given a preliminary account of the nature of the self that is to be found let me now attempt to clarify the process by which it is found. I have said that the essential condition is the presence of another person, in this case the person of the mother. This by itself however is not enough. The acquisition of self-consciousness is not a consequence of discovering in one's environment a special sort of being, that is, a person, then discovering that they are self-conscious and finally coming to the realisation that one is the same sort of being that they are and therefore self-conscious too. That would be an entirely fanciful supposition. It would moreover presuppose sophisticated cognitive activity which is only possible once self-conscious-ness has been achieved. The sufficient condition for the real acquisition of self-consciousness is that one is oneself present to the person who is present to one. There are two aspects to this presence. First there is the personal presence of the mother as such and then there is the existence of the child in the consciousness of the mother. By becoming present to the mother who is present to it, it becomes present to itself; it discovers itself as the object of the mother's activity. As such it is not yet fully aware of itself as a person or agent. But the first step has been taken, a step that is of the piece with all that is to follow. Each element of full personal self-consciousness has to be acquired from the consciousness its mother has of it, since it is not actually present as such in any other place, least of all in its own as yet unactualised capacities.

It is for this reason that I cannot accept John Heron's suggestion, in his otherwise wholly admirable study 'The Phenomenology of Social Encounter: the Gaze'[7], that in an interpersonal encounter

7. J Heron, 'The Phenomenology of Social Encounter: The Gaze', in *Philosophy and Phenomenological Research*, 10 (1970): 243–264.

a person 'retains his own sense of identity by virtue of his external perception of the body of the other and of his inaccessibly private kinesthetic sensations of his own body' (1970: 253). This suggestion is in fact out of line with the rest of the article which offers strong support for the view that strictly personal self-awareness is gained only from the mutuality of personal relation. There would seem to be no connection between the 'kinesthetic sensations' referred to and one's sense of being precisely an agent. Kinesthetic sensations are certainly always an aspect of an action, yet by themselves they simply declare the existence of movement or behaviour, not action proper. Furthermore when Heron adds that they are sensations of one's own body, he in fact presupposes what has to be shown, viz. that one is conscious of having an own body, which implies of course that one is conscious of oneself. Against all this his study supplies ample foundation for the sense of identity in the intersubjective relation itself, in the experience of the directed gaze. In experiencing the gaze of the other, one experiences oneself as the object at which it is directed.

We now have to enquire into the necessary conditions for the child to become aware of himself as an agent in the strict sense of the term. In order to do this I shall describe a transaction between the child and the mother. It must be remembered that this is not a pseudo-scientific account of child development, and that the elements that I shall distinguish as parts of a process are in fact simultaneous aspects of the common experience of being an agent, seen in relation to their necessary conditions.

In the mother-child model the child must be seen as a representation of the pure natural capacity for being an agent; it is a wholly helpless and needy being. The mother on the other hand is a representation of a fully developed person.

If the child has needs then either they can be met or not. The child is conscious. His consciousness is thus either of lack or fulfilment, pain (in a very general sense) or satisfaction. In the case of a simple physical need we can see that the child's lack is of three things: of something other than the child (say, food), of a state or condition of itself (being well-fed), and of power to get the first to satisfy the second. When the child's need is met by the mother consciousness of lack is replaced by consciousness of fulfilment. This changed state of the child is brought about by the activity of the mother so even if the child is conscious of the process of change there is nothing in that to counter his own sense of impotence. How far children actually do have a sense of impotence with respect to meeting their physical needs, and therefore a source of dissatisfaction in addition to the physical needs themselves, is of course a question beyond the competence of a philosophical study.

At this stage one might perhaps say that the child is conscious of activity without an owner. Insofar as an agent is present at all in the fulfilling act it is certainly not the child, since his impotence, and whatever consciousness he has of it, remains. To the mother however the child is not simply a being of physical needs that requires her care but a person, in the sense at least of one who has personal capacities. Her recognition of it as a person is the foundation of another sort of activity in its regard: she values it, and this fact too finds expression in her acts. Thus one can make a primary distinction in the mother's attitude to the child: it is both the object of her care and of her value. This distinction is not founded on two radically distinct types of needs, physical and personal. To see it in that way would be to put the cart before the horse and would involve an unnecessary dualism. The one child has many needs, but the child itself can be seen in two ways: as an object of care or an object of value. The same acts answering the same needs can and do express two different motives stemming from two different attitudes. The acts that express the mother's recognition and consent to the child's value can be the same acts that answer its physical needs. But the single act has now a double function, to meet the need and to express the value. If we consider a limiting case, and refuse to postulate in an a priori way a distinction between physical and personal needs, a machine (or a wolf) could care for the child and meet its needs. The mother does that of course but at the same time does what no machine could do. She has a belief in the existence of personal capacities in the child and for that reason is able to value it.

I have used the term 'value' to distinguish the mother's attitude to the child as a person rather than simply a being of needs. It is very general term and one needs to specify it a little more in order to account for the special role it plays in the development of the child. By 'care' I mean to indicate simply an activity that is directed towards the meeting of needs; the term says nothing of the motive of the activity. The caring mother could be preparing her child for immolation on the altar. Or simply ministering to her own self-esteem. 'Value' on the other hand refers primarily to the motive. The child itself is seen as valuable irrespective of any relation it might have to the mother and her own desires and intentions. Accordingly the caring acts performed in its regard are seen at the least as duties. The person who performs them and who at the same time recognises an obligation to do so is expressing in however minimal a degree consent to the value of the child and therefore to its existence and development as a person. To the extent to which they do this they are presenting themselves to the child as the person that they are rather than simply the fulfiller of his needs. Perhaps it is a trifle difficult to see this in the very minimal case that I have sketched. It is one that would be exemplified by an unenthusiastic nurse in an orphanage. The normal case is one in which this minimal sense of duty and responsibility is merely a structural element in more or less whole-hearted mother-love. Where the essential recognition and consent to the value of the child as a person is embodied in actual love then the active presentation by the mother of herself in her caring acts is much more clearly evident. In this the normal case, acts of care become inadequate to express the true motive of the mother's activity with regard to the child. Another class of acts comes into being whose sole purpose is the expression of love. They have no pragmatic purpose at all. In such acts the mother is much more personally present, in the sense and to the degree that they are the expression of a full *consent* to the active relation to the object of the act. She is thus available to be known as a person and not merely as a meeter of needs. This primary sense in which she is personally present to the child is the most important as far as its personal development is concerned and should be sharply distinguished from all others, even from such secondary quasi-personal presences as for instance that other and often deliberate self-presentation whose motive is the meeting of a normal mother's *own need* for love.

It is in the mother's presence to the child as one who recognises and consents to it as a person that the child is finally able to discover itself as the person to whom her activity is directed. And this is moreover the only place in the world where it can exist as an object for consciousness before it exists as such for itself.

The possibility of acquiring that self-consciousness that is a necessary element in being an agent in the strict sense of the term depends on the presence of one who recognises and consents to one as a person. That in itself is however not enough to make the child an agent, since this also requires that it be conscious of itself as having power or as being a cause of an occurrence in the world. We have therefore to discover within the mother-child relation the origin of such causality and such a sense of power. And as before it is in the person of the mother that it must be found.

The motive of the mother's love goes beyond consent to the mere existence of the child. It is after all a person only in the sense of the possessor of personal *capacities*. Its mother's love thus necessarily wishes the development and perfection of these capacities for its own sake, so that it becomes an actual person in full possession of its powers. To the extent then that it becomes conscious of her presence and responds to it with consent of its own, consent that can take such various forms of fascination, adoration and delight, it realises her ambitions for it. She discerns the dawn of self-consciousness in it and the self-communication of consent. As it develops its distinctively personal characteristics it does the one thing needful to satisfy her love. No-one else has such power. The child is thus the possessor of a special sort of power which it possesses through a combination of personal capacities and the mother's love. It is the cause of an occurrence in the world and through its consciousness of the mother's joy it has the necessary condition *for becoming conscious of itself as such.*

It is important to see why only a positive, loving attitude on the part of the mother is able to impart to the child the consciousness of agency. First of all it is only because she wills the development of its personal capacities that its exercise of them is able to cause her joy and give the child the power over her that it has. Secondly, the development of its personal capacities answers a natural inclination of the child, has its own satisfaction for it and inevitably makes for its consent. The inclinations of the child's personal nature and the mother's love coincide so that this real mutuality of satisfaction in its development of self-consciousness as an agent is able to be the necessary stepping stone to an eventual consent to her as a person. The child after all does not simply respond to the mother, it responds with grateful love. And this is a further degree of mutuality, and also a further degree of self-development. It consents both to its own development as a person and to her existence and value as a person who exists for it.

If on the other hand the mother's attitude to the child had been one of rejection and hostility then her consent to its existence and status as a person would have been lacking, she would not have been present to the child as a person herself, and the whole dialectic of development would have been subverted from the start.

W Ver Eecke (1975)[8] agrees with our emphasis on the necessity for a positive, loving attitude on the part of the other if a person is to become properly aware of himself as an agent. He bases his conviction moreover on a detailed analysis of the experimental work of Spitz and others in child development and pathology. Spitz's study concerned anaclytic depression and hospitalism in babies. Babies who, for administrative reasons, were removed from their mothers in an institution showed all sorts of emotional and physical symptoms. They cried more than other babies and suffered from insomnia. They showed a greater susceptibility to colds and lost weight. In general they showed symptoms of withdrawal and retardation of personality growth.

In the case of the hospitalism observations, where the babies were removed from their mothers after the third month, the results were even more drastic. Ver Eecke (1975: 231) sums them up as follows:

> 'During the first three months of separation the symptoms were very similar to those of anaclytic depression. After the third month, the children showed excessive motor retardation. They became completely passive, lying on their backs without being able to turn themselves into the prone position. Their faces had an imbecilic expression, eye co-ordination was defective, fingers showed bizarre movements and the children were sometimes subjected to 'spasmus nutans'. At the end of their second year, these children had on the average a development which would classify them as idiots.'

Ver Eecke's conclusion is the 'child needs a mother or a mother substitute and not just a nurse' (Ver Eecke, 1975: 237). This is equivalent to our distinction between care and value or love. His purpose in his study is to counteract Sartre's notion that authentic subjectivity can exist only in opposition to other subjects by means of objectifying them, that, in short, genuine subject-subject relations

8. W Ver Eecke, 'The Look, the Body and the Other', in D Ihde (ed), *Dialogues in Phenomenology* (The Hague: Nijhoff, 1975), 222–246.

are impossible. He concludes, in terminology very similar to our own that 'real subjectivity is only possible within the context of intersubjectivity... The other is therefore not the enemy of my subjectivity, he is the condition for my becoming a subject' (Ver Eecke, 1975: 245). In the course of his study however, because he has to deal with the emphasis on negativity that is characteristic of Sartre's account of relations between persons, Ver Eecke is also able to find the proper place for opposition between self and other in the achievement of self-consciousness. He identifies opposition as a moment within a relation that is primarily one of mutual acceptance. In mutual acceptance self-consciousness as an agent is already achieved. The opposition that so often expresses this (the period of 'No'-saying in young children) is, in the case of 'healthy' development, not real opposition at all but symbolic opposition, an exercise of autonomy in a relationship of trust in an almost game-like manner. This insight is important for us since it provides a counter to those theorists who maintain, contrary to our own position, that a real struggle between subjects is necessary for the emergence of a genuine awareness of oneself as an autonomous agent.

In my description of the mother-child model of the intersubjective relation of persons I have given my own account of how and why it is that persons depend on other persons for the exercise and development of the distinctively personal powers. I am very conscious that what I have attempted in this article is only a beginning of what could and should be done if my general project is well-conceived. I have considered only the bare minimum exercise of personal powers. But there is also the question of their development beyond this bare minimum, the question of personal growth. However one ought in the last resort to understand this, it would clearly include moral and even religious elements as well as psychological and social ones. It is this complex area that Macmurray's second intersubjective model, that of 'community', is constructed to deal with. I hope to deal with it myself at some future time.

For the present—and in conclusion—I would like to comment briefly on one aspect of my initial account of persons in relation. As we have seen the presence and influence of another person is necessary if our distinctively personal capacities are to develop. An impersonal environment is inadequate for this. This suggests that there is a sense in which persons, individual persons as well as the whole intersubjective realm, transcend the impersonal world. It would seem that no amount of causal influence of the impersonal world is sufficient to effect or activate the personal. If this is so then the descriptive terms we have used, 'self-conscious' and 'self-determining'—and 'self-enacting' too, have an ontological as well as a phenomenological status. The nature of persons is such that their behaviour cannot be reduced to the effect of impersonal causality. Being self-enacting means being capable of transcending the whole system of impersonal causes.

That might not seem so large a claim if the causal influence of *persons* on one another is thought to be of a piece (metaphysically) with that of impersonal causes; if the personal influence of other persons on us may have some distinctive features but these are ultimately metaphysically irrelevant. The description I have given however contains features which suggest that the matter cannot be fairly dismissed in this way.

We are considering the strictly personal influence of one person on another, the influence of fully developed personal powers on as yet undeveloped ones. The peculiar feature of this intersubjective transaction is the way in which the influence of the one augments the *self*-enactment (which is to say, the *autonomy*) of the other. Put otherwise, it is the case that self-enactment increases in direct and not inverse proportion to the personal influence of the other. Leaving aside the question of how there can be an increase in self-determination at all (it must be remembered that we are dealing with the radical self-determination involved in agency, not merely freedom from some or other constraint), it does seem that we have evidence here of a kind of causality that it quite *sui generis*. In the realm of impersonal causes (the realm of physics and biology and even perhaps empirical psychology too) the degree to which the influence of an exterior cause is undergone by something is the degree in which its behaviour is not its own. It becomes the instrument of the other. In the mother-child model the opposite is the case. Without the influence of the mother the child would be less capable of its own self-enactment, not more.

Of course the causality we are considering here is a queer sort of causality. It is that effective in personal attitudes, such as the mother's love for the child, rather than in bodily movements as such, such as those involved in feeding it. If the mother feeds the child, the child does not feed itself; if the mother treats the child as a person it gradually begins to behave as one. One might be tempted to say 'Oh, but the influence of the mother's love is not a physical influence.

And so to call it causal is misleading'. But that seems unfair. It is real enough. And if it is *really* not physical then the fact of its reality has metaphysical implications for the nature of persons.

I am not alone in picking out something philosophically peculiar about what could I think be called 'personal causality'. John Heron, in the article already referred to, feels obliged to use language that suggests a line of thought very similar to my own. He is describing the quite specific phenomenon of mutual gazing (me gazing at you gazing at me) as an example of intersubjective encounter between persons. And in the course of a very careful account of the relation set up and the effect this has on each person, he uses, a number of times, the term 'transphysical'. He speaks (Heron, 1970: 255) of the 'transphysical streaming' of the gaze of each person, and also of a 'transphysical unitive reality of a field' that is set up by the mutual gazing.

Language like this is perhaps unavoidably metaphorical. Yet it does point—so it seems to me—to a feature of personal reality which is not patient of ordinary physical description and scientific explanation. It seems that a philosophical consideration of the intersubjective relations of persons such as I have attempted in this article is capable of bringing this feature to the fore.

If the project begun in this article were successfully carried through it would, as I said at the outset, have consequences important for theology. If the necessary intersubjective conditions for the growth and fulfilment, as well as for the mere exercise, of our distinctively personal powers were described in a manner somewhat similar to that in this article, a view of interpersonal reality, of persons and the milieu of persons, would result that was totally antipathetic to that encouraged by the materialistic scientific ethos of our culture but yet capable, I am convinced, of strict philosophical justification. It would give us a basis for a natural theology that issued in something much more like the God of Christian tradition than the unmoved mover of the cosmological proof. It would help us to re-work the central Christian doctrines concerning the relations between God and us. It might even (I have claimed so much already, I might as well be hung for a sheep as for a lamb!) help us to say something fresh about the doctrines of the Trinity, something that could bring closer together an Augustinian account (with its 'subsistent relations') with an Eastern 'collegial' one.

But there, having blown my theory's trumpet more than is modest, I will let the matter rest.

(1984)

Chapter Eighteen
Persons are Transcendent

In this paper I want to present and argue for a truth about the nature of persons that is largely overlooked or forgotten in our scientific and technical culture. The dominant feature of our culture is materialism, in both its theoretical and practical sense. Our world-view is materialistic: to be real is to be perceptible and measurable. And our goals are material too: new products, greater control of our environment. We are aware of other cultures, '*undeveloped*' African and Eastern ones, that are different but they are usually dismissed as primitive. We often tend to forget however that the central tradition of Western Philosophy, the tradition that is the foundation for twentieth century science and technology, is also opposed to materialism. From Plato and Aristotle, through Augustine and Aquinas to Descartes and Kant, however different individual philosophers might have been, there is a remarkable consensus in their understanding of persons. And this has centered on the view that in some way or other persons transcend the material realm. Historically this view has been expressed by the term 'rational animal' to describe human persons. The term 'rational' means different things to different people. In this paper I am going to argue that it is because persons are rational beings in the sense of being able to do things *for reasons* that they transcend the material realm. I should say that in talking of persons I don't mean human beings. I do of course think that human beings are persons. But in calling us persons I am saying something special about our nature; my chief interest is in what that is. It may be that it is something that we share with certain kinds of animals such as chimps or whales, or certain extra-terrestrial beings, or even certain kinds of computer, but I am not interested in that question. I leave it open as to whether there are other kinds of person as well as *human* ones.

The bulk of this paper will be about an aspect of what it is that makes us persons, but towards the end I shall have to refer to the peculiarity of being a human person too. What it means to say that persons are transcendent will become quite clear in the course of this paper. In particular I hope to show the importance of recognising this truth about persons, since it has some far-reaching implications for the way we live. It must not be thought that in speaking about something transcendent in the nature of persons, I am speaking about something strange or unusual. I am speaking about something very ordinary, something that is part of our everyday experience. But the fact that we all experience it does not necessarily mean that we all have a correct notion of it. By seeing it in the right light I think that one will recognise that this very ordinary aspect of our lives does have a mysterious dimension to it; it is like the tip of an iceberg, nine-tenths of which is hidden beneath the surface.

To give you an idea of the connection between being transcendent and being rational in the sense of being able to act for a reason let me tell you the following story. Hellenic football team are playing Kaizer Chiefs. Teenage Dladla gets the ball on the right wing and sends in a cross. Ace Ntsolengoe accelerates up the midfield just in time to meet the ball outside the penalty area and get in a blazing volley. The ball curves low across the area, eludes the outstretched fingers of the Hellenic goalie and enters the net just inside the right-hand upright.

A goal!

The above is a brief description of the event such as might be given in a newspaper report. Typically newspaper reports on soccer matches also try to explain how or why it was that goals came to be scored. And clearly other explanations of the same event could be given as well. A purely physical one for instance. This would be in terms of the trajectory of the winger's cross, the acceleration of Ntsolengoe, the point of impact and impact velocity of boot and ball, the coefficient of friction between ball and boot, the angle of the shot, the ball's weight, the elasticity of the goalie's muscles, the length of his arms. One could also give a chemical account of the same event, in terms of the blood sugar in Ntsolengoe's veins, the composition of the ball, the condition of the goalie's legs and lungs. A psychological account, in terms of the motivation of the players, the effect of the coaches pep-talk the previous evening, the importance of the game, and even certain details of the goalie's private life, could also be given. And a sociological account, bringing in the history of the rivalry between the two teams, the social pressures on teams in the championship, the peculiar factors obtaining when a predominantly black team plays one that is mainly white in an apartheid society. It is quite clear that each of all the sciences could give its own description and explanation of the event under discussion. Of course the different explanations are not mutually exclusive. They each add something to our understanding of the event. But no matter how many explanations of the scientific type were given they would be unable together to constitute a full or sufficient explanation of the scoring of the goal. No explanation of this event that left out a mention of the *rules of football*, according to which a team can only win a match if it has put the ball between the goalposts of its opponents at least once, would explain why after leaving Ntsolengoe's boot the ball travelled towards the Hellenic goal instead of away from it. In short, however long the list of causes, immediate and remote, of the goal, the list could not be complete unless it included the rules of football. It should however be obvious that the rules of football are a cause of the goal in a radically different sense from all those of the sciences.

They only act as causes insofar as they are part of the mind and will of a player who understands them and plays the game according to them. To mark this radical difference they are usually called '*reasons*' rather than causes. But whatever we call them, because they are a crucial part of a person's thinking, choosing and acting, they are effective in getting things done in the real world, the world that science also tries to describe and explain.

The moral of this parable is that human actions transcend any conceivable scientific explanation, that is explanation in terms of causes, and therefore that they transcend any conceivable system of such causes. Which is to say, they are free. Freedom is such an important aspect of our transcendence that I will deal with it in greater detail. 'Free' like 'rational', is such an ambiguous word that I will usually speak of our *capacity for self-enactment* rather than our freedom. In any case my example will make it clear what I mean.

The two most common signs of freedom or self-enactment in our everyday lives are our capacity to know the truth and our sense of responsibility. In everyday life we take both for granted. We would in fact be stupid not to. Total skepticism about our ability to know the truth about things is a self-refuting attitude, as Aristotle showed when he got the skeptic to speak: even the skeptic meant his claim 'There's no such thing as truth' to be taken as true. And there is something similarly indubitable about our sense of being ultimately responsible for certain of our actions, namely those we have deliberately decided on. However much we believed in determinism of some kind or another we would still retain this sense of responsibility for those acts we had deliberately decided on.

What both these unavoidable and undeniable experiences show is that persons have a capacity for what I have called 'self-enactment'. In judgements of truth and deliberate decisions, I am self-enacting both in the sense that it is me and not another that is responsible far the act, and also that whatever the object of the act may be, in performing it I also act upon myself. I am both free from the influence of external causes and able to determine the sort of person I shall become.

These are such important claims to make about persons that we must consider the evidence for our being self-enacting more closely. Why does being capable of knowledge and responsibility imply all that? To answer that question let us consider what happens when we come to know something or make a decision.

In making a judgement about the world (say 'That is a cat') we certainly do claim to have grasped reality, even if sometimes we have to qualify what we say with a 'probably'. Even if we always had to say (which we don't) 'It only seems so to me' we would still be claiming that it *really did* seem so to me, and not that it only seemed to seem so. One cannot ultimately get away from the scandalous claim to truth. And in claiming truth for one's judgement one is simultaneously affirming the distinction between one's own ideas and the real world. Truth is the correspondence between our ideas and the world and for there to be a correspondence there must be a distinction. And because there is distinction there can also be error: one's ideas could fail to correspond to reality. In making a judgement one stands back from one's ideas about what one has experienced and asks whether they are true of the experience. Eventually something is discovered that constitutes evidence for the truth of the idea and we judge it to be true *for that reason*. We may later have to change our judgement, admit we were wrong, but when we do it will again be for a reason.

There are two things I want to draw attention to in this account of making a judgement. The first is that judgement always involves a reason; even it is not explicitly adverted to. If you were asked afterwards 'Why do you think that?' you could give a reason, even if only an obviously bad one. It would always make sense for someone to ask you 'Why?' The second point is that in making a judgement I become present to myself and act on myself in a rather peculiar and radical way. It is my own idea that I am judging, and my own experience that provides the evidence for my judgement's truth; the content of the idea and the judgement are the same, all that is added is the affirmation. In making a judgement of truth I assess my own beliefs against a criterion that I impose. In doing so I take up a point of view that is beyond my whole system of beliefs in order to survey them and assess the coherence of the belief I am assessing with the system as a whole. This capacity to objectify and critically assess one's own beliefs is often called the ability to abstract. In any case it is an example of one's ability to act upon oneself and be present to oneself as a whole.

So it can be seen how our capacity for logic (our demand for reasons for belief) and our capacity for self-enactment are closely connected in the making of a judgement. The same is true in the making of a deliberate decision.

Here it is our desires that we have to consider rather than our beliefs. In making a decision we have to choose between a variety of different and often competing desires. This choice of what desire to act upon is called *consent.* By consenting to this or that desire I allow it to determine how I shall act. Of course my desires and my consent only exist in a context of beliefs. I consent to a desire *for some or other reason*, because I believe such and such to be the case, such and such a state of affairs will make me most happy. Consent is not the same as having a reason but it always takes place for a reason. Once again it can be seen that in consenting to this or that desire that I happen to have, I act upon myself. I have the capacity to create an internal division in myself and let the one side act on the other. This is an inadequate way of putting it since it is not a part of me that acts on another part but my whole self that acts on myself. I as consenting act upon myself as desiring; the actual content or object of the desire and the consent is the same. A consented-to desire is simply more my own, more me, than one that has not been consented to. Here, the way in which, by consenting to my desires, I bring myself to act is especially clear. I am self-enacting in a very complete and comprehensive sense. And at the heart of my self-enactment is my capacity for logic, my acting *for a reason*.

Thus it appears that whenever we make a judgement or a decision we are both acting for a reason and, precisely because of that, are self-enacting in the radical and comprehensive way that I have described. This is such an important point that I want to prove it beyond reasonable doubt. You see it is possible for some one to say 'Well you have given a fair description of how it feels to make a judgement or a decision, but that is all that it is—a description of feeling, the way one experiences the happening *from the inside*. In actual fact a judgement or a decision is an event like any other and has the same sort of causes. If neurology were further developed we could say just what those causes were.' And I want to claim that such a view is seriously mistaken, that it cannot possibly be true.

It is because judgements and decisions are both things that we do far a reason that they cannot possibly be the result of external causes acting upon us, but instead are examples of our capacity for self-enactment. The reason why no non-rational or external cause of a scientific kind can cause my grasp of a logical relationship between beliefs, whereby one of them could serve as the reason for the other being true, or the reason why I should decide on one thing rather than another, is because the act of *grasping* can only properly be described in logical terms and not in psychological or physical ones. Psychological and physical explanations of my judgements will of necessity always leave out that I am doing what I do *for a reason*, that is because I have grasped a logical connection between one belief and another. Because physical and psychological events cannot be described in logical terms they cannot be sufficient causes of events that can only be properly so described.

I can make this rather tricky point clearer with an example. Two people, A and B, have the same belief, namely that the black dog in the corner house is dangerous. A believes this because he has noticed that whenever the dog is taken for a walk it is muzzled. B believes it because he was bitten by a black dog in childhood and ever since then has been afraid of black dogs. Let us suppose that both men are equally committed to their beliefs. A however believes what he does *for a reason*. He believes that the dog is dangerous because he believes that dogs wear muzzles to stop them biting and the black dog wears a muzzle. His belief about muzzles provides a logical link with his belief about the black dog. Because he sees this link and believes what he does because of it his belief is reasonable. It has been caused by his grasp of the logical link. And this is just as true even if the black dog wears a muzzle not to stop him biting but because he has to keep his mouth shut to allow an ulcer in his mouth to heal. In the case of B however a psychological account of the causes of his belief is sufficient. He has no reason for belief since his belief is the result of mere association of ideas and is as such devoid of a logical connection to another belief that could act as its foundation.

It is thus because persons have the capacity to believe or decide things for reasons that their judgements and decisions transcend any conceivable system of external causes of the kind discovered by the sciences. In fact the law of non-contradiction that is the foundation of logic is simply an abstract formulation of the normal demand for coherence of belief and consistency of action that is characteristic of persons. And this lack of contradiction in oneself, in one's own belief and decision systems—even the natural dynamism that produces the demand for such a lack of contradiction, is what is meant by being self-enacting.

I have up to this point tried to show the connection of rationality with transcendence by showing that because persons are able to act *for reasons* they are self-enacting. And as our account shows, there are two aspects to being self-enacting.

The first is being free, free from external causality, free from the physical and psychological causes that the sciences are able to discover. By saying that we are free in that sense, I do not of course mean that in human persons the laws of physics and biology cease to hold. We are also not free from the law of gravity or the second law of thermodynamics. But I do mean that our behaviour cannot be fully accounted for by the laws of physics and biology or even by any conceivable set of the sciences. Sometimes it is true in special cases we lose this freedom—as in cases of brain damage or mutant births or even under the influence of certain kinds of drug. In those cases purely scientific explanations of our behaviour are often sufficient. But that is precisely because those capacities that define us as persons have been either destroyed or rendered inoperative. The best way of course to make a person's behaviour completely explainable by the sciences is to kill him.

The second aspect of being self-enacting follows from the first. If the laws of the sciences cannot properly explain our distinctively personal behaviour then it follows that the concepts of the sciences cannot properly describe what we are. In other words persons cannot adequately be described in physical or biological or even psychological terms. And hence it follows that we are not simply physical or biological beings. The true picture of human persons is I think as follows: we are complex many-levelled beings. Physical descriptions are true of us and so are biological descriptions; the same is the case with sociological and psychological descriptions too. But none of these accounts of persons need make the others false. Each deals with a more and more complex level of personal reality. A problem arises however when we come to the final level, that of our rationality. This is the most comprehensive perspective on persons since it is that which actually makes us persons. And the problem here lies in the capacity for self-enactment that I have tried to describe. Persons are, as I have shown, so radically self-enacting, that in the case of such activities as making judgments and decisions, they act upon themselves in a complete and total way. It is not the case of one part acting on another part, as in bodily movements, or even of one sense acting on another, as when we mentally compare the way something feels with the way it looks. In judgment and decision the whole person acts on the person as a whole, or rather the person acts as a unity of an extremely radical sort. Every physical being, on the other hand, is made up of parts and the same is true of every biological organism. It is thus inconceivable for such beings to act in this way. And this suggests that persons when they do are really free of such laws altogether, and are in that respect not physical or biological beings at all. The words to describe this characteristic of persons since the time of the Greeks have been 'immateriality' and 'spirituality'. It is this line of thought that has given rise to various kinds of idealism or dualism, namely the claims that persons are really immaterial beings or else that they are composite beings of spirit and matter. All material things have parts. Persons are capable of an activity that excludes parts. They are therefore possessed of the property of simplicity. They are therefore immaterial.

The battle between dualism and materialism regarding the nature of persons is very much in the centre of philosophical debate at this time all over the world. I can't enter into this debate now but I will at least: show where my view of the nature of persons fits in.

In claiming that persons are transcendent I do not want to suggest that that is all they are. I am making that claim because I think it is a forgotten or suppressed truth in our culture. We *are* self-enacting in the strongest and strictest possible way. We are also—at least *human* persons certainly are—dependent on our environment, our physical and biological environment, for everything we do. Even in our most self-enacting acts we are dependent on causal contact with our environment. We can't entertain concepts or make judgements without images and sensations caused by physical processes. Nor can we make decisions apart from desires caused in us by genetic and social conditioning. In view of this, and seeing that my notion of self-enactment excludes materialism, am I condemned to dualism? I think not. I think my view of persons finds a path between materialism and dualism. In order to follow it, all one has to do is to change one's usual way of thinking about mind and matter.

What I want to claim about human persons is that we are both self-enacting and other-dependent. That sounds like dualism. But we are self-enacting *by means of* being other-dependent. That sounds like nonsense. What I mean is that unlike other kinds of being in which dependence on what is other than themselves makes them less in control of their own acts, we become more ourselves, and more in control of our lives the more we are involved with what is other than ourselves in a certain way. I say 'in a certain way' and this must be spelt out. We only become aware of ourselves as knowing subjects insofar as we have knowledge of objects other than our own minds. We only develop our own power of self-determination insofar as we respond to the influences of our environment; the presence of what is other than ourselves is what makes free action possible. All this is especially true in the case of our relations with other persons. It is in these relationships that our personal nature is expressed most fully. In fact if we did not exist in dependence on other persons and their personal influence we would never be able to develop our capacity for self-enactment at all. 'Wild' children never learn to speak. Babies deprived of all mothering become imbeciles. And we can only grow as persons insofar as we respond to the influence of other persons who have already developed their capacity for self-enactment to the full. The formula 'self-enactment through other-dependence' is the law of life for human persons. It may sound paradoxical, but it is not contradictory.

The apparent paradox disappears when one understands that the dependence involved derives its character from our nature as persons. There are many ways of being dependent, and only one of them is capable of developing our capacity for self-enactment. Yet one is all we need to prevent our theory from being nonsense. We are thus not dualists; nor are we materialists. A way of visualising imaginatively what my view of persons is, is to use such images as inner and outer, or centre and circumference. There is an inner and an outer aspect to personal life, a centre and a periphery, yet these are two aspects of an irreducible unity. The trouble about such images is that they are images of a static reality. A better image would be that of a movement, originating from a centre, travelling outwards and then returning. The centre is the self, the movement is towards what is other and then back again. The return to self is only made possible by means of the movement towards what is other. So the very notion of self-enactment, when it is understood as a description of personal life, includes a reference to otherness. There is a duality in personal life, but that is because personal life is reflexive, subject and object at the same time. And such a reflexive unity is the most radical unity there can be. A self-enacting unity has an inbuilt duality to it, in its very heart as it were. This is not the dualism of mind and matter or body and soul or whatever, since it is a duality within the most spiritual, immaterial aspect of persons. In human persons however this duality expresses itself in a movement from inner to outer, from self to other, mind to matter, and back.

All this might seem unnecessarily complicated. A formulation such as this is forced on us however if we wish to affirm both that persons are transcendent and that human persons, in spite of being material, nevertheless are possessed of a radical unity. No one would deny that human beings are extremely complex creatures; one should thus expect any adequate understanding of them to be pretty complex too.

My interest in this paper is the fact that human beings are persons, and I have tried to say something about the nature of persons, namely that they are transcendent in the way I have described. The discussion has inevitably been abstract and for that reason might seem unimportant. This would be false. The transcendence of persons is really the most important thing about them and has many practical consequences as well.

To start with, if persons are transcendent in our sense, then the sciences, even the human sciences, cannot give full knowledge of them. The sciences cannot know them precisely as persons. Because all science is based on the data of sense it cannot include the data of the consciousness that persons have of themselves and that forms the foundation of their mental life. A psychologist for instance can study himself as an object from a variety of scientific viewpoints. In each case however he remains the same *subject* of his scientific operations, the one who is doing the study. He can't study himself precisely as the one who *produces* science and still preserve the scientific point of view. An example of this is the inability of any science to study scientific method itself. So all the sciences added together will still leave this crucial, central area of personal life out of account. This is the area that is in fact left over for philosophy. Philosophy however is merely a more systematic form of the common intuitive self-understanding that is gained in one's ordinary personal growth. Philosophy might seek the ultimate principles of all our knowledge and our system of values; they are however already operative in our lives and we are already vaguely conscious of them.

In general it can be said that there is a knowledge of persons, of oneself and others, that emerges in the experience of being a person in relation to others. It is not just an unfortunate fact that it only emerges in this way. It is a knowledge that can only be gained in this way—and that precisely because persons are transcendent. It is knowledge gained by a certain kind of *involvement*, whereas scientific knowledge depends on the strict separation of the scientist and the object of the science. Personal knowledge of the non-scientific kind is not less knowledge than scientific knowledge. The proof of this lies in its predictive power. Intimate friends are able to predict the behaviour of their friends far more accurately and comprehensively than any scientist. Possibly the most important implication of this insight into the knowledge of persons is its limitation of the claims of the human sciences to any total understanding of personal reality. It is not only such total ideological quasi-scientific systems as psychoanalysis and Marxism that are dethroned; even the humbler claims of the ordinary social and human sciences to explain human behaviour are set in a context of understanding that reveals their partial and provisional character better. I do not want to deny that the human sciences, and Marxism and Freudianism too, contain many illuminating insights into human nature. But these particular insights can only be properly appreciated and weighted appropriately when seen against the background of the transcendent nature of persons. Seeing them in this context really does transform the way in which they are understood. The Marxian and sociological discovery of the effect of economic factors and sociological determinants such as class on our lives can only be properly integrated into an understanding of humanity when it is relativised by the insight into our freedom to change society in a way that is genuinely new and the expression of values that are not the product of what has gone before.

It is not only the theory of the sciences but also the practices based on them that would be affected by our understanding of persons. Psychotherapy is an obvious example. In general however any practice that recognises that persons are transcendent will tend to be less committed to purely physical techniques (such as drugs) and emphasize the part played by meaning and understanding on human health and well-being. The methods used will also be less manipulative and more inter-personal in recognition of the freedom that alone can act as the foundation for personal growth and integration. Such practices would often be less 'efficient' than those presently preferred. But what we call efficiency (in, say, medicine) is often a mask for the control of a tiny factor to the massive detriment of the whole human system. The whole modern western conception of a 'hospital' is an example.

It is not only in strictly scientific theory and practice that our understanding of persons as transcendent would have implications. It would also have implications in the fields of education and politics. Once again our understanding of persons would rule out all deterministic ideologies and manipulative systems of government. At first sight our conception of persons would seem to be more at home in a capitalist than in a communist society. To be sure communism denies transcendence in the most forthright way. But both communist and capitalist societies are equally materialistic. The dominant ideology of capitalism is dualism, and that we reject. How dualism and materialism are able to go hand in hand in capitalist societies is a long story and one that I cannot go into here. But I think the Marxist critique of capitalism throws a great deal of light on this paradox.

It must be remembered that the understanding of persons presented here includes the view that we can only exercise or develop our capacity for self-enactment in a certain kind of dependence on others. Persons can grow as persons and find fulfillment only in a certain kind of personal community. The description of the characteristics and the forms of a community that is genuinely personal is the task of ethics; our account of persons can thus provide a foundation for an ethical system that links qualities of character with forms of inter-personal transaction. And this avoids both the individualism of much liberal ethical theory as well as the collectivism or communism.

That community with others can really enhance rather than prevent individual freedom might appear a paradox. But it is a consequence of our theory of persons. It is in fact only a possibility if persons are transcendent in the sense I have described. To undergo the influence of a transcendent being is to develop one's own capacity for self-enactment rather than lose it. This is especially true of our relationship with God.

(1985)

Chapter Nineteen
How Jesus Saves Us

In this article I make much use of St Paul and especially of his letter to the Romans. It is not however primarily an article of exegesis. I am approaching Paul as a fellow Christian rather than as a scholar. As such I assume a shared experience. His attempt to understand this helps me. But the language I use to express my understanding of our common faith must be very different from his.

If one asks Paul to explain how it is that Jesus saves us, one must expect a reply couched in the terminology of the Jewish and Middle Eastern thought of his time. These categories are already there for him to use. I in turn cannot simply repeat them since that would not provide me with any real understanding. It would instead be a sort of intellectual tourism. I must interpret them in categories that 1 can explain in terms of my twentieth-century experience of the world. The foundation for this interpretation is unchanging human nature and its needs, and the way in which Jesus meets these needs, which is the same 'yesterday, today and tomorrow'.

According to Paul, what we are saved from is a predicament that is best described in terms of slavery, or subjection or even possession. What we are enslaved to or in subjection to or possessed by is sin. 'Sin' is course the general biblical term for what is wrong with humanity, but because of its generality it is ambiguous. It refers first and foremost to the attitude (and the acts that express that attitude) that destroys the image of God in humanity. It is also used to refer to the result of such an attitude and act.

At one level (the story-telling level; the narrative of the transaction between God and Israel), sin is seen simply as action deliberately contrary to the will of God. (And sometimes not even as deliberate!)

Remember, however, that God is the creator and fufiller of humanity. Thus his will can't be correctly seen as some arbitrary set of purposes expressed in a set of positive laws that he wishes humankind to keep. Both the content of God's will and the nature of the punishment for infringements of it must be seen as intrinsic to human nature. So the sin can't be conceived of as a matter of breaking rules and then suffering the punishment that happens to be set for them. All legal and forensic models for sin and punishment are woefully inadequate for this very reason. So too are interpersonal models that envisage the relationship between the sinner and God on the analogy of that between king and his subject or a feudal lord and his vassal. Here again a particular social convention is pressed into service for the unique relation between creature and creator. Nevertheless we are not limited to such extrinsic models by means of which to understand the reality of sin. We can use genuine psychological and social-psychological categories provided they are related to some critical metaphysical framework and are not simply derived from empirical science. We have in fact an example of precisely this in the theology of Paul, though of course the metaphysical framework within which his categories are applied is largely implicit. I shall attempt to interpret these, using a different framework.

A final preliminary remark must be made concerning the Pauline language that implies that the human predicament is a state of slavery to the devil and his powers. Whatever one believes about the reality and activity of angels and devils, in the last resort they do not affect the fundamental notion of sin. Sin, to be sin, must be a freely and personally chosen act or attitude, and all peculiarly sinful consequences must flow from this. So one cannot avoid having to give an account of the reality of sin in psychological and inter-personal terms.

The human predicament: division in the soul

As far as the predicament itself is concerned Paul himself seems quite clear that it is a psychological state, though it expresses itself in inter-personal attitudes and acts. The state is one of deep internal division within a person. The classical description and analysis of this division is in Romans 7, where Paul presents, as his own experience, an account of the predicament humanity is in as a result of sin.

In Paul's case the division is between covetous desires and the desire not to covert. He really wants not to covet but finds himself unable to stop doing so. That at least is his situation prior to salvation. Now that he has been saved, the division has been healed and he is able to do what he really wants to do. The experience of salvation has given him insight into the predicament from which he has been saved, how he had got into it, why it was impossible for him to get out and how Jesus managed to do for him what he was unable to do for himself.

As I understand Paul, the division within him was between deep desires or fundamental tendencies of his nature, such as the desire to be generous or unselfish, and other desires that he had developed in the course of his life. These other desires are not specified but the whole habitual system of them is described as covetousness. These desires are different in kind from the other sort, the natural ones, since those are expressive of human nature as being the image of God. The natural desires thus point towards human fulfillment, the perfection of human nature in God's image. The ultimate point of this perfection is that it will enable a person to participate in a transcendent fellowship and communion with God. The human predicament is the sheer inability to consent to and follow these natural desires, but rather to indulge and follow their opposites, so that the very possibility of developing towards the perfection of nature and the communion with God is lost.

The first question that such an account of the human predicament immediately suggests is why should people have so universally gone against desires of their own nature and built up habitual desires that are opposed to their real fulfillment? Paul certainly thinks that *all* of us are in this predicament, not merely the majority. A second question that suggests itself concerns the seriousness of the predicament. Granted that things are as Paul describes them, why is it not possible for a person simply to change? Once he sees where his desires are leading him, surely he can choose to take a different direction. Is the predicament simply one of ignorance? Now that Paul has discovered what is really going on he can let people know and then it is up to them to change, if they want to. But this is certainly not how Paul sees the predicament. In his view it is impossible for persons to overcome their own predicament; it is something that only a transcendent power can do. This is why they need a saviour, and a saviour that is a truly transcendent being.

The answer to the second of these two questions seems to be as follows. The division in the self is so deep that our very heart is affected. We have lost the freedom to choose what we want; we are unable to consent properly even to that which we see and feel to be the best for us. This is why Paul describes the division as a form of slavery. We have lost our freedom because one part of us is in subjection to another part. Paul has various ways of describing the opposed parts of ourself and these throw some light on how radical the division in us is envisaged. 'I do not do what I want, but I do the very thing I hate.' This is the starting point. Here the opposition seems simply to be between what I want to do and what I don't want to do; the predicament is that I actually do the latter. Paul then proceeds to argue: 'if I do what I do not want, it is no longer I who do it, but sin which dwells within me.' This formulation expresses well the idea that in some way I have lost my freedom, my ability to choose. My behaviour has become compulsive. What is meant by sin 'dwelling within' me? Paul is making a distinction within the self between something that remains incorruptible, an ineradicable tendency towards and consciousness of what will fulfil my deepest needs, and a power of consent to this that can be destroyed or corrupted. He uses the terms 'spiritual' and 'carnal' to designate these two elements of the self. These terms must not be taken to imply a dualism of body and mind or soul, such as is common after Descartes or even such as is found in Plato. Paul inherited the fundamentally unitary conception of human nature that is typical of Judaism. The terms are available in the thought-world of the time and Paul uses them to describe these opposed elements in the self. The distinction they describe seems to be one of what is absolutely fundamental to the self, in the sense of being part of one's human nature, and of something else that is less so; Paul says, 'I delight in the law of God, in my inmost self, but I see in my members another law at war with the law of my mind and making me captive to the law of sin which dwells in my members.' Here we have the one side of the opposition described as my mind or my inmost self while the other is described both as my members and as sin. It would seem that the contrast between 'inmost self' and 'members' is that between centre and periphery, or even between foundation and building. In itself this does not take us any further, but the repeated use of the world 'law' in the above quotation does point the way to a solution.

The term 'law' was of course a highly significant one for the Jewish Paul. It refers in the first place to the Torah, the law of Moses. *Here* however it means something like a principle or active power. The connection between the two uses is that the law of Moses is, at least in its fundamental principles, an objectification, a revealed account, of the law of human nature as made in God's image. The distinction is between the actual tendencies and capacities of the human nature that God has created in his image, and the consciousness of them that has been gained in the history of Israel and formulated in, say, the Decalogue. So for Paul to say that he delights in the law of God in his inmost self is to refer to the ineradicable desire to follow the deepest desires of his nature. That makes sense. What on the other hand, is the *other* law that makes him captive to the law of sin that dwells in his members? The answer to this question solves the whole riddle. We can provide an answer to it by means of an understanding of what Paul says about the Jewish law itself and his own attitude to it.

One has only to read Romans in the most cursory manner to realize that Paul's attitude to the law of Moses is ambiguous. On the one hand it is the revelation of God's will for humanity and thus of what will perfect human nature as the image of God. As such it is 'holy and just and good'. On the other hand 'the very commandment which promised life proved to be death to me'. The law promises life in the sense that it is a prescription for how humanity must live in order to find fulfillment. It proved to be death to Paul in the sense that it was the cause of his subjection to sin and the loss of freedom that ensued. How could it do this if it was holy and just and good and, moreover, the law of God?

Paul tries to explain his ambivalent attitude to the law of God by contrasting his life before he was aware of it with his life as a Pharisee who was dedicated to following it. 'I was once alive apart from the law, but when the commandment came, sin revived and I died . . . sin, finding opportunity in the commandment, deceived me and by it killed me.' The expression, 'finding opportunity in the commandment' to describe the relation of sin and law is one he uses more than once. It is as though the holy, just and good commandment, precisely because it is all those things, is an occasion of sin. This hypothesis is confirmed if we take the case of Paul's covetousness to fill in the 'before and after' framework that he uses to bring out the connection between sin and the law of God. This is what he says: 'If it had not been for the law I should not have known sin. I should not have known what it is to covet if the law had not said, 'You shall not covet.' The meaning of this is not that he would not have eve coveted if he had not known the law. He would have coveted, and to the extent that coveting is against his God-created nature, he would have perverted that nature and prevented it reaching its fulfillment. But he would not have known that coveting *was* against his nature, since the law of Moses is precisely a revelation of what his nature is. He now knows that coveting is against his God-created nature and this is opposed to God who wills that nature's fulfillment. And that is to know it as sin. As against his nature as such it is bad; because God wills his good it is against God's will and that is sin. Now when he covets, he is conscious that he is going against his nature and against the will of God. The extraordinary thing however is not simply that although he now knows that coveting is against his nature and the will of God he continues to covet, but that the knowledge actually *increases* his covetousness. 'Sin, finding opportunity in the commandment, wrought in me all kinds of covetousness.' Now that he knows that covetousness is against his nature and God's will and he has a real motive for not coveting, Paul finds he covets more than ever. The more he tries not to covet, the more he covets. 'So I find it to be a law that when I want to do right, evil lies close at hand.' Paul's wanting to do what the law commands is the very thing that ensures that he will fail. To see why this is so takes us to the very centre of Paul's understanding of sin and, in the process, his understanding of human nature.

The Cause of the Predicament: Sin as Idolatry

For Paul the essence of sin is idolatry. All mankind is in a state of sin because everyone in one way or another has 'exchanged the truth about God for a lie and worshipped and served the creature rather than the creator' (Rom 1:25). The objects of our idolatrous worship are 'the elemental spirits of the universe' (Eph 2:1). These are 'beings that by nature are no gods [but] . . . weak and beggarly elemental spirits' (Gal 4:8). He takes pains to assert that 'we know that "an idol has no real existence", and that "there is no God but one"' (Cor 8:4). The notion of idolatry suggests an image of a person kneeling before a statue. The statue or what it represents is the idol. But it must be remembered that the statue or the thing it represents is worshipped for what it can do, let us say bring health, or wealth. So it is truer to say that it is health or wealth that is the real object of our idolatrous worship. In fact it is more exact to say that it is being healthy or being wealthy that is the real object of idolatrous worship. Being healthy and wealthy are good things for human beings and so the object of natural needs and desires.

What is it then to value them in an idolatrous way? For Paul the real objects of our idolatrous worship are not the statues or the things they represent but the 'principalities and powers' that rule our lives, the 'elemental spirits' of the universe. These, I think, must be seen as fundamental psychic and cosmic powers that make up and underlie our nature. They could even include social and cultural forces that have developed in the history of humanity and which are capable of exercising a super-personal influence on individuals. Nevertheless, whatever they precisely are, the power they have over us comes from the fact that we worship them, give them an unconditional value.

As 'principalities and powers' these 'elemental spirits of the universe' are present as elements in our lives, controlling us and making us their 'slaves'. This way of speaking should prepare us for the insight that the ultimate object of idolatrous worship is oneself. Idolatry is putting one*self* in the place of God. To take the case of Paul himself, one can say that he made an idol out of the law of Moses. The fact that he took the law of Moses to be the law of God illustrates the true nature of idolatry very well. There could appear to be nothing worthier of unconditional worship. In fact Paul's case presents us with the phenomenon of idolatry in its most radical form and so reveals its essential nature perfectly. In Paul's case, more clearly than in any other, he is putting himself in the place of God. The law which is supposed to reveal the conditions of our dependence on God for our ultimate fulfillment, becomes for Paul a means for his own self-glorification. As a keeper of this law he deserves God's respect and reward! He wanted to keep the law so as to prove his own power to himself not in order to express his unconditional dependence to God. So his failure to keep it was not an invitation to depend more completely on God and trust in God's power to fulfil what was required; it was rather a source of utter despair.

If this account of the real position of Paul the Pharisee in respect of the law of Moses is accurate, then it follows that self-worship is the source of slavery to the elemental spirits that he speaks of, and the division in the self that we have described at such length. How this is so can be seen by looking more closely at the notion of idolatry as self-worship. How is it possible? And why should it occur?

Humanity is the image of God in the thought-world of the New Testament. A consideration of the first eleven chapters of Genesis shows this to mean that humankind occupies a creator-like position in the world. Humanity transcends the realm of finite realities, being free of total determination by them and so able to control its own destiny in the world. But it has this freedom of self-determination only in dependence on the creator. Humanity is incomplete and can only grow to completion in dependence on God; it needs the continuing creative power of God to develop as the image of God until this is perfectly realized. The appropriate attitude of humankind is a complete reliance on and devotion to God. Such adoration of our creator is an expression of the same capacity that gives us freedom of choice and the ability to determine our own lives. The fact that we can give unconditional worship to anything is a reflection of the fact that we are made in the image of an infinite being. But it is also true that the only being that can be rightly worshipped in this way is God alone. If we transfer this unconditional worship to ourselves a total disintegration of psychic order takes place in us. Vis-à-vis God we are dependent, and we treat ourselves as independent. We are incomplete, and we treat ourselves as complete. We can only find our ultimate satisfaction in an infinite being and we try to find it in ourselves, who in spite of our capacity for entering into relationship with an infinite being are irreducibly finite. The change that occurs has its own modalities. It involves self-assertion and pretence at wisdom instead of receptivity and the desire to learn. Fundamentally it means that we cease to grow, since our development depends on our openness to God's creative influence. Instead, because our fundamental relationship to ourselves is fundamentally wrong, the way we pursue all our objectives in the world and all the value judgements that we make are wrong as well.

When our capacity for unconditional self-donation is referred to God (in whatever of all the many possible ways in which this can take place in the world of space and time) then we are able to exercise our freedom in the world so as to fulfill our real needs in the proper way and to grow in wisdom and appropriate feelings, valuing various things in proper proportion, according as they are satisfying to our true needs. When our capacity for unconditional worship is referred to ourselves we are fundamentally unsatisfied in the most important sphere of our emotional and intellectual lives. *In fact* we have to rely on other things for the satisfaction of our needs, on God as well as the things in our worldly environment. Since we refuse to recognise the fundamental dependence on God, which has an unconditional character, we transfer the unconditional *dependence* to some or other finite source of satisfaction some state of affairs or object or power in the world (for example, our job, our children, our nation, our own moral principles). This then becomes the idol. But it is in fact only the external objectification of our own *self*-worship. We project this onto something other than ourselves, since we are deeply unsatisfied and in fact need *another* (of some kind or other) to satisfy our needs. We choose a finite other because it is in fact in our power and the (illusory) self-surrender to it is not a real surrender of one's worshipped self-sufficiency at all. Of course in all this there is a great deal of self-deception, but the fundamental form that idolatry takes is the same in all cases. It is never simply a case of ignorance of what will truly satisfy our deepest desires; beneath whatever ignorance there is, is the determination of the will to be wholly independent and to be its own absolute good.

Of course once the attitude of idolatry has developed and some finite good has had projected on it the unconditional worship that we give ourselves, then our psychic balance and integrity is forever lost. All our valuations are wrong; emotions conflict with one another and we will incompatible things. Crucially we have lost control of our lives, our behaviour is compulsive and we are prone to believe illusory notions that happen to fit in with our disordered will. This is the state of division in the self that Paul documents so faithfully. It is not mere division either; from the nature of the case it is progressive, a process of disintegration.

The Need for the Transcendent: the Idea of a Saviour

The above account could serve as an answer to the question why the human predicament is so radical and so dangerous, why it is beyond human power to overcome. If Paul's biblical anthropology is correct, human fulfilment is always the work of God. An infinite capacity can only be developed and perfected by an infinite being. Within the actual circumstances of our worldly environment the slavery of sin can be seen as a developed, freely chosen, inability to choose wholeheartedly the infinite good that alone can satisfy us. We are so divided in mind and heart that although we are always capable of free choice, and indeed of unconditional worship, we are not able freely to choose to give unlimited worship to the being that alone could receive it. The very unconditional nature of our capacity for self-donation and the fact that it has been applied to the wrong object, with the consequence of a total disorientation of our psychic life, is what fixes us in a situation from which we cannot extricate ourselves. It is not simply that a change of object of our devotion is required. It must be remembered that our worship of God is *always* mediated through our evaluation of and behaviour towards finite objects (including images and ideas). It might well be thought that a little change of value here and there could put the situation right. This is to forget the fact that idolatry is fundamentally *self*-worship. The worship of particular objects in the world is just a projection and objectification of this. Hence what is required is a fundamental and complete change of direction of worship, from inwards to outwards, from self to God. It would thus appear that as in the case of creation, as in the normal necessity for transcendent power to bring finite beings into being, so too in the case of sin, it is only God who can overcome the predicament that humanity is in. He alone can be our saviour. Thus far Paul's account of sin and the necessity for a transcendent saviour appears to be coherent.

But what of our other question: why is it that *all* of us are in the predicament of sin? Is sin then necessary? If it is how can we be judged to be guilty? From what I have already said of Paul's theory of sin and the notion of human nature on which it is based, it is possible to see why, although not necessary, such idolatry is highly likely. As finite worldly beings we are in full possession of our finite powers; as beings capable of a personal relation to God we are radically incomplete. The very capacity that makes us capable of knowing and loving God and so wholly dependent on him in this respect, makes us capable of understanding and controlling the world. We are incomplete in our knowledge and love of God. Growth in that is only possible by means of God's influence on us, mediated through the ordinary circumstances of our worldly environment. Hence there is always a possibility of ignorance and error. We may make mistakes in particular circumstances as to what is of God and what is not; as to what God requires of us and what he does not. But sin and idolatry do not consist in, nor are they caused by, mistakes. They are caused by a turning of the will away from what is of God towards what will foster our own worship of ourselves. How can this come about? The possibility for this exists in the fact that growth in the self-donation to God requires moral effort. It is the effort of turning away from the natural self-love of a finite being to the love of something infinite. Natural self-love can easily become idolatry. It only requires that we choose to *prefer* the self to everything else. Love of God on the other hand only requires that one *prefer* God to oneself. What happens is that the order of preference is inverted. In the ordinary circumstances of life the development of a preference for God, and a corresponding love of oneself for God's sake, takes place bit by bit. Each bit involves the effort of self-negation; of preferring the side of oneself that is dependent and powerless (although it has an infinite capacity) to the side that is powerful and in control. This process is that of moral effort. It *need* not be unsuccessful but one can see why it inevitably is, especially when it is taken into account that one's actual situation is full of sin and the results of sin. Pressure is brought to bear on us to fit in with habits of sin. The basic fact however is that successful growth in the love of God involves a preference of our infinite tendency to our finite ones. The finite ones are in principle capable of satisfaction, whereas the infinite one's satisfaction is not in our hands. We appear to have to go against our nature to love the creator. In fact it is only that we have to go against our nature's tendency to make an absolute claim on us to satisfy those needs that are well within our power.

We have not yet quite finished our consideration of Paul's account of the human predicament. According to Paul we are in a state of slavery not only to sin but also to death. Salvation, to be worthy of the name, must also involve the overcoming of death. To understand Paul's attitude to death one must see it as fulfilling a function in the physical realm somewhat similar to that of the law of God in the moral realm. In itself it is simply part of the human situation; in connection with sin it becomes a dangerous and destructive power. Whenever Paul talks of death as something from which we need to be saved it is closely connected with sin. Paul never considers the possibility of there being no sin in the world. The real world is always a sinful world. But one must not imagine that therefore death is only capable of having a negative meaning for human kind. On the contrary, just as it derives its negative meaning from its connection with sin, so it can gain a positive meaning from its connection with Jesus' salvation. In fact it is precisely the *death* of Jesus that is the cause of our salvation (though this can only be appreciated by those who have faith in his resurrection). Hence we must take a brief look at Paul's conception of death; our death as well as that of Jesus.

Paul inherits the Genesis perspective on death. In fact whenever he refers to the 'commandment' in Romans, meaning the law of Moses, I can't help feeling that he is also thinking of the 'first' commandment, namely the one that God gave to Adam. The consequence of breaking that was precisely the loss of everlasting life. Therefore, in terms of my own understanding of the Adam and Eve story, I see death as simply yet another aspect of the 'test' situation in which incomplete humanity has to grow towards fulfillment. As a sheer factual element in the human situation it has the meaning of a total loss of control or power over one's environment and oneself. It proves one's inability to achieve fulfillment. It also means separation from all the good things under one's control and which one can achieve with one's own powers. But because humanity, as the image of God, also transcends its worldly environment, death can be seen in two different ways and humankind can take up two different attitudes in the face of it. It can be seen as an invitation to trust in the transcendent power of God to achieve for one a fulfillment beyond one's own power, or it can be seen as the destruction of all one's hope for fulfillment. Does one continue to rely on the transcendent power of the wisdom and love that one has experienced in one's life, believing in its ability to overcome even that total lack of power one experiences in the face of death, or does one lose faith in the transcendent source of such power, believing that it too is impotent in the face of death? Thus it can be seen that one's attitude to death is either an attitude of faith or lack of faith in a transcendent power. Because the state of sin is essentially an attitude of self-worship, which involves an unconditional reliance of one's own powers, death is an event of total despair. The idols, the principalities and powers to which the sinner is subject, cannot save him from death because they are nothing but objectifications of his own finite powers. So death at once reveals his apparent security and fulfillment as illusory, and denies him any hope of real fulfillment. Conversely, being saved from death means being granted a fulfilment beyond that which one could oneself achieve.

One's trust in the transcendent power of the wisdom and love that does appear in human life, is justified by one's resurrection to a life of eternal wisdom and love.

The Transcendence of Love

We now have before us an account of the predicament from which Jesus saves us. Our next concern is to understand better how he does so.

For Paul the actual process or achievement of salvation has two sides to it. The first is what Jesus does in his death, something that is only fully revealed by the resurrection. The second is our response to this 'work' of Jesus. This two-fold process has effects in us and our lives which we can try to describe. What Jesus does in his death is to bring to perfection in his own life an unlimited devotion to his 'Father' and to us. The transcendence of this life (its 'divinity') is revealed by his resurrection. It is physically transcendent in that it is not destroyed by death; it is morally transcendent in that it is completely without sin, the fulfilment of the Law. As has been said, Paul's anthropology is non-dualistic. The resurrection reveals Jesus' life as being triumphant over both sin and death. It is by trusting ourselves completely to the moral and physical power expressed in Jesus' death that we are saved. This act of trust involves all the powers of our person, mind and heart and will: Paul calls it faith. He puts it thus: 'we are justified by faith' (Rom 5: 1). What he means is that by our act of faith in Jesus and the power and holiness of his life we become like him. Our act of identification with him enables him to communicate to us the personal qualities that make him holy. His part in this is called grace and is a direct effect of his love for us: 'by grace you have been saved through faith' (Eph 2:5). This formula is a summary of the essential inter-personal transaction between Jesus and us that constitutes salvation. The result is that we 'become obedient from the heart' (Rom 6:17) to what the Law commands, because we have been 'strengthened with might through his Spirit in the inner man' (Eph 3:16). We have in fact, through Jesus' grace and our faith, become sharers in his own spirit, the spirit of his transcendent life. Paul even speaks of Jesus as having become a 'life-giving spirit' (1 Cor 15:45). So much then for the moral consequences of salvation: we become doers of the law. But there is a physical consequence of salvation: we are to overcome death. 'If the spirit of him who raised Jesus from the dead dwells in you, he who raised Christ Jesus from the dead will give life to your mortal bodies also through the spirit who dwells in you' (Rom 8:9). So we are brought to perfection. Everything the law demanded is now achieved. The law couldn't give us power to fulfil it; having the spirit of Jesus' transcendent life in our hearts does just that. We no longer see death as the enemy of our fulfillment but trust in the power of Jesus' life to overcome it.

This is very nice and neat but questions remain. If all this is gained by faith in Jesus then surely such an attitude must be difficult to attain. If we are capable of generating such a profound act of self-donation how come we are not capable of fulfilling the Law? A partial answer to this is that there is all the difference in the world between trusting someone else to do something for you that you are unable to do, and trying to do it for yourself in spite of everything. If the one thing that is really preventing persons from keeping the Law is their own self-worship then relying on someone else for the power to do so is the perfect antidote. The mechanism of transformation consists in the compelling power of an unlimited love. Paul experiences the death of Jesus as the expression of an absolutely unlimited love of Jesus for him. If one is loved in that way there is nothing in the attitude that one need resist: Jesus makes his, Paul's salvation, the motive of his whole life and death. To be able to get and give love like this corresponds to the deepest desire of his nature. Consenting to it is not hard since it acts as the basis for a complete unification of all the desires of his heart. Covetousness is dissipated. Jesus' love is the cause of this but insofar as Paul consents to it, it becomes his own. A critical question nevertheless remains. How does such an attitude differ from sheer inauthenticity, a handing over of personal responsibility to another? Putting one's absolute trust in Jesus to do for one what is most intimate and essential for one's personal fulfillment is not an act either of idolatry or of immaturity since it is his death, or 'him crucified' as Paul says, that is the focus of one's trust. *That* is quite void of any suggestion of finite powers other than our own, as well as being the symbol of our own utter impotence. All this needs to be said to save the integrity of the act of faith. Nevertheless when all is said and done, it must be understood that, like any actualization of our created capacity for a transcendent life, faith is the expression in us of God's power. The self-donation it involves, although it is the cause of all that follows in us by way of holiness and integration, is itself the effect of a transcendent causality working through the ordinary events of our lives, amongst which will surely include our efforts and inability to be holy, and the suffering that our sins cause us. It is precisely this that reveals the strictly transcendent nature of the power that is communicated by Jesus' love: it does not contradict our freedom but brings it into being.

All this is to say that the spirit of Jesus' life that is communicated to us is the spirit of a transcendent being. Paul's experience of salvation is the same as that of the other witnesses of Jesus' resurrection. His coming to believe that Jesus has overcome the negative meaning of death and affirmed its positive meaning in his own (Jesus') life and that this life is one of unconditional love for him (Paul), is the effect of a necessarily transcendent power at work within him. So the subjective transformation he undergoes is fitted to the objective content of his belief concerning Jesus and his resurrection and his goodness. The transformation in Paul is an occurence which, if it is correctly understood in the way that has been described, could only have been produced by a transcendent power.

The essence of the transformation is the replacement of his idolatrous self-worship by the adoration of another, namely Jesus. This avoids inauthenticity since it is the adoration of the crucified Jesus who is alive with an eternal life, and this is to adore a truly transcendent power and not a mere objectification of one or other human power. Nor is the adoration the projection of a merely human hope, since both its physical and its moral character is derived from the fact of death. The fact that its moral character is derived from death is the guarantee that the victory over physical death is not 'cheap' victory, a bare fact of physical power divorced from moral integrity. As I have stressed, the moral and physical aspects of death must be understood in relation to each other. It is only the dualism and materialism that results from a modern scientific outlook that falsifies the picture by separating them.

As a result of his experience on the road to Damascus, Paul has come to believe that Jesus has fulfilled the law and triumphed over death. He has also come to believe that Jesus is able to achieve both these things in him, Paul, too. What is more, his experience of being transformed in himself is proof for him that this achievement has at least begun. The division in his heart has been healed; he is able to fulfil the spirit of the law. Above all he is capable of a genuine adoration of God and a compassionate love of other persons. Because of the way in which he conceived his former slavery to sin, he is obliged to recognize the transcendent nature of Jesus' life and of the power at work in him. The resurrection of Jesus and the transformation of Paul are equally effects of the power of God.

In all this the absolute centrality of love as the mechanism of salvation stands out. Love is seen not as one emotion among others but as the absolutely central and definitive attitude of a person regarding another person. In the famous hymn to love in 1 Corinthians, both faith and hope are seen as temporary forms that love takes before our transformation and union with God is complete. Love remains, as Paul says. This is because it is not only the dynamism of our transformation but the expression of our nature once it has been transformed. Salvation is *for* something, and this something is life in the family or the community or the fellowship of God. The result of Jesus' resurrection is for him a communion. And the result of our salvation is a sharing in this transcendent communion. Paul uses all sorts of metaphors to express the personal community with Jesus and his Father that we are able to participate in as a result of our salvation. 'All who are led by the Spirit of God are sons of God' (Rom 8:14). 'You have received the spirit of sonship. When we cry 'Abba! Father!' it is the Spirit himself bearing witness with our spirit that we are children of God', (Rom 8:15) 'because you are sons, God has sent the Spirit of his Son into our hearts, crying 'Abba! Father!' So through God you are no longer a slave but a son' (Gal 4:6).

An interesting feature of Paul's experience of salvation is that he never knew Jesus before his death. His only contact with him before his 'resurrection experience' was with his followers. Thus his knowledge of the quality of Jesus' life and the nature of his claim and his promise were all gained from Christians and not from Jesus himself. Paul's situation in this respect is in many ways a sort of bridge between that of the first followers of Jesus and ourselves.

This is the bridge of the tradition of the Church that enables St Paul and ourselves both to share a common faith and also to approach a common understanding of it.

(1986)

Chapter Twenty

A New Argument for the Existence of God

In this article I wish to present an argument for the existence of God as the one who alone is able to bring about personal growth in us. In outline the argument is as follows:

> Human persons depend on other persons to develop as persons.
> If all persons absolutely were dependent in this way then no personal growth at all would occur.
> Personal growth does occur.
> Hence there must exist, as its sole sufficient cause, at least one person who is not dependent for personal development on others, an absolutely independent person.

This is what Christians recognise as God.

I shall begin with an exposition of this argument. Its force depends a great deal on the conception of personal growth on which it is based, so I shall have to set out in some detail my view of the nature of persons and of the necessary conditions for their development. I shall then discuss some of the issues raised by the argument. Why is a 'new' argument being attempted? What is there to recommend the argument that I have chosen? What is the nature and purpose of an argument for the existence of God? What is its cognitive status? In the course of this discussion I will put forward a view as to how philosophers ought to approach the question of God, a view that I take to be more compatible with Christian faith than is commonly the case.

In an earlier article (Shutte, 1984[1]) I have presented a philosophical account of the necessary conditions for personal growth which, if sound, would go some way towards establishing the first (and fundamental) premise of the present argument. I mentioned there that that account could be used as the basis for an argument for the existence of God. I did not however feel able to attempt it there and then. Now that I am attempting it I shall take what I have already written as read. Apart from a brief summary of the earlier analysis I will concern myself wholly with new material in order, I hope, to gain deeper insight into the nature and conditions of personal growth.

In my earlier article I investigated the necessary conditions for the minimum exercise of those capacities the possession of which makes us persons in the strict sense of the term. The capacities were identified as those for self-consciousness and self-determination, as are revealed in our making judgements and decisions. In judging and deciding, it was argued, we are involved in an activity that is self-referential in a peculiarly radical way. We are in fact self-enacting in the sense both that our acts are free from external determination and also that, whatever the direct object of our act, in acting we also act upon ourselves. It is this feature of persons that entails our dependence on the personal influence of other persons for our development. An impersonal environment is insufficient. To develop our capacity for self-consciousness and self-determination to the level common in normal adults we require to be recognised and valued as persons (in at least a minimal degree) by other persons.

To establish this conclusion I followed John Macmurray's method of using an ideal (and abstract) model of a pair of persons, a mother and her child.[2] The child represented the mere capacity for personal life, the mother the total personal milieu required for this capacity to develop to fulfilment. In practice of course we develop in relation to a multitude of other persons, and the essential requirements for personal development are obscured by the quantity and variety of relationships. The model has the effect of simplifying and so clarifying the essential elements in personal development of this fundamental sort.

1. Shutte, A, 'What Makes Us Persons?', in *Modern Theology* 1 (1984): 67–79; Chapter 17 in this volume.
2. Macmurray, J, *Persons in Relation* (Faber, 1961).

I will adopt the same method in this article, an abstract model to represent the ideal conditions necessary for personal growth, but here it will be that of two 'adults' or 'friends' rather than a mother and child. This is because the personal growth I am concerned with now is that consequent upon the development that enables us to make judgements and decisions in a normal adult way. It is, in other words, the growth that takes place (or doesn't; it is not, alas, inevitable) after we have reached physical maturity. It could be called psychological or moral or even spiritual growth. All these terms are appropriate but all are imprecise. Few people would want to deny that there is a sense in which persons can grow as persons but most would be unable to explain precisely in what such growth consists. A variety of 'maps' of personal development are available: from empirical psychology, from moral philosophy in the form of lists of the virtues, and above all from the theology of the spiritual life. There is also a great deal of useful material in literature, especially in novels. I wish however to concentrate on the development of those capacities that define us as persons since it is only these that, in my view, absolutely require the influence of a transcendent person if they are to grow. And these are the capacities, as I have said, that make us self-enacting.

That being the case, it might appear that the question of growth as a person is ruled out from the start. The capacities in question are after all those for self-consciousness and self-determination. And surely these have already been developed to the full in all normal adults? We are all capable (at least most of the time) of judgement and decision. In what sense could we become more self-conscious or self-determining?

Putting it like that does indicate the way in which I think one can usefully speak of our further growth as persons. It is focussed on our conception of persons as self-enacting. As I have said, this implies our being in a way both subject and object of our own acts. In the normal self-consciousness involved in judgment and decision we are aware of ourselves as the 'owners' or 'origins' of our acts. This is a real though minimal form of self-knowledge. And clearly in the realm of self-knowledge there is room for growth. The same is true of self-determination. Every decision, whatever its special object, is always also a decision about oneself, an affirmation of oneself in some or other respect. Such self-affirmation is however always only partial and discontinuous, its completeness and integrity prevented both by lack of insight into what we really want and by a real conflict of desires. A whole-hearted self-affirmation untroubled by either illusion or division remains only an ideal.

It thus appears that self-knowledge and self-affirmation have a special status as indicators of personal growth. This derives from the fact that they are, like self-consciousness and self-determination, elements in the self-enactment that is the defining characteristic of persons. They are in fact fuller realisations of this capacity and therefore better suited to reveal the nature and requirements of personal growth. This special status of self-knowledge and self-affirmation can be seen more clearly if one thinks of personal growth as in some sense a growth in the unity or integrity of the person. Self-knowledge and self-affirmation are, I think it can be shown, the essential principles of such integration. In order to show this I must say a little more about them.

An important clue to the true nature of self-knowledge and self-affirmation is given in the following quotation from DH Lawrence[3]:

> All that matters is that men and women should do what they really want to do. Though here as elsewhere (he is discussing our sexual life) we must remember that man has a double set of desires, the shallow and the profound, the personal, superficial, temporary desires and the inner, impersonal, great desires that are fulfilled in long periods of time. The desires of the moment are easy to recognise, but the others, the deeper ones, are difficult. It is the business of our Chief Thinkers to tell us of our deeper desires, not to keep shrilling our little desires into our ears (1931: 52–53).

It is, I would maintain, precisely these 'deep' desires that form the essential object of both self-knowledge and self-affirmation. They are not desires produced in us by particular circumstances of a cultural or social kind; they are rather built into our human nature and pre-exist any social or cultural conditioning, whether we are aware of them or not. In fact, seen as a system of dynamisms or tendencies towards a certain kind of life, they actually constitute our human nature. For this reason knowledge of them is the essential ingredient in self-knowledge. I do not mean a generalised knowledge of human nature

3. DH Lawrence, *Apropos of Lady Chatterley's Lover* (Penguin, 1931).

such as a philosopher might have, (the kind I am trying to reach in this article) but the particular knowledge of one's own nature, of what one really wants and what would most truly satisfy one.

Of course this is not the only ingredient in self-knowledge. One must be aware of one's other, superficial, wants too, as well as one's beliefs about matters of fact (especially those facts relevant to the satisfaction of one's desires). But insight into the nature of one's 'deep' desires is the most important for determining the whole character of one's conception of oneself. This is because such an insight embodies a judgment of value and is thus capable of determining how one will act. In recognising a desire as 'deep', as what one really wants, and as built-in to one's human nature, one is evaluating it as central or foundational to one's fulfilment. The set or system of deep desires, once brought to light, will constitute a criterion of what is worthwhile, of what one ought to do and how one ought to live.

An example may make this point clearer. In the sphere of our sexuality, for instance, we may be aware of a number of desires. We may have a desire for frequent casual sexual intercourse with a variety of partners, as well as a desire for an enduring, whole-hearted sexual communion with one other person. Self-knowledge here would consist in being aware of both desires but in recognising the superficiality of the one and the centrality and importance of the other. One would have to become aware of the compulsive and dissipating character of the superficial desire as well as of the enduring and unifying character of the deep desire. And such an awareness would issue in a judgment of value concerning the role to be played by the different desires in one's life, of the degree to which one ought to consent to them in the decisions that one makes.

Clearly it is possible to be mistaken about the nature of one's deep desires and of the relative importance of different desires. It is also possible to be simply unaware of certain desires, especially the deepest and most central. And both forms of failure in self-knowledge will produce conflict within the person, since lack of understanding and mistaken judgments of value will tend to produce wrong and conflicting choices, which will in turn create conflict and incoherence in one's emotional life. True self-knowledge will of necessity embody an ordered system of value judgments and it is this alone that can integrate the cognitive, the volitional and the emotional dimensions of the person. Within each of these dimensions of the person the principle of integration is thus self-knowledge of the kind I have described.

As far as self-affirmation is concerned, it is no less true that these deep desires are the key to genuine growth. For unless they are the primary object of self-affirmation, our self-affirmation can never be whole-hearted or complete. Self-affirmation consists principally in our power of consent. We can consent both to our judgments of value and to our desires. And we can consent to a greater or lesser degree, or refuse consent entirely. It is thus not difficult to see that unless we consent properly, which is to say fully, to our deep desires we can have no hope of affirming ourselves as an integrated whole. The deep desires will persist in any case, whether we consent to them or not, but they will persist in opposition to those superficial desires to which we have more fully given our consent. And as long as such opposition persists and is ratified by our power of consent there can clearly be no true self-affirmation and hence no growth in the integration of the person. Unless there is harmony in the emotional dimension of the personality—and this cannot exist unless the deep desires are allowed to prevail in the ordering of our emotional life—there can be no question of real self-affirmation.

Something of the same is also true of the cognitive element in self-affirmation. Unless we consent to the judgments of value that we make concerning our desires, and especially our deep desires, and so ratify the hierarchy in which they are placed, there will be conflict and opposition between the cognitive and the volitional dimensions of the person. We will judge one thing and affirm another; the self of our self-knowledge will not be the same as that of our self-affirmation. Of course if our judgement concerning the relative importance of our desires is mistaken then the lack of consent is all to the good. The opposition between the cognitive and the volitional dimensions of our personality nevertheless remains. And that has serious consequences for the integrity of the person. (It is well said that a wrong conscience obliges.) True integration of the person requires both that we come to a true awareness of our deep desires, recognising their centrality and importance, and that we affirm them in accordance with such judgments of value.

I hope it is now clear why I regard self-knowledge and self-affirmation as the fundamental principles of the integration of a person and hence as the essential indicators of personal growth. Introducing the notion of deep desires of our human nature has helped me to show this. There is not the space here to go into greater detail as to the nature of such desires and their relative importance. Lawrence was concerned primarily with the sphere of sex. And one could produce examples from other fundamental areas of human life. I shall presently have to consider at least one such example. But let me say here that I think that, in spite of appearances, we have a deep desire for self-knowledge of the kind I have described, and for self-affirmation. And, if I am right, this is really a desire to develop as a person, to be integrated, to be fully self-enacting. In this process self-knowledge is the principle of integration within the cognitive, volitional and emotional dimensions of the person, and self-affirmation is the principle of integration between them. Growth in both is necessary if the normal conflicts and contradictions that characterise human life are to be overcome.

I have spent as much space as I have in discussing the nature of personal growth because it is only on a certain understanding of it that the necessity of the personal influence of other persons (and ultimately of a transcendent person) will become apparent. I must now proceed to show why this is so.

I want to claim that it is only by making the self-knowledge and self-affirmation of another person one's own that one is able to grow as a person oneself. I will make use of a two-person model to describe the interpersonal transaction necessary for personal growth. In the model one person is already possessed of self-knowledge and self-affirmation, the other is not, except in the minimal sense of being self-conscious and self-determining. The model is as I have already said, abstract and ideal. We are concerned only with the essential necessary conditions for the development of our capacity for self-enactment. In real life personal growth is a good deal more problematic. Not only do we develop in relation to a number of other persons, but from the time that we become capable of such growth there have already been set up within us certain impediments to it. The normal adult situation is one characterised both by a lack of self-knowledge and defective self-affirmation. And these constitute a vicious circle. Defective self-affirmation makes self-knowledge more difficult to attain and vice versa. But we shall return to the concrete details of the predicament in which persons actually exist when we consider whether personal growth as here described actually occurs. Here we are considering an ideal case of a person who lacks self-knowledge and self-affirmation but in whom no impediments to these have yet been set up.

In order for me, who lack self-knowledge and self-affirmation, to acquire them I must come to know and affirm a person who already has them. And I can only do this insofar as I am empowered to do so by that person himself. This he achieves by his knowledge and affirmation of me.

The key to this interpersonal transaction is the account I have already given of the special place occupied by our deep desires in both self-knowledge and self-affirmation. It must be remembered that these desires are those inherent in human nature as such. And as such they are common to all human persons. Thus it is because self-knowledge is primarily knowledge of these deep desires as they express themselves in me that I can grow in self-knowledge by coming to know them as they express themselves in another.

It is for the same reason that the other's self-knowledge enables him to know me. He is in fact able to know me better than I know myself since, although I may know more details about myself than he does, my awareness of my deep desires is formless and incoherent and does not add up to any real understanding. He on the other hand is able to grasp the essential structure of my character since it underlies all that I do or say, and his view of it is not spoilt either by the bias of superficial desires or a fog of irrelevant detail.

And similarly it is because self-affirmation is primarily affirmation of these deep desires as they reveal themselves in me that I can grow in self-affirmation by affirming them in him. So too, it is his own self-affirmation that enables him to affirm me, even when the actual immaturity or disintegration of my life and my lack of interest in or rejection of him make such affirmation apparently impossible. He knows what I really want, knows it to be good, and so is able to affirm it in spite of the misleading or repulsive forms the misunderstood or devalued desires may give to my emotional life.

Thus far I have been explaining why it is that in coming to know and affirm one who knows and affirms himself I also grow in my capacity to know and affirm myself as well. I must now explain how it is the other person, and he alone, that enables me to do this.

In order to enable me to know and affirm him, the other person has to know and affirm me; it is precisely the sense of being known and affirmed that enables me to both know and affirm him. Since he understands the deep desires of our common nature the other is able to recognise the position they hold in my own life and so is able to understand me, often better than I can myself. He knows what to look for: the essential indicators of my growth or decline. He is moreover able to affirm me more properly than I can affirm myself, since his affirmation of me is focussed on the same desires that are the central object of his own self-affirmation. Admittedly his affirmation of me will take the form of willing my growth, of the development of aspects of my life that are not dominant. Nevertheless to the extent that he truly understands me his affirmation of me will be referred to what is genuinely and uniquely mine.

The other's affirmation of me is, because of the accuracy of his insight, an affirmation of what I really most deeply desire. Because of this it makes for my consent, my consent, that is, to his affirmation of me. And to the extent that I do consent to this, I come to affirm him. This affirmation of him opens the way for me to come to know him as he really is, to share in his own self-knowledge. To the extent that I share in his self-knowledge I come to see myself as he sees me. The self-knowledge that this entails, being primarily a recognition of my own deep desires, opens the way to a greater self-affirmation, and a more whole-hearted consent to his affirmation of me. And thus the transaction continues.

It is important to realise that the initiative in this transaction must come from the person who already has self-knowledge and is self-affirming. It is only his realistic and whole-hearted affirmation of me that can both 'open him up' to be known by me and encourage me to affirm him. His deep desires coincide with mine; his knowledge and affirmation of them enables me to know and affirm them too. A consideration of the nature of these deep desires would make this conclusion even more evident. We shall presently do something in this regard. But the definition of persons that we are working with enables us to identify at least—and right at the centre of the system—a deep desire for self-knowledge and self-affirmation. The other person is only able to affirm me in this way—as I really am and solely for my own sake, because he already has self-knowledge and is truly self-affirming. If he were not his insight into the deep desires of our common nature and his affirmation of them would be defective, and hence the basis for the mutuality and reciprocity that makes the transaction possible would be lacking.

This requirement is so important for turning our account of the necessary conditions for personal growth into an argument for the existence of God that we must examine it very carefully. I have now completed my account of the interpersonal transaction necessary in order to bring about personal growth. We must now see in what sense it entails the existence and causality of a transcendent person.

We should note at the outset that a person who both knows and affirms himself is required as much for the initial stages of personal growth as for the ones that I have been examining in this article. We tend to take for granted the existence of 'grown-ups' in relation to whom children can develop. But grown-ups were not born grown-up. Nor is it enough that they should have merely grown to physical maturity. The child requires, at least to a certain minimal degree, to be recognised and valued as a person if it is to develop the self-consciousness and self-determination definitive of personal existence. And to provide this the parents must, as I have shown, both know and affirm themselves. This could only have been achieved, moreover, in relation to other persons already possessed of self-knowledge and self-affirmation. Who in turn could only have acquired them from others. The conclusion seems inescapable: unless someone somewhere is capable of self-knowledge and self-affirmation without the assistance of others who already are, no self-knowledge or self-affirmation will ever be acquired. If it is true, as the first premise of our argument has it, that human persons depend on other persons in order to grow as persons, then it follows that unless at least one person is not thus dependent, is fully developed as a person without the help of others, then there is no possibility of personal growth occurring at all. Such a person could not of course be a human person since he would transcend that dependence for personal development that characterises all human persons. When we reflect that human persons, as self-enacting, transcend the causal determination of everything but that of other persons, it can be seen that the transcendence attributed to the ultimately sufficient cause of personal growth in us is an extremely radical transcendence indeed. I shall presently argue that it is the transcendence that Christian faith recognises in God.

The logic of our argument is in fact the same as that of the cosmological argument. Our requirement of a transcendent person corresponds to that of an uncaused cause. And in both cases the force of the argument derives from an understanding of the impossibility of a so-called 'infinite regression'. This is so regularly misunderstood that I must explain it in its application to my present argument.

The impossibility in question is not that of a series of causes going back in time without end. There is no reason why there should not be infinitely many causes in the series. What is required rather, for the existence and operation of the whole series, however long, is the existence and causality of another kind of cause altogether, namely one that is uncaused. In a train the last truck is moved by the pull of the second last and so on. But there will be no movement at all, however long the train, if it consists only of trucks. There is needed a different kind of mover, namely an unmoved mover, a locomotive, that can pull without being pulled. It is not a question of pre-existence, of an original cause that is first in time, but of a different order of causality, a transcendent one. This is the logic of the cosmological argument and it is the same as what I am arguing in the personal realm.

If my analysis of the necessary conditions for the development of our capacity for self-enactment is correct, then we depend on the personal influence of one in whom it is already developed. But he in turn can have achieved full development only under the influence of another fully developed person. Hence if the development of this capacity is to occur at all there must be someone somewhere who is not similarly dependent, a fully self-enacting person who is not dependent on anyone else for his self-enactment. Such a person would correspond to the uncaused cause of the cosmological argument. He would, as I have said, be possessed of an independence so complete that not only would he not be subject to the limitations of human nature, but—the capacity for self-enactment being what it is, namely freedom from other causes—he would be free from the influence of all finite causes whatsoever. He would (as we shall see) be transcendent in the sense required by the Christian notion of God as creator. He would of course have to exercise his causality within the realm of finite persons and their relationships with each other. How that is possible is another matter. Nevertheless if our analysis of the necessary conditions for the development of our capacity for self-enactment is sound, then it follows that the causal influence of a transcendent person is required if such development is to take place at all.

A critic of my argument might grant all that I have said about the necessary conditions for personal growth but object that the sort of personal qualities that our analysis requires need not be found all together in one individual. After all we do not in real life develop only in relation to one other person but to many. Could not the necessary ingredients of self-knowledge and self-affirmation be distributed across the whole acquaintance of the developing person? I do not find such a suggestion plausible. It is logically equivalent to the notion that a large number of fairly kind and clever people will constitute a reservoir of extreme kindness and cleverness. I do not think that personal qualities of this sort can be added up in this way. And furthermore, in the case of such fundamental and pervasive qualities as self-knowledge and self-affirmation, I do not see how they could be present in fragments that could be subsequently combined in a single character. Such qualities are aspects of that indivisible whole that is a person's character. They are either present all together, at a certain level of development, or not at all.

Another critic could grant us even this but still object to the suggestion that the 'first cause' of personal growth be fully self-enacting. Full self-knowledge and full self-affirmation might well be ideal goals of personal development, but surely they are not strictly necessary for it to take place. Is it not sufficient that I am able to develop in relation to one who is merely more highly developed than I am? He does not have to be perfect! There are I think two difficulties with such an objection. Firstly it would mean that my personal development would always have a 'ceiling', namely the level of development of the most highly developed person I know. And, apart from the prima facie implausibility of this, such an arbitrary limit would, I shall presently argue, contradict a fundamental dynamism of personal life. Secondly there is the question of how, on this supposition, the most fully developed person got to the level he has if there were not someone at least as fully developed already there. And how did he get there? How did the whole process of personal development get off the ground?

Such replies to our critic may not be conclusive, but I do not think that really matters. As we shall see, there are other grounds for believing that a sufficient cause of personal growth must be fully developed as a person, possessed of full self-knowledge and fully self-affirming. But the purpose of my argument is not to establish this but only that, if personal growth occurs, a transcendent person must exist as its sole sufficient cause.

To conclude our exposition of the argument we must now address ourselves to the question of whether personal growth as I have defined it does in fact occur. It seems to me that my analysis of the necessary conditions for its occurrence gives prima facie support to the common conviction that there is some sense in which persons are able to grow as persons and do often in fact do so. Although my account of the interpersonal transaction necessary to produce personal growth is an abstract one derived from my definition of persons as self-enacting, surely it contains enough material borrowed from experience to support the conviction that personal growth can and does occur more or less in the manner described. Even if this were so, it might be said that that is a very weak way to end an argument for the existence of God, which ought as such to manifest a certain metaphysical rigour. This is a fair point and deserves a response.

I have in fact already compared the logic of my argument to that of the cosmological argument, in order to emphasize the similarity. There is however also a difference. The cosmological argument is based on our experience of causal interaction and dependence. And this is something one cannot reasonably doubt. Causal dependence of this kind is a general feature of our universe; there are no exceptions. The same is not true of personal growth. Not only is personal growth not universally necessary; it is not necessary at all. In fact it even makes sense to doubt whether it ever occurs. Thus, even if it does occur, our grounds for justifiably believing that it does will have a very different logical status from those for assenting to the cosmological argument. If one demands that sort of rigour one is bound to be disappointed. Still, as Aristotle said, it is a mark of an educated man that in every subject he looks for only so much precision 'as nature permits'! He was speaking about ethics but I think his advice applies to our present topic as well. I will accordingly describe three kinds of experience that I consider provide evidence for the justified true belief that personal growth does in fact occur.

The first experience is that of desire, the desire for personal growth. This desire is so ineradicable and so imperious in us that it is difficult to believe that it does not express a fundamental capacity of our nature. Its universality across cultures and historical periods would also seem to indicate a basis in human nature. And if a desire is natural in this way then it would seem to follow that the conditions for its satisfaction must exist. I am not saying that the existence of a natural desire for something is evidence that the desire will be satisfied. But it is evidence that the conditions for its satisfaction do naturally exist.

The existence of suitable nutriment in our environment is a necessary correlate of our desire to eat. And this is true even if most, or even all, people die of starvation. Hence if being a person entails having a desire that only a transcendent being can satisfy then such a being must exist.

It is perhaps difficult to feel the force of this argument as long as one considers the desire precisely as a desire for personal growth. Do we all in fact desire this? Isn't it really merely the fruit of a particular form of western culture? And even there isn't it rather rare? How many of us really desire self-knowledge? I think it is easier to grasp the inevitability and ineradicability of the desire for personal growth if one considers it from the perspective of the growing person. Our account of the necessary conditions for personal growth was that of an objective observer, a third person account. And we identified the knowledge and affirmation of the other as a means to the self-knowledge and self-affirmation that constitute personal growth. In fact that is not how it would have appeared to the persons involved. In actual life one seeks the knowledge and affirmation of others for its own sake. If one replaces the words 'knowledge' and 'affirmation' by 'understanding' and 'love', this becomes clearer; one wants both to be understood and loved, and to understand and love another (or others). More precisely, one wants to be understood and loved by one whom one loves and understands.

Such a desire is surely part of our human nature. But, as our analysis of the interpersonal transaction showed, the knowledge and affirmation of others is inseparable from the knowledge and affirmation of oneself. Whether the knowledge and affirmation of others is the cause of one's own self-knowledge and self-affirmation or its expression, the two cannot exist apart. Hence in desiring the understanding and love of others one is in fact desiring to know and affirm oneself whether one is aware of it or not. One's ultimate desire is to participate in a community of mutual understanding and love, and the necessary condition for this is self-knowledge and self-affirmation. Such community is a historical relation of persons, but it cannot exist except on a foundation of the full development of the capacities of our human nature. So even if one is unaware of a desire to grow as a person it is included in one's desire for true personal communion with others, since if one didn't develop in that way one would not be able to participate properly in such a level of life.

Also included is the desire that the others with whom one is to be in communion have developed their personal powers to the full, since it is only to the extent that they know and affirm themselves that they can truly understand and love others as well.

The desire for personal community with others that I have described is a natural desire in the sense I want to claim. It is one of the 'deep' desires Lawrence speak of. In fact it is arguably the 'deepest' of these deep desires. Certainly it stems from our specifically personal nature. In the actual circumstances of human life it is however often difficult to discern. Any actual human community or relationship involves persons who are not fully developed as persons, in whom therefore various desires are in conflict with the desire for true personal community. In particular the very absoluteness of the desire for personal community and the personal growth that makes it possible, coupled with a lack of self-knowledge and self-affirmation, is what ensures that all sorts of inadequate and illusory substitutes will be found. It is the very imperiousness of the need that ensures people's inability to satisfy it. We desire self-knowledge and so we canonise inadequate self-images, putting them in a position that cannot be questioned. We so want to affirm ourselves to the full that we do so, giving inadequate values our unconditional consent. We want so much to be loved for our own sake that we are unable to love others for theirs. Everyone is in the same situation; each person needs to be understood and loved if he is to be able to love and understand others. What is required if our desire for personal community is to be fulfilled is that someone is able to love without being loved, to understand without being understood. It is the same requirement as that for personal growth, namely the existence and activity in the lives of human persons of a personal power that transcends these limitations. In the case of personal community it is more clearly necessary, since personal community implies not merely our development as persons (to a greater or lesser degree) but our full development. The desire for personal community I have described is not a desire for partial fulfilment of our personal powers but their complete fulfilment in the service of a form of personal communion that is correspondingly complete.

And this is the real reason why the transcendent person must be one who is fully developed as a person, completely self-enacting, perfect in self-knowledge and self-affirmation.

It may be that our re-description of our deep desire for fulfilment as persons has made it appear more truly natural. I hope that is so. But even if it is, and even if the existence of a natural desire implies the existence of the conditions for its satisfaction, is this enough for us to conclude that personal growth does in fact occur? Clearly not. It is enough for us to conclude that an infinite being exists that could bring about personal growth but not that it actually does so. Nevertheless it does seem to me that the experience of the desire for personal communion (and growth), coupled with the judgment that it is indeed natural, entails an understanding of our own nature as persons that is a positive and sufficient basis for the belief that personal growth can be expected to occur and even, in some sense, ought to.

This experience is admittedly a largely negative one. We experience a longing and a lack. Yet the insight into one's personal nature that this can provide if taken seriously, and not dismissed as neurotic or compensatory, is able to create cognitive space for the full and settled conviction that personal growth does actually occur.

This settled conviction grows from the second kind of experience I wish to describe. This is the experience of the ability of others to love us unselfishly and to understand us better than we understand ourselves. It is an experience of their goodness, of the fact that they have already grown to the point where the fulfilment of their personal powers can show itself in relation to us. (A concrete example of this would be the experience of genuine forgiveness.) The unconditional or absolute quality of the goodness manifested in their lives makes itself felt in the trust and certainty they inspire in us. We cannot prove that they are good; yet we are certain that they are. Our certainty shows itself in the determination that whatever happens to us, whatever choices we are offered, we want to be 'on their side', to have a similar character, to be the sort of people they would want to love.

This experience is also an experience of self-affirmation. Even if it coexists with all sorts of contrary behaviour and incompatible desires its unique character shows itself in its moral force in our lives, its sense of an unconditional obligation. If we betray its promptings we feel shame and remorse.

Finally there is the experience of communion with other persons, a communion that is felt to bear the sign of personal fulfilment, and which—since we are capable of sharing in and enjoying it, is also an assurance of our own. Admittedly such an experience is difficult to describe. It is always transitory, a matter of 'hints followed by guesses'. It can however reveal its character by its overwhelming effect on the whole character of our emotional life. It shows itself in the dissipation of fear, especially the fear of death. We feel empowered by something 'stronger than death', a death-transcending life—and hence the presence of something transcendent, of one who has this life and can share it with us.

These three kinds of experience are not in fact unrelated to each other. In the order in which I have described them they are related to one another in a progression of depth and comprehensiveness. The final, most interior and inclusive, emotional experience cannot occur without the consent embodied in the second. In the second experience the will is dominant; we make an option for what we see as good. But such an option includes, even if it does not actually follow on, a vision or understanding of what is genuinely desirable. And this is what is predominant in the initial experience of lack and need. The three experiences together ground a total personal attitude—cognitive, volitional and emotive—that includes the belief that personal growth occurs. This belief is thus simply the cognitive effect of growth having actually occurred in us. For the person concerned it is conclusive and morally compelling. He needs no argument to justify his belief and no argument could change it. And in the nature of the case one could not ask for more. Personal growth is not necessary or universal. But when it does occur it includes the justified true belief that it does.

What then is the cognitive status of a belief in the occurrence of personal growth? The peculiarity of such a belief is that the evidence for it can only be the experience of its occurrence in the person of the believer. There is thus no neutral way of a third person checking up on this that is detached from personal growth in himself. I do not think that this undermines the rationality of such a belief. All strictly personal knowledge of other persons entails, I would want to claim, the personal involvement of the knower. It does however prevent any quasi-scientific justification of it. The only good grounds for belief in the occurrence of personal growth is its occurrence. Each of us must verify this occurrence for himself in himself. What the whole of the above argument has shown is that if we do, then we are also committed to a belief in the existence and activity of a strictly transcendent person who alone is sufficient to cause personal growth in us.

It seems to me that belief in the occurrence of personal growth is in fact a minimal and anonymous form of religious faith—at least as this is understood in Catholic theology. Its object is not merely the existence but the actual active presence of an infinite person. As such it is the cognitive aspect of a total personal attitude that is directed towards a personal community made possible by this activity and this presence. This has a striking formal similarity to Christian faith. Insofar as it is merely belief in the occurrence of growth it is perhaps not fully-formed as faith, since that would have as its object not merely personal growth but the fullness of personal community. Still the fact of personal growth is an indication of the possibility of personal community. A justified true belief in the reality of a personal community of human persons with one another and its transcendent cause can only be based on its occurrence. And this is what Christians do believe took place in the experience the followers of Jesus had of his resurrection.

Having concluded the exposition of my argument for the existence of God I wish to add some remarks by way of explaining why I feel the need to present what I regard as a new argument and why, since my argument is so lacking in logical rigour, I have chosen the argument that I have. In the course of these remarks I hope to clarify the conception of God to which my argument concludes, as well as to explain what I take to be the function of arguments for the existence of God in general.

What precisely is it that one wants from an argument for the existence of God? If one simply wants to know whether or not a transcendent being exists as the cause of our existence then any of the classical arguments would suffice. I am not one of those who feel that they all fail of their purpose. It seems to me however that one ought to want—and people who go into the question of the existence of God normally do want—to know more, namely whether there exists a being capable of making us happy. If there is anything common to all conceptions of God it surely is the notion of a being with power sufficient to make us happy. No religion worthy of the name recognises a God unable to do that. Thus even if we are convinced that a transcendent being exists we will want to know if such a being is capable of making us happy, if (in other words) he is worthy of being our God.

Western philosophy, having grown up in the milieu of Biblical religion, Christian, Jewish and Islamic, has taken a certain conception of God for granted, a sort of highest common factor of a Christian, Jewish and Muslim conception. It is self-evident that the God of these religions is understood to be capable of satisfying our deepest desires. It is not similarly evident that the uncaused cause or the supreme being of the philosophical arguments is. It might I suppose be thought that being supreme or the cause of the universe it could do anything it pleased. But does even that follow? A strict notion of the uncaused cause or a supreme being is so spare as to give one next to no idea of what one could expect of it in the sphere in which one is really interested, namely that of our desires. In the 'ages of faith' when the classical arguments for the existence of God were formulated it was taken for granted that the being that appeared in their conclusions was the sort of being that could satisfy our deepest desires. In a secular age it is not. Now a good argument must show both that a transcendent being is necessary to satisfy our deepest desires and also that such a one exists. In an age in which the connection between metaphysics and religion has been broken it is always possible to agree with, for instance, the cosmological argument and still ask 'So what?' The importance of the existence of an uncaused cause is not immediately evident. That should not be possible with a good argument for the existence of God; it is not possible with the argument I have put forward here.

Clearly the transcendent person of my argument is capable of satisfying our deepest desires, at least as I have defined them. But is he transcendent in the sense required by the Christian conception of God? Assuming that my argument is sound, does it really demonstrate the existence of God in the Christian sense? It is my view that it does, and indeed does so better than the traditional arguments.

Christian faith conceives of God as our creator. As such he transcends the universe in a peculiarly radical way. The nature of this transcendence is perhaps best brought out by the notion of incommensurability. The universe and its creator are incommensurable in every way. They cannot be opposed to or compared with each other. They cannot even be added together so as to make two. Real plurality always presupposes some category that can be shared. You can add one apple to another because both are apples. You can even add an apple to an orange because both are fruit. In the last resort you can add anything in the universe to anything else because both are things. In the case of the creator, however, this fundamental community does not exist. He is not part of the universe, does not exist as things in the universe (or the universe as a whole) exist. Hence you cannot add the universe and its creator and make two.

Another way in which the radical nature of God's transcendence of the universe is traditionally brought out is by seeing it in relation to the notion of immanence. As referred to God the two notions are complementary. Both refer to the peculiar causal dependence of the universe on its creator, namely its dependence on him for everything it has or is or does. To say that God transcends the universe is to deny that he is part of it or shares any of its properties; to say that he is immanent in it is to say that he is the cause of its existence at each moment that it exists, and that all the reality it has derives from him.

We must now tackle the question of whether the conception of transcendence required by my argument measures up to this.

In my earlier article on the initial stages of personal growth I drew attention to a distinctive feature of the interpersonal transaction required for the production of self-consciousness and self-determination. This was the fact that the child's capacity for self-enactment increased in direct and not inverse proportion to the strictly personal influence of the mother. When it is remembered that the notion of self-enactment implies freedom from determination by external causes, such a conclusion appears contradictory. It certainly contradicts our common notion of causality, reinforced by that of the physical sciences. According to that notion in order to accomplish any finite work the more that is done by one cause the less is required of any other. If two oxen pull a plough and one ox does three-quarters of the work, the other ox need do only a quarter. Such a mathematically quantifiable causality is certainly contradicted by the causality apparent in our interpersonal model. Nevertheless if our account of the interpersonal transaction is correct it is precisely because of (a certain kind of) effort on the part of the mother that the child is enabled to act freely. The one's causality does not prevent but produces the freedom of the other. The apparent paradox is removed however if it is indeed the case that in such an interpersonal transaction the causality of a transcendent person is at work since, as has just been pointed out, such causality would be incommensurable with and so in no way opposed to or in competition with that of finite persons. It would in fact be creative of their personal act in all its integrity in the same way as it is creative of their natural capacity to act in this way.

This feature of what I would like to call 'personal causality' is even more marked in the transaction in which self-knowledge and self-affirmation is produced. This is the model case of personal growth in all its fullness. And here it appears that the more one is influenced by another in a strictly personal way, the more one comes to gain possession of oneself, the more completely self-enacting one becomes. The more I am affirmed by the other, the more I am able to affirm myself; the more completely the other knows me, the more I am able to know myself. One could even formulate a 'law of personal causality' thus, that persons develop in direct and not inverse proportion to the strictly personal influence on them of other persons. A condition of such a law holding however would be that the system of interpersonal relations includes a person who is transcendent in the manner of the Christian God. Thus my argument not only concludes to a conception of God that measures up to that of Christian faith. Such a conception is also implied by the account of personal growth on which it is based. In fact it is such a crucial feature of it that one could regard an account such as this not simply as grounds for the belief in the existence of a transcendent person but also as a model of how such a person could be expected to operate within the lives of finite persons and even, in general, in relation to all his creatures.

This latter point seems to me especially important. The 'personal causality' that characterises the above account of personal growth seems a much better model for the relation between God and us than the common physical model. In fact I do not see how the traditional problem of the relationship between God's grace and our freedom can be solved except through coming to understand the kind of personal causality revealed by our description. The traditional problem associated with human freedom is at its sharpest in relation to God. Because of course all our actions are caused by God. Anything God does not cause, in all its reality and operation, simply does not exist or operate, since he is its creator. No sense at all can be given to the common attitude that sees the creator as causing our existence but not our activity as well. Such a view is a consequence of thinking of creation solely in regard to the beginning of things, and not as the permanent relationship between God and the universe. In this fundamental sense we can never be free of God, nor would we ever want to be. But our model of inter-personal relations can show how God's causal action on us in fact creates the real freedom that we do have as persons, namely freedom in relation to other creatures, other persons included. If it is the case that the strictly personal influence of other persons on us augments rather than diminishes our freedom of action then God's influence on us in our actual lives, his saving grace, can be understood as the limiting case of such personal causality. In fact the personal causality of other human persons is simply the created form that God's causality takes in bringing about our growth towards our fulfilment as persons.

Our interpersonal model for the activity of God in bringing about (in fact creating) the development of our freedom, is also a useful model for the relationship of creation as such. The paradox inherent in the notion of the creation of freedom brings out the radical transcendence of the Christian God in a far better way than such physical analogies as the potter and his pot.

There is another advantage that my argument has over the classical arguments. They are all in a general sense 'cosmological', that is they were elaborated in a philosophical climate that was realist in a broad sense, concerned with reality as such, the nature of things and their causes. Metaphysics was, precisely, meta-physics. After the Renaissance philosophy underwent a shift of focus, becoming increasingly centred on humanity, especially humanity as the subject of knowledge. Hence the anthropological slant of modern philosophy. Against this shift in background the usefulness of the classical arguments needs to be re-assessed.

It is always the function of a philosophical argument for the existence of God to tell us more about our own experience than about God. I find no fault with the austere agnosticism of the classical proofs in this respect. Rightly understood they are all different ways of revealing in the very fabric of our most ordinary experience the mysterious presence of a different dimension altogether. The result of such an intellectual exercise is not that we now see something new that we hadn't seen before but that we see all the old things in a different way. The cosmological argument, for instance, reveals the mysterious depths in our ordinary experience of the physical world—not the spurious mysteriousness of infinite time and infinite space but the real mysteriousness of contingency, the lack of self-sufficiency. And in so doing it opens up a place for religion and religious experience in the midst of our ordinary experience of the world.

The argument from personal growth performs a similar function and, to my mind, performs it better, since the experience with which it deals is our experience of ourselves—and we are after all the subjects of religion and religious experience. In it I want to reveal the mysterious depths of our personal natures and our community with other persons, not the spurious mystery of biological or psychological complexity, but the genuine mystery of the presence and power of something transcendent in our personal relationships. Although my argument concludes to a transcendent cause of personal growth that is capable of satisfying our deepest desires, its real point is to throw light on our own natures and the nature of those relations with others in which we are able to grow as persons.

To put it like that is perhaps misleading, since it suggests that it is not my aim to argue for the existence of God. In fact the two aspects hang together. It is only insofar as we come to understand the true nature of persons and personal growth that we realise the mysteriousness of our ordinary human relationships and community. And it is this mysteriousness that is the empirical root of an intellectual assent to the reality of a transcendent person in our lives. The better we understand persons and personal growth the more convinced we shall be of the activity, and therefore of the existence, of one who is not limited in any way as we are and who is the sole sufficient cause of our growth and community and therefore entitled to be recognised as God.

I am often struck by a disparity between contemporary theology and contemporary philosophy, even philosophy of religion. It is not simply that theology is concrete whereas philosophy is abstract. It is rather that, even when both are dealing with the question of God, they are doing so in so different a context and with such dissimilar interests, that it scarcely seems that they are dealing with the same object. In particular it is the case that one can be a highly acclaimed philosopher of religion without any interest in (or even apparently any understanding of) religion as such. In speaking of an interest in religion I do not mean this or that religion but that sphere of human life that could be fairly called religious and the features of human nature that underlie it. I have put forward the argument I have in the belief that the understanding of God in theology and in philosophy must be connected. One is more concerned with the data of human history, the other with that of human nature. But both are merely different perspectives on the same single human experience.

In theology and philosophy of religion we have to do with two complementary forms of wisdom that cannot properly be developed apart. The conviction that underlies my present argument is that the philosophical wisdom most relevant to deal with the question of God in a philosophical way is an understanding of the 'deep' desires of our nature and the way in which other persons can help us to satisfy them. The human sciences can of course contribute to this understanding, as indeed can literature of all kinds. There remains however a task that philosophy, in both its metaphysical and ethical competence, alone can fulfil, namely the rational justification of the truth and the importance of belief in God as the one who alone can bring human nature to its fulfilment.

From the point of view of theology it could be objected that the argument I have presented in this article goes beyond the boundaries of philosophy. After all it concludes to God not merely as the cause of our existence but as the cause of our fulfilment. And this is precisely the perspective of theology; can there possibly be a natural knowledge—a knowledge not founded on faith—of God's historical activity? Because the foundation of my argument is the affirmation that personal growth actually does occur this does imply knowledge of the actual historical activity of God and not merely knowledge of his natural causality. And this sort of activity is what is commonly known as grace, reckoned as supernatural and so beyond the scope of our natural cognitive powers. Personal growth, in my understanding of it, is such a comprehensive notion and since it entails the fulfilment of our distinctively personal powers and the completeness of personal community with others, it is virtually synonymous with what theology understands as 'salvation'. Does my argument thus provide us with rationally justified knowledge of salvation, either in general or even in particular cases?

As I have already admitted, our knowledge of personal growth—whether our own or that of others—has certain peculiar features. It is only available to those who have in fact grown as persons. And it exists always and only as a part of a comprehensive personal attitude that includes volitional and emotional elements as well as purely cognitive ones. In fact this comprehensive attitude has the same basic character as what theology knows as 'faith', save that its object is not the person of Jesus. The affirmation of the reality of personal growth is thus a form—anonymous if you like—of Christian faith. That is not a preposterous idea if it is accepted that personal growth can in fact only occur as the effect of the personal causality of a transcendent person. And it does not therefore imply that such an affirmation is arbitrary or irrational. It is certainly not scientific, but I hope my descriptions of the conditions under which it can be made, show it as coherent and reasonable in the context of the personal knowledge of persons.

There is a great deal more that could be said concerning the way in which persons know one another that would be relevant to this topic. But I cannot do that here. I am sure however that one must do away with the chimerical either/or between reason and faith, where reason means only science or logic and faith means miraculous illumination. Reason and faith, nature and grace, cannot be separated in reality as their concepts can be distinguished in theory. What we have to try and understand is a single phenomenon, a single history of human nature, of personal growth (or decline). Natural insight into the nature and occurrence of personal growth and the understanding of faith cannot be discontinuous; nor can grace bring it about except within the integrity of human nature.

Such an understanding of the relation between faith and reason, grace and nature is, as far as I can see, thoroughly traditional. There are in addition two theological indications that encourage me to hope that my argument doesn't confuse philosophy with theology. The first is the doctrine that all genuine moral or spiritual virtue in persons is the fruit of grace. This doctrine has sometimes been interpreted to mean that unless we know that a person possesses grace (because he explicitly confesses Jesus as his personal saviour, or whatever) we cannot tell whether his apparent holiness is the real thing or not. I cannot accept such an interpretation. I understand it in what I take to be the orthodox sense, namely that insofar as we are able to discern real goodness in a person, we are to that extent able to claim him to be in a state of grace. Human goodness wherever it shows itself is a sign of grace. And that is just what my argument claims to show.

The second theological vindication of my method in this article is the doctrine that all persons are given sufficient grace for an ultimate personal union with God. I understand this doctrine as implying that grace is in a sense a 'natural' gift to human persons. The doctrine of original sin notwithstanding, each human individual is born in a state of grace, in the sense that his personal nature is open to the presence and the power of God. And God's grace exists as an immediate and continuous pressure upon him through his normal relationships with other persons and the whole personal milieu. Grace can of course be resisted. But it cannot cease to exist as the ever-present dynamism of the personal relationships in which 'we live and move and have our being.'

This presence of grace in the normal circumstances of personal life is the 'normal' state of affairs in human history. And this is just what my argument presupposes and, in a sense, describes. What I would most like my argument to do is to provide a link between normal and religious experience, especially in the heart of our experience of other persons.

(1987)

Chapter Twenty-One
Understanding Forgiveness

Forgiveness does occur. I wish to reflect on the offering and accepting of forgiveness for the light it throws on human nature and its needs. It is my view that the familiar interpersonal transaction of forgiveness is the most typical form of personal growth, both on the part of the one who offers and on the part of the one who accepts, involving as it does the most central human capacities and the enduring constants of our interpersonal relations. Not that forgiveness is always, or even relatively frequently, given and received, or given, or received, but it is always a possibility and, as I hope to show, a demand of our human nature. And as such it is a revelation of a certain unlimitedness as well as the finiteness of that nature.

The better to understand the nature of forgiveness and to distinguish its various elements let us have in mind a concrete case. In order to highlight what is essential it will be a case of perfect forgiveness, and the acceptance of forgiveness will be correspondingly complete. This will of course have an adverse effect on the realism of our treatment but that can't be helped. The concrete details of our case-history are intended simply as a stimulus to the imagination and more powerful imaginations than mine will be able to provide their own.

Here then is our story: A much-loved colleague of mine are the only applicants short-listed for the same position. Through devious machinations whose details do not concern us he manages to convince them of a certain falsehood that leads them to prefer him to me, whereas if the truth of the matter were known I would have been chosen. Afterwards I discover what he has done.

Eventually I come to forgive him and he to accept my forgiveness. Let us now consider the nature of this transaction and the conditions of its possibility (both logical and psychological). Let us consider first the offering of forgiveness. I will in what follows refer to myself as the victim and to my colleague as the enemy.

First there is my enemy's act. What precisely is it that makes it a matter for forgiveness? Harm is not enough; there must be ill-will and it must be directed at me in person if it is I who am to forgive. The harm to me, though it is necessary if there is to be matter for forgiveness, is an insufficient condition if it is not the end at which the harmful action aims.

Ill-will, on the other hand, by itself is also insufficient. It must at least be expressed, by speech or instrumentality, both in order to reveal the character of the intention and as the final stage of consent to it. The revelation of ill-will, constitutes the necessary minimum of harm to require forgiveness. For to be aware of ill-will directed at me is in fact to suffer harm of a sort.

Knowledge of the ill-will directed at me is only one part of the knowledge I require if perfect forgiveness is to be possible. I require also knowledge of the history and character of my enemy, of the degree of ill-will and the circumstances of the act. In general it would be true to say the fuller this knowledge is, the greater the possibility (and the necessity) of complete forgiveness. Not by way of providing extenuation in either the background or the circumstances of the act. Extenuation would of course simply lessen the need for forgiveness. But rather that my forgiveness may be offered precisely to the person of my enemy in all his historical particularity on the occasion of that very act.

We come now to the most obvious condition for forgiveness, the volitional and emotional response of mine to the harmful act and the person who performed it. At first sight a condition of this sort appears to be very different from those already discussed. It is subjective, they objective. It is psychological, they are logical. It is contingent, they are necessary. But these oppositions are only apparent. We are not concerned only with the conditions that make the concept of forgiveness logically applicable, but with the total personal transaction including what is psychologically normal or even necessary for it to take place. For instance, in regard to the conditions already established, of harm and ill-will, it is not enough that they be present; they must also be known or at least judged to be present by the victim. Indeed, if we were only concerned to analyse the offering of forgiveness, it would not matter whether they were really present as long as the victim judged them to be. But because we are interested in the total transaction in its typical—though in this case abstractly perfect—structure, feelings as well as facts are relevant. Feelings are facts too in the actual performance of the transaction.

So I have made up my mind concerning the reality of harm and the degree of ill-will. The first consequence of this is detestation of the person corresponding to the degree of ill-will I believe him to have towards me. To the extent that my judgment allows I oppose and repudiate his will. My own attitude of will is one that absolutely opposes his. I would that it had never been and insofar as it persists I will its annihilation. Secondly, I detest the act itself in both its universal aspect, as something objectively unjust, and in its particular effects on me. I sorrow at the deprivation and diminution of the possibilities of life and would restore, if it were possible, my life's disrupted order. This double detestation of my will has the emotional concomitant of the desire to punish. And this also has two, though intimately related, aspects: retribution and vengeance. The only proper response to ill-will is its destruction, and the demand for retribution is the first step in this attack. It is a gesture towards that depth of my enemy's will where the ill-will is rooted for the purpose of its destruction. The means is harm to him, harm necessarily in excess of what I have suffered. Vengeance, which is the vehicle of retribution, demands this excess since the harm I suffered was the expression of ill-will against my person, and I am not entitled to respond in similar fashion (that is, with ill-will). This is the essence of vengeance.

The picture we must entertain of my response to my enemy's act is of an attitude of repudiation and disgust focused on his person through the circumstances and character of his act, but which nevertheless is entirely devoid of ill-will. It is easy enough to see that a purely moral detestation can be devoid of ill-will. But I wish to picture the appropriate response to moral evil as one that involves the whole person, even those levels of life that usually appear only in drama and not in philosophy. Even vengeance is part of an appropriate response to evil, and not to feel the desire for vengeance is not to recognise the evil fully for what it is, or to recognise it in a purely notional way. Insofar as my will itself is really opposed to evil, movements of retribution and vengeance must be included in my response. Individual psychological characteristics may of course rule out such emotions, but that would point to a lack of psychological integration on my part. The appropriate disruption of my emotional life caused by the desire for retribution and vengeance is not something pathological but entirely 'natural' as a response to an evil act. But as such it is also part of what needs to be forgiven. I should not have to suffer such disruption. Nevertheless the integrity and indeed the legitimacy of my response depends on the fact that it is without ill-will. What precisely this entails and what are the conditions of its possibility I hope to make clear in due course.

We have now described the conditions that make perfect forgiveness a possibility for the victim. And they have turned out to be almost wholly negative. So they pose this crucial question: how is the transition achieved from the almost wholly negative attitude of will that has been described to the wholly positive one of forgiveness? We have now reached the point where the transition must take place. Let us see what it must comprise.

First it must be noted that it is forgiveness that is to be achieved, not forgetting. It is surely true that one of the effects of forgiveness is something like forgetting. But forgetting is no part of the act of forgiveness itself. On the contrary I must be explicitly aware of what precisely I am forgiving my enemy for if forgiveness is to be offered, and he must be sure of this if it is to be accepted. Further, the positive activity in forgiveness is not that of overcoming my anger or regret about the effects of his action on me. There is no reason why these attitudes may not remain indefinitely. For although the matter of forgiveness is the evil act and its effects on me, the object of forgiveness is the person of my enemy. Forgiveness is an essentially person-oriented movement of the will. This is why forgiveness has nothing to do with resignation, implying as that does the passive acquiescence in evil. Nor has it anything to do with a refusal to punish the offender. I may well lose interest in punishment once I have forgiven my enemy; on the other hand I may decide that a certain punishment is in his best interest. But the whole issue of punishment is in fact secondary. Punishment is not even considered unless ill-will is present, so if it is the person of my enemy who is to be forgiven then it is the evil quality of his will that is the only ultimate concern of my forgiving act.

As a guide to our grappling with the problem of the transition from negative to positive attitudes of will in the moment of forgiveness I want to describe my final attitude towards my enemy once he has been forgiven.

I have forgiven him completely. This is equivalent to saying that I wholly will his personal fulfilment and happiness. I use the word will not to exclude feeling but to emphasize the way in which, in such an attitude, I put myself at the disposal of or dedicate myself to my enemy's good. As far as his genuine well-being is concerned, as I judge it to be, I wish to promote, further and maintain it, desire it when absent, sorrow in its loss, rejoice in its presence. In a word I identify myself in all my parts and powers with it. This is a description of the love of friendship as defined by Aristotle and Aquinas: to will good to someone in the most far-reaching way. It is, let us assume, the initial attitude I had towards my colleague before he became my enemy. What is it that now permits us to identify it with forgiveness? Just this, that its immediate formal cause is his evil act. If forgiveness is to bear the fullest weight it is capable of, then it is in the hostile act itself and nowhere else that we must look for its specifying ground and motive. His deliberate intention to do me harm must become the cause of my regained love for him.

The clue to the solution of this paradox is in my attitude towards my colleague before the murder. It was as we have said one of pure love of friendship as described above. This love is the steady dedicated willing of his good. And then I am confronted by a revelation of his deliberate ill-will towards me. I have various motives, as we have seen, for repudiating the act. My judgment of it as evil however must bear ultimately on the quality of my enemy's will. And here, in the case we have constructed, is a peculiar source of suffering. To the degree that I genuinely will my enemy's good I will suffer in the revelation of this evil quality. A peculiar sort of suffering indeed, and one that is perhaps rather rare. But one should not doubt its reality and intensity. Imagine the person you love most in the world turning against you with deliberate malice. The horror and pain of such a revelation would be of a different order to any caused by the effects of his hostile act. The more evil I judge him to be, the more I will suffer on his behalf. And this suffering is the essential foundation of forgiveness. It is the suffering of compassion. The meeting of the love of friendship and the detestation of evil in a single object, namely my enemy's hostile act, is what makes up this compassion. His ill-will certainly does him harm and I suffer in this. That is one side of compassion, the negative side. The positive side is pity, an other-centred movement of sorrow. This is the necessary foundation for forgiveness.

In all this it is important to be quite clear about the objects of love and hate in this transition and how their meeting is the foundation of a single coherent attitude. It is no good postulating a general benevolence coupled to a particular detestation. If it is a particular act that is to be forgiven then both the love and hate must have that act as their specifying object for forgiveness to result. It is not enough, for instance, to make a distinction between the act that I repudiate and other acts of my enemy, actions, inclinations and habits, for which I love him, and see forgiveness as merely balancing the one against the rest and allowing the rest to prevail in my will. For forgiveness must be specified by the hostile act itself. Nevertheless the traditional notion of hating the sin while loving the sinner does indicate the place where I consider the solution to the problem is to be found. My enemy's act is a revelation of his will and ultimately of himself. And my forgiveness, though necessarily focused on the act itself, is ultimately directed at him. A distinction between act and person is necessary. Yet for it to be possible to love a person while hating the ill-will revealed by a hostile act, in even a notional, much less a truly personal, way, it is necessary that the act reveal more than merely malice. It must reveal something good. Why is this necessary? Because insofar as the act reveals only ill-will, loving the person in the sense of willing their good means simply that one wills them to change. Insofar as a single act reveals a person there are three possibilities. One could idly wish that they were different persons who would act differently; that is mere fancy. One could wish that they didn't exist—in an act that was the expression of pure ill-will it seems to me that this is all that one could will. Or one could will them to change. Insofar as this third alternative is different from the other two it presupposes something in the act that is capable of development for the good of the person concerned, a potentiality, that is, for good. It is this that is the object of one's love.

It must be remembered in all this that in talking of ill-will we are concerned with the centre of the will, that which is most of all the origin of a person's acts. So we are talking of the person himself. If it were the case that a person's will, and so the person, was wholly specified by ill-will, forgiveness would really be impossible. The question at once is raised as to whether this is possible, and the answer must be in the negative for the reason set out below.

We have arrived at the conclusion that if forgiveness is to be accomplished there must be something in the evil act that can be legitimately valued and so fostered or developed for my enemy's good, since forgiveness, as it is an expression of love, ultimately has this as its aim. If my enemy wholly wills the ill-will in the act, then forgiveness is impossible. Therefore if forgiveness is to be possible in every case, even the most extreme, he cannot wholly will the evil act. If no object of any evil act can wholly determine or unify the will then there is always something left over as it were, or some division, that leaves room for goodness.

To say that there is division in the will, which is the self-conscious origin of a deliberately chosen act, is to point to division in the person himself. If it is impossible for him wholly to will a particular act, it can only be because his will is in opposition to a natural dynamism that expresses itself in all his acts but does not find an adequate object in any. To call such a dynamism natural is to specify it as good. What precisely it aims at is difficult to say. In a purely formal way we could say that it aimed at the exercise of a choice and the performance of an act that was the product of a completely unified will, integrating all the powers and desires and habits of the person, at something that was absolutely good. Whether such a capacity, dynamism, deep desire, for an unlimited good exists in us as part of our human nature is a good question. If our account of forgiveness implies that forgiveness is always a possibility, and hence that a wholly evil will is an impossibility, it suggests an affirmative answer. At any rate it suffices to identify the opening for forgiveness as a necessary division in the subjective springs of the act. To the extent that each act of a person is the expression of a natural dynamism towards the perfection of that person's capacities precisely as an agent capable of choice and action, and so of an ultimate unification of volition in an wholly adequate object, there is always open the possibility of forgiveness when his acts contradict or destroy the unification of his will.

In other words I have to be able to make the Socratic distinction between what my enemy *really* wanted to achieve in his harmful act, and what he thought he wanted.

Wherever there is forgiveness there must be a dynamism in the evil act itself that qualifies the ill-will with its ever-present pressure for the integrity of the person and his will.

To sum up then: I am able to value something revealed in my enemy's act and thus to will his good as aimed at by that very act. This loving identification with him and his own personal fulfillment is the movement of forgiveness. I suffer his deprivation of good in the division of his will and will that it be overcome. One could say that compassion at his self-destruction, containing as it does the positive power of will for his good, overcomes my hatred of his evil will and its hostile act, and my anger and sorrow at its effects.

So forgiveness is achieved. There is a change of heart in me insofar as I discern in my enemy's hostile act the deeper desire for an object capable of wholly unifying the will, a dynamism for an unlimited good. Why should such a revelation move me so? We must postpone the answer to such a question. But it must be remembered that in the example we have set up I am entirely without ill-will. The anger, the repudiation, consequent on my enemy's act does not alter this condition. So I will my enemy's good throughout. It is the possibility of directing this love at something in his evil act that makes my settled will forgiveness. So my change of heart is not a radical change in my will, it is merely the discovery of an appropriate object at a deeper level in my enemy. Nevertheless the alteration in actual attitude and emotion is enormous.

To see forgiveness in terms of the movement of the will consequent upon an insight into the desires of my enemy embodied in his evil act explains also why forgiveness cannot be completed in a subjective alteration of disposition. It cannot stop short at the achievement of an inner attitude but, because its motive is my enemy's good, naturally issues in an act that attempts to bring it about. Is there a general form that such an act must take? Of course there is: it is the revelation to him of my forgiveness. It is precisely his ill-will towards me that requires forgiveness. Hence the revelation of my will for his good is the first step towards its achievement. Whatever his good actually consists in, I have committed myself to the attainment of it. So if he comes to consent to my love of him, having discerned my good will, he will be in fact opening himself once again to his own genuine good. The ill-will that causes the fatal division in his will, will be replaced by another attitude. The motive of my revelation of forgiveness is precisely to overcome the division in his will by removing the ill-will, not for my sake primarily but for his. By revealing my attitude of love I reveal that he has specious grounds for ill-will. Of course because my love in this case takes the form of forgiveness my judgment of his hostile act is also revealed. And I will that he come to share that too. By revealing my judgment of his act and my identification with his good I show him that his ill-will towards me is a hatred of his own good too.

How can such a revelation take place? I have written as though it were a thought-out technique of a therapeutic kind, as though it were the object of a deliberate decision on my part additional to and consequent upon the forgiveness it is intended to reveal. That may happen in particular cases but in fact in all cases of forgiveness there is a natural means of the revelation of the attitude without which forgiveness is not complete. This is simply the suffering that I undergo as a result of my compassion. Insofar as my enemy understands this suffering, both my repudiation of his ill-will and my will for his good, are revealed. This suffering, and especially its coexistence together with the original suffering caused me by his hostile act, is the natural revelation of forgiveness. It is essentially a private affection but issues naturally in an outward act, ideally an act of some actual self-sacrifice for him. Here both the suffering and the pity, which are the negative and positive parts of compassion, become visible. As such they can be the effective sign of forgiveness, and an invitation to repentance on my enemy's part.

This completes our analysis of the offering of forgiveness. We have now to consider the acceptance of forgiveness and the conditions that make it possible. What are the different elements involved in the acceptance of forgiveness and what sort of transition must I make (I am now the enemy) if my acceptance of it is to be complete?

First of all I must come to know that I have been forgiven. And ideally, if my acceptance of forgiveness is to be as complete as possible, I must have full knowledge of my victim's mind. We will not go through the list again. Instead we note that my access to it is barred by my ill-will. The recognition of the truth of his judgment of me, a truth that repudiates my will, as well as of his will for my good, requires good-will. Therefore if my ill-will is pure I am shut off from the revelation of forgiveness. We have suggested that there can be no such pure ill-will, but at any rate the purer the ill-will the more difficult it will be to understand my victim's self-sacrifice on my behalf (and hence his compassion and his good will). I will be possessed by bias. But insofar as my will is not wholly determined by ill-will there is an opening through which objectivity can shine.

So I must come to know his judgement of my act and will, as well as his good will and compassion, if it is truly *his* forgiveness that I accept. And then I must be able to make his judgement of me and my act my own. I must share his judgement of my ill-will. This is a necessary first step towards the contrition that is the heart of repentance. But it is only a first step. It is insufficient because by itself self-condemnation produces only regret. I judge myself to be evil and wish I wasn't. I recognise my responsibility for my act and am sorry for its consequences. But it is only when I come to share in my victim's judgement *that I did not wholly will* the evil that I did, that I can achieve that remorse that is the heart of contrition. For it is only when one realises that one did not really or wholly or in the last resort *want* to do what one has now come to repudiate that one can feel remorse. One has to recognise one's selfdestruction of one's own will. The remorse that follows is the negative side of a willing of the lost good *as good*. This is what makes it a form of suffering and why without it contrition is impossible.

Let us now consider the actual movement of my will (that constitutes remorse) under the influence of what my victim has revealed. Knowledge of and sharing in his judgement of my act and ill-will is a necessary condition for remorse. But remorse can only be actually achieved when I share in his compassion. Indeed remorse is nothing other than a sharing in my victim's compassion. The object of the attitude is the same—the good (my own) I really want but which I wilfully destroyed—and the suffering at its deprivation are identical. The only difference is in the persons. If he suffers in willing my good in my evil act it is compassion, if I do it is remorse. And remorse is to contrition as compassion is to forgiveness, as negative included in positive. Contrition is the remorseful consent to the love that is the positive foundation of forgiveness. Thus, unlike remorse, but like pity, it is other-centred. It is a sharing in my victim's will for my good that is revealed in his forgiveness. Because knowing that he has forgiven me includes knowing that he wills my good precisely as aimed at by my hostile act, (that is he loves me precisely as the performer of *that* act) I am presented with the actual dynamism towards goodness that was present together with the ill-will in the act. It is what he loves in me and it is mine. Acceptance of his forgiveness is thus consent to the dynamism of mine that is opposed and obscured by the ill-will. It is not a notional act but a movement of the will. To the extent that I allow myself to be forgiven, I accept my victim's love, his will for my good, and, in so doing, *will* it for the first time. My consent to my own good is thus mediated by my consent to his will for my good. Contrition is always derived from another and regards the other. What makes possible my acceptance of forgiveness, and the consequent transference of good-will is of course precisely the residual dynamism towards what is good that was in opposition to the ill-will of the act. If that did not remain then my attitude would not be open to change. If 1 had wholly wanted to do what I did I would continue to do so. As it is I am able to respond to forgiveness since my victim's will for me coincides with my own actual deep inclination. Admittedly this identification is complete only if my victim's will is pure, and perhaps it never is. Still a wholly good will is not a logically contradictory notion as is pure ill-will. In our example the victim does indeed will my good, and to the degree that he does so I am able to identify completely with him.

The transformation of attitude involved in the acceptance of forgiveness is more extended yet. Contrition, though often spoken of as though it were primarily a form of sorrow at one's own fault, is in fact essentially a sorrow directed at one's victim. One is sorry for what one did to him, sorry 'for him' as it is said. I have come to will his good precisely through accepting his good will for me. There are two moments in my acceptance of his love: the first is self-oriented and involves the repudiation of my ill-will, the second is other-oriented and involves the reversal of my attitude to him. Ill-will is turned into love, normally in the form of gratitude. This is a sort of adoration, in that I love him as the one who has restored me to myself, unified my will, made me whole. This adoring gratitude issues in a desire to make reparation. This will include restitution if that is at all possible. But always it will include something extra, a symbolic gift or act of generosity beyond any justice. The object of this is to express and communicate the destruction of the ill-will. It is the opposite of vengeance but answers to the same need. In the giving and receiving of this symbolic gesture reconciliation is achieved. Reconciliation is not only a state of mutual love but also the possession of a common mind. The history of conflict has now through the transaction of forgiveness become a source of intimate knowledge for both enemy and victim. Both can truly see the malicious act as a 'happy fault'.

The foundation for the whole transaction is clearly the steady love of the victim and the fact that it has a greater scope than his enemy's ill-will. But it would be powerless to effect reconciliation were it not for the residual tendency to goodness, the desire to wholly will what one wills, in the enemy. It is this division in the enemy's heart that makes the transaction possible, since it means that the victim's love is not merely fanciful (there is something he can value, can rely on, can foster) and it provides the essential ground for identification, the union of wills, that brings about the change of heart of the enemy.

Of course it is only when, as in the case we have visualised, the victim wholly wills his enemy's good that there can be a complete identity of aim between his will and the enemy's residual desire for an unlimited good. If the victim's will is mixed with self-centred spite or wounded agression towards his enemy then there would not be the possibility of an identical response in favour of the enemy's good, and so reconciliation would be imperfect.

I wish now to address myself to a closer examination of this residual desire in order to specify it more concretely and so to show how it, as an object for the victim's will, will have a value that outweighs the ill-will of the enemy. And we need to see too how it can continue to co-exist in the enemy's heart together with ill-will. Since in the end this previously unrecognised desire is preferred to something deliberately and willfully chosen, the residual desire must be for an object that is really the end to which the evil act can come to be seen as a (mistaken) means. The change of heart in the acceptance of forgiveness is not simply the recognition that I want something more than something else, that I was mistaken in what I willed. That would be tantamount to saying that I didn't really intend to harm my victim. But I did. It remains true however that in the success of my act I did not achieve what I really wanted. In fact the whole dialectic of forgiveness ultimately entails that ill-will is self-defeating.

We have said again and again that pure ill-will could not be forgiven, and indeed that it could not exist. We must now see why this is so by analysing the notion of malice. I use the term to denote the highest possible extreme of ill-will, something our example does not express.

Malice gets its true character not from the character of the harm willed but in the fact that the harm is directed at a person. It is not the particular quality of harm in itself that is important but the extent to which this is an appropriate sign of an attitude towards the victim. Fundamentally malice is a repudiation and rejection of the victim as such, in the fullness of his historical existence. To say that it is a will that he not exist, does not adequately capture the sense of the way in which he is de-valued. It is not just the fact of his existence that is hated but his total all-inclusive person and history. He has a negative value for the enemy, not only a zero value. His existence is seen as a positive threat, having a power over me mere death cannot efface. In malice the other person appears as a power that totally opposes and undermines my own value and power. His existence and well-being is the total exclusion of my own. We cannot co-exist.

The fixation of malice on its victim will be better brought out if we visualise the total environment of enemy and victim as each other. Their universe is a universe of two. This is not meant to be realistic. Yet the device is essential. For if others are present in the enemy's world it is always possible that the malice of his will is diverted. I hate A but love B. Of course that is the usual situation but it does not help us understand malice.

In this situation the threat to me of my victim is total and there is no recourse to palliatives in relation to others. His power and value negate my own. So he must be negated. Sheer non-existence, however, would be no solution since then my power and value would have no fuel for their exercise and expansion. He must live to suffer. He must remain close at hand to be totally and eternally repudiated. Like the characters in Sartre's *No Exit* we must be together to be painfully apart. The fixation on the victim that is characteristic of the person possessed by malice establishes the necessity of the victim's continued presence. There must be continual communication in order that any community of life and mutuality be destroyed. The situation has a paradoxical, indeed a contradictory character, which is highlighted if we visualise a universe of two.

The fact is that malice reveals the real need of the enemy for community with his victim. So a desire for continued communion is present even in the very attitude that most repudiates it.

Is it realistic however to suppose that, even in malicious acts, this is the real, though unconscious, goal of the act? Another consideration may help here. As we have described it malice can be seen as an expression of a desire to be unlimited by the presence, power or value of another person. The desire to exercise unlimited power, to possess a positive freedom of self-actuation where one is master of one's life, though apparently antithetical to a tendency towards loving communion, is in fact merely the same feature looked at from the side of the subject rather than the object. If in fact the transcending of limitation depends on the co-operation of others (if, that is to say, I am finite) then there is no contradiction between the two aspects. But calling the desire a desire for transcending limitation shows why it is that it can co-exist with every particular (which is to say limited) means that is chosen towards its fulfilment. If there is such a desire or natural dynamism in persons then it *can* be pursued without regard for the only conditions under which it can be satisfied, in contradiction of the person's finiteness, and hence as malice towards the threatening others. My whole account of forgiveness, given and received, presupposes its reality and power in our lives. Sartre would agree. But I think it can be satisfied, and that in the real world of interpersonal relationships it is precisely in the interaction of forgiveness that it is. This Sartre would deny.

(1987)

Chapter Twenty-Two
Community, Apartheid, and the Metaphysics of Humanity in Genesis 1–11

The images of Genesis 1 to 11, the days of creation, the garden of Eden and its snake, the flood and the ark, the tower of Babel—and all the rest, are so much part of one's mind that it is easy to miss the distinctive and profound conception of humanity that they are intended to express. In this article I want to present my understanding of this conception, both because I am convinced of its truth and importance, but also because it is a conception that we fail to make sufficient use of in theology and even, possibly, in our lives. And that is a pity since it has great explanatory power.

The key to this conception is the idea that God is part of the definition of humanity. Of course it is true of every religious tradition that its notion of God is intimately connected with its notion of human nature and its needs. This is because in all religions God is conceived of as the one with power sufficient to meet our needs, especially those we are incapable of meeting ourselves. No religion worthy of the name would worship a God unable to fulfil the fundamental needs of humankind. I take this to be a classical feature of religion as such: the idea of a predicament in which we are involved which only one with power transcending our own can overcome.

The religion of the Bible is no exception. But here the notion of God is connected even more intimately to the conception of humanity than in this classical scheme. Here, especially in the first eleven chapters of Genesis, humanity is seen not only as needing God but as the *image* of God. In the following pages I will attempt to unpack some of the riches bound up in this conception to show how it is capable of illuminating the predicament in which humanity seems inevitably to find itself.

Genesis and the Human Predicament

What we have in the first eleven chapters of Genesis is an explanatory account of the human predicament as seen by the composers of the Old Testament. (I prefer generally to think of its composers rather than its authors. Among such I include the following: those who first thought up the stories or the ideas or who experienced the events that are referred to; the tellers of the stories and the recounters of the events and the singers of the songs; those who first wrote things down; the collectors of the writings; the arrangers and the editors, and, last but not least, the authorisers, those who settled the Biblical canon.)

The composers of the Old Testament, especially those responsible for giving the Bible its final form in the period after the Exile to Babylon, were primarily interested in the predicament of Israel. The stories in the first eleven chapters of Genesis serve to explain that as well. But in the minds of the composers the predicament of Israel and that of humankind are intrinsically related; the explanation of the one is the explanation of the other.

We have in these first eleven chapters a description (actually a number of complementary descriptions) of a predicament together with an explanatory account of how it came about. The explanation not unnaturally takes the form of a narrative about 'how it all began.' Myths of origin always have an explanatory purpose directed towards the reality of the present. Nevertheless the causal origins of anything are not necessarily temporally but only ontologically prior to their effects.

It is in this sense that I propose to understand the stories in this section of Genesis. Their real point or purpose—even for their composers—has nothing to do with long-ago events as such. Everything in them that has this character I shall ascribe to the narrative form of the writing rather than to the content the composer wishes to express. Of course as a matter of sheer logic there must have been a first man—whether or not humanity began in one place or in many. And if there is sin in the world now then once again, logically, there must have been a first sin. But neither first man nor first sin have any special importance theologically. The question about the necessary conditions for the existence of humanity as well as that about the necessary conditions for the existence of sin, is just as appropriately addressed to any person in any age as to the first. And this is the question that the composer of Genesis is really concerned to answer.

It is much easier for imagination to deal with questions about ontological conditions in terms of historical events and, provided we know what we are doing, we don't need to give up our myth-making activity. The trouble starts only when we take our productions literally—as the theological history of nineteenth century and contemporary fundamentalism shows. Even now it is difficult, and necessary, to abstract from the imaginative details of the narrative in order not to be seduced into the literalistic attitude of thinking of past events. Particularly dangerous in this regard has been the idea of a 'Fall'. This archetypal notion (present in most mythologies in some form or other) is so powerful that in spite of the fact that it is nowhere mentioned in Genesis—or in the Bible itself for that matter—it has so firmly attached itself to the story of Adam and Eve that this story is usually referred to (even in the added sub-headings of actual Bibles) as the story of the Fall. And of course bound up with the idea of a Fall is an image of Higher and Lower Levels, the first of primitive innocence, the second of the experience of guilt. The notion of an age of innocence followed by a fall simply reinforces the idea that the stories are really about doings in the early days of the Earth.

The first eleven chapters of Genesis comprise what I take to be three carefully composed stories about the human predicament, the Story of Adam and Eve, the Story of Noah, and the Story of Babel. The stories are clearly divided from each other by three genealogies. I propose to discuss only the first and the last, the Adam and Eve story and the Babel story. Their position, as first and last, is as we shall see not accidental; and they are in fact complementary.

The Adam and Eve Story

In the Adam and Eve story the actual human predicament, the real situation of every person, is depicted in the list of God's curses at the end of Chapter Three. It has two sides to it, one that concerns the relations between persons, the other concerning the relation between humanity and the rest of creation. Between persons there is disorder and conflict. As the Cain and Abel story (which is appended to the Adam and Eve story as a sort of dramatic illustration) makes clear, such disorder involves domination and subjection and ultimately violence. And humanity is unable to exercise control over the rest of the earth, which dominates and enslaves humanity. The fruit of both oppositions, that between individuals and that between humanity and the earth, is a lack of freedom on the part of humanity. And in both cases the ultimate expression of this is death: people kill one another, and the earth overcomes humanity: 'you are dust and to dust you shall return.'

What is the cause of this predicament? In terms of the story it is disobedience to God's command not to eat of the fruit of the tree of knowledge of good and evil. The snake also plays a part in this since it is its lying promise that actually provokes the disobedience. God is also involved since it is God who makes the rules, pronounces the curse and metes out the punishment. But what does all this mean?

The key to the meaning of the Adam and Eve story is the conception of humanity that underlies it. This is the conception of humanity as the 'image' of God: 'God created man in his own image, in the image of God he created him; male and female he created them.' The notion of image contains two essential elements; an image is like what it is an image of, and it is wholly dependent on it for this likeness. It is fairly clear in what sense humanity is reckoned to be dependent on God, though, as I hope to show, there are aspects to this relation that are not usually taken into account. It is the dependence of creature on creator. When it comes to the element of likeness, however, there is a much wider range of possibilities to choose from. There is a sense in which the whole of the Old Testament is a character-study of God. Here however the context makes it clear that God is being regarded primarily as the creator of the universe. And it is precisely as such that humanity is said to be God's image.

Within the universe humankind occupies a creator-like position of lordship and control. Immediately after saying, 'Let us make man in our image;' God goes on to say 'let them have dominion over . . . the whole earth.' This idea is repeated more than once in this section, and echoed too in the detail of God's planting a garden and putting Adam in charge of it to tend it. Human creativity is seen as expressing itself not only in the control and ordering of the whole earth but in the creation of a family of humankind. Indeed the two functions are linked. The creativity of humanity consists in making the whole earth a home for the human family: 'Be fruitful and multiply, and fill the earth and subdue it.' Humanity's lordly position in the world is charmingly illustrated by the detail of God's bringing all the animals to Adam for him to name them, 'and whatever the man called every living creature, that was its name.'

The Meaning of Image

I have said that the conception of humanity as the image of God is the key to the meaning of the Adam and Eve story. And at first sight that is paradoxical, indeed doubly paradoxical. For the motive for disobedience turns out to be, precisely, the desire to be 'like God.' And that is paradoxical, since if Adam already is like God why should he still want to become like God? It is doubly paradoxical, since it turns out, as I shall presently show, that this is just what God wants as well—so why should God forbid and punish it?

The paradoxical character of the story is essential to it for it illuminates the deepest reaches of the conception of humanity as the image of God. The conception is this, that humanity as it issues from God's hand is incomplete, does not fully realize God's image. If creation consists in fully establishing God's image, then creation itself is incomplete. What God creates in the first instance is the mere, though real, capacity for being God's image. What remains to be done is the fulfilment of this capacity, the complete realization of the image. And as in the case of the beginning, so too in the case of the completion, of creation—it can only be the work of God. The only difference is that in the first case the creation of humankind is begun by the transformation of the sub-human world, the 'dust of the earth', whereas in the second it is human life and activity itself that is to be transformed by God's creative power.

The creation of humankind, precisely because it is the creation of a free being (which is what being the image of God ultimately entails, as will be more fully shown in a moment), must contain two aspects, one of which can only be realized within the acts and decisions, the history, of humanity itself. I shall discuss more fully in a moment the form that this aspect of creation, as envisaged by this story, is supposed to take. One should however note, in passing, that the notion of creation we are dealing with, once stripped of its narrative form, is that of a permanent causal relation between God and the universe. Creation is most emphatically not an event, 'in the beginning'. If one wants to distinguish between a beginning and a completion of creation then one can only point to the distinction between the creation of the capacities and their fulfilment, which is of course a process that 'takes time'. The whole process is however, equally 'creation' in that it expresses the same relation between God and humankind. There is of course from the side of humanity a beginning to the process; it is not some long ago event of prehistory, but the conception and birth of each human child.

With this clue to its meaning let us now look more closely at the details of the story to see how they express it, and to gain a fuller insight into the overall conception it contains.

The nakedness of Adam and Eve is an important element in this story and one which our key enables us to interpret. It is not a sort of pre-Raphaelite symbol of innocence as is sometimes suggested, an interpretation that fits in well with the idea of a primeval age of innocence. It is rather a symbol of incompleteness. In the Old Testament the full, complete or proper person is the person plus his or her clothes. Their clothes give persons their identities. After they have eaten the fruit, Adam and Eve realize their incompleteness. In the situation they are now in—which, as we shall see, involves a knowledge of what their completion consists in and a corresponding awareness of their impotence to achieve it—this realization is a source of shame. Their compulsive effort to achieve, or to pretend at, completeness takes the form of clothing themselves with leaves from the trees. God, however, clothes them after driving them from the garden. This is of course what God intended to do all along, but with the glorious robes of God's bride that appear again and again in the Old Testament writings as the fitting adornment of one whose 'creator has become her husband'. The white robes of the blessed continue and constitute the climax of this idea in the New Testament as well.

The Meaning of the Trees

Considering the nakedness of Adam and Eve has involved mention of the trees. There is a superabundance of trees in this story. The garden is full of trees. And the point is repeatedly made that the trees are there for food, to feed the life that God is intent on establishing. They are thus, in our interpretation, a symbol of the good things of the world that are available to supply the needs of humanity. We are incomplete, needy beings and the materials with which we must fashion our fulfilment are present round about us in the world. And that is why Adam and Eve are depicted as turning to the trees for help once they have become aware of their incompleteness.

What, however, of the two mysterious trees in the centre of the garden? Does this interpretation apply to them as well? I think it does. Like the other trees they are there as an answer to Adam's needs, but in this case the needs are very special ones. They are the needs he has precisely by virtue of being the image of God. This is why they are taboo. They can be used to bring about his fulfilment only in a very special way or else they will produce the opposite.

My stress on the paradoxical elements of this story should prepare one for paradox in the behaviour of God. In my view God *intends* Adam to eat of the trees of the knowledge of good and evil, and indeed of the tree of life as well. A 'straight' reading of the story however would suggest just the opposite. God tells Adam that he must on no account eat of the tree of the knowledge of good and evil. God punishes him when he does, and puts him out of the garden at the end precisely so that he won't be able to get at the other tree, the tree of everlasting life. In the face of all this, why am I so sure that Adam is intended by God to eat of the fruit of both of the 'supertrees,' as well as all the others in the garden?

The reason for my near-certainty on this point is the slant given to my reading by the conception of humanity as the image of God. If this conception is indeed the 'key' to the story then the two trees in the centre of Adam's garden appear as a very powerful symbol of those characteristics that are definitive of God, the creator, and so of Adam, God's image. The story itself says as much. As appears in the dialogue between Adam and the snake, to know good and evil is to be like God. And God acknowledges it; it is one of the grounds God gives for putting Adam out of the garden. As for the tree of life, this is really what God is trying to defend, since as it turns out at the end of the story, it is in fact the tree of '*everlasting* life', namely God's own life, the life of the creator not the creature. Everlasting life and the knowledge of good and evil, these are the essential attributes of God, the creator—and of God's created image, Adam. So the eating of the fruit of these two trees is in fact an apt symbol of the final realization of the image, that fulfilment of incompleteness, that I have presented as the ground plan of this story.

If this interpretation is to stand we must make sense of God's prohibition. An objector might allow us our paradox but claim that that appears as a flat contradiction of what I have said. How can God's clear prohibition to Adam regarding the tree of the knowledge of good and evil be understood as consonant with an overriding intention that he should indeed eat of it?

The coherence of my interpretation depends on the recognition that Adam has capacities that only God is able to develop. This is certainly implied by the 'image' notion, an image being *dependent* on that of which it is a likeness for its realization of that likeness. But it is not elaborated on in the Adam and Eve story. There is, I think, a reason for this. As we shall see, the rest of the Old Testament is an account of how God strives to create humanity as God's own image. This idea is contained in the notion of 'promise' which looms so large in the Old Testament and which is already apparent even in these early stories. But more of that presently.

The Paradox of the Prohibition

The prohibition to Adam I interpret as follows: Adam is to find completion by a free response to God. Because it is free there is the possibility that it will not be made. His incompleteness makes such a response both necessary yet not inevitable. This 'project' character of human existence, the fact that it is a task or a challenge, is expressed by the prohibition. In terms of the logic of the story itself, God must be seen as forbidding Adam to *take* the fruit because God wishes to *give* it to him. Because the fruit symbolizes God's own power it is something that cannot simply be acquired by Adam by his own efforts; if he is to get it at all (and he must have it if he is to be God's image) then he must be given it by God. What is required from Adam is faith in God, trust that God will give what God has promised. Instead of this essentially waiting, receptive attitude towards God, Adam (or rather Eve!) takes matters into his own hands and attempts to find fulfilment on his own.

In terms of the 'image' notion, what is required of Adam is his free consent to being dependent on God for the fulfilment of his most fundamental needs and his complete realization as God's image. His disobedience is the expression of his refusal to give that consent. To put this another way: there are two ways in which Adam can want to be like God, for God's sake because God wants it and God's will has absolute value, or for his own because he wants it and he places an absolute value on his own will. Adam chooses the second way and thereby destroys the very possibility of achieving what he wants. Because he is the *incomplete* image of God he has to choose; because he is the image he cannot choose not to want to be like God. *That* is not a possibility for him; so it cannot possibly be that which constitutes his disobedience.

I have made a lot of the notion that the two trees in the centre of the garden are symbols of Yahweh's own attributes as creator, and hence of the human capacities too that make Adam like God. But what is it precisely that they are symbols of? In the case of the tree of life the answer to this question is fairly clear. God transcends death; God's life is everlasting. There is even a suggestion that Adam too would not have died if he had not been disobedient. There is something unnatural about death even for God's image. It is more difficult to be sure what precisely is meant by the knowledge of good and evil provided by the other tree. If however one reflects that it is God's knowledge that is being talked about and that in this story God is essentially the creator, then one can understand the expression as referring to the sort of understanding or insight involved in creation, namely a grasp of the nature and purpose of everything, of each specific thing and of everything altogether.

Knowledge of good and evil thus means knowing what is good or bad for anything because you are its creator and know what it needs to be what you intend. If this is so, then God's prohibition concerning this tree signifies Adam's ignorance of his real nature as God's image. By eating of the tree he comes to know what God intends, and realizes as a consequence his own incompleteness. He also of course realizes that he has gone against this intention, but that now he is impotent to do anything about it.

The Symbolism of the Snake

The figure of the snake is an enigmatic one in this story. It is important to remember that it is a creature (this point is explicitly made), and not therefore some heavenly evil adversary of God's. Nor indeed is it especially evil. It told a lie to be sure. But it told an important truth as well. Its essence is perhaps deceptiveness rather than falsehood. In any case I see it as closely associated with the trees. Its conversation is all about the trees. In the tradition of Christian art too this connection is often made. The snake appears wound round the trunk or a branch in close proximity to the fruit. Sometimes it is even offering the fruit to Eve. I think that, like the trees, the snake stands for the world as the source of supply for all humanity's needs.

All the goods of the earth are good insofar as they can be used by humankind for its fulfilment. Because humankind occupies a creator-like position in the world, as lord and controller of it, everything in it is under our power. It is precisely this fact that tempts us to find in it the fulfilment of *all* our needs, including those we have as the image of God. However, as we have seen, God alone can fulfil those. But humanity, seeking complete fulfilment, can attempt to achieve it by means of what it can control, the worldly things about us. If we can find fulfilment in this way, through our own power, we do not have to rely on God and our self-sufficiency will be complete. We will be lord of all we survey and that will be enough. The snake is the capacity enjoyed by things under our control to offer us the illusory promise of fulfilment.

The Essence of Idolatry

Our interpretation of the trees and the snake fits in well with another central Old Testament theme, namely that of idolatry. Idolatry is the greatest possible sin in the eyes of Israel's legislators; together with injustice (with which it seems to have some special link) it is that against which the prophets most frequently and forcibly inveigh. On my interpretation Adam's sin is precisely that of putting himself in the place of God, seeking to be like God in independence of God instead of accepting likeness as a gift. In fact that self-worship is the essence of all idolatry. Although on the face of it some or other created object or cause takes the place of God as the object of Israel's worship, the worship is ultimately directed back at the idolater.

The *point* of idolatry is self-assertion, the sense of lordship and control. It is for this reason that the idols are always created realities that are in fact in the control of mankind. Humanity is (under God) lord and controller of creation in the eyes of Genesis. Idolatry is the attempt to make this lordship an absolute one. Of course there is self-deception in all this as well. Idolatry necessarily involves a false consciousness: the idols are experienced as having power of their own, although the power is in fact that of their worshipper. The idolater hides from this and from the real insufficiency of the idol to do what is required of it. This is the ceaseless taunt of the prophets in the face of Israel's idolatry, that the false gods are no gods at all, are impotent and lifeless. What is more, their makers will become like them. In our interpretation of the Adam and Eve story it is because Adam is the image of God that he can in fact be satisfied by nothing less than God. And because he has the capacity to respond to the unconditional value of the creator, when he chooses in a spirit of defiant self-assertion something other than the creator in which to put his value, he likewise values it without limit.

In the story it is the trees (and perhaps the snake as well) that become the idols. In the middle-eastern country trees are of course well fitted to be symbols of power and life, In arid desert lands trees are the signs of an oasis and the life-giving water. It is surely no chance that Israel's neighbours set up their idolatrous shrines 'under every green tree:' This is a standard formula of the prophetic denunciation of idolatry.

The Promise to our Finitude

The story of Adam and Eve ends with a promise. That at any rate is what my interpretation makes of the detail of God making the guilty pair clothes of skin before driving them from the garden. First of all the clothes are a gift, as the realization of the image was intended to be; and they cover the nakedness, provisionally overcome the incompleteness, of humanity. The story of Cain and Abel, which is a sort of rider to the story of Adam and Eve, also ends with such a provisional gracious gesture in the detail of the 'mark' of Cain, through which he is prevented from being killed.

We have come to the end of our consideration of the first of the Genesis stories. The account of the human predicament that it contains is seen to be derived from a conception of humanity that is both complex and comprehensive. Abstracting now from the details of the story one can say that the centre of this conception is the idea that humanity has the capacity to transcend the rest of nature, both in the sense that it is able to *control* it rather than be controlled by it, and also in that mankind is capable of *insight* into the nature and purpose of everything, God included. The other side of humanity's transcendence is incompleteness. It is precisely because we are transcendent that we are incomplete; it is precisely that capacity that entails a need that neither we nor the world under our control can fulfill.

The transcendent character of humanity is associated with a special kind of relationship to the creator of the universe. This relationship is such that it is only within it that human nature can find fulfilment, a fulfilment moreover that depends on *historical* activity of the creator, that is activity beyond that of the sheer bringing into being of human nature. This is certainly mysterious. And yet the fundamental characteristic of the human predicament, the enslavement of mankind by and within the created universe, does suggest that human fulfilment consists in the opposite of such subjection. Our lack of freedom in the world is unnatural because by nature we are capable of controlling the world. And this capacity entails a real transcendence of the rest of nature.

Incomplete Because Transcendent

What could be the foundation of such transcendence except a special relation to the transcendent creator? There is however more to this special relationship with the creator than this. It is also the key to the explanation of how the human predicament comes about. As I have already said, it is because we are transcendent that we are incomplete. And it is humanity's incompleteness that makes a human predicament possible. For we are bound by nature to seek fulfilment. The only place we can seek it is in the world in which we find ourselves. But because of our transcendent nature nothing in the world as such is able to afford the fulfilment we require. It is the activity of the creator alone that can fulfill us. And it is a necessity of our created nature that we must discover and respond to this activity within our worldly situation. We have to learn to see it there and we have the choice of responding to it or not. Because of our transcendence we are free to refuse. We are not free however not to desire the satisfaction of our capacity for transcendence. So we project a transcendent power onto one or other object in our world, thereby giving it an unconditional value and so subjecting ourselves to it. Although its transcendence is an illusion, we really lose our own.

So the conception of human nature in Genesis does afford an explanation of the human predicament as it is conceived by the composers of the Adam and Eve story. The predicament is not presented as an inevitable consequence of human nature, since that nature is presented as free. Nevertheless the incompleteness of human nature, an incompleteness that is the other side of its freedom, makes a vocation to grow an inevitable aspect of the human situation. And the rejection of this exigence can be fairly seen as all too likely, since the condition of growth is a paradoxical relinquishment of power and control. Humanity is and is intended to be in control of everything within the world, but it is and intended to be subject to its creator. If however our creator must act to bring about our fulfillment within our world environment (as God must if our response is to be a free one) then there is the possibility of our habitual attitude of dominance prevailing over the need to be dependent. So the two attitudes are combined and confused, the desire for an absolute value and the desire to control, and something within our control is given an absolute value. The result is loss of freedom.

Now there is a further element that must now be considered. This is the sexual (and so the social) element of the story. It appears in the account of the human predicament as a certain opposition and lack of freedom between Adam and Eve as a result of their disobedience. It also appears in the transaction with the snake. It even appears in the accounts of the creation of humanity which contain the key to the whole story.

Image of God: Sexual, Social, Creative

From the first account of creation it would seem that part of humanity's likeness to God consists in its being sexually differentiated. I think that is partly due to the connection between creativity and sexual fertility; Adam and Eve are after all commanded to 'fill' the earth with a human family. It is also, and more importantly the sheer plurality of persons in humanity that is significant, the tact that *mankind* is essentially a community. This seems to mirror something in the creator that is often referred to in plural terms. The second account of creation stresses this communal character of humanity. God says that 'It is not good that the man should be alone,' and in the creation of Eve from Adam's body it appears that the human race is conceived of as a unity, both in origin and destiny, since they are to become 'one flesh' again in marriage.

In the transaction with the snake Eve plays a crucial role, she is both tempted and tempter. In a way she is partly on the side of Adam and partly identified with the snake. This detail I take to point to both a division within the fundamental unity of humanity and to a sense in which humanity itself, like the rest of creation, the trees and the snake itself, can be considered as 'food' for humankind, as offering some sort of answer to our need for completion. For each human person, at any rate, the world in which they must seek fulfilment contains other human persons too. But these others have a special position, and perhaps a special role as well, since they are co-seekers as well as possible providers; they too are in the image of God.

I do not wish to develop this particular theme further here since it seems to be a subordinate one in this particular story. It is important enough however to stress before leaving it that in this story the explanation of the human predicament has as its heart a transaction *between* persons in which humanity manifests a dual role, being both seeker and (illusory) provider of fulfilment.

The Story of Babel

One reason why there is no need to delve more deeply into the social side of the Adam and Eve story is that it is explicitly treated in the final story in this section of Genesis, that of the Tower of Babel. I call the sexual element in the Adam and Eve story social deliberately since I think the significance of the sexual differentiation of humanity in this story is referred precisely to the communal character of humanity both in nature and destiny—and in its actual predicament. After all what is sexual differentiation but sociality as a fact of human *nature.* In the Tower of Babel story the fact of human sociality is the dramatic centre of the scene.

The structure of the Tower of Babel story is similar to that of the story of Adam and Eve. There is a description of the human predicament, and an explanation of it based on a specific conception of humanity and what would constitute its fulfilment. A difference of emphasis is the detail that the conception of humanity is contained in a description of its fulfilment rather than, as in the first story, its capacities. But that is a function of the position of this story in this section of Genesis. The section is in fact a prologue to the whole Old Testament, and this story concludes the section with a fore-shadowing of the God-provided goal of the history that is just beginning.

In this story it is the disunity of humanity that constitutes the human predicament. This disunity is depicted in the powerful image of a confusion of language. The actual situation of humanity is a division into many nations and many languages. And this is unnatural and a predicament to be overcome. Being 'scattered' is itself seen as a bad thing, but the additional implication is that there is a lack of understanding as well as separation. The disunity is not just a physical state.

Human Disunity and God's Community

If this is the predicament, then the overcoming of the predicament lakes the form of building a universal human community. This conception of the goal of history is given powerful symbolic form, both in the image of the city where all live together and that of the common name all come to share, as well as the over-riding conception of a single language uniting humanity in a common mind.

In this story as in the former the paradox appears of God apparently preventing what God really intends. But as before I consider it is not humanity's project that God wishes to alter or prevent, but the way in which it is attempted. Following my theory of interpretation it is clearly the case that mankind is meant to speak one language, to have one name, to inhabit one city. The reason that they do not is a failure on the part of humanity. To depict it as the work of a jealous God is to point to the cause of the failure, as it would necessarily appear to the composer of this section of Genesis.

As in the first story, it is humanity occupying the place of the creator. Here it is the creation of the human community that is at issue. As God's image, humanity is to become a true community. But, as the symbol of the tower 'with its top in the heavens' is intended to convey, humanity attempts this task without reliance on God. A single language, city, name, is beyond human power as such to create. It is only in dependence on God that it is possible at all. Humanity however is accustomed to its creator-like status in the world and so its attempt to achieve what in fact lies beyond mere human power—the fulfilment of humanity as the image of Cod—takes the form of self-assertion. Once again it is idolatry. Here it is the tower of the city that is the idol. Here too it is even clearer than in the first story that the ultimate object of humanity's worship is humanity itself. What humanity is after in this story is unlimited power, not over the world but over itself. It is this desire that lies at the root of the political divisions and the failure to reach a common mind that constitute the human predicament. In the political communities that it does bring into being humanity worships its own power. It is for this reason that none of these communities can constitute the community of humanity, they exist only in separation from and in opposition to each other.

I hope that this brief sketch of the interpretation of the story of the Tower of Babel brings out sufficiently its connection with the story of Adam and Eve. It presupposes many of the ideas contained in that, particularly the understanding of humanity as the image of God that is so central there. I do not really think it could be understood on its own, without reference to the other.

On the other hand it supplies something that the Adam and Eve story lacks. For all its detail and charm the Adam and Eve story is a highly abstract one; it is very much a depiction of the metaphysics of humanity. The Tower of Babel story is much more concrete. This, one feels, is the actual form that the metaphysical drama takes in human history. The form that the realisation of God's image takes in human history is the creation of human community. This in the last resort is the view of the Bible. And not of the Old Testament only! I feel sure that Luke's account—that of the apostolic experience of the coming of the Holy Spirit is presented with the story of Babel in mind. The story of Pentecost is the story of how all peoples on earth, each with its own language, culture, character, can be united in one community by one new language that all can understand, the language of the Word preached by the apostles.

Humanity and Transcendence

I must now set out in summary what I believe my unpacking of Genesis 1 to 11 to have produced. In essence it is a conception of the human predicament and a conception of humanity that both explains it and explains how it might be overcome. The conception of humanity is centered on the notion of transcendence. Human nature transcends the rest of nature in the sense that non-human nature is by itself insufficient to account for either the existence or the activity of human beings. Nor is it sufficient to satisfy our deepest desires. This freedom or independence from all finite causes which human beings enjoy is a direct result of the peculiar immediacy of their dependence on the causality of something that is not finite. Thus the conception of humanity in Genesis 1 to 11 not only does full justice to the fact of human freedom; it offers a metaphysical foundation for it. No doubt this is presented in symbolic terms. Nevertheless it is clear enough to be formulated in rigorous fashion, as the history of Christian metaphysics has shown.

To see human beings as transcendent in the sense of self-determining has nothing 'mythical' about it. And it is the only adequate foundation for a theory of morality and an actual system of ethics. Contemporary forgetfulness of this crucial dimension of human nature must be seen as a threat to the human values that only it can justify, values such as meekness, humility and readiness to forgive.

The notion of transcendence has another side to it, namely the implication that humanity can understand and so, in principle, control the rest of nature. And it is not difficult to see this idea as the ultimate root of the science and technology that has developed in those cultures influenced by biblical religion. Power over nature that comes from a God-like transcendence of it also implies responsibility for it. There is nothing Promethean about the biblical conception of humanity. Unfortunately this element of our transcendence is usually overlooked. Which brings us to the predicament.

As we have seen, the human predicament is depicted by the composers of Genesis 1 to 11 as an inability to form true human community, either sexual or social. Added to this is the state of war between between humanity and the rest of nature, a war that produces only suffering and ultimately death. The conception of humanity outlined above both explains how such a predicament comes about and shows the way in which it can be overcome. As transcendent beings we have desires that no finite goods can satisfy. And we have an inescapable need to value something unconditionally. It is ultimately this need that accounts for the compulsive, assertive, dogmatic commitments that we make, whatever their particular objects might happen to be. However different the circumstances of these attachments might be it is always the 'dear self' that is the ultimate recipient of our worship. And that is why the most typical consequence of such 'idolatry' is the destruction of genuine community in every sphere of human life.

The conception of humanity in Genesis 1 to 11 provides one with a profound explanation in terms of the essential dynamics of human personality of why genuine human community is so difficult to achieve. It is a conception that could certainly be elaborated in detail in quite ordinary psychological terminology. To a certain extent it already has been in the scholastic categories of Aquinas. But a great deal has happened in the field of psychological study since Aquinas's day. Surely a 'theological' psychology could be developed using this biblical conception as a foundation, but borrowing from all the secular disciplines that have something to offer. Aquinas's Aristotelian notions retain their power. Then there is existential philosophy and phenomenology, not to mention psychoanalysis and the various theoretical and practical psychologies produced in the twentieth century.

With all this it ought to be possible to develop a systematic account of human motivation and the dynamics of personal growth that could connect our understanding of such different fields as psychotherapy, morality, the spiritual life, and even dogmatic theology. Indeed it is difficult to think of important areas of thought and practice to which a profound and comprehensive theory of human nature is not relevant. The conception presented in Genesis 1 to 11 should not be dismissed as irrelevant simply because it is elaborated in mythical terminology and inseparable from the notion of God.

I have said that the conception of humanity found in Genesis 1 to 11 both provides us with an understanding of the human predicament and also shows us how it might be overcome. And it is this of course that is the area of really crucial interest. Does Genesis 1 to 11 have anything significant to say?

Contemporary Political Applications

According to UNESCO's Figures, in 1982, 528 million people lived on less than 100 dollars each. During the same year 5 million children died from starvation. Nearly all of these very poor people and dead children belonged to the 'third world' or the 'south' of the north/south divide. That is to say, they come from the 'undeveloped' parts of the world. So the UNESCO figures, and others like them, support the view that the gap between the haves and the have-nots is in fact continuing to widen. And this in spite of technological progress and aid-programmes. Again, this occurs in spite of widespread awareness of the fact.

I am not an expert in economics but it seems clear that the problem is not one of a sheer lack of resources, or even of the inability of our technology to cope with the difficulty of distribution. According to economists such as the late Barbara Ward-Jackson the problem is fundamentally a political one, and that not in some intractable technical sense of the term but in the sense that it concerns the making of a common decision. In short the problem exists because a common will to solve it does not exist, at least among those people who are in a position to do something about it. And this means ultimately that the people who could do something about it do not want to enough.

Put like that what I am saying seems too simple to be true. But I do not think it is. If I consider South Africa as an example of this widening gap between haves and have-nots, and my own position in it, I think I can see the issues more clearly. I certainly would not want to say that I have no will to close the gap between, in this case, black and white—the gap in power, opportunity, money, and prestige. I can fairly say that I very much want it to be closed. Its existence causes suffering of extraordinary kinds and causes me moral trouble too. And yet if the strength of my will to change it were to be tested in some way I doubt if it would come out very high. If, for instance, I had to decide what proportion of my income I would be prepared to contribute toward closing the gap, I know it would not be very large. Of course that is partly because of uncertainty as to whether my sacrifice would really help.

For a change of this kind to occur a common will at least of those in a certain position in society (say, in South Africa, white voters) is required. And my willingness to make my own sacrifice could be quite reasonably reckoned to be dependent on how sure I was that everyone else would make theirs. And if I were sure? Well, believing that our common sacrifice would be effective in closing the gap, let us assume more or less permanently, would certainly remove one obstacle to me making my own. But the assurance of a common will to achieve the objective would fortify me in a way far beyond simply encouraging the belief that our scheme would work. It would inspire me, literally, to be unselfish. It would affect not only my action but my will; it would change the quality of my desire to end injustice. And it would do this simply by the revelation of that quality of will in others.

That is what must happen, whether in my own case, or in that of the 'haves' in the world-wide situation. We have to change the quality of our desire for justice. And that, it is not too difficult to see, is not such a simple thing. In fact, if my own case can be taken as typical, it can only be brought about by an encounter with that very quality in another, or in an overwhelming number of others. In fact this doesn't happen. And it doesn't happen because a real desire for justice doesn't exist, in anyone, let alone in large numbers—or it doesn't exist enough.

The point of this political excursus is to provide some concrete reference for the solution to the human predicament that is at least suggested in Genesis 1 to 11. The solution is that humanity must direct its capacity for adoration away from itself and towards God instead. Only then will our hearts be set free for the desire for justice. And only then can the hostility in the human family be overcome. Put like that the solution seems, like all purely religious solutions, too simple to be true. We must not forget however the psychological transformation that such a change in the object of our worship will entail. If we follow the understanding of Genesis 1 to 11 it would be difficult to conceive of anything more radical. The real difficulty with such a solution is not that it is too simplistic but that it is beyond human power.

If we are to believe the composers of Genesis 1 to 11 such a conversion can only be achieved by God. And in Genesis 1 to 11 there is only the promise that this will be done but no suggestion as to how. The last verse of chapter 12 does however contain one. God promises Abraham that he will make 'of him a great nation'. 'I will bless you and make your name great, so that you will be a blessing. I will bless those who bless you, and him who curses you I will curse; and by you all the families of the earth shall bless themselves.' This however is only a suggestion. It is only in Jesus that the method of overcoming the predicament is fully revealed, namely the historical presence of God as the medium of true human community. This idea is high-lighted in Vatican II's preferred, and novel, definition of the Church: 'By her relationship with Christ, the Church is a kind of sacrament or sign of intimate union with God, and of the unity of all mankind. She is also an instrument for the achievement of such union and unity' (*Lumen Gentium* 1.1). Novel though the definition is, it fits in well with the conception of humanity and its predicament contained in Genesis 1 to 11.

(1987)

Chapter Twenty-Three
The Great Story: Creation

The first eleven chapters of the Book of Genesis, the first book in the Bible, are not really about things that happened long ago at the beginning of the world. They are really an attempt to explain why it is that humanity is in such a mess and what is needed to overcome it. This explanation all depends on a single profound insight into the nature of humanity itself, an insight expressed by saying that humanity is 'the image of God'. All the stories, the story of Adam and Eve, of Cain and Abel, of Noah and of the Tower of Babel, that make up these eleven chapters, are put there by the writers of the Book of Genesis because they each express one or other aspect of this basic insight into humanity.

All the great thinkers of the Church have understood this: the early Christians who wrote the books of the New Testament, later theologians like St Augustine and St Thomas Aquinas, and people writing today. Of course the New Testament writers and St Augustine and St Thomas also thought that the stories in Genesis were literally true. In the days before people learnt to do science, everybody did. The difference between stories that were literally true and stories that told a truth (like the parables of Jesus) was unimportant to them.

Although all these early thinkers believed that these stories were literally true, none of them thought that that was what was *important* about them. What was important about them for St Augustine and St Thomas, and St John and St Paul too, was the truth they told about humanity—that we are 'the image of God'—and the way this throws light on the mess humanity is in and how we can overcome it. Even so it is still true to say that if they had believed these stories to be literally false it would have been more difficult for them to take seriously the insight into humanity and the human predicament that they contain.

That presents us with a problem. We know that these stories are not literally true. And that makes it difficult for us to take them seriously. We tend to treat them as fairy stories, appropriate only for children and not for adults. And that is just wrong. The truth they are intended to express is something that can only be properly understood by adults. The great thinkers of the Church have tried to do just that in their theology. They have picked out the jewels of truth from these stories and filled countless books with them.

What we need to do, in our own time, is to tell a new story to express these self-same truths. We need to tell a story that we can believe, a story that is more or less literally true. So it must be a scientific story—not just plain science, but a story based on science. It doesn't have to be absolutely accurate. We are not trying actually to do science. But it has to be more or less true to the truths of science so that we can see how the truth that it is meant to express, the truth about humanity as 'the image of God', fits into the real world that science has helped us to understand more fully.

Chapter One: The Story of Creation

As far as I have been able to discover, it happened something like this. Long, long ago the universe consisted simply of energy. This energy was all there was. There were no real things of any kind, no shape or form, nothing definite at all. Even space and time were not yet real. When modern physics explains the different fundamental particles that make up atoms as forms of energy, it is energy like this that it is speaking of.

From this fundamental energy came movement and change. Things began to exist and, with them, space and time. Infinitely small, infinitely many, particles swarmed in infinite space through infinite time. And throughout infinite space through infinite time, in a wholly mysterious way, things changed into other things. Particles combined with particles to form atoms. Over further huge stretches of time, filled with countless contacts of atoms with each other, new combinations of atoms formed a new kind of things—the molecules. These were capable of combining in even more complex ways to make up the different substances that modern chemistry is able to discover. Then the chemical substances that made up the universe combined to form all the elements known to us: solids and liquids and gases, earth, air, fire and water. Huge reactions and explosions took place: galaxies, stars, planets were formed; and on the planets, seas and volcanoes and solid land.

Millions of years went by and the reactions grew more gentle, more orderly. In the cooling waters on the earth chemicals combined; huge mega-molecules were transformed into simple cells, tiny crystalline, jelly-like units of life.

A Different Kind of Energy

At each stage of the change—from energy to particle, from particle to atom, from atom to molecule, from molecule to cell—the new kind of thing that came into being was quite different from what had gone before. At the same time it contained everything in it that had been there before. Cells are composed of molecules, which are made up of atoms, which are made of particles, which are from energy. Yet cells can do things that molecules can never do. Each kind of thing can do more than the kind of thing from which it is made.

This shows that the power of the thing does not come only from the things of which it is made. At each stage there is something more, something really new. This is called creation. More cannot simply grow from less. The things in the universe aren't simply being rearranged into new combinations; the whole universe is changing, becoming something new. And the change, the becoming new and different, can't be explained simply by what the universe already is. A different kind of energy altogether is at work, one capable of producing something really new. Creation is taking place.

When we say that creation is taking place, we mean of course that the universe itself is being created. Creation isn't something that happens inside the universe; it is something that happens to the universe. This means that creation is caused by something that is not part of the universe, by a quite different kind of power. And that is very mysterious.

One can grasp this point more clearly by means of a simple example. Think of a long train of goods trucks. The last truck in the train moves because it is coupled to the second last. This is turn moves because it is coupled to the third last and so on. It is not difficult to see that there will be no movement at all if the train consists only of trucks. For the trucks to move one needs an entirely different kind of thing, namely an engine. That can move itself and so move all the trucks as well.

The different things that make up the universe are like the trucks. None can really change itself—not even engines, not even people (if you think about it carefully). We all depend on other things in order to change, or even in order to continue to exist at all. But if there were nothing else, if the universe of dependent things were all that there was, there would be no change. There is change though; really new things come into being, and old things change beyond recognition. These changes therefore show that another kind of thing altogether must exist, a thing quite different from the things that make up the universe. And its power is the ultimate source of all the changes in the universe, because it is the source of the universe itself.

In fact we could have discovered this in a simpler way altogether, right at the beginning of our story. That energy we started with, from which everything that exists has come—how did it come to exist? It couldn't cause itself; that doesn't make sense. It must have been created by something else, something quite different from anything in the universe.

The Direction of Evolution

After millions of years living things began to grow on the earth and in the sea and sky: plants and trees, fish and animals and birds—millions of different kinds of living things. Each member of a living species is connected in some way. Every living thing is capable of reproducing its own kind, either by seeds or by sex. And every living thing is a thing that dies. Life and death are created together.

Over huge stretches of time even species change and die. Modern biology has discovered the way in which species change and die out, through tiny mutations that are either well- or ill-adapted to its survival. In this way death becomes part of the mechanism of development. For at the stage of creation that we are speaking about it has become quite clear that there is a direction to the process.

Each new stage of the universe is a development of the previous stage towards greater complexity in things. This feature of the process has such important consequences that I must explain it more fully. A molecule is more complex than an atom; a living cell is more complex than a chemical substance; an animal is more complex than a plant. That is clear enough. But the more complex a thing is, the more it is a single whole. That is not so clear at first. It will become clear if you think of the difference between a cow and a stone.

The cow is more complex than a stone not just because it is bigger but because the different parts all play different parts in the life of the cow—the heart, the eyes, the feet, each has its own special function. This is why we call the parts of a living thing like a cow, organs and the cow itself an organism. The complexity is precisely the organization of the parts into a single whole. In a stone every part is the same as every other. So it is not a single whole in the way a cow is. If you break a stone in half you will have two (smaller) stones. If you break a cow in half you won't have a cow at all.

Finally, the more of a single whole a thing is, the more it is in control of itself and its life, or self-determining. Being self-determining means being free of influences from outside oneself, to a greater or lesser extent. Think of plants for instance. They are to a certain degree self-determining. Of course they still depend on their environment for support and food and so on, and they are influenced by it in many ways. But they can also influence it and make it serve their own needs. An obvious way they can do this is by moving. Plants can't move from one place to another, but they can move their roots towards moisture and chemicals in the ground, and they can move their leaves and blossoms towards the light.

Freedom is even more marked in animals. Animals, after all, have feelings. They can feel things outside themselves; that is they have senses and sensations. They can feel things inside themselves; they have desires and emotions. And so they can take their environment into themselves—not physically, as food, but mentally, as perceptions: sights and sounds, tastes and smells and touches. And they can move into their environment, not only physically, but by desiring things in it and trying to get them, by choosing things and doing things to get them, and so even changing the environment itself or choosing a new one.

Animals can also learn to do new things and form new habits. They have memories and so can teach other members of their species, their young, how to do these new things too. They have language—which is to say they can use bits of their environment (sounds usually, but also movements and even objects) to communicate with other members of their species. Because they can communicate, animals can be together in more than just a physical way: they share their feelings with each other and in this way recognize and get to know and feel affection for each other. Animals and animal life are a sort of model of humanity. That is why we find animals so interesting and why so many children's books are about animals. We see ourselves in them and can learn a lot about ourselves from them.

Animals show clearly the direction that creation takes, and that direction points to us. The way animal life moves ahead we usually call evolution. Evolution is not something different from creation: it is the main method of creation once the biological level, the level of life, has been reached.

The Creation of Humanity

Once animal life had been created it was many millions of years before humanity itself evolved. The most complex, conscious and creative animals were the mammals and amongst the mammals the anthropoids, from whom both the great apes such as chimpanzees and gorillas and ourselves have come. So it is not quite true that humanity is descended from the monkeys. Both humanity and the monkeys are descended from something else. We have a common ancestor, one that has since died out.

After many more millions of years the hominids began to appear. We know a bit about them from the fossil records studied by paleantologists such as Teilhard de Chardin. And then suddenly, about 250,000 years ago, according to the fossil records, humanity itself appears. How do we know the exact time? The signs of humanity that scientists recognize are such things as rock-paintings, stones chipped to form tools and weapons, graves, fireplaces. And the place? Almost certainly in Southern Africa!

How was humanity created? It is impossible to say for certain. But just like the creation of living things from non-living, so the creation of humanity from animal life is the creation of something quite new, another case of more coming from less, of the kind we have seen happen at every stage of creation. A simple model to give an idea of how creation works is that of ice changing to water and water changing to steam under the influence of heat. Solids, liquids and gases are really different and behave in different ways. Yet each can be produced from the other by an external power such as heat. Note that an external power is necessary: ice can't become water by itself although it is made of the same chemical substances. Heat is necessary too.

The same is true with creation. At every stage an 'external' power is required to cause the change. Energy, the energy from which all things are made, is just energy. It has no shape or character. To get shape or character, to change the energy into definite forms of energy (physical, chemical, biological forms) another kind of power is required. Energy can't of itself produce things. Things don't of themselves turn into living things. Living things don't of themselves become persons. At every stage of creation an 'outside' power is required.

What sort of power could this be? The idea of an outside power is certainly mysterious. Especially since 'outside' here means outside the universe, and how can anything be outside the universe if the universe is everything that exists, including time and space. It is for this reason that I have put 'outside' in inverted commas—to show that there is a question to be answered about this. We will try to do so as we go along.

How then did humanity come into being? It emerged out of communities of hominids over a long period of time. The outward sign of the development of humanity was the development of language.[1] Language is not just a kind of tool for practical purposes. It is also used to express thoughts and feelings for their own sake. Singing and chanting especially are used in this way. Somehow or other in the communal celebrations of our ancestors (celebrations of birth or death, or success or anxiety), out of the dancing and the singing, emotions, sounds and objects were connected to each other and recognisable human language was born.

From then on words had meanings; they stood for ideas. And gradually our ancestors became aware of a new realm of reality, the realm of meaning. Everything could have a name. So our ancestors named everything. And in doing this they discovered themselves as the creators and possessors of meanings. They were alive in a new way, a truly human way. They were persons—in charge of their own lives, able to make up their own minds about how to live because able to create ideas out of what they had experienced. So they were able to judge whether ideas were true or false; they were able to decide what would be good or bad to do.

1. S Langer, *Philosophy in a New Key* (Harvard, 1984) Chapter 5, 'Language', especially 126–135.

All this happened about a quarter of a million years ago, which, although it is a period that quite dwarfs the period of which we have any historical record, is fairly recent when the age of the earth is taken into account. But the huge periods of time must not be allowed to obscure the unique importance of the creation of humanity. It is important because is sums up everything that has gone before. And it is important because it is the beginning of the end of the final phase of the process of creation. The next chapter will continue the story of creation. But now this story has become the story of humanity.

Chapter Two: The Story of Humanity

In the first chapter I tried to tell the story of creation in a way that fits in with all that science has taught us about the universe. I reached the point where humanity appeared on the scene for the first time. And I concluded by saying that the creation of humanity had a unique importance in the story of creation. It is important because it sums up everything that has gone before. And it is important because it is the beginning of the final phase of the process of creation.

Everything is Contained in Us

Just as vegetables contain all the simpler and more primitive levels of reality: the cellular, the chemical, the physical, and energy itself, so do animals contain all the levels that vegetables do. Of course the simple organic character of vegetable life is transformed in animals to become capable of feeling and knowledge. In human beings animal life too is transformed by its involvement in thinking and choosing and acting. But it is still an ingredient in human life, as are all the other levels as well. So humanity is a microcosm of the universe, the thing in which every other kind of thing is included. And in our thoughts, in the realm of ideas, everything is included in a different way. The whole universe can be reflected in our thoughts and come to exist in a new way in us.

The process of creation, and the way in which each stage of the process is contained in the last, is not just something that belongs to the past. It continues, and is repeated in the development from conception to birth of every human child. In the bodies of the parents chemical substances are converted into a living cell. And in the womb of the mother a new organism is formed. First it is like a little jellyfish.

Then it becomes something like a fish with a spine and an eye. Then it looks like a hairless monkey with a tiny tail. Then it is recognisable as a human baby. Finally it utters a cry.

The baby is of course a person, not an animal. But that is not the end of the story. Babies cannot speak or think. Like humanity as a whole, each human child has to discover the world of meaning, of ideas, and so discover itself as well. For most of us this happens during our first few years of life when we are too young to remember it properly. We do however have an account of how it happens from someone to whom it happened quite late in life, someone who never learnt to speak when she was little because she was blind and deaf. The person was Helen Keller. She not only learnt to speak, she remembered how it happened, and wrote about it afterwards in her autobiography:

> We walked down the path to the well-house, attracted by the fragrance of the honey suckle with which it was covered. Some one was drawing water and my teacher placed my hand under the spout. As the cool stream gushed over one hand she spelled into the other the word water, first slowly, then rapidly. I stood still, my whole attention fixed upon the motions of her fingers. Suddenly I felt a misty consciousness as of something forgotten—a thrill of returning thought; and somehow the mystery of language was revealed to me. I knew then that 'w-a-t-e-r' meant the wonderful cool something that was flowing over my hand. That living word awakened my soul, gave it light, hope, joy, set it free! There were barriers still, it is true, but barriers that could in time be swept away.[2]

I have said that humanity is of special importance in the process of evolution because it is the final product of the process, the culmination of evolution in which everything else s contained.

If one asks the question 'Where is evolution going?' the answer is that it moves always in the direction of complexity, and therefore towards ever greater unity and freedom. It moves from very simple things of very few kinds to more and more complex things of many different kinds. The more complex a thing is, the more of a unity it is and the more freedom it has from the influences of its environment. Human beings are the most complex beings that exist, and so of course we have the greatest freedom too.

---

2. Keller, H, *The Story of My Life* (Doubleday, 1936), 23–25.

So humanity is at the centre and the peak of the evolutionary process. In fact in humanity evolution, properly so-called, has come to an end. To the extent that they are truly self-determining, human beings are free of the forces of nature. In fact through its understanding of nature humanity can control nature, and shape it according to its own purposes. This is what modern science and technology enable us to do. At least they give us the power to do this. Thus far we haven't used this power very well. But more about that later.

The Beginning of History

A famous evolutionary scientist, Sir Julian Huxley, has said that in humanity evolution 'has become conscious of itself'. That is a good way of putting it. It follows that from this point on a new process has begun. We call it history. Creation continues, but now it is to a certain extent in human hands. What happens to the world depends on us. We can blow it up or poison it—or we can make it a home for humanity to live in.

History is different from evolution because it is a process in which new ideas rather than new things are created. From the beginning of human history we can see this; an arrow-head made out of a stone by chipping it is not really a new thing. At least the stone it is made of is the same stone. But now the stone embodies an idea. It has a purpose: killing. The new form it has been given by the arrow-maker expresses this purpose. And it can express this purpose well or badly. Every arrow-head is either well-made, good for killing, or not.

Of course the most important way in which things can come to embody ideas in the course of history is in the way that sounds and marks on stone or paper do when they are turned into words. By using this special kind of thing called words we are able to fill our minds with ideas. Words are the tools we use to make ourselves.

Our earliest ancestors looked very different from us. And they lived very different lives. Yet in all sorts of ways they revealed that they were truly human, in exactly the same way as we are. They buried their dead. For them as for us death was the one event in their lives that made them see their lives as a whole, with a beginning and an end. It also forced them to ask the question about the meaning and value of their lives. For a being with limited powers over its own life, death is naturally a threat. For a free being such as humans are, death reveals the limits of our freedom.

Yet the practice of burial shows the existence in our ancestors of a desire to make sense even of death. Death is a problem not just because it is a threat, but because we feel that there is an answer to it, though one that eludes our grasp. Death reveals the presence in our hearts of a nameless desire, a limitless longing for we know not what, for completeness, for happiness, for knowing the meaning of the universe and knowing it to be good. Death seems to contradict this many-faced desire; and yet humanity seems unable to rid itself of it, our stone-age ancestors just as much as we ourselves.

The Origin of Religion

The way our ancestors tried to make sense of life, and to express what they found good and beautiful in it, is revealed in their art and in their ceremonies. To celebrate great events, or certain times and things, they danced and sang, and they painted on walls of caves. They made pots and tools to be beautiful as well as to be useful. And they made all sorts of little figures, animal and human, that expressed the power of their ideas, their hopes and fears, and what they valued most. The stories they told, myths, were their way of expressing their understanding of life, of where they had come from and where it was going. The ceremonies they performed, magical and sacrificial, were their way of expressing their desires and their hopes that the power that determined the order of the universe would fulfil them. Such ceremonies were also their way of expressing joy and thankfulness for deliverance from danger or for success in hunting or in battle.

Because our ancestors, being human, were able to reflect on themselves and on their lives as a whole, they were conscious of their needs and of their lack of power to fulfil them completely and perfectly. In their rituals and ceremonies, in their art and image-making, they expressed their desire that the powers of nature that had brought them into being and that would one day bring about their deaths, would fulfil their needs perfectly and completely. This was their religion.

Many of the needs of our ancestors were natural needs. There was not enough food. Tools broke. Prey escaped. Babies got sick. There was no rain. But some were caused by themselves: people fought, stole, were jealous, ran away. One need stands out as being both: the need of each person for other persons, not just for what others could do for them but for their own sakes. This shows most clearly in the sexual habits of the earliest human beings. Animals mate only when there is a chance of procreation. And this they know by instinct. Humans however make love all the time. This shows that the natural need that love-making satisfies is not simply that of procreation. It is a need for the other person—as a person, a need for love—to be loved but also, simply, to love.

From the very beginning, this need proved very difficult to satisfy. It is the cause of all sorts of fear and despair, hostility and domination. It is the cause also of all sorts of social institutions: rules about marriage and family life, and political arrangements too. The desire to be loved and to love, to be valued by others whom one values too, shows itself at every level of human society, from sex right up to international politics. It is probably the deepest of all our desires regarding other persons, and so appears at the heart of all the religions that have developed in human history.

The Two Great Struggles

Wherever they lived and whatever they looked like our earliest ancestors were involved in two great struggles. There was the struggle to control nature, and however cleverly this struggle was engaged in, it inevitably ended in suffering, sickness and death. And there was the struggle to control themselves. For of course the greatest danger to humanity was humanity itself. When food was scarce people fought for food. Men fought over women and men and women fought each other. This second struggle, humanity's struggle to control itself and live in peace and harmony, also seemed doomed to failure. Whatever clear social and political and family arrangements our ancestors made these tended to disintegrate into conflict and oppression and war. In their religion they developed images of gods who could save them from these evils, gods who were powerful enough to be lords of nature and kings over human society.

These two basic struggles in which the earliest humans were involved arose from their two basic needs, a need for nature to keep them alive and well, and a need for each other in order to be happy. But the two struggles were connected with each other. Without some degree of cooperation between people there is no hope of controlling nature. If people are not able to live together peacefully there is no possibility of organizing their powers to make the world into a home.

Language, which enables people to think and plan, and so make tools and weapons to satisfy their needs for food and shelter, also provides a way of organizing and controlling people themselves, of making common decisions and coming to agreements, of making rules and laws to live by. So as our ancestors developed their use of language they were also able to try new ways of winning the struggle to make earth serve their needs and the struggle to live and work together in a peaceful and happy way.

Of course in the beginning humanity was not just one big family. After the last Ice Age in the Neolithic period, human society developed in various different parts of the earth in different ways over a period of about 20,000 years. There were five main centres of human development: Central America, with its Maya civilization; the South Seas, with Polynesian civilization; the basin of the Yellow River, with Chinese civilization; the valleys of the Ganges and the Indus, with Indian civilization; and lastly the Nile valley and Mesopotamia, with Egyptian and Sumerian civilization. Each of these ancient civilizations had their own language (or languages), their own technology for trying to control nature, their own social organization for trying to control people, and their own religion in which they created images of gods powerful enough to succeed in winning the struggle where they had failed.

The real problem, of course, in each of these civilizations, and the reason why their technology and social organization and religion never really worked, was that human beings are, as we have seen, free to choose. Because they have the power of thought, they are able to make up their own minds. It was for this reason that people couldn't be completely controlled and organized, even by rulers or laws. And as long as people couldn't live together in peace and co-operate, nature herself could not be controlled. Even religion is not powerful enough to control beings that are free. People can always rebel against religious rules, make up their own minds and even worship new gods that seem better able to meet their needs.

The Goal of History

In all these civilizations religion was the way in which people expressed their deepest longings and their hopes of winning the struggle to control their destiny. It was also the way in which people mobilized themselves to do what needed to be done. But religion was also the expression of the conviction that what needed to be done could only be done by more than human power. We do have needs that are part of our human nature, but which human powers are not sufficient to fulfil. The most important of these needs are the need to create and participate in true community with others, and the need to somehow deal with suffering and death. All our other needs seem to be subordinate to these.

The history of humanity is a history of struggle. But it is not just a history of failure. There was progress as well as decline, progress in technology, progress in social organization, progress in religion. Humanity progressed by a series of experiments: experiments in thought, experiments in politics, experiments in religion. Some of the experiments did not really work and gradually a civilization passed away. This happened to both the Maya and the Polynesian civilizations. Others worked in part, but seemed lacking in some respects, and progressed more and more slowly. This seems to have been the case with the ancient Chinese and Indian civilizations. In the West however, in the area round the Mediterranean, the pace of progress seems to have increased by leaps and bounds in the last 6,000 years, which is the period for which we have any genuine historical evidence.

It was in this area, in the desert country at the eastern end of the Mediterranean, about three thousand years ago that there occurred a breakthrough in the history of thought, an insight into history itself that was so illuminating that it changed the course of history and has made the world what it is today. It was an insight so profound and so far-reaching that it deserves the name of revelation.

It was the discovery that a power capable of winning humanity's struggle to control nature and itself did exist. This power was real—not just a projection of people's hopes and longings. It was a power capable of overcoming suffering and sickness and even death because it was the power that controlled the universe. It was a power capable of creating true community among people because it was a power that could control our freedom. It was all this because it was the power of an absolutely transcendent being, one without any limitations whatsoever.

How this discovery was made, the astonishing discovery that this sort of power was actually at work in human history in the lives of particular people, is another story, a story we will tell in the next chapter.

(1996)

Chapter Twenty-Four
The Possibility of Faith Today

This article is about faith, and the possibility of faith, in a secular age such as ours. It is also about humanity and the conceptions we have of it in our secular culture. To me it seems impossible now to treat the one without the other.

In an age such as ours, after Kant's 'Copernican Revolution' and the discovery of humanity as the creative subject rather than merely the object of the sciences, a proper study of anything (religion included) both depends on and augments our understanding of ourselves. More particularly the following thoughts on faith are derived from reflection on three different themes.

The first is the question of how one acquires faith. This is a very contemporary problem. There are many who although they see faith as something desirable (even especially so) also see the acquisition as forever beyond them. 'If only I had faith' they wistfully say. The traditional Christian assurance that 'faith is a gift' serves only to make this hopeless nostalgia more hopeless still.

Then there is the question of how one recognizes faith when one has it. If faith is a supernatural gift, does it nevertheless reveal its presence in a naturally discernable modification of outlook or behaviour or character? Is there some humanly administrable test for genuine faith?

Finally, the relation of Christian faith to other faiths is an inevitable question in a culture that is as conscious as ours is of pluralism of every kind, and not least in religion. It is a question for the academic study of religion, but also for the ordinary Christian believer and for would-be believers too.

In this article I am putting forward a synthetic overview of the relation between our conception of humanity and of Christian faith that would provide a conceptual tool for working on these questions. Of necessity such an overview will touch on many topics and deal with none in detail. In spite of that I feel that this kind of synthetic approach has value. The best way to find one's way through a wood is to see it from above.

The Secular World-View

Religious faith, of whatever kind, poses special problems for many people today. The growth in understanding and control of the world made possible by modern science and technology, together with the growth in awareness of human freedom that is inseparable from this, seems to have made faith more difficult for us.

In the third world, in South Africa for instance, religious faith still seems a natural and easy thing to most people. But I think that is so only to the extent that people have not yet been deeply influenced by first-world culture in the form in which it is spreading across the globe. Third-world culture, and third-world peoples too, are still going through the 'brook of fire' of scientific consciousness. There is no way of avoiding this fire that seems to burn up the world's religious past. We must go through it.

One of my aims in composing this article has been to formulate an understanding of faith that will go through the fire. If that is possible then the firs of secularisation may prove to have been purifying rather than destructive.

In initial impediment preventing people from grasping the truth of faith is our general twentieth-century view of the world. It is a secular view of the world. And it has its own special illusions. It is inextricably bound up with modern science and technology. It is intimately connected with the Western (European) culture that goes wherever science and technology go, and is at present re-colonising the world.

In criticising this secular world-view I do not want to suggest that we return to the sacral world-view of pre-scientific societies. This is the outlook that sees the world as full of supernatural powers, of devils and angels, and supernatural places, both infernal and celestial. It is a world in which myth and magic and—so it seems—religion too are at home. Perhaps that world has gone forever. Yet it was part of humanity's childhood, so it is part of our psyche. We must not deny or repress it. But it must not continue to control our lives, what we believe or how we believe.

We have to live in a secular world. In order to do that and be open to the truth of Christian faith we must free ourselves from its illusions. One of these illusions is that humanity has grown out of religion. The different sciences have different interesting, and often important, things to say about religion. But in a scientific culture there is a general belief that because religion, like every other social institution, is a human creation, it cannot therefore (strictly speaking) be true. It is something we have made up. Marx and Freud and Sartre each give different accounts of why we do this, and do it so desperately. But they all agree in thinking that in religion we depict and enact reality as we would like it to be rather than as it really is. Religion, as is often said, is wish-fulfilment.

The biblical writers, both Old Testament and New, would of course agree with Marx and Freud and Sartre about this. But they would prefer to call it idolatry. This is because, although they judged most of human religion as self-deceptive (and self-destructive) fooling with illusions, they did not think that it need be that. To the question as to why people in every time and place have constructed images to worship, they would have replied that they did so because they had been created with a capacity and a need for worship—to value absolutely something of absolute value.

The Reality of God

The biblical writers believed that there was something of that sort, namely God, the creator of humanity who could neither be imagined or controlled. Modern atheists like Marx and Freud and Sartre, and those who have been influenced by their style of thought, reject the idea of God not because they have not been able to verify it by the methods of science or philosophy but because of what they think they have discovered about humanity and human religion. Humanity has the capacity for freedom, but not if God exists. In fact, according to them, humanity has enslaved itself—and largely through religion. It is largely because of religion that human beings are not free, in society, or in their minds, or in their personal relations with each other.

I think we have here a clue to the real reason why a secular culture like ours rejects the idea of God. It seems to be incompatible with the reality or the possibility of human freedom and hence of our ability to control both the world of nature and ourselves.

So it is not enough, in order to remove the impediments to faith, to try to prove (as Aquinas tried) that God is real. One also has to show that his reality is compatible with human freedom. I think it is. I even think that if God is not real then human freedom is impossible. The idea of freedom is so central to a secular conception of what it is to be human that I must indicate briefly how it is linked with God in each of these two ways. Only then will one be in a position to link the experience of faith with the experience of one's own humanity in a secular age.

As regards the first point, if God is truly transcendent, his power or influence cannot be measured against or compared with (either adding to or taking away from) the power or influence of any created thing—including ourselves. If he acts upon us, whether by way of creating us or of keeping us in being or of bringing us to perfection, his influence in no way adds to or disturbs or competes with our own. Our free acts are as much dependent on his creative power as anything else is. To be free of *that* would simply be not to exist at all. This is a paradox but it is a necessary consequence of the notion that God is our creator. In the last part of this article I will be considering a feature of the way in which persons influence other persons that provides evidence that this paradox is the expression of something real. But for the moment let us just admit it and address the second point, namely that the reality of human freedom depends on the reality of God.

There are fairly clear negative grounds for thinking that this is so. Our free acts are those that are not sufficiently explained by finite beings other than ourselves. To say that we are free is to say that *we* are the origin of the act. Nevertheless we are not the cause of the *capacity* for free action, the capacity that makes us different from other animals and which is developed in us as we grow up. To be that we would have to cause ourselves, since the capacity is part of our nature. But no other finite being could be the cause of this capacity either. For it is the capacity for *free* action. And what holds for the act holds also for the capacity, namely that an over-riding influence of external causes would prevent its being free. Hence the capacity itself, that aspect of our human nature that makes us free, could not have been produced by any series or system (evolution let us say) of finite things. Still it is real. Therefore it must have been brought into being (through the evolutionary process no doubt) by a being that is not finite.

Such an insight into the necessary conditions for human freedom makes us at once aware of the way in which we transcend the world shown us by science. And this gives us an intuition of a realm of reality, of which we as free beings are part, which though real is essentially mysterious to us. It is, as it were, too deep for the clear light of science to reach. Without any intuition of this dimension of reality it is difficult for a person to be open to the truth of faith. They would be out of touch with an essential truth about themselves.

To sum up the point I have been trying to make, recognition of our freedom is not a barrier to belief in God but rather a proof of the reality of a realm that transcends the world shown us by science. If this realm is real then God may be too.

Life Beyond Death

The truth is that although the secular view of the world gives freedom such a central place, its understanding of freedom is seriously flawed by the materialism that seems inseparable from a world-view of this kind. A scientific approach to reality seems always to produce a materialistic view of the world. It is this materialism that prevents an adequate understanding of persons. Its inadequacy is illustrated in an especially striking way in regard to death.

According to a materialistic understanding of persons, human consciousness is produced by nerve activity in our brains or, more properly, in our whole central nervous system. The nervous system, like any other organic substance, is made up of complex physical units interacting with each other. When the units are separated and the interactions cease, consciousness ceases too. That is death. Death is the final annihilation of human consciousness.

Strangely enough that is not quite the whole materialist story. Since the brain is a purely physical structure, the precise neuronal pattern that produced my consciousness of myself could be reproduced in some other material (silicon chips let us say) that is more durable than flesh and blood. And this could exist, and be repaired, indefinitely. My consciousness would thus continue forever. All this strange scenario requires to become fact is sufficient advance in neurology to discover fully the workings of the brain, and sufficient advance in computer technology to be able to programme the pattern that produces the consciousness that is uniquely mine.

Even if it did become possible to make a brain and it were true that human consciousness is simply the product of brain processes I do not think that we would find that kind of 'eternal life' at all satisfying. Apart from incidental difficulties arising from the kind of body one would have, there would be the over-riding problem of never having died. The life one would be living would be the same kind of life that one had been living all along. But the universal human desire to overcome death is not the same as the natural inclination of all living things to avoid it. It is rather the desire for a different kind of life, a life that is not limited in the way that a life that is ended by death is.

This desire to overcome death is in fact a manifestation of a peculiarity of human beings, something one could call a lack of limitation. In this case the lack of limitation shows itself in the desire for something unlimited. Death, after all, is the most obvious proof of the limitations of human power. In dying we are forced at last to surrender our attempt to control our own destiny. And in this lies death's real importance. In accepting our finiteness and our impotence in the face of death and relying on a power that is infinite (and hence able to transcend death) we are enabled to express and so realise the unlimited side of our own nature. Dying becomes an act of self-offering, whatever the actual circumstances of our death may be. Without death, such a radical act of self-donation would be impossible. So it is only in death that our need to give ourselves completely, the need that is central to our being persons, is able to be fully and perfectly fulfilled.

The life beyond death that we desire would be a life built on that foundation. It would be a state that could be reached only through death, and would manifest the qualities that a 'good' death expresses so well. It would of course be a life made possible only by the creative power of God, sustaining us through the crisis of death, transforming and perfecting our humanity in the way that he has planned. But it would still be a human life, lived in a human world, the familiar world we have come to know, though transformed and glorified. It is because contemporary materialism cannot envisage a future such as this, either for us or for the world, that it misunderstands death in the way it does.

I hope I have succeeded in showing how and why our secular culture makes it difficult for us to believe in the existence of God and in the possibility of life after death. I also hope I have shown how closely these two beliefs are related to the understanding we have of our own human nature. If we recognise something unlimited in our own nature these two beliefs will fit in. If we don't, they won't.

The Impediments to Faith

Although not believing in the existence of God or in the possibility of life after death makes it difficult to have faith, faith itself is not simply having these two beliefs. Faith is not simply an intellectual attitude. It is an attitude involving the whole person, mind and will and feelings. And in addition it is also an attitude to a person, to God or to Jesus. For this reason even the intellectual element in faith won't be primarily a matter of believing certain truths or doctrines but of knowing a person. It will be experiential rather than theoretical, knowledge by contact or familiarity.

So faith requires an attitude of the will and the emotions as well as an attitude of the mind. And because it is an attitude to a person, the non-intellectual element in faith is really fundamental. It is only a certain disposition of the heart that really gains one access to the intimate knowledge of God that faith involves.

But here too, in the sphere of the heart (the will and the emotions) no less than in that of the intellect, a secular culture produces formidable impediments to faith. The challenge to faith in the sphere of the heart is the challenge of commitment. We have the capacity for making an unconditional commitment, the capacity for worship. Do we keep this capacity open for God or do we fill it with idols? The pressure towards idolatry is universal to humanity. But in our culture it seems to have a peculiar intensity. A secular culture is so conscious of humanity's own value and power that it would seem especially prone to foster a spirit of self-worship in us.

A world created by science and technology, a 'developed' world, gives one the illusion of self-control, in particular it suggests that happiness is a problem for technology rather than for morality, that peace and prosperity can be achieved without moral effort and growth. And an artificial environment that is all-embracing, affecting one's imagination as much as one's diet, creates artificial needs. The deep enduring needs of our human nature are lost to consciousness and remain unsatisfied. Think of the need for solitude, for instance, or the need for sustained and serious conversation. How easy is it to satisfy such needs in our secular society? How many people even recognise that they have them? And think of sex. How easy does our kind of culture make it for us to discover our true desires there?

Implicit Faith

We have been considering the impediments to faith thrown up by our secular culture. They are so many and so serious that it is not surprising that many people find faith a problem. I do not think, however, that this means that there is less real faith in our time than in former times. Ours is a secular culture so the symbols of faith have been removed from public life to a large extent. A consequence of this is that people find it much more difficult to recognise and identify faith either in themselves or in others. But this does not mean that the actual attitude of faith does not exist in them.

Because faith is a form of personal knowledge of a person it can exist even if it is not properly understood or is mistakenly described. I can have a deep understanding of my wife in spite of the fact that I may be mistaken in some of my ideas about her. So, in the case of faith, I can recognise the mysterious and transcendent power of real forgiveness between people without connecting it in any way with God or Jesus, concerning whom I may well be very seriously misinformed.

Because faith is not only a matter of knowledge, however personal, but also a matter of the will and the feelings, it is possible that these elements of faith may be well developed although the intellectual element has not been, or has been perverted. It is even possible to have real love of God, real charity, while at the same time thinking that the whole idea of God is simply an outdated myth.

For both these reasons real faith can exist in a hidden way, hidden even from itself. There is no reason to believe that it does so less in a secular society than in any other. In fact the ingredients for real faith in God always exist in every society, however disguised or misinterpreted they may be by the dominant culture. I will now say what I think they are and describe them in some detail.

The First Ingredient of Faith: Desire

The first ingredient of faith is the desire for something of absolute value. This often shows itself negatively, as dissatisfaction with or frustration at illusory substitutes such as fame, wealth, power, prestige or success of various kinds. On the other hand it can take positive forms, such as real indignation at injustice, remorse for harm one has caused, the yearning for 'true love' or the desire for liberation from weakness of will.

Insofar as the desire for something of absolute value is present in all these forms, they can be seen as expressions of a desire for God. It is only God who can be the ultimate cause of our fulfilment. Just as only a transcendent being can create free beings, so only a transcending being can bring such beings to fulfilment, perfecting their freedom without violating it. We find faith then, in spite of all we might say or think, to the extent that we recognise this desire in ourselves and consent to it, or at least don't attempt to destroy it or to replace it with another more easily satisfied.

A natural desire, in the sense of a desire that springs from human nature and is universal in all human beings, is evidence for the existence of its object. If a new species of bird were discovered (on board a ship at sea let us say), and it could only stay alive on a diet artificially created for it by scientists, this would be a sign that somewhere in the world (on a remote island perhaps), food containing the same chemicals and vitamins existed in a natural state. So if it is the case that all human beings by nature have desires that only a transcendent being could satisfy, this is solid evidence for the reality of such a being. It is not of course proof that the desire, in this or that particular individual, will be satisfied. But it is proof that it can be, that the conditions for its satisfaction do exist.

The Second Ingredient of Faith: Power

The second ingredient of faith is the experience of a certain kind of power. It is strictly personal power which either brings about or expresses our growth as persons. It enables us to know ourselves more truly and to affirm ourselves more fully. Such a power can only be produced in us by a transcendent being since personal growth is a growth in freedom.

We experience this power at work in our own decisions and dispositions: in forgiving others, in loving the unlovely, in working for justice, in all one's genuine moral effort. Or we experience it in the decisions and dispositions of others: in their love and forgiveness and their loyalty to oneself. In either case the power is expressed in relations between persons, and it is often difficult to tell whether it is incoming or outgoing. When one experiences it in oneself it seems to have come as a gift through the influence of others; when one experiences it in others one seems to be oneself empowered by the experience. The transcendent nature of the power is shown by the lack of opposition between the one who gives and the one who receives, a mutuality and reciprocity in which personal freedom is augmented rather than decreased.

Another way of describing this experience of the power capable of producing personal growth (and so of freedom) is to say that it is the experience of goodness. To experience real goodness in persons is to experience the result of personal growth in them and hence the reality in their lives of the power necessary to achieve this. In their ability to love us unselfishly and to understand us better than we are able to understand ourselves, we experience an unconditional or absolute value that makes itself felt in the trust and certainty they inspire in us. We cannot prove that they are good; yet we are certain that they are. Our certainty shows itself in the determination that whatever happens to us, whatever choices we are offered, we want to be 'on their side', to have a similar character, to be the sort of people they would want to love.

It should not be too difficult to see this experience of power in ourselves and in others as an experience of charity, whereas the first, the experience of desire, was one of hope. Although hidden by the circumstances in which they exist, and as it were anonymous, these two dispositions are theological virtues (they cannot come into existence except for grace), and so form the foundation for genuine faith. Where they do not exist genuine faith is impossible, whatever doctrines one may believe.

The Third Ingredient of Faith: Knowledge

The third and final ingredient of that attitude of the whole person that is faith in the broad sense, is faith in the narrow sense, an attitude of the intellect as such. It is coming to believe that our desire for something of absolute value is not empty. We see that it points to something real though transcending the world that we can control or the ideas that we can comprehend. And we come to recognize the transcendent origin of the power that produces personal growth in us. But there is also something more. True faith, however implicit, is never only concerned with ideas, however profound, or truths, however important. It is a response to a person.

So somehow or other, in our relationships with other persons—and indeed with the whole impersonal world as well, as it forms a medium for our society with others—we become aware of more than merely the power of a transcendent being. We become aware of a personal presence as well. Not as one person among others, but as present in the personal presence of all the others, especially the good. This presence doesn't take away from the immediacy or fascination of theirs but enhances it.

It is difficult to describe this identity-in-difference, but one can illustrate it. For instance, in a painting of a Madonna and child the genius of the painter has been able to show in the still-unformed features of the baby's face the likeness and the character of the mother. In something of the same way it is possible for faith to find in human faces the features and the character of God.

From what I have said it can be seen that I do consider faith still to be a possibility for people in a secular society, in spite of all the impediments to it. I want to stress that I am talking about real faith, what Christians call 'saving faith', the kind that can be produced in us only by grace, that makes us sharers in an eternal sin- and death-transcending life and unites us to God himself. The question therefore arises as to how the implicit faith I have been talking about is related to explicitly Christian faith and to Jesus himself.

Christian Faith

The first thing I want to say is that without Jesus' revelation to us, I do not think that one would be able to identify this 'anonymous' faith for what it really is, namely a real discovery of and response to the real God. It is Jesus who has taught us how to recognize faith, hope and charity for what they are. People with the kind of implicit faith I have been describing certainly don't recognize it as such. Since the time of Jesus, however, this insight into humanity, its needs and possibilities and what is going on in each person's life, has been kept alive. It is still alive in contemporary Western (European) culture. It is embodied in many institutions (hospitals, legal systems) and even exists in a hidden way in new developments that seem to contradict it altogether like communism. Essentially, however, it remains alive in the Church, in spite of the deformations and exaggerations peculiar to our time. In any case, wherever a person picks up this self-knowledge, this insight of faith, it will refer them back to the Church as its origin, insofar as they come to discover that what they have is faith, they will discover the Church as well.

Here is the logic of how faith comes to discover itself in discovering the Church. First of all, the Church's claim to know the truth about God being present in human history is derived from the story told by the apostles. It is only true if that is true. The apostles' story is the story about Jesus, and it is based on their actual experience of him. According to them, Jesus told them this and they believed him because they trusted him absolutely. So assenting to the Church's claim one is also accepting the authority of Jesus. At least one is if the apostles did understand and report Jesus correctly, and if the Church is doing the same as far as the apostles are concerned. For it to be quite certain that one's assent to the Church is in substance an assent to what Jesus himself believed there must be at least some kind of infallibility of Church tradition involved. Faith in Jesus will thus include faith in this infallibility on the part of the Church.

What are the grounds for such an act of faith? Consider first the apostles themselves. In their case it is quite clear that they accepted what Jesus had to say about God simply on his authority. There was no way of checking up as to whether what he said was true. Moreover in view of what he was telling them, namely the truth about God, their acceptance of his authority had to be unconditional if it occurred at all. It would have built into it the belief that Jesus spoke with the authority of God. Thus putting their faith in Jesus was putting their faith in God.

Putting it like that brings us to the heart of the matter. The apostles coming to believe in what Jesus told them about God was part of their whole response to him as a person and, in particular, to what had happened after his death. Because they had also come to believe that in their relationship with Jesus they were in personal contact with God. They had come to know about God not simply because of what Jesus had told them but because of what they themselves had experienced. Their knowledge was not merely inferential but direct, immediate, knowledge by acquaintance. They believed that God was present and powerfully active in human history because they believed that they met him there.

So whatever the apostles claim to know about God is derived from their belief that they have personal knowledge of God acquired from their relationship with Jesus. This experience of God is different in kind from the experience of God in creation as the creator. It is also different from the experience of God in history in human actions and relationships. In this case God is present as a historical person and thus in the fullest possible way for human persons. Yet as a result of this experience it becomes possible to recognize the other kinds of experience as experiences of God. The transcendent power experienced in creation and in personal growth and community is seen to belong to the one they have come to know in their relationship with Jesus.

Grounds for Faith

That is how the apostles came to faith. What of those who come to believe through them? What are the grounds for their faith? First, the story told by the apostles must strike them as true. It must present a view of life that corresponds to their experience and, moreover, promises to fulfil their deepest desires. With regard to identifying Jesus as the one in relation to whom one can come to know God as a person, no evidence or reason or general truth can be sufficient, not even claims about the truth of the resurrection or the forgiveness of sins. The grounds for accepting claims such as those can only be a conviction of the truthfulness and integrity of the apostles themselves. In other word, the crucial claims contained in the apostles' story must be accepted on their personal authority alone. And because of the content of the claim, accepting it is recognizing their authority as absolute, as being the authority of God. What could possibly justify such acceptance?

Only conviction of their goodness. Not only must the apostolic body be judged wise and truthful; it must also be judged to be holy. Only if it seen to be the embodiment of all these personal qualities can assent to its testimony be an act of genuine faith. Their claims about Jesus entail that his transcendent power is alive in them, and if this is not evident how can one believe what they say?

Even if their lives do reveal the presence of God's transforming power, that does not prove that it comes from Jesus. But if their lives do not reveal the influence of such power then questions about its origin do not even arise. Further, it is only insofar as one does feel that it is God's power that is revealed in the goodness and truth of the apostles' lives, that accepting them as a sign of God's presence is not idolatrous but an authentic act of faith.

It follows from all this that the only adequate cause of Christian faith would be entering into a personal relationship with the apostles, a relationship that is the embodiment of the spirit of Jesus himself. The apostles offer both truth and forgiveness by offering themselves. And in that way they enable the spirit of Jesus to evoke faith in those to whom they preach. Only such an interpersonal transaction could be an adequate medium for entering into the personal relationship with God that is fully-formed faith.

Faith is Given

The same must be true for us and our contemporaries as well. The only sufficient grounds for faith in Jesus are the wisdom and understanding, the holiness and forgiving love that one may find in members of the Church. Only in that way, in responding to a personal relationship offered by members of the Church, and so entering into the personal community of the Church, could one come in touch with the spirit of Jesus they claim to be alive in them, and so with Jesus—and so with God himself. Fully-formed faith is a personal relationship with the person of God. A personal relationship of a human person to God cannot be fully realized in anything less than a personal relationship of a human kind, whether to Jesus, the apostles or to the present members of the Church.

If God's plan for humanity and for human history is what Christians say it is, then it must be fulfilled in something like the way that has been outlined above. He must make himself present to us in our human world. And he can do so in the fullest possible way only by entering into a personal relationship with us, as a person among persons. And if this particular presence and its influence is to be communicated to others in other times and places, it can only be by means of a particular personal community carrying it through time and space in a continuous tradition of personal life.

It is not enough that the Church know and proclaim the truth about God. The truth about God that is all-important for us is that he has come into the world. The Church is there not merely to tell us this so that we can know the truth with our minds. It is there to enable us to experience God's grace made real in the members of the Church.

Saving faith can only come about as the effect of grace. In other words it must come as a gift. Thus it must come to one from another. Ultimately the other is God, but immediately it is some human other. As such it comes in the fullest possible way as a gift from the Church, who has it as a gift from the apostles, who were given it by Jesus. So the search for faith, in our time as in others, is the search for someone, or some others, who can give it one. And the only way they can do this is by giving one themselves.

(1992)

Chapter Twenty-Five
Euthenasia and the Theology of Death

The substance of this article was originally produced for the Southern African Anglican Theological Commission, which was considering proposed new legislation on euthanasia. It was felt that a Christian response to this question had to be based on a theological understanding of death.

In composing this sketch of a theology of death I also had in mind the Draft Bill, 'The End of Life Decisions Act', of the South African Law Commission, produced in June 1997, and the paper 'Comments on the Draft Bill on End-of-Life Decisions' by the UCT Bioethics Centre at Groote Schuur, of which I am a member. The issue of euthanasia, like that of abortion, is a moral issue that is at the centre of awareness at the moment, and it is important that Christians reflect on it deeply and not just superficially. Issues like these can so easily produce thoughtless habitual responses.

Our Culture Can't Cope with Death

It is difficult to make the Christian understanding of death one's own in a scientific and technological culture. This culture, which is the dominant culture of our time, and spreading across the world wherever science and technology go, can't cope with death. Death is trivialised in popular art and literature and reduced to a peripheral position in social life. Our culture is built on the myth of our control of our own destiny through the power that science and technology give us. But death escapes our control and so embarrasses us, giving the lie to our dreams and undermining our self-confidence.

Our culture is unique in this. All societies since the beginning of human history have found death mysterious. The earliest signs of humanity include ritualised burials. And in every culture known to us death is seen as posing a question to be answered or problem to be solved, as part of a predicament universal to humanity. It separates us from those we love; it puts an end to our efforts to make something of enduring value. Every religion worthy of humanity offers its own answer to the problem of death.

What Happens When a Person Dies?

Our understanding of what happens when a person dies depends on our conception of what a human person is. Our culture embodies a materialist conception of persons. Human beings are understood as merely complex constructions of the same physical particles as everything else. When the organisation of these particles is destroyed through accident or disease our consciousness, which is dependent on this organisation, is annihilated beyond recall. That is death.

In view of this understanding of death the most that one can hope to do is to put it off as long as possible. And this is a dominating aim of medicine. There are even hopes that advances in science and technology could succeed in putting it off forever—at least for a select few. Whether even that would provide the answer to the question of death that humanity looks for remains to be seen.

Materialism or Dualism?

The materialist understanding of persons is however mistaken. Human persons are not only objects the sciences can study and technology control. They are also the subjects who produce science and technology, devising appropriate methods for discovering new truths and worthwhile goals for technology to pursue. As thinking and choosing subjects we transcend the whole realm the sciences are able to know or technology to control. It is not that the laws that the sciences are able to discover break down in us; they are merely insufficient to explain our distinctively personal acts, our judgments and decisions.

The materialism of our culture is ideological in character, an uncritically accepted system of thought that rules us in spite of its theoretical weaknesses, controlling the imaginations of most people. The only alternative that is recognised is some kind of dualism, between mind and matter or body and soul. Dualism is often favoured by religions in our culture since it holds out more hope than materialism for providing an answer to the question of death. Dualistic conceptions of human persons usually see the immaterial mind or soul as the real person and the body merely as an instrument or the means for our participation in a material world. Death, for such dualists, is thus merely a change of state. The material body disintegrates and corrupts; the immaterial soul lives on by virtue of its own inherent power.

Dualist theories of human persons have their own built-in weakness. They fail to do justice to the radical unity of a human person, the inextricable involvement of bodily and mental elements in all our thought and action. As one goes up the ladder of being, from simple organisms, through plants and animals, to persons, the unity of the individual is intensified, not decreased. Dualism is deeply mythological in character, incompatible with the genuine discoveries of science. And in a religious context it could be judged as a form of idolatry. In many quasi-religious sects this is the case. The soul-self does not need a god to overcome the threat of death. It is immortal of itself. In the bleak materialist universe shown us by science, esoteric knowledge of some kind can give us an ultimate security in this vision of our immortal selves.

In spite of the inadequacy of both materialist and dualist conceptions of human persons each contains an insight that is importantly true. The truth of materialism is that human persons are inextricably engaged with the rest of the universe, connected to our natural and social environment by all the causal links the different sciences discover. There is only one world and we are intrinsically dependent on it. The truth of dualism is that in our deliberate thought and action we transcend these causal links and are self-determining. These two truths appear contradictory: we are both self-determining and dependent on what is other than ourselves for what we are and do. The traditional Christian conception of persons however recognises both these truths and offers a way of reconciling them.

The Christian Conception of Persons

The Christian conception of human persons follows from the belief that humanity is 'the image of God'. An image is both like what it is an image of, and wholly dependent on it for what it is. As far as likeness is concerned, God is, for us, the transcendent creator. Humanity shares in these attributes and expresses them in relation to the rest of creation. As transcendent we transcend the causal systems of nature and society. We are self-determining. And so we have creative power over the impersonal world, to understand its dynamisms and direct them, to make it a home for the whole human family. We are also dependent. And this too is expressed in our dependence on what is other than ourselves, our natural and social milieu, for our existence, growth and fulfilment.

We are self-determining by virtue of an immediate constitutive relationship with the transcendent creator. No system of finite causes, evolutionary or environmental, could bring a free being into existence. But as finite persons we can only exercise, develop and perfect this capacity for self-determination through our dependence on our environment, natural and social.

This self-determination through other-dependence is revealed most fully in our personal relationships with other persons. The more we are influenced in a certain kind of way (by being known and valued as the persons we are for our own sake alone) by other persons, the more our actions are our own and the more self-determining we become. This paradoxical phenomenon is evident from the earliest stages of infancy, in adult experiences of personal growth and empowerment, and in those experiences of reciprocity and mutuality that come as the fulfilment of our personal relationships with others.

The apparent contradiction of freedom-in-dependence is explained in the Christian understanding, as the effect of the presence and operation within our interpersonal relationships of the transcendent personal power of the creator himself. Just as no finite power is sufficient to create our capacity for free action, so no finite being is capable of developing and perfecting it.

The Christian View of Death

This conception of persons provides an alternative to materialism and dualism that is rationally coherent and which, moreover, is able to reconcile the truths in both while avoiding the mistakes. It provides the foundation for a Christian understanding of what happens when a person dies.

This is traditionally expressed as the separation of body and soul. The dualistic language must not however be allowed to obscure the fact that a dualistic conception of human persons is incompatible with Christian faith. The classical tradition of Christian theology is not dualistic: soul and body are related as form and matter, two constitutive principles of a single being.

The Christian view inherits the Biblical emphasis on the unity of the human person. There are not two different kinds of thing, spiritual and material, much less two different spheres, a natural and a supernatural, in which each is at home. At the most there is the duality of inner and outer, of inner life and outward expression, of heart and limbs in the imagery of the New Testament. The soul is the inner principle of unity of the person as a whole; the body is the whole person in outward manifestation. So when body and soul are separated at death a person is, as it were, separated from themselves. The whole person loses their life and ceases to live.

It is better, in view of the dangers of dualistic language, and also in order to get a realistic rather than a merely mythical picture of death, to avoid talk of soul and body. In any case these terms correspond to the self-determination and other-dependence described above. And these categories, though more technical, are less misleading.

In death our connections with our environment, both natural and social, are broken. But because our self-consciousness and self-determination depends on these, they cease too. We cease to be the self-conscious, self-determining subjects of our lives. Yet we do not cease, because of that, to exist. The internal relationship to the transcendent creator is not affected by death, and it is what gives us existence as well as our capacity for self-consciousness and self-determination. So death in itself is not annihilation. But it is not something that power other than that of the creator could overcome, certainly not some inner power that human persons themselves might possess. As dead we have neither consciousness nor power to act. If death is to be overcome in some sense it must be by means of God's creative power.

The Human Predicament: Death and Sin

This account of what happens when a person dies is the bare bones, the skeleton as it were, of a view of death compatible with Christian faith. Thus far it owes nothing to faith and is justifiable by reason alone, though going beyond the limitations of science. Before I can present the full Christian faith regarding death I need to put flesh on this account, so that we have a better picture of death as a central event in human life and a deeper understanding of its meaning. Here we leave the philosophical domain, which is concerned with the necessary and universal, and enter the realm of history. The account I shall give is based on the biblical view, including that of the New Testament, but it is not precisely a matter of faith. Though providing the means for the expression of Christian faith, it is something that any one could understand and accept quite apart from faith.

Death is a fundamental aspect of human life. And human life, in every time and place, has the character of a predicament. Since its origins humanity has been involved in two great struggles, a struggle with the impersonal world to make it a permanent home for the human family, and a struggle within humanity itself to make it a true community of persons. And success in the first struggle depends on success in the second. The Bible documents the facts that the first struggle produces suffering and death, while the second produces conflict, conflict between people and conflict within each person.

The reason for this, in biblical terminology, is sin. The essence of sin is idolatry: according finite powers infinite value. In fact, as the first eleven chapters of the book of Genesis make clear, the ultimate object of idolatry is humanity itself. Knowing ourselves to be the image of God, we worship the likeness without recognising the dependence. Thus instead of being open and receptive, responsive and obedient to the only power capable of developing free beings to fulfilment, the transcendent power of the creator, we close ourselves against it. And so we lose our freedom, subjecting ourselves to the finite powers under our control.

This loss of freedom expresses itself firstly in inner conflict: we are unable to do what we really want to do, and act in opposition to the deepest desires of our nature. It also expresses itself in conflict between ourselves and others. Imprisoned by our own self-worship, we are unable to affirm others for their own sake and as they really are. And so the project of creating a single unified community of humanity, and making the world a home for that community to live in, is doomed to failure. This is the predicament from which humanity needs to be saved, in the vision of the Bible.

Death is part of this predicament, and gets the negative meaning it has for us from it. The natural meaning of death is the ultimate impotence of our finite powers to bring about our own fulfilment. In the situation of sin, where we only value what is under our own control, this means the utter loss of all we value, and hence despair.

In the vision of the Bible only the transcendent power of the creator is sufficient to overcome sin and death. To a superficial understanding this would seem to be clearly true in the case of death, though less so in the case of sin. In fact in the biblical world-view the opposite is the case. The overcoming of sin is only possible for a transcendent power since it involves the restoration and development of freedom, something beyond the power of any finite cause, human persons included. Death, on the other hand, only requires a transcendent power to overcome it if overcoming it means not just preventing it, but the establishing of a life 'beyond' death that transcends death altogether in some way. It is quite conceivable that human power might one day be capable of preventing death altogether through scientific and technological means. But that would not be overcoming the negative meaning of death as seen by the Bible.

The Christian Faith

The Christian faith is that God is able to save humanity from its predicament, and does so. The first followers of Jesus came to believe this through their experience of this salvation in their own lives, an experience that came to them through their fellowship with Jesus.

As far as sin was concerned, he converted them from the idolatry of self-worship to a devotion to the transcendent power and goodness manifested in his own life. He achieved this by virtue of a whole-hearted and realistic love of them as images of the transcendent creator. He loved them for what they had it in them to be, and this enabled them to be it. This love expressed itself primarily as the forgiveness of their sins, an intimate personal interaction that transformed them from within, overcoming their inner oppositions, and freeing them to enter into a community of mutual knowledge and love, with him and with each other.

This is what the apostolic community came to believe that Jesus had done in saving them from sin. And, although it had all happened through their ordinary human contact with him, because it was sin that had been forgiven and freedom that had been restored it could only be the work of the transcendent power of the creator himself. The effect of this salvation was a radical change of heart, an opening towards and reliance upon a personal power transcending anything under their control.

They expressed the spirit of this new life as dying in order to live, becoming small in order to become great, being last in order to be first. Such paradoxes were necessary to convey the fundamental paradox of an experience of the transcendent creator's presence in the interpersonal transactions of finite human beings. The spirit of this new life required embodiment in new virtues: faith in, hope for and love of its transcendent source and its image in the world.

The followers of Jesus also came to believe that God had saved them from death. This faith too came to them through their fellowship with Jesus, a fellowship they continued to experience even after he himself had died. As a result of their experience of his resurrection they came to believe that the community they had enjoyed with Jesus, and which had seemed ended by his death, would never end. The same transcendent power that had brought it into being by forgiving their sins and changing their hearts would keep it in being forever.

They had learnt that a kind of death to oneself was the way to fullness of life. Now, as a result of their experience of Jesus' real presence in their midst in spite of having died, they came to see death itself as the way—for finite and sinful creatures—to sharing the transcendent life of the creator. As a result of this experience of the transcendence of death in Jesus they came to look forward to a death- (and sin-) transcending life of their own, in a community of humanity perfected by God's power, in a world renewed and transformed by that same power.

The Christian Church has inherited this faith of the apostolic community and the understanding of death that it includes. We need to find a way of expressing this understanding in our own secular culture so that it does not sound merely mythical.

Life After Death[1]

The conception we have of a death-transcending life will inevitably be symbolic and mythical. But the Christian understanding of human persons outlined above can however supply constraints on our imagination and an organising principle for interpreting the biblical material in the language of a secular culture.

1. See also J Pieper, *Death and Immortality* (Faber, 1968).

Firstly it needs to be said that life beyond death cannot be life in 'another' world. There is no other world, but only the universe in which we live and which God has created. The 'new creation' cannot be new in the sense of another different one. It is of course life 'with God'. But God is not in some other place. The only place where God is, in the sense that he can be in a place at all, is here. But he is in the universe not as a part of it, or even as the whole of it, but as its creator. He is also, according to our faith, incarnate in it as its saviour. So if we go to God when we die, we don't go away, we stay here.

Of course we expect the world to be transformed in some unimaginable way, but however it is transformed there must be continuity. It is the world that was created that has been redeemed. And the same must be true of us. It is the person I have become by the end of my life that will live after death. As far as we are concerned the principle of continuity is our capacity for self-determination, our personhood, since this only exists by virtue of an immediate relation to the creator that no finite cause, such as whatever caused our death, can affect. Everything that has been built up during our lifetime on this foundation must remain. It is of course inoperative in death, since the relation to otherness, to the whole of the rest of the created universe, has been removed. This is why the Christian answer to the problem of death is described as the 'resurrection of the body'.

It must be remembered that in a non-dualistic understanding of human persons the body is not a part of a person, joined (for instance) to another part—the soul. It is the whole person, but in its relation to what is other. The resurrection of the body thus describes the restoration of this relation, and so the reactualisation of the relation to self: (self-consciousness and self-determination) that depends upon it. With this the whole universe is given back to us, albeit in some unimaginable new way, and we are reintegrated into it.

The created universe is finite. It is not God. Space and time are perhaps not necessary conditions of finiteness but only of change. Still, some analogy of space and time seem essential to the distinction between self and other which presumably will remain, and to the notion of created life. We shall not become gods. But perhaps the limitations of space and time will be to a certain degree removed. There is a sense even now in which each of us, through our consciousness of the universe as a whole, is coextensive with it. Perhaps the resurrection-life will involve being present to every part of it at once.

Less speculatively and more importantly, life beyond death cannot be temporal in the sense in which it now is, though of course we can only imagine it in that way. For this reason it is better to refer all that Christian faith teaches about this life to the event of death itself. This is the event after all that is the entry into it. This is helpful in that it does away with the idea of a time lapse between the separation of soul and body in death and their re-connection again in the resurrection. Whatever happens, happens all at once. The disruption and the reintegration are two aspects of the same event, or perhaps the single event seen from this side and from the other. The event of death from our side is the purifying dispossession of our finite powers; from God's side, as it were, it is our final transformation and completion. All the Christian myths, of purgatory and so on, of the after-life are possibly representations of one or other aspect of the meaning of death as the method of this transformation.

Our Attitude to Death

We come now to consider the Christian attitude to death and the part it should play in the moral and spiritual lives of Christians.

As we saw when looking at the response of the disciples to Jesus, the fundamental moral consequence of Christian faith is the self-donation involved in genuine love. And it is the universal experience of the Christian moral tradition that this has the character of a kind of death. This is the equivalent in the moral life of the real death at the end of life. Both are deaths 'on a cross'. This moral attitude is simply the full expression of that active openness and receptivity to the recognition and affirmation of us as persons by others that enables our personal growth. It is the essential dynamism whereby finite persons respond to the initiative of a transcendent power. It would, moreover, be wholly ecstatic were it not for our idolatrous attachment to illusory identities and securities that we have built up by sin. As it is, the movement of self-transcendence feels like self-negation. But insofar as it is achieved in us, insofar as a disposition to self-donation is created at the centre of ourselves, the final dispossession of death is not something to fear. It is of a piece with a movement of the spirit we have learnt to trust. We know our fulfilment lies in hands other than our own and are able to surrender to their support. This is death as transformation and self-donation, as purgatory and heaven. On the other hand it is possible that we have in the course of our life constructed a false security so strong that we are unable to put our faith in anything beyond our own control. We have built a walled city with a tower reaching (so we believe) to heaven, constructed for ourselves an identity that will endure for ever. And this is death as ultimate imprisonment and loss of self, as hell.

Throughout our lives the drama of growth or disintegration continues. The self-worship of sin is so difficult to be honest to oneself about that it is always possible to fool oneself that one is indeed 'dying to self'. In a theological perspective death and dying is God's way of ensuring that we see things as they are and make a genuine decision about what we want, to be with God or not. Christian faith in Jesus encourages us to trust that we will choose God.

Death in Health-Care

With this Christian understanding of death as a background it is now possible to indicate the place and importance of death in health-care.

It is necessary to state the obvious for the sake of emphasis: death is not a disease. It is a crucial, and natural, part of human life, as indeed it is part of the life of every living thing. It marks the point at which the creation of an individual life is completed and the individual is able to enter into a full relationship with the universe as a whole.

Because this consummation and transition is the work of a transcendent power it is experienced as surrender and loss of strength by finite persons. Insofar as we are also sinful as well as finite, such self-surrender will also involve real suffering and mortification. So death will often involve the suffering of loneliness, impotence, loss of looks, over-taxing of those who care for us, as well as shame, guilt, a sense of failure and loss of self-respect.

But the suffering in death that is the result of our finiteness and sinfulness must be distinguished, at least notionally, from the suffering produced by the circumstances that cause our death, sickness or trauma or whatever: physical pain and discomfort of all kinds, nausea, breathlessness, dizziness and mental confusion, loss of memory, terrifying dreams.

Medical science and technology does not have as one of its proper aims the actual prevention of death. Even if that were possible it would not be good, in the Christian view. Death has a God-given meaning for us, and we must learn to understand and embrace it, in spite of the fearful aversion of our culture. Medicine does however have as its proper object those circumstances that cause death and the character of a death, and produce the sort of suffering described above.

The function of health-care in the strict sense is to foster personal growth and fulfilment through attention to the bodily and psychic factors that influence or prevent this. A humane health-care practice will recognise the place of death and dying in this process and not fear or avoid thinking about it. Instead it will use all the scientific and technological resources at its disposal, as well as the essential resource of caring and competent personnel, to ensure that patients die good deaths, as far as possible conscious, pain-free and cared-for.

In all that scientific health-care is able to do for patients it is a mistake to make a distinction between the technological interventions of human medicine and natural processes that come from God. Science and technology are the products of human insight and activity and thus expressions of our nature. And that too comes from God. Apart from sin, it is a mistake to make a distinction between what comes from human powers and from God. Whether we are considering sickness or death, health-care professionals are responsible for what they do. And one cannot contrast human freedom with God's activity. The more directly and fully our acts are caused by God, the more they are our own. To speak, in the context of health-care, of 'leaving it to God' or 'letting nature take its course', cannot remove the responsibility from human subjects for their acts and omissions.

This applies to death as well as to any other part of human life that can be influenced by human acts, and hence by those of health-care professionals. It is, from a Christian point of view, part of the responsibility of health-care professionals to participate in decisions as to when and how people are to die. Insofar as the Christian view of life and death influence their decisions, and the spirit of Christian morality inspires their actions, their patients can have nothing to fear from their interventions or advice.

Having a theology of death can help one make up one's own mind on the question of euthanasia—for others or oneself.[2]

(1998)

---

2. Background reading for this paper: B Davies, *An Introduction to the Philosophy of Religion* (Oxford, 1993); PT de Chardin, *Le Milieu Divin.* (Collins, 1960); S Moore, *No Exit* (Darton, Longman and Todd, 1968); J Pieper, *Death and Immortality* (Faber, 1968); K Rahner, *The Theology of Death* (Burns and Oates, 1965); A Shutte, *The Mystery of Humanity* (Snailpress, 1993).

Chapter Twenty-Six
Dialogue Between Religions

At the beginning of the third millennium it is quite clear that the earth has become a global village, with all the positive and negative consequences of this. Certainly it is true that increased closeness has meant increased conflict. The prime example of this is the built-in conflict between the developed and the undeveloped parts of the contemporary world. Development in this context means development by the science and technology that originated in Europe during the modern period and has since spread across the globe. Wherever it has gone it has carried with it its own culture. So development also includes the swamping of traditional cultures by this new world-culture rooted in science and technology. I am using 'development' in a neutral way to refer to a phenomenon we all recognise. In fact it is more accurate to speak of *over*development and *under*development, because this makes it clear that something is wrong.

South Africa has a special, and symbolic, place on the world's development map. Not only do we embody overdevelopment and underdevelopment in one country to a unique degree, but the opposition between the two has until recently been embodied in the idea and the reality of apartheid. White South Africa was overdeveloped, Black South Africa underdeveloped. Opposition and conflict defined our way of life. I am sure it was for this reason we became so famous. We were a microcosm of the rest of the world. Apartheid was a perfect name for the disease from which humanity was suffering at the end of the twentieth century. That is why the world is so interested in our recent changes. And that is why it is so important what we do now. I think we have the opportunity to attempt a crucial experiment from which the world as a whole could benefit.

This is the situation in which we are now discussing dialogue between religions. As we know from recent and present history, religion can be a powerful factor in, and even a cause of, conflict between individuals, groups and nations. But I am sure we all believe that it can also be a powerful force for overcoming conflict. It is this belief that has motivated this meeting of the Goedgedacht Forum. It is also the belief of the Parliament of the World's Religions that is at the moment preparing for its millennial meeting in Cape Town later this year. I am going to suggest some of the conditions that must be met if religion is to play this role successfully. But before I do that I must say something about how I am using the term 'religion'.

I am using it in an absolutely general way to refer to a specific sort of human activity. I am not presupposing any particular view of the world or reality. Religion, as I understand it, is the expression in thought, feeling and action of our natural desire for complete fulfilment. Human beings have the capacity to see their lives, or the world, as a totality. This limitlessness of human nature is not only a characteristic of our minds but also of our wills and our desires. We are able to envisage, to desire and to strive for a fulfilment that is a fulfilment of every part of us, a perfection or completeness that would satisfy the whole of what we are.

Typically the fulfilment that religion aims at is felt to be beyond human power to achieve, or at least beyond our natural or unaided powers. Hence the idea of a god or gods, namely a source of power transcending our own and sufficient to fulfill those fundamental desires of our nature which we are unable to. However I do not want to limit religion only to those traditions that refer to a god or gods. It is the basic human attitude and activity that I am concerned with, and not the particular form it takes. So Buddhism can be seen as a religion. Perhaps even Marxism. Two things however are essential. Religion is concerned with fulfilment of a total kind. And it seeks to access and enact the power necessary to achieve this. Religion, as distinct from philosophy or science, is not primarily directed towards knowledge but towards power. It is for this reason that it is such an important factor in our present situation.

The rationale for such organisations as the World Conference of Religions for Peace and the Parliament of the World's Religions is more or less this: there cannot be peace in the world unless there is peace between the world's religions; there cannot be peace between the world's religions unless there is dialogue between them; this dialogue is the reason for their existence. It is also the reason for this meeting of the Forum. The goal of all these initiatives is not the unification of all religions into one super-religion. We have come to believe that pluralism in the sphere of religion is not only inevitable but a sign of reality. We have also come to recognise that the different traditions can provide complementary insights into reality and as to how one should live. But, more importantly, we are being forced to admit that reality is so rich and inexhaustible, and life so infinitely open to newness, that no one tradition could possibly contain everything. A plurality of religions is a positive benefit.

What we are hoping to achieve is a kind of marriage, a marriage of many partners. As in a marriage we aim at a community that will enhance, rather than submerge, the identity and character of the partners. We want to achieve real mutual understanding, real sympathy, real co-operation, real solidarity. Those who have already set out on this path will have discovered that it is precisely those who have been most true to their own tradition who are closest in spirit to those in another tradition who have been similarly faithful to theirs. We meet at the centre, not on the periphery. For this to be possible we will have to choose an appropriate strategy and develop certain dispositions of character to make our marriage work.

Every religion has beliefs about what is real and what is good, beliefs about human nature and its needs and how they can be satisfied, beliefs about the source and kind of power necessary to do this. And such beliefs can differ from one religion to another. But there is a fact of the matter, whether we know it or not: either there is a god or there isn't, either death is the end or it is not, either all our natural needs can be satisfied or they can't be. So if religions differ in belief they can't be equally right about those things on which they differ. Just as is the case with different cultures, each will' be a mix of truth and falsity, good and bad. Giving each equal respect does not mean regarding each as equally true, equally good. It means taking each equally seriously, making the same genuine effort to understand, the same honest critical appraisal, of each of them—especially one's own.

The fundamental psychological conditions for genuine dialogue between religions is to be able to be open to other religions and critical of one's own. These are the basic virtues needed, a spirit of genuine receptivity to the insights and influence of other traditions, and a readiness to adopt a self-critical attitude towards one's own. Such virtues are not the enemies of authentic faith but a sign of it.

The fundamental objective foundation for dialogue between religions is the humanity we all share. All religions have this in common: they seek the fulfilment of our humanity. However they may differ in their view of the world or how we ought to live, whatever different customs and ceremonies their adherents may practise, whatever different lifestyles they may have, this common reference point remains: human nature with its capacities, desires, needs and powers, the single source of every culture and religion.

Of course different religions may have different ideas about our human nature. But at least we all have the same objective reality on which to test them. Even ideas about the gods or life beyond death can be tested against our experience of our humanity, since they must be related to it in some way to play any part in our religious life at all. For this reason the aspect of religion that is most important as far as dialogue between religions is concerned is values—ethics and morality. It is here, in the sphere of practice and action, rather than in the theoretical sphere of belief, than one can most clearly see the connection (and the relevance or irrelevance) of religion to humanity.

Every religion I have come across sees values and morality as having their basis in our human nature rather than being merely conventional, the contingent customs of this or that culture, this or that society. Even religions that stress the divine source of moral laws and values recognise that they are not merely arbitrary edicts. They are commanded so that those who keep them will become 'holy' or 'like God' or attain to some kind of fulfilment or salvation. They are commanded for the sake of those who are to obey them, and so are intrinsically connected with our humanity. The commandments are good not *because* God commands them; God commands them because they are good *for us*.

Fundamental human values thus form the best foundation for dialogue between religions. Each religion will express them differently in its life, will use different terminology to define them. And each may emphasise particular values to a greater or lesser extent. But all have the same source, the same experience, on which to base a shared reflection and critical evaluation. In this area our dialogue is about something we all share and to which we can appeal. We can begin and continue it with a confident trust that we are not simply imposing fabrications of our own tradition on our partners in dialogue, or being required to surrender to some dogma of theirs.

I have said that we in South Africa are well placed to perform an experiment from which the rest of the world can learn. I think that this is true with regard to dialogue between religions too. South Africa is after all one of the most religious societies left on earth! But it is also a place where the dominant scientific secular culture of our time exists in close contact with the traditional culture of Africa. And this contact I believe, if we can make it fruitful, holds out great promise for our project.

I have spoken critically of the scientific secular culture. This is because it is part of the humanly destructive power that is re-colonising the world. It is also because the main form it takes at the moment, as it spreads across the world, is such a degraded and brutal one. But it need not be. There are immense riches in European culture. There is nothing wrong with science or secularisation as such. I want to explain this idea more fully.

The European discovery of freedom in the modern period represents, I believe, a real deepening of insight into a central aspect of our humanity. It is one which we cannot go back on. It provides a solid signpost for our journey of dialogue together. But there is another that we, here in South Africa, have privileged access to. It is the idea of humanity, central to traditional African thought, embodied in the well-known saying *umuntu ngumuntu ngabantu* (a person is a person through persons). This is the idea that we depend for the exercise, development and fulfilment of our humanity on others, that our humanity itself is a gift. In this view the human self only comes into being in relationships with others.

Such a view can appear the exact opposite of the European insight: other-dependence versus self-determination. They look contradictory, but I do not think they are. In fact I would like to claim that it is only by virtue of a certain kind of influence of others that we are enabled to be, empowered to be, self-determining. The more we are dependent *in this way*, the more—not the less—self-determining we become. This is not the place to work this idea out fully and argue for its truth. I have done that elsewhere. But if it is true then it provides another marker for a dialogue between religions.

Religions have always emphasised the communal nature of humanity. If one can show that this is compatible with the self-determination of a secular view then one will have laid a solid foundation for understanding and living one's religion in a secular world. It must be remembered that what I have referred to as self-determination and other-dependence are not intended to be merely facts about our humanity but values as well. If morality is something naturally expressive of our humanity and not a mere convention or dogma then truths about human nature are also moral truths. To say that someone shows humanity is to make a moral judgment as well as a factual one. *Ubuntu,* the key moral conception in traditional African thought, actually means humanity. Each of the two insights I have highlighted, the secular and the 'religious', comprises a whole constellation of human values. Self-determination includes such values as authenticity, integrity, willingness, conscientiousness, courage, self-control and a host of others. Other-dependence, in the sense I mean it, entails unselfishness, openness, justice, sympathy, faithfulness, compassion, consideration and the like. None of these is new. What is new is to see that the one list is bound up with the other. In any case it is values such as these that must form the basis for dialogue between religions.

This is true not just in the sense that such values make dialogue possible and fruitful. They also constitute a standard that a religion has to measure up to if it is to be worthy of our allegiance and devotion. Religion is capable of undermining our humanity, dehumanising us, as well as perfecting it. I am not thinking of what is actually done by religious people. We all suffer to a greater or lesser extent from weakness of will. We all have psychic wounds. We are all subject to social conditioning and pressure. We all fail to practise what we preach. I am thinking of what religions say we ought to do. And clearly there is a religious justification of inhumanity that we must recognise and try to overcome.

In South Africa we are all aware of the religious justification of apartheid. But there are many other kinds of religious justification of inhumanity. Discrimination between the treatment of the faithful and others is a particularly insidious one. There is the justification of unjust wars. And the pacifism that turns a blind eye to human poverty and suffering. Each of us could contribute our own short-list.

The reason I am stressing this point is that it illustrates so well the fact that we cannot avoid the apparently presumptuous business of having to pronounce judgment on the world's religions. In living our own and in dialogue with others we are bound to use our critical and moral powers to the best of our ability. We cannot simply obey.

Dogmatism and idolatry are very close together. Thomas Aquinas taught, and the Catholic Church still (reluctantly) teaches, that a wrong conscience obliges. In other words it is more important to be true to what you honestly and genuinely believe than to be right. It could be necessary for your eternal salvation to leave the Catholic Church!

This is not presumption but the recognition that, wherever the power released in our religion comes from, its goal is the growth and fulfilment of our humanity, not its destruction. If this is so then it means that we can all approach this momentous matter of dialogue between religions—momentous because it is the first time in the history of humanity that it is happening on a universal scale—with confidence and a sense of freedom. If only we are true to ourselves we will be open to the truth of others.

(1999)

Chapter Twenty-Seven
Evil and the Christian Response: Science, Philosophy and Theology

A Christian attempt to deal with evil, in oneself and in the world, is not a purely intellectual exercise.[1] There is of course an intellectual element in it, inasmuch as any adult engagement with a basic and demanding feature of one's life involves an attempt to gain a deeper insight into its true nature, and also in this case as well, some insight into how to deal with it. Christian faith however supplies two further elements, namely the belief that evil can, and therefore ought to, be overcome, and also to a greater or lesser degree, the ability to do that. This faith is based on the experience of the capacities of human nature and the power necessary to develop and fulfill them that the followers of Jesus have gained in their relationship with him, an experience understood as the empowerment of fundamental capacities of human nature, both in Jesus and in them, through the closest possible personal union between it and its transcendent source.

This paper has a number of parts. The first concerns the definition of evil, especially when it is considered from a religious—and Christian—perspective. The second deals with the way in which a scientific worldview can, and ought to, change our understanding of evil, and in particular evil in relation to God. (When I speak of God in this paper I am speaking of the one Jesus called 'Father') The third part is philosophical. I outline a philosophical understanding of human nature, its capacities and needs, in order to provide both an explanation of and a standard for judging evil done. This conception

1. A number of recent books on evil have made this point. In particular Ken Surin's *Theology and the Problem of Evil* (Blackwell, 1986) and Terrence Tilley's *The Evils of Theodicy* (Georgetown University Press, 2002) warn readers against the inauthenticity of a purely intellectual 'solution' to the problem of evil.

of human nature will also provide a conceptual framework for the final theological section of the paper. In this final section I set out my understanding of the Christian faith in God as saviour from every form of evil.

From a religious point of view evil must be understood in a very general sense, as referring to everything that is wrong with us and the world. In the Christian tradition the classical definition of evil is 'the privation of some particular good'.[2] The notion of privation or lack must not lead one to think that this tradition regards evil as in some way unreal, in the manner of Christian Science or, perhaps, Buddhism. The privation or lack in question must be understood in relation to the idea of nature, as being a lack of something that a particular kind of being ought to have in order to fulfill its nature. A diseased plant, for instance, might lack its natural ability to produce flowers and so seeds to propagate its species. Even a faulty machine would be evil in this sense, since it would be incapable of performing the function for which it was made. So evil, in the sense in which I mean it, does not mean 'very or especially bad' as it often does in common usage.

A distinction is often made between moral and natural evil. I prefer to speak of evil suffered, whether as a result of human agency or not, and evil done. Human beings are, after all, part of nature. And moral evil could be mistakenly understood in a purely conventional sense and not as a real quality of the agent. To make it quite clear that in speaking of evil in terms of privation or lack I am always thinking of something with a particular nature that is incapacitated by this, I am going to use the idea of harm. The privation or lack is something that harms the thing that suffers the lack. And this is so as much in the case of evil done as in that of evil suffered. Awareness of this latter point is lacking in much contemporary writing on the topic. It was not always so. Since the time of Plato in fact the notion that it is worse to do wrong than to suffer wrong has been a leading idea in the European ethical tradition.[3] And worse here has always been understood in the sense of harm to the doer, psychological rather than physical harm but harm nonetheless.

2. This is Aquinas' formulation in his *On Evil*, Q.1, Art. 1. But he quotes Augustine as an authority to the effect that 'evil has no positive nature, but the lack of good has received this name' (1995: 4).
3. Socrates, speaking to Polus in Plato's *Gorgias*, 'I think that both of us—and everyone else as well in fact—believe that doing wrong is worse than suffering wrong' (Oxford, 1994: 48).

Let me reinforce this intuition by means of an example. Imagine you are a parent whose small son is a bully. He bullies the other children at his preschool mercilessly, especially the smallest and most timid. His teacher arranges a meeting with you and reveals the facts: children unwilling to go to school, wetting their beds, miserable. As a responsible parent you would be rightly horrified at the harm your son was doing to these children. But you would also be horrified at the harm he was doing to himself. And this second kind of harm is of a much deeper and more sinister kind that the other. If your son were not persuaded to change his ways he could grow up into an evil person. The damage his behaviour does him is potentially far more dangerous than the sufferings lie caused the others.

Take a further step and consider our reaction to atrocities such as the Holocaust and Hiroshima. It is something more than the quality and quantity of the suffering of the victims that horrifies us. Natural disasters could produce suffering of a similar kind and scale. The real horror is that this suffering was deliberately caused. We call the perpetrators monsters because we feel that they have almost ceased to be human, have undermined their own humanity. It is this feeling that they are no longer human, but monsters or demons, that makes it possible for some people to want to inflict the worst conceivable punishment on them—hell for instance. In fact their humanity, though diminished, is not lost. Their development towards fulfilment is arrested; they can never be humanly happy unless the wounds they have done themselves are healed.

In our present climate of thought it is the harm that we do to others that has taken centre stage—as well, of course, as the harm caused by nonhuman causes such as earthquakes and tsunamis. If however we consider the history of religious, and certainly of Christian thought, the opposite is the case. It is the harm we do ourselves by means of our evil acts that is seen as the biggest problem. Deliberately harming others is certainly an exampIe of being an evil person. But there are many other examples of evil in the subject that do not have others as their object. Attitudes such as covetousness (think of St Paul!), greed, cynicism, envy—and lists such as the 'seven deadly sins'—all identify evil aspects of a person's character that may never issue in harmful acts towards others.

So evil must always be understood as harm. In the case of evil done it is harm to the doer, deep harm to their own humanity. In the third part of this paper I will examine this idea in greater detail.

I now turn to the contribution made by the sciences to our understanding of evil. As with most theological topics, the Christian understanding of evil has been formulated in premodern and—to a certain extent—mythical language. In our contemporary scientific and secular culture we have to find new ways to formulate the essential Christian insights into evil.

We now have a far deeper and more comprehensive understanding of the actual conditions that make the existence of human beings possible.[4] This knowledge must be allowed to put constraints on theological speculation around the topic of evil. The question, for instance, of whether God could have made a different world, can now finally be seen to be an empty one. Too often in the past thinking about evil has been plagued by the tendency of otherwise able minds to indulge in the most bizarre fancies about what they would do if they were God, the kind of world they would make and the kind of abilities and character they, being God, would have. Above all such thinking has produced an abstract monstrosity of omnipotence and

---

4. It perhaps useful to consider at this point in some detail the actual conditions that make human life possible. 'The structure and function of a single cell is immensely complex. But a human grows to an interconnected set of ten thousand billion cells, all working together as a single purposive and conscious organism in hierarchically controlled way, put together according to instructions in the DNA molecules that are read out and executed in an order that depends both on time and position, able to function continuously all the time as the number of cells increase coherently from one to ten thousand billion in a highly organized fashion, passing through different stages of maturity, all of this happening in an interacting set of organisms of similar levels of complexity within a hospitable environment, this system itself developing from a single cell to the level of complexity we see around us today, all the while remaining functional. All of this is possible because of the nature of quantum mechanics and of the forces and particles described by physics (essentially the electromagnetic force acting on the proton which together control the nature of chemistry and hence of biological activity. They all fit together as required because of the precise values taken by the fundamental constants that control the strengths of physical interactions, which also happen to allow the functioning of stars as required in order to produce the needed elements, and allow development of the solar system (which is made possible through the force of gravity), with a hospitable surface for life on Earth . . .' George Ellis, *Before the Beginning* (Boyers, 1993), 90–91.

omniscience allied to absolute benevolence and justice to do service in the role of God. Science now puts constraints on this kind of theodicy. The sum total of the sciences reveal humanity as a microcosm of the universe and the product of a process of increasing complexity that is still continuing If this is the effect of God's creative activity, then these are the necessary conditions for the creation of humanity. God's decision to create humanity is of course free (a work of 'grace') but we have no reason—or right—to assume that this is possible in any way other than through the immensely complex, finetuned causal chains the sciences have revealed. God's creative power remains mysterious, but science is a pentorch beam of light.

With regard to the nature of evil (both evil suffered and evil done) the relevance of the sciences can be summarised as follows: in the first place the worldview presented by the sum total of the sciences establishes an evolutionary process filled with prehuman harm and suffering All of this is however the result of the working of the laws of nature together with the initial conditions that they work on. To that extent it is inevitable, even necessary if the process is to result in us. Even death plays an essential part in the process of the development of species. All prehuman evil, being inevitable, is natural and necessary to the production of something good.

This picture changes with the appearance of humanity on the scene. This appearance is of course a progressive one, not instantaneous. Gradually the necessary conditions for free decision, and so for deliberate evil, evil done in the full sense of the term, are assembled. As in a growing child, so in early humanity, the physical and psychological conditions for the capacity for real selfdetermination develop bit by bit. And when they do, what was inevitable ceases to be so. Evil done by humans because it is freely done is not necessary and does not of itself lead to anything good at all.

Understanding the origin of humanity in a scientific way does however go some way towards explaining the possibility of evil done by humans. The prehuman evolutionary forces, biological and psychological, involved in the production of the first humans remain alive in them. Kinds of aggression and selfcentredness necessary for the development of our immediate ancestors do not suddenly disappear with the coming of *homo sapiens.* But they need to be integrated into and transformed by the new nature with its new capacities that has come into being. There is real newness, to be sure, but there is also continuity with what has preceded it. And this process of integration and transformation will, one must suppose, take time and the effort of will. The perspective opened up by the evolutionary worldview is of a humanity that is radically incomplete, a humanity that is still in process of construction (of creation?). And because of the nature of humanity (as we shall see) this means that this process is one that must be managed by humanity itself. In an evolutionary perspective humanity confronts itself as a task.

As well as revealing the presence of prehuman elements in us that can only be made fully human by the exercise of something newly produced by evolution, namely human will, science also reveals the constraints on this exercise resulting from the causal connections, both social and biological, that are necessary (though not sufficient as we shall presently show) for the existence and activity of our wills. The human will has the capacity for free decision but this freedom is limited by genetic and psychological factors as well as by the situation in which we exist and the resources at our disposal. In considering the question of evil done, and the related issue of moral responsibility, it is very important to remember this. We now realise far better than in previous ages how diminished our responsibility for our life choices is. Depth psychology as well as sociobiology, have made this very clear. The typical situation of a moral agent is to be under pressure from all sorts of psychic forces, many of which one is unaware of.

A final factor that the scientific worldview contributes to a realistic approach to evil from the point of view of Christian faith is its insistence on the solidarity and integrity of worldprocess. We live and act in a delicately balanced and finetuned environment, where everything that happens has an effect however small on everything else. The fabric of the universe is a seamless robe. Respect for the integrity of the causal networks that constitute the universe will make one less than ever inclined to appeal to a 'god of the gaps' to explain things we don't understand, less inclined to look for or to expect 'miracles'. Science thus reinforces the traditional view that God works through secondary causes and not as one cause among others. This insight is especially important if one is to assert that creation is a continuing process, not merely in the sense that God's creative activity is necessary to keep the universe in being at each moment that it exists, but that it is responsible also for real newness in world process, a newness that is not 'miraculous' but which respects the solidarity and integrity of secondary causes. In this way a scientific worldview is the enemy of idolatrous conceptions of God and God's activity, which reduce this to some 'supernatural' force *within* the world.

We turn now from science to philosophy in order to see what help this can provide to a Christian engagement with evil. And here it is the conception we have of human nature that is our focus of attention. At the outset one must distinguish the way in which philosophy can give one insight into human nature from that of the sciences. Because humanity is a microcosm of the universe in the sense that all levels of reality are represented in us every science has something to offer towards understanding human nature. Each science however can only offer insights that are limited by its methods and point of view, scientific knowledge is always perspectival, aspectual and therefore abstract. It is always also provisional and therefore partial. And every science presupposes that there is a way of judging its methods and their results, that its methods meet some normative standard of thinking and choosing. In other words every science takes for granted the thinking, choosing person of the scientist. No science deals with thinking and choosing as such. Thus when dealing with human nature the whole sum of sciences is insufficient. Each science can deal with an aspect of humanity as its proper object. Only philosophy can deal with humanity as the subject of all the sciences, the one who invents, produces and judges science. And in this way it deals with that aspect of our human nature that science cannot reach because it always presupposes it. It is precisely this aspect that makes us capable of science, and morality, and religion.

The insufficiency of the sum of sciences to reach, deal with or explain this dimension of our humanity already indicates an important truth about human nature: we transcend the kinds of reality that science is able to engage with. The clearest sign of this transcendence is of course our ability to do science. But the fundamental character of this transcendence is our capacity for freedom, for acting and judging for reasons rather than under the influence of the kinds of causes the sciences deal with, for real selfdetermination. When we decide to do something or judge a belief to be true *for a reason* our act transcends any conceivable scientific causality. Not that the causes that the sciences discover cease to operate in us, that there is a break of some kind in the seamless robe we have spoken of. Those causes are still necessary but they are insufficient to explain my act. This is because an intrinsic element in my choice or judgment is logical rather than causal. It is nonetheless real and has power to change the world.

I have laboured this seemingly abstract point because it is so often overlooked in our scientific culture, And it is the tip of an iceberg of insight into our human nature that is of the utmost importance both for our understanding of our capacity for evil and of the Christian faith in God as saviour. The fact is that there is something in human nature that transcends everything else in the universe that the sciences reveal. It is therefore intrinsically mysterious though as normal as life itself. For if the causes revealed by science are insufficient to explain our capacity for freedom it follows that they are insufficient by themselves to bring it into being—for then it wouldn't be a capacity for *freedom*. This points to the existence and operation of another kind of causality altogether, a causality that has its origin in something that is neither other than me in the way that anything in the universe shown us by science is, but nor me or part of me, since I depend on it for my existence. This can only be because it is incommensurable with me in the way that Christians understand God as our creator to be incommensurable with creation.[5]

According to this conception of God as creator one cannot add God and creation and get two. One can add one orange to another orange and get two oranges because they are both oranges. One can even add an apple to an orange and get two fruit because they are both fruit. In general one can add anything in the universe to anything else because they are both things. But one cannot add God to anything because there is no class to which they both belong. This is what it means to say that God is the *creator*. God both transcends the universe—that is, God is not the universe, nor part of it, and is immanent in it—not as one thing among others but in everything as what causes it to be. This relation of incommensurability between creator and creature is at its clearest and sharpest in the case of human beings insofar as they are selfdetermining, since our free acts are free precisely to the extent that they are caused not by any other thing but solely by the creator. Being free does not of course mean being free of God; such freedom simply does not exist. But because God is my creator, the more God

5. For a detailed treatment of the necessity for the influence of a transcendent cause if real becoming in world process is to be possible—including the evolution of humanity from pre-human beings—see Karl Rahner's *Hominisation* (Burns and Oates, 1965).

alone is the cause of my acts the more they are my own. We shall presently offer something that will lessen the strength of this paradox. But we cannot remove it altogether because it is the sign of something that is genuinely mysterious in human nature.

Up to now I have considered our capacity for freedom in an essentially negative way, as freedom from the causality of the sciences, a freedom entailing humanity's transcendence of the rest of the universe the sciences reveal. But there is a positive aspect to human freedom, namely selfdetermination. There is a sense in which human nature is an unfinished thing. Because of our capacity for selfdetermination we are in the position of having, in a sense, to make ourselves. Of course each of us is under all sorts of genetic and psychological constraints, but within that framework there is a real sphere of creativity open to us. We have the freedom, and the responsibility, of determining the sort of persons we will end up being, of fashioning our own identity. As the existentialist philosopher, JeanPaul Sartre (*Existentialism and Humanism*, Methuen, 1970: 34), expresses it: 'man is condemned to be free'. This expression brings out well the crisis of having to choose oneself and the anxiety it can cause. Our freedom presents us with a virtually unlimited horizon of possibilities. This unlimitedness of our capacity for choosing ourselves makes itself felt in a desire for something—a situation, a state of affairs, a life—we can value without limit, something of absolute and permanent value with which we can wholly identify ourselves so that we can be all that we could really and fully want to be.[6]

The pressure of this deepest desire of our human nature can take strange forms in human history and in the lives of individuals. Fundamentally it is a desire to realise our unlimited capacity for selfdetermination by an affirmation of something of a correspondingly

6. 'Insofar as man is a transcendent being, he is confronted by himself, is responsible for himself, and hence is person and subject. For it is only in the presence of the infinity of being, as both revealed and concealed, that an existent is in a position and has a standpoint from out of which he can assume responsibility for himself. A finite system as such can experience itself as finite only if in its origins it has its own existence by the fact that, as this conscious subject, it comes from something else which is not itself and which is not just an individual system, but is the original unity which anticipates and is the fullness of every conceivable system and of every individual and distinct subject.' K Rahner, *Foundations of Christian Faith* (Darton, Longman and Todd, 1978), 34.

unlimited value. However nothing in our concrete situation offers us an unlimited fulfilment. Our response to this situation is often one of despair, though not necessarily recognised as such. In desperation we make of some limited value—money, health, security, fame or whatever—an absolute value, attaching ourselves to it as the final source of our identity and the goal of our selfcreation. Alternatively our despair can take the form of a depressed selfhatred: 'it's not good to be alive'.[7] In either case we actively go against our natural desire, inhibiting its authentic expression and in the last resort diminishing it to vanishing point. In so doing we are diminishing our humanity as such, since this desire is so central to our nature. This is thus the essence of evil done, evil in the subject that harms the one who does it. The paradox is that it is the most essential, and the most valuable, thing about us—our capacity for selfdetermination—that makes it possible. I want now to consider the concrete situation in which this dramatic struggle in the soul actually takes place so as to show that it is what I have described as an insight into a genuine predicament which confronts humanity.

The situation in which we gain the most intense awareness of this desire and in which, inevitably, we attempt to fulfill it, is that of our relations with other persons. In fact it is only in relation to other persons that I become aware of my capacity for selfdetermination at all. Both in the history of humanity and in the life of the individual subjectivity is the result of intersubjectivity. 'Wild' children, children who have been left to die at birth and have not died but grown to physical maturity totally outside human society show no signs of a sense of self, of being a responsible origin of action. In the relationship with the other, in which awareness of my capacity for selfdetermination is born, it is the other that has the initiative. It is by virtue of being recognised and affirmed by the other that I am able to recognise and affirm myself and in doing so, I become aware of my radical dependence on the other for this.

What I really want from the other is an unconditional, unlimited love of me for my own sake, as something of absolute value. However no human lover is in a position to give me this. Because of the conditions

---

7. For a brilliant and insightful discussion of the origin of sin, both in the individual and the human race, from this standpoint see Sebastian Moore's *Let This Mind Be In You* (Darton, Longman and Todd, 1985).

of human existence that we have remarked on above—insufficient knowledge, incompleteness, inner conflict—other persons are in the same position as I am, driven by a selfcentred need for genuine love that inhibits their ability to give it. There thus exists a vicious circle in this most fundamental intersubjective situation. And it is the source of unending conflict between persons and within them.[8]

Another way of seeing this essential intersubjective situation in which we seek fulfiliment is to say that what we really desire is a form of community with the other characterised by mutual recognition and love. This would be a community of free beings in which the freedom of all was exercised and fulfilled. Because of the dynamism outlined above this seems beyond human power to achieve, whether at the personal or the political level. The history of humanity is a history of conflict between persons and groups that is the external form of a conflict within persons caused by attempting to satisfy a limitless capacity with objects of limited value. In this way evil done, which essentially harms the doer, is also the cause of similar harm to others.

It should not be too difficult to see the similarities between this philosophical account of the nature of evil and its origin and the Biblical conception of sin. This gets its classical formulation in the powerful myths of the first eleven chapters of the book of Genesis. These stories have been gathered together from four different oral traditions by the editors of Genesis to provide an account of the human predicament, its causes and how it might be overcome. It is, if you like, a kind of prologue to the whole Bible presenting the problem to which the rest of the Bible—and especially the New Testament writings for Christians—supplies the answer.[9]

The problem is sin, and sin for the Biblical tradition is essentially idolatry. And idolatry is fundamentally, beneath the great variety

8. The most famous philosophical account of the intersubjective situation of persons is that of Sartre in *Being and Nothingness* (Routledge, 1969). It is not, in my opinion, the best. Among the many authors I am aware of who have tackled this topic the following stand out: John MacMurray (*Persons in Relation*, 1959), Maurice Nedoncelle (*La Réciprocité des Consciences*, 1966), John Heron ('The Phenomenology of Social Encounter: the Gaze,' 1970), Robert Johann (*The Meaning of Love*, 1975) and Andrew Tallon (*Personal Becoming*, 1979).

9. The discussion of the Genesis material that follows is a summary of a more extended treatment in a 1987 article of mine in *Philosophy and Theology*, 'Community, Apartheid and the Metaphysics of Humanity in Genesis 1–11' (Chapter 22 in this book).

of forms it takes, selfworship. The idol is valued for the power it is thought to have to enable it to fulfill the desires of its worshipper, hence the ultimate object of worship is the self. And the key to the Biblical notion of sin as idolatry is its conception of humanity as the image of God. 'And God said, "Let us make man in our image, after our likeness . . ." So God created man in his own image, in the image of God he created him' (Gen 1:26–27).

In the Adam and Eve story the serpent tells Eve that if they eat the fruit of the tree of the knowledge of good and evil they 'will be like God, knowing good and evil' (Genesis 3:5) Paradoxically this is the truth. The trees in the story are symbols of everything in the garden which the world provides to fulfill our needs. This is true too of the two mysterious trees in the centre of the garden that they have been forbidden to touch, the tree of the knowledge of good and evil and the tree of eternal life. But whereas the other trees are there to supply our ordinary everyday needs, these two trees are there to fulfill those needs that we have precisely because we are the image of God. They are in fact symbols of God's own eternal, meaninggiving life that God intends to share with us. Created in God's image humanity has the capacity for sharing in God's transcendent creative life but this is as yet undeveloped. The incompleteness of Adam and Eve in the garden is symbolised by their nakedness. In the world of the Bible a complete person is a person plus their clothes; clothes define the identity of the wearer. So we see Adam and Eve using the trees to cover their nakedness and God making them clothes of skins when they leave the garden. These foreshadow the glorious robes of Israel as God's bride that appear again and again in the Old Testament writings as the fitting adornment of one whose 'creator has become her husband' (Isa 54:5). The white robes of the saved continue and constitute the climax of this idea in the last book of the Bible when creation is finally complete.

God intends to fulfill the capacities that make humanity the image of God by the *gift* of a share in God's own life. Humanity attempts to achieve the same goal in a different way, by *taking*, or attempting to take, this life for themselves. An image can only exist in dependence on that of which it is the image. Humanity tries to realise God's image in themselves in independence of God, by means that they can control. The world (in the person of the serpent) makes the lying promise that this is possible. The prohibition regarding the two trees signifies that it is not. The result (described in the list of curses that ends the story) is conflict, conflict within humanity and between humanity and the world, a conflict that ends in death.

The same pattern appears in the final story of the sequence, that of the Tower of Babel. Here however the drama takes a much more concrete form, the form it actually takes in history in the eyes of the biblical authors. Here humanity as the image of the transcendent creator God of the Bible attempts to realise its own transcendent creativity by creating a community of humanity in which it is finally complete. This completed community of humanity is symbolised by the city with a tower reaching heaven in which the whole of humanity is unified as one nation with a single name and a common language. This indeed is God's plan for humankind in the mind of the biblical authors. And once again the story is told in paradoxical fashion, with God—as in the case with Adam and Eve—appearing to put a stop to humanity's efforts. And the result is the human predicament as it actually appears in human history: misunderstanding and hence disunity and conflict. The figure of God, in both these stories, should not be seen as Yahweh, the real God of Israel, but rather God as God appears to the eyes of sin, of idolatry. For here as before it is not what humanity is seeking to achieve, solidarity and identity in a transcendent community of the whole of humanity, but *how* they try to achieve it, through the assertion of human power over things we can control rather than by a receptive openness to and trust in a power that exceeds what we can control. It is precisely this power that the author of the book of Acts in the New Testament believes to have been made available through the influence of Jesus on his followers. In the story of the descent of the Holy Spirit on the apostles, so that they are able to speak a language that people of every different language can understand, Luke clearly has the story of Babel in mind. In Jesus, he believes, God himself has spoken a Word that all can understand and so understand each other.

We have come to the final section of this paper. The result of our philosophical consideration of the nature of evil and its causes has been to see that it is precisely the most profound and powerful capacity of our human nature, taken together with our incompleteness and dependence on others for its development, that makes evil possible. And our brief look at the biblical view of sin as idolatry corroborates this view from within a religious tradition. I now want to outline a specifically theological account of the Christian response to evil. Christians understand God as in some sense saving us from evil. What does this mean? And how does God do it?

The philosophical conception of human nature I have outlined in the third part of this article provides me with the tools for answering these questions. For me the key that can enable a Christian response to evil is to see God and his power, especially as it is exercised in creation and salvation, in strictly personal terms, namely in those terms that make us God's image and likeness. The authors of Genesis might have derived their understanding of human nature from their conception of God as their transcendent creator. We however with the help of a philosophical conception of human persons and their relationships with one another, something that can be tested against our experience of being human, can use these insights into our own being to indicate the character of the mystery that is God.

Christianity is that religion which, in recognising the nature of God's presence in Jesus, recognises the personhood of God. To say, as Christians do, that God is personal is not just to treat God as a person, as one like us who can both listen and speak to us. All religions envisage their gods like that. Our imaginations are inherently anthropomorphic. For us to say God is personal is to say that God and God's power is best conceptualised on the analogy of those capacities that make human beings persons in the strict sense, selfdetermining with an unlimited scope to their creativity of meaning and value.

At the same time as insisting on the strictly personal character of God and God's power we must also take human persons as our model for what is real, the created universe as such. I mean we must try to see the universe as a multitude of persons rather than a quantity of atoms or stars. Individual human person, after all, are—as I have said—microcosms of reality, containing every level within themselves and integrating them into a unity that transcends them. Moreover all human persons, through our capacity for knowledge and value, contain the whole universe within ourselves as the object of our thoughts and desires. The universe is thus essentially an aggregate of persons in relationship with each other through the medium provided by our spatiotemporal environment with all that it contains. Each of us is thus a centre to the universe as a whole. And through our bodiliness the whole universe is our common body. Being a centre is a consequence of the reflexive relationship to ourselves, the relationship of selfawareness and selfdetermination that makes us persons. Being a part of the universe as a whole is a consequence of an equally primordial relationship to what is other than ourselves which is our bodiliness. The traditional African worldview, in which the universe is seen as a field of living force with vortices or focuses rather than an aggregate of things, has much to recommend it. With these two guidelines let us now attempt to deal with the questions we have asked.

The necessary first step in this is to formulate the essential content of Christian faith by recalling the events that brought it into being.

The followers of Jesus came to believe, as a result of their experience in their relationship with him (before, in and after his death) that God had become present in the person and life of Jesus, so that in their relationship with him they had knowledge, intimate personal knowledge, of God. This was a wholly novel experience of God. It wasn't that God had ceased to be the transcendent origin and support of their lives, as conceived by the prophets of Israel and recognised by Jesus himself. But now they felt they had come to know God with the kind of knowledge one person might have of another, knowledge by acquaintance and contact, the kind of knowledge they had come to have of Jesus. They signified the meaning of this unique experience by naming Jesus the Word of God, meaning God the Father as knowable and known.

Through their knowledge of Jesus and their consequent identification with him they had come to know both God and themselves as sharers in Jesus' intimate personal knowledge of God. When it is a question of the personal knowledge of a person (which is the kind of knowledge that is Christian faith) love and knowledge are very close. One cannot know a person fully unless one opens one's heart to them in love. But one can only open up in this way if one's knowledge of the other permits it, the other too must open up, be willing to be known. Love and knowledge are thus two elements in an interpersonal movement of communication and identification: knowledge is the invitation, love is the response. In their response to Jesus his followers experienced something in themselves they came to call the Holy Spirit. It came to them from Jesus and was experienced as a sharing in his own obvious love of the Father. For this reason they called the new spirit in their lives, which was defined by their experience of Jesus as God's Word, the Holy Spirit. It was God the Father in the form of God's love.

From the above account of the events that brought Christian faith into being it can be seen that the essential doctrines that define this attitude to God and the conception of God it contains, namely those of the Incarnation and the Trinity are inseparably linked. The central idea of the first is that the transcendent creator is really and fully present in Jesus and his life (and because of that to his followers and the rest of creation as well), and this gives one the specific conception of God spelt out in the second, as able to unite himself to his creation without ceasing to be God and to unite his creation to himself.

So God is not just a creator, but one who includes creation in God's own life. The best example of this—and this is where the *Christian* conception of God goes beyond that of others—is the Incarnation. Karl Rahner (1978: 222) comments that:

> This brings one to an ontological ultimate which a merely rational ontology would perhaps never suspect . . . the absolute One in the pure freedom of his infinite unrelatedness, which he always preserves, possesses the possibility of himself becoming the other, the finite. He possesses the possibility of establishing the other as his own reality by dispossessing himself, by giving himself away.

The Incarnation is seen as including within itself the notion of creation in such a way that the concept of creation is extended to include its point or purpose. Thus God

> creates the human reality (of Jesus) *by the very fact* that he assumes it as his own. He, the Logos, constitutes the differentiation from himself by the fact that he retains it as his own, and conversely: because he truly wants to have the other as his own, he constitutes it in its genuine reality . . . . Therefore his capacity to be creator, that is, the capacity merely to establish the other without giving himself, is only a derived, delimited and secondary possibility which ultimately is grounded in this real and primordial possibility of God, namely, to be able to give himself to what is not God, and thereby really to have his own history in the other, but as his own history (1978: 222).

This conception of God as creator, one that is derived from the doctrine of the Incarnation, is best formulated in personal and interpersonal terms, as a person who knows and loves another as they know and love themselves. In the case of God, however, God's selfknowledge and love do not only include the other (the whole of creation and especially created persons) but create it to be known and loved as well. If we take the intersubjective relation of human persons as the model for God's relationship to humanity (and the rest of creation) in the Incarnation then one can see how it makes sense to speak of God's selftranscendence and selfdonation on the analogy of our knowledge and love of another person. But our knowledge and love, though constitutive of our personhood (as modes of selfawareness and self-determination), are not the ontological foundation for that (which is our created human nature). In God's case it is really God that is communicated in God's knowledge and love, since these are identical with God's being. In the Incarnation this selfcommunication consists in the creation of a human being who is able to share perfectly (because it is God who is communicated) in God's self-knowledge and self-love, and so know and love himself as God does. In this way it can be seen that the personal model for creation, because it does justice to the Incarnation, is the best model we can have. Creation without the selfcommunication of the Incarnation would not exhaust the fullness of what is possible to God in relation to creation.

The doctrine of the Trinity is simply the formal expression of the conception of God derived from the experience of the followers of Jesus as formulated in the doctrine of the Incarnation. As indicated above their experience involved a three-fold relatedness to God. As inheritors of the Jewish religious tradition they were conscious of themselves as held in being by their creator, the one known to Jesus as Father. In relation to Jesus they had achieved a new identity (selfknowledge) through knowledge of God's Word. And finally, as sharers in the spirit of Jesus' life, they were moved by God's Holy Spirit to love God as Jesus did. Because the term of each of these three relations, though formally and experientially distinct, was God, the threeness entered into their very definition of God. As traditional theology would say the 'economic trinity' is the 'immanent trinity'. In this perspective the unity and reality of God can only be adequately expressed with a personal model, as the unity of consciousness, knowledge and love that is definitive of persons.

Understanding God's (continuing) act of creation from the standpoint of the doctrine of the Incarnation gives one a quite special slant on the notion—and on the conception of God that it involves. From this perspective one can understand the whole history of the universe as the bringing into being of the human person of Jesus through the Incarnation of God. God is of course present in the whole process as its creator, both sustaining and directing it, bringing newness into being. There is nowhere else for God to be. But in the Incarnation this presence becomes personal in the strict sense, in a human person. If a strictly personal relationship with God is to be possible for human beings then God must meet us where alone we can exist, namely in the one universe that God has made, and he must be present in a strictly personal way.

God's presence in Jesus is in fact the ultimate case of that incommensurability which we saw was implied in the notion of creator. The idea that God can have a human nature while remaining God, although quite mysterious, is not contradictory as it would be if God were some finite being. Being incommensurable with any created nature, God cannot be added to or subtracted from anything. God, in Jesus, is as human as we are without ceasing to be God.

We are now in a position to formulate a nonmythological conception of salvation—which is the Christian response to evil. And we do this by considering the paradigm case, namely that of Jesus and his followers.

As we have seen, the situation from which humanity needs to be saved is one characterised essentially by sin and death. To this we must add the suffering produced by sin. For unlike the suffering produced by natural causes, as well as that produced by nonsinful human acts, the suffering produced by sin (both personal sin and the social and cultural formations that are the embodiments and prolongations of personal sins) is not only not an inevitable aspect of the creation of humanity (including tile sinless humanity of Jesus) but unnecessary and in themselves serving no purpose.

There is a sense in which God's purpose in creation is achieved in the sinless humanity of Jesus. But this achievement is an aspect of the Incarnation rather than of salvation as such. Jesus had to work out his 'salvation' through sweat, tears and blood. He had to learn obedience through suffering, obedience 'unto death'. But his sinlessness was a necessary though not a sufficient condition for our salvation. If we consider this in the situation of the relationship between Jesus and his followers we can summarise it as follows: with regard to their sins and sinfulness Jesus' response was forgiveness. As to the potentially destructive power of death Jesus offered them a share in his deathtranscending life. And as far as the suffering caused by sin, their sin and the sin of the world, was concerned Jesus offered his own suffering brought about as the direct result of his compassionate love.

Let us consider each of these in turn. With regard to the first, the salvation from sin, the sketch I am about to give is a summary of the evidence supplied by the writings of the New Testament and of my own more detailed treatment of this in two former publications.[10]

It is often overlooked that the paradigm case of salvation from sin is that of the sin of Jesus' *disciples*. And their salvation must not be seen in mythical, or even in legal or moral terms, but as a real change in them, a change in the quality of their will and character, a change referred to in the New Testament as *metanoia*—a change of heart. This was effected by Jesus through their relationship with him by an attitude of his to which they eventually responded. The attitude was that of forgiveness. And once again I must stress that this was not a merely juridical transaction but a real interpersonal influence. The New Testament calls it love, but love in a special sense of the term, an unconditional affirmation of a person for their own sake. When those who had been followers of Jesus came to write of their experience many years later this was the thing that stood out, the thing that had made all the difference.

'When Jesus knew that his hour had come to depart out of this world to the Father' they wrote, 'having loved his own who were in the world, he loved them to the end' (Jn 13:1). 'To the end' means to the end of his life, but it also means 'to death', enough to die for them, absolutely. 'Who shall separate us from the love of Christ? Shall tribulation, or distress, or persecution, or famine, or nakedness, or peril or sword? No, in all these things we are more than conquerors through him who loved us' (Rom 8:35). The force of this memory animates all the New Testament writings.

The centrality of love in the Christian scheme of things is well known. But one often overlooks the experience to which all the great texts and hymns and doctrines concerning love refer back. The ultimate origin of the disciples' conviction that 'God so loved the

10. A Shutte 1986 'How Jesus Saves Us' (Chapter 19 in this book) and 1993, *The Mystery of Humanity*.

world that he gave his only Son that whoever believes in him should not perish but have eternal life' (Jn 3: 16); and that 'God's love has been poured into our hearts through the Holy Spirit who has been given to us' (Rom 5:5); that 'love is of God, and he who loves is born of God and knows God' (1 Jn 4:7); so that 'if I have not love I am nothing' (1 Cor 13:2); that 'love never ends' (1 Cor 13:8); and finally that 'God is love, and he who abides in love abides in God, and God abides in him' (1 Jn 4:16)—the origin of this conviction is their experience of Jesus' love form them in the time they spent with him before he died. They only came to believe that 'God is love' because they had experienced Jesus' love and he had come to occupy the place in their lives and in their hearts that was reserved for God.

It is love of this kind that is able to discern and value the person of the sinner in the very act or attitude of their sin. Moreover when Jesus claimed to be able to forgive sins he was claiming to be able to do something that only God could do. As we have seen the notion of sin as idolatry, or selfworship, involves a real disintegration of the ability of a person to will the good. Their ability to freely choose the good is affected. And just as only a truly transcendent power is required to bring freedom into being, and to fulfill it, so a similarly transcendent power is necessary to restore freedom once it is lost.[11] This is the metaphysical root of the disciples' eventual belief that in their relationship with Jesus they were in personal contact with God.

The interpersonal transaction between Jesus and his disciples that resulted in this transformation of themselves in the depth of their will and character was not complete at the time of his death. It could not be. Only his death, the apparent failure of his promise on which they had come to set their deepest hopes, the promise to inaugurate 'the kingdom of God', could finally purify their attitude to him of the last traces of idolatry and selfworship. It was the death of any selfish hope because it was the death of the one they had come to worship. This needs explanation. The disciples were ordinarily religious Jews, worshipping Yahweh in the rituals of their religion. But in the course of their acquaintance of Jesus he had come to take the place previously occupied by their religious symbols and rituals, he a real

11. For the intersubjective transaction by means of which personal growth is exclusively possible see the works referred to in footnote 50 as well as Chapter 2 of Shutte 1993. The interpersonal causality involved in these entails the incommensurable influence of a transcendent source.

living human person. Not that they ceased to believe in God, but Jesus had now come to occupy that place in their lives. At the time of his death the disciples did not, could not, realise this. It was only as a result of the mysterious experience they came to call his resurrection that they came to understand what had happened to them under the influence of Jesus.

Whatever the actual experiences were, their result was that the disciples came to believe that Jesus was alive with a death and sintranscending life and that he was sharing it with them. If before his death they had undergone a change of heart that was only fully established by his death (although they thought he had failed they were unable to cease to believe in the absoluteness of his love), the resurrection experience resulted in a change of mind, a change of mind that finally completed the change of heart, producing the full acceptance of Jesus as the Word of God and themselves as sharers in God's Spirit.

Though a strictly transcendent power is necessary to overcome sin this fact is not as obvious as the necessity for a similar power to overcome death. The disciples' faith in Jesus' resurrection did not mean that they believed him to be now alive in the way he was before he had died, in the way Lazarus is depicted as coming back to life for instance. That would have been a miracle but it would not have produced or justified the attitude to him that his resurrection did. As a result of that they had come to believe that he was alive with an altogether deathtranscending life, 'eternal life', the life of God. And what is more, he was sharing it with them.

The overcoming of sin and the overcoming of death can thus be seen to be intrinsically related. Death, though an entirely natural element in worldprocess and human life, gains its negative meaning for us through its connection with sill. If during the course of our life we have come to put an idolatrous trust in finite goods death, as the end of our power to control our lives, will appear as an ultimate loss of all we have come to value. If on the other hand we have come to put our trust in a transcendent power, revealed in the unselfish love that others have for us, then dying and death will be an occasion, and an opportunity, for a wholehearted selfsurrender to it and whatever it can effect in us. This in fact is precisely the essential character of the New Testament ethic, the moral paradox of 'dying in order to live', of 'losing one's life in order to save it', loving God more than oneself.

In showing the significance that Jesus' death and resurrection had for his followers we have in fact presented the Christian response to the first two kinds of evil from which we need salvation. Forgiving love is the only adequate, hearttransforming response to evil done. The power of this attitude is, for Christian faith, greater than the power of an evil will. It is an article of faith that no will can be so corrupt that it cannot be reached and changed by genuine forgiveness, for this is the form that God's love takes in sinful human life, Of course such an attitude, and power, has been a reality in human existence since the beginning of human history. But like every created reality it has shown a development in the course of history. In the history of Israel, and its religion in particular, a deepened understanding of this is evident.[12] Finally, for Christian faith, in the (sinless) life of Jesus the nature of this attitude is fully revealed. In the life of persons understanding is always able to add something to an attitude of the will and the affections that is without it. Thus though the life of Jesus reveals the truth of something that has always existed, knowledge of this truth enables us, other things being equal, to embody this attitude better than in the past. The actual presence of Jesus in the world and in human life (God, having become incarnate, remains incarnate.), though now only sacramentally realised, can empower us to do this in a way that nothing else can.

The revelation, through the resurrection, of the reality of a deathtranscending life is not only the confirmation of the transcendent power of Jesus' attitude to sin in us, namely towards evil done. It also has an important role to play in our attitude towards evil suffered, whether as a result of evil done by others or of natural causes.

The fact that death has a positive meaning for human persons and a role to play in our development as persons is crucial to a Christian response to evil in all its forms. This fact is embodied in the traditional doctrine of purgatory. Apart from its mythological expression this doctrine embodies the conviction that further development is possible for human persons through or 'after' death. Thus both the damage done by sin to the sinner and those others affected by the sin, can be repaired. This work, for a Christian, must be seen as following from the solidarity of all who have died with the resurrected humanity of

12. Especially in the 'Songs of the Suffering Servant' in Deutero-Isaiah, and in particular, Isa 53:1–12.

Jesus. It is through this that all are in touch with the power of God to overcome sin and to bring good out of evil. For a Christian, Jesus remains the model of how God deals with evil, whether in this life or in the life to come. Thus the notion that God always acts through secondary causes is not contradicted. The resurrected human person of Jesus is the secondary cause *par excellence*. It is in the face of Jesus that other human persons can see the full glory of God (2 Cor 4:6).

We come now to the final aspect of our consideration of Jesus as the revelation of how God deals with evil in all its forms, with sin and the harm and suffering caused by sin, and. indeed, the humanly destructive effects of suffering however caused. Two features especially, in the case of Jesus, stand out: his sinlessness and the fact that his suffering and death were caused by sin. The sinlessness of Jesus is a human achievement gained in the struggle against sin and the effects of sin, and in his suffering and death. At the same time it is God's achievement, both in changing the hearts of sinners and in identifying with those who suffer, by actually suffering the worst effect of sin, rejection by the humanity that God loves. The greater the love, the greater the suffering. In the death of the sinless one the 'mystery of love' is revealed, that it is stronger than sin and can transmute evil into good. One can see how destructive of the authenticity of the Christian understanding of evil it would be to separate the humanity of Jesus from the person of God. Only if Jesus' humanity is God's humanity do its qualities and powers have a transcendent scope. On the other hand, because it is God's humanity, the humanity of Jesus is a realization of humanity as the image of God. The way he deals with evil in all its manifestations is able to be a model for Christians, shaping both their faith and practice.

I want to acknowledge my debt to John Hick's profound and sane treatment of our topic, *Evil and the God of Love* (Collins, 1970), by ending this article with an extended quotation from that work. He sums up the Christian response to evil in words that I cannot better:

There are, then, two attitudes to evil within the Bible, one based upon the dualistic view of evil as the irreconcilable enemy of God and man, and the other upon a profound sense of the sole ultimate sovereignty and responsibility of God. These two attitudes reflect, I would suggest the characteristic duality of the religious and especially the Christian life . . . Through our immersion in the tensions and pressures, the terrors, pains and anguishes of our frail, sinful human life, we see evil as a deadly threat not only to our own welfare but to the very meaning of human existence; and in Christ God himself shared this temporal standpoint, struggling with us and for us against the powers of darkness . . . And yet we are also and at the same time conscious by faith of the eternal being and love of God, holding both ourselves and the whole creation securely in his grasp and exercising his sovereignty over the entire course of time and history.

I suggest, then, that these two contrasting biblical attitudes to evil reflect, on the one hand, our existential involvement in the long, slow, difficult, painful process of 'soul-making' and, on the other hand, our faith that such a process is in fact taking place within and around us, and that both attitudes are wholly valid . . . However the question still remains: What is the relation between these two points of view?

> The bridge between the two standpoints is provided by the Christian hope of the kingdom of God. The compatibility between the 'existential' view of evil as utterly malevolent and harmful and the theological view of its as divinely permitted and overruled, is a form of the compatibility between the temporal process which we know by our own present immersion within it, and the future completion and transformation of it which we affirm by faith . . . (These evils) do not merely seem to threaten us with ultimate destruction; they really are such a threat. And yet precisely because they really do thus threaten our deepest good we may by God's grace so repent of our sins and so bear our sufferings that they become elements within something else, namely our reconciliation with God and our growth into the finite 'likeness' of our maker. We thus have to say, on the basis of our present experience, that evil is really evil, really malevolent and deadly and also, on the basis of faith, that it will in the end be defeated and made to serve God's good purposes. From the point of view of that future completion it will not have been merely evil, for it will have been used in the creation of infinite good. (Hick 1970: 393–400)

(2005)

Chapter Twenty-Eight

Telling the Christian Story–By Karl Rahner and Me

This is the story of my theological relationship with Karl Rahner. His influence on me has been such that often the reader will not be able to tell whether it is I speaking or he. However I do not think this an entirely bad thing. I do not claim to be as great a theologian as Rahner but I have no doubt that I am a better writer. Rahner is one of the most horrifically ponderous and prolix writers that ever came from that supremely ponderous and prolix tradition that includes Hegel, Husserl and Heidegger. Even Hugo, Karl's brother, admitted that he could only understand what Karl was saying when he read him in English.

There is another reason why Karl Rahner is so difficult to read. In all his writings he is walking a tightrope stretched across the rubbish tip where lie the remains of writings forbidden by Vatican officialdom. Rahner has to bend over backwards to keep his balance between communicating the Christian faith to a scientific and secular culture, and negotiating the minefield the history of the Church has left for the theological explorer to cross.

In most of what follows I will be expounding Rahner's ideas in my words. The reader will have to take on trust that I am thoroughly grounded in both Rahner's philosophical and theological works. Not that I would claim to have read all several hundred of them. But I have studied the most important ones exhaustively: *Spirit in the World, Hearers of the Word, Hominisation, The Christian of the Future, The Church and Sacraments, The Theology of Death, The Love of Jesus and the Love of Neighbour, The Practice of Faith, The Trinity* and countless articles in the twenty-four volumes of his *Theological Investigations*, not to speak of all his contributions to dictionaries and encyclopaedias such as *Sacramentum Mundi* and *Mysterium Salutis.* If I intended to try and reference everything I say, not only would I never finish this article; I would never have begun it.

I first discovered the work of Karl Rahner in the late sixties when I was a member of the Dominican community in Stellenbosch. The Dominican Order was founded by St Dominic in the thirteenth century, and Thomas Aquinas—by far the most celebrated philosopher and theologian in the Catholic Church—was one of its early members. So as a Dominican student I had intimate contact with his thought. And so did the Jesuit Rahner. But in addition to a common philosophical background we also had something more important in common: a desire to make sense of Christian faith in our contemporary secular culture and to formulate its basic doctrines in terms that were compatible with our contemporary world-view.

No-one in the Catholic church has done more to achieve this than Karl Rahner. At that time the Second Vatican Council was in session and Rahner was the leading theologian engaged in what Pope John had named *aggiornamento*—the bringing up to date of Catholic life and thought. No-one was better fitted for this task. Not only was Rahner prodigiously learned and so intimately familiar with the theological tradition (he was the then editor of *Denziger*, the classical compendium of authoritative Christian doctrinal texts). He was also a philosopher of the first rank, steeped in the classical tradition of European philosophy, and author of original work of his own that brought Thomist philosophy into contact with existentialism and phenomenology.

What struck me most at that time about Rahner, and filled me with admiration and the desire to emulate him, was the way he combined philosophical rigour with an absolute commitment to Christianity. He gave reasons for everything he said, never arguing from authority but from experiences that anyone could refer to in order to corroborate his arguments. And yet he simply took the tradition of faith (including its traditional formulations) as an authoritative given that needed to be explained. His articles and books were thus a continuing dialogue between the traditional language of scripture and church doctrine and the language of his own contemporary philosophy. They were works of both 'translation' and 'inculturation'.

I had come to faith in God through philosophy in the classes of Professor Martin Versfeld at UCT in the late fifties. I was an Anglican at that time and proceeded to study theology at Oxford with a view to ordination in the Anglican Church. While in England I became a Catholic. One of the things that I missed in the Anglican Church was a lack of a philosophical dimension in its theology. But in Stellenbosch we were encouraged to develop a philosophy of our own. Rahner was an ideal partner in this endeavour. I plunged myself enthusiastically into the vast sea of this writings. On the one side there were specifically philosophical works such as *Spirit in the World*, *Hearers of the Word* and *Hominisation*. On the other were the twenty-odd volumes of his *Theological Investigations*. But in the theology of Karl Rahner philosophical reflection and Christian faith are inseparably united.

As far as the philosophy is concerned Rahner has translated the philosophy of Aquinas into a modern idiom. Medieval philosophy was metaphysical in Aristotle's sense, namely the identification of the most fundamental concepts one has to use in thinking of anything at all. Physics, for Aquinas and Aristotle, was the application of these concepts—such notions as existence and essence, act and potency, form and matter—to the things of nature. Psychology was their application to living things, including us. Philosophy was thus, in this sense, cosmological. Everything was included. In the modern period, with the development of the natural sciences, this complete and unified system was abandoned—forever. The natural sciences would never be complete but continue to grow—forever. And philosophy now was able to focus on its proper object, the only thing left over because beyond the reach of science, namely human subjects who invent the sciences' methods and judge their results. The modern period saw philosophy's discovery of subjectivity, culminating in Kant's Copernican Revolution, the so-called 'transcendental turn'. From now on, starting with Hegel, and continuing with phenomenology and existentialism and linguistic philosophy, philosophy would concern itself with the exploration of human interiority. Philosophy was no longer cosmological but a kind of anthropology.

Rahner's philosophy represents a culmination of this process. One can recognize all these developments beneath the finished product. And his philosophy provides him with a medium for his theology. In what follows I will be attempting to give, in summary form, the theological vision I have acquired from, or at least share with, Karl Rahner.

1.

Human beings have a dimension that transcends anything the sciences can know since it is what produces and judges the sciences. It is what makes us self-aware, self-determining subjects of thought and action, and is the source not only of science, but of morality, art, religion and, in general, culture. It is this transcendent subjectivity that makes us persons in the technical sense, spiritual as well as material beings. To say that we are spiritual is to draw attention to the peculiar internal relation human beings have to themselves (self-awareness and self-determination) that is not merely some part of us related to another part, but of ourselves as a whole in relation to the whole of ourselves. This is contrasted with our materiality which refers to the equally constitutive relationship in which we stand to all that is other than ourselves, the whole universe in fact, personal and impersonal. As spiritual beings we transcend the whole of the impersonal universe in the sense that it does not explain our existence and cannot fulfill those desires that we have precisely as spiritual beings. It must however be pointed out that we are unable to exercise, develop or fulfill our spiritual capacities except through our relationship to the rest of the universe, both personal and impersonal, and in dependence on it.

This insight into our human nature does not depend on faith but on philosophical reflection on experience. But unless one recognizes this dimension to our human nature it is not possible to understand adequately the essentials of Christian faith.

2.

In the light of the above philosophical anthropology a quite distinctive worldview emerges. The well-founded theories of contemporary science have enabled us to understand that the universe is an evolutionary process in which, over time, progressively more complex forms of being come into being through a real transformation of what preceded them. Humanity is the most complex (in its materiality) and the most simple (in its spirituality) being known to us. As such we contain in a transformed unity all the preceding forms of being discovered by the sciences. Though they are part of us we are not reduced to them but transcend them. In addition we are able to contain the universe as such in consciousness and endow it with meaning and value in our decisions and our acts. Thus the universe as a whole is most properly understood as a plurality of persons. It is the object of our thought and choice, and its impersonal aspects constitute the milieu in which a plurality of persons can exist and a medium in which interpersonal transactions can bring about our development and fulfillment. Put simply, there is more of reality in a person than a fundamental particle or physical force.

Again it must be stressed that such a world-view, with its metaphysical implications, is a purely philosophical one and owes nothing to Christian faith. But if one does not share it, understanding the essentials of Christian faith will be difficult. In fact it is probably the dominance of different conceptions of human nature and worldviews that make authentic faith difficult in our contemporary scientific and secular culture.

3.

We experience our transcendent subjectivity in all our cognitive and volitional activity. And at the same time we experience our openness to and inclination towards something absolutely transcendent that is immanent in our activity. I say 'something' because it is not any specific object of knowledge or desire; nor is it simply we ourselves as the knowing, acting subjects. It is however inherent in our conscious free activity as the condition that makes it possible, not merely as a 'logical' condition but as a reality that is essentially mysterious.

There is an unlimitedness to human consciousness and desire that indicates an unlimited reality and value as its source, an absolutely transcendent reality and value that is nevertheless immanent in our experience of ourselves as knowing, choosing subjects.

A reflection on our capacity for free choice will make this clearer. When we deliberately affirm something as true or choose something as good our act transcends all the causal networks the universe contains and the sciences are able to discover. Not that the laws of nature break down in us, or the social influences that have formed us cease to operate. Indeed they are absolutely necessary if we are to act at all. But they are not sufficient. If they were we would not be free. And what holds for the free action must also hold for the capacity to act freely that is part of normal human nature as outlined above. It follows that causal networks of the universe (such as are necessary to produce human beings from pre-human nature), though necessary are themselves insufficient to produce beings like us with the capacity for free action. There must therefore be another kind of causality at work, within the evolutionary process though beyond the reach of science, that is absolutely transcendent of the universe though immanent in its processes to bring us into being.

4.

The production of beings with the capacity for free acts such as ourselves is only the clearest case of a feature that is universal in the evolutionary process uncovered by modern science. This is a process in which really new forms of being are continually coming into existence through a transformation of what preceded them. The most dramatic examples, apart from the emergence of humanity, are those of consciousness from preconscious being, of living from non-living, and of the universe itself from an initial singularity. In general cosmic evolution is from the homogeneous and dispersed to the complex and centred. And at every stage the new form of being is not simply the product of what previously existed. Though necessary, physical things and forces are insufficient to produce biological organisms. Something more is required, a causality that transcends the cosmic process our science can investigate though immanent in it. A number of examples from contemporary science lend support to this philosophical position.

5.

Human beings, though transcending impersonal reality, are nevertheless dependent on it for all we are and do. There is no thought without images, no images without sensations, no sensations without sense organs sensitive to a spatio-temporal environment in which alone we can exist, express ourselves and communicate with others. This is what is known as our historicity. As transcendent beings we are able to develop an inner life, to live by meanings and values. But we can only do this in a process that unfolds in time and in a milieu that identifies us in space. We develop ourselves only in dependence on what is other than us. And, most importantly, through our relations with other persons, in a social and cultural milieu that humanity itself has constructed. Historicity is a feature of the life of individuals and of humanity as a whole.

6.

For beings such as we are our relations with other persons are crucial for the exercise, development and fulfilment of our distinctively personal capacities of self-consciousness and self-determination. And a philosophical phenomenology of intersubjectivity shows that certain definite kinds of relationship with others are necessary for this. It reveals that the more we are influenced by other persons in whom these capacities are already developed, the more self-determining we are enabled to be. Apart from such influence we are unable to grow as persons. This can appear to contradict the fact that the capacity in question is that for self-determination, for action that is free. But careful analysis of experience proves the contrary: the more I am influenced by the other in certain way, the more the act is my own.

This is in fact what our philosophical anthropology should lead us to expect. For we saw there that the existence of beings with a capacity for self-determination was only possible as the effect of an absolutely transcendent cause immanent in the evolutionary process. And in our experience of ourselves as knowing, choosing subjects we are conscious of an apprehension of reality that is absolute and of a desire for something of absolute value. This experience is however not objective; the transcendent source of our knowing and valuing is only implicit in our experience of ourselves. Here however, in the relationships with others in which we exercise develop and fulfill our capacities for self-knowledge and self-affirmation, we actually experience in an objective way the power and presence of an absolutely transcendent personal reality immanent in the very relationships themselves. It is precisely this that explains the paradoxical 'interpersonal causality' whereby the more we are subject to the influence of the other, the more self-determining we become. If the influence exercised on us was simply that of a finite cause other than us, the more it caused us to act, the less the act would be our own. But the opposite is the case.

We are thus bound to recognise that within the relationships in which my capacity for self-determination is developed there is a truly transcendent personal cause at work, whose influence is incommensurable with that of finite causes, personal or impersonal.

7.

This notion of incommensurability is of the utmost importance for dealing in a theological way with Christian faith. It arises however through a philosophical phenomenology of intersubjectivity and is founded on our actual experience of personal growth in relationships with other persons. The fact that this is something universal to humanity and not exceptional should not blind us to its essentially mysterious character. If the analysis is true than it is indeed the case that we have real experience of something absolutely transcendent, and therefore mysterious, in our ordinary interpersonal relations.

Rahner corroborates this insight and its importance in his treatment of the notion of creatureliness and our experience of this. Being a creature in this context entails a unique relationship to our transcendent creator, a relationship that is traditionally expressed by the notion of incommensurability. The notion of the incommensurability of creature and creator is central to classical theism and taken for granted by Aquinas. One cannot add God and the universe and make two. This is not because either is unreal, or that God and the universe are identical, but because there is no common measure in terms of which they could be added to or subtracted from one another. The reality of each is too different. An analogy would be that of a poet composing a poem about himself. One cannot say there are two poets, the one composing and the one in the poem. But to say there is only one is misleading because the poem already exists in the poet's mind. Rahner makes use of this idea in his discussion of our creatureliness. The following quotation serves the purpose of making the connection with the idea of 'interpersonal causality' outlined above.

The radical dependence and the genuine reality of the existent coming from God vary in direct and not in inverse proportion. In our human experience it is the case that the more something is dependent on us, the less it is different from us, and the less it possesses its own reality and autonomy. The radical dependence of the effect on the cause and the independence and autonomy of the effect vary in inverse proportion.

> But when we reflect upon the real transcendental relationship between God and a creature, then it is clear that here genuine reality and radical dependence are simply just two sides of one

> and the same reality, and therefore they vary in direct and not inverse proportion. We and the existents of our world really and truly are and are different from God not in spite of, but because we are established in being by God and not by anyone else. (1978: 79).

The best example of this apparently contradictory, but in reality paradoxical, relation is that of the human capacity for self-determination. In our discussion of Rahner's philosophical anthropology it was pointed out that only an infinite cause could be sufficient to bring beings with the capacity for freedom into existence, albeit through the causal mechanisms of evolution. It follows that even the exercise, development and fulfillment of our capacity for self-determination is the effect of the creative causality of God. Human freedom means freedom from total determination by worldly causes not freedom from God. It is precisely this paradoxical truth that my analysis of interpersonal causality is intended to substantiate.

With this we come to the end of my account of the philosophical foundations of Rahner's theology. An important element in it is his notion of historicity. This, in Rahner's words, means that 'man as subject and as person is a historical being in such a way that he is historical precisely *as* a transcendent subject; his subjective essence of unlimited transcendentality is mediated *historically* to him in his knowledge and his free self-realization' (1978: 140). It follows from this that what we call history is not just a succession of events, as might be said of pre-human evolution. It is only history insofar as it is a process endowed by humans with human meaning and purpose. It is this that historians must engage with, not only list the events. In fact even to list the events involves naming them and thus engaging with their meaning. To an account of human history we now turn.

8.

The philosophical conception of human nature and analysis of experience given above is one that has, of course, been developed in history and in quite recent history at that. And as outlined above it contains, as an essential element in it, a conception of a transcendent creator of the universe immanent in all that happens but incommensurable with it. Such a conception approximates closely, though not completely as we shall see, to the one Jesus called

Abba and which Christians recognize as their god. (I use the term 'God' as a proper name to designate precisely this same one.) So for Christian theologians human history is studied from the viewpoint of faith in Jesus with all that that entails. All human history is thus seen as 'salvation history', in the sense that we believe that God is still continuing his creative engagement with the world, though now principally through the exercise of human freedom. Put otherwise, evolution still continues. But now it is an evolution of human consciousness, culture and community. And it is not simply progressive, but proceeds by fits and starts, both development and decline. In its early stages humanity is largely undeveloped as far as its central capacities are concerned. Its knowledge of the universe is very limited. And in its life it has to struggle to personalize the instinct it has inherited from its prehistory. There is space for ill-will as well as error in the incompleteness of its development. Powerful emotions of fear and anger rather than insight and responsibility can direct the course of history. This is why creation in its human stage does not proceed at a constant or increasing rate. There is immaturity to educate and spiritual ill-health to heal. In the real universe, whose latest form is humanity, creation is salvation.

Early humanity reveals quite clear signs of religious experience and behaviour, attaching particularly to death but also manifesting in art and ritual. The notion of a god is that of a source of power transcending human power but capable of fulfilling deep desires that emerge in all cultures from our common human nature. Religion is the human attempt to access and enact such power in the service of this fulfillment. Because of the transcendent dimension of our human nature this fulfillment is always seen in absolute terms, as complete and enduring, whatever particular need happens to be the present focus of concern. But in the history of religion two needs, and hence two desires, emerge as fundamental: the desire to overcome all forms of disunity between people and the desire to overcome sickness and death. These two fundamental projects of human life can be seen as the expression of the duality of human nature already described, our relation-to-self and our relation-to-the-other, our spirituality in self-consciousness and self-determination, and our bodiliness in dependence on other persons and our impersonal milieu for its enactment. And they are beautifully depicted in the story of Adam and Eve and the story of the Tower of Babel. For Rahner, and for me, the built-in goal of human history, is well expressed in the novel definition of the Church contained in the *Dogmatic Constitution on the Church* of the Second Vatican Council: 'By her relationship with Christ, the Church is a kind of sacrament or sign of intimate union with God, and of the unity of all mankind. She is also an instrument for the achievement of such union and unity.' (1966: 15).

As humanity develops in the course of history so too does its conception of its gods. One must therefore speak of a history of revelation, where revelation refers to insight into the nature of our god and its relation to us. This history is part of the history of salvation and it too is an evolution, though not one of a steady increase in insight. In primal cultures the world-view is mythic, sacral. The gods are personified powers of nature. But always they are conceived of as transcendent in the sense of possessing powers that transcend the human but which we need to fulfill our deep desires. For that reason they are regarded with a special awe, as holy, wholly other. In different cultures they have different names and are described in different ways.

Though the gods of primal cultures are transcendent in the sense that they transcend human power they are not transcendent in the strict sense. The power they are believed to have may be sufficient to fulfill human nature as that is understood in that culture. But primal cultures do not have insight into human freedom and spirituality. And as such, human beings have deep desires that only a truly transcendent being, incommensurable with us, could fulfill: the desire for a true and hence universal community of persons and the desire for a death-transcending life.

Historians speak of an axial period of human history, and in particular in the history of religion. This is usually dated from about 1000 BCE to 300BCE. During this period there occurred in several different traditions (Hindu, Buddhist and Jewish are usually mentioned, and sometimes also that of Greek philosophy) the beginning of the realization of the existence of a genuinely transcendent being. For our purposes the Jewish tradition provides the best introduction to Christian faith. In this tradition Moses is credited with this revelation. And this revelation is developed by the Jewish prophets. In Jewish history by the time of Jesus, the conception of our humanity and our god that has developed has become the foundation for a whole edifice of related ideas concerning the intentions of our god and the character of our relationships with our god and one another. In short there has developed a whole conception of the meaning of human life and history that is centred on the conception of our god. The Jewish people are to become the nucleus of a universal community of humanity that is united and ruled over by Yahweh, their god. Indeed Yahweh is understood as planning to be present himself in the midst of his people to inaugurate a kingdom in which he will rule forever. In this kingdom not only sin but also death itself will be overcome. The organizing principle and fundamental law of this kingdom will be the law of love. The process whereby the kingdom of Yahweh will be established, and sin and death overcome, will involve Yahweh somehow taking the effects of sin and death upon himself and in this way destroying their negative power over humanity.

In the Jewish scriptures these ideas are given graphic expression by the prophets. There are the Suffering Servant Songs of Deutero-Isaiah, the story of the Tower of Babel in Genesis, and the prophetic visions of the City of God and the Resurrection of the people of Israel. The whole of history is seen as moving towards a climax in which their god himself appears to inaugurate a never-ending rule. In this way the Jewish religious and cultural tradition gives powerful expression to the deep desire of our transcendent human nature for a community of complete reciprocity and mutuality that is not brought to an end by death. And it is in this form that it is understood by Jesus and his followers.

9.

And this brings us to the theology of Rahner. This theology is of course based on Jesus and our experience of him. It might seem unnecessary to stress that Rahner understands that Jesus was, is and will always be a real human being. But two thousand years of theology have produced many other views, ranging from some or other kind of 'superman' (*ubermensch*) to a mere humanoid apparition of God. Strange though it may seem Christianity has been dogged from it's beginning by monophysitism, the 'physis' in question being not human but divine. Some of the trouble no doubt can be put down to technical theological language being misunderstood by non-theologians: the word *hypostasis* for instance, or even 'person'. But most of it has, I think, a more sinister source: the universal tendency towards idolatry.

Rahner puts the matter with admirable clarity. For instance, to say 'Jesus is God' is dangerously misleading. 'For when we say that Peter is a man, the statement expresses a real identification in the content of the subject and predicate nouns. But the meaning of 'is' in statements involving an interchange of predicates (*communicatio idiomata*) in Christology is *not* based on such a real identification. It is based rather on a unique, otherwise unknown and deeply mysterious unity between realities which are really different and which are at an infinite distance from each other. For in and according to the humanity which we see when we say 'Jesus', Jesus 'is' not God, and in and according to his divinity God 'is' not a man in the sense of a real identification. The Chalcedonian *adiairetos* (unseparated) which this 'is' intends to express (*Denzinger-Schonmetzer* 302) expresses it in such a way that the *ansynchtos* (unmixed) of the same formula does not come to expression. Consequently, the statement is always in danger of being understood in a monophysitic sense' (1978: 290).

For clarity's sake in what follows I will always use the name Jesus to refer to the human person who lived, died and now lives a death-transcending life with the one he called Father and whom I call God. The Incarnation of God in the universe and in human history is indeed mysterious, but the mystery is all on the side of God and not at all on the side of Jesus. We know what Jesus is. We know nothing of what God is except that God is mysterious. But the mystery that God is, is revealed for Christian faith in the (human!) person of Jesus.

For Christian faith God (as the one Jesus called Abba) has a quite distinctive character and relationship to us. In the first place it is God who is now recognized as the source of our existence and the one whom we experience in our experience of ourselves as knowing, choosing subjects involved with other persons in a milieu of culture and of nature. And it is God whom we experience especially in those relationships with others in which we exercise, develop and fulfill those capacities that make us subjects, and, in particular, our desire for the fullness of personal community and death-transcending life. For Rahner nobody is without this experience, and it is in this sense that he uses the term 'anonymous Christian'. Of course experience is not knowledge, and primal cultures had only inadequate ideas of God, as are expressed in their religion. But for Rahner the whole of human history can be seen as an evolution towards the true understanding of the power that moves history towards its goal through the insights and freedom of humanity. And this is because he believes that human history is the history of *God's self-communication* to humanity. The notion of God's self-communication to humanity is the fundamental conception in Rahner's theology. It is this idea that defines both salvation and revelation for him.

The salvation of humanity consists in the creation of 'the unity of humanity in union with God', to paraphrase the expression used by the Second Vatican Council. For Rahner the way to this is God's self-communication to us throughout human history, but finally and fully in the life of Jesus. For a union between God and humanity to exist it must be achieved in our human world, the world God created for this purpose. It cannot take place anywhere else, for human beings cannot be real anywhere else. We are 'evolution become conscious of itself'. However transformed, it is this universe that is our eternal home. And it has been created by God with the purpose of making it a home in which God can be with us. We don't go to God; God comes to us. This is the import of Rahner's idea of God's self-communication. And so the Incarnation (the complete and therefore unsurpassable form of God's self-communication) is seen as the purpose of creation, and salvation as the purpose of the Incarnation. One must of course add that the notion of salvation is only appropriate because of sin; it is God's continuing creation and self-communication in the process of overcoming sin and the effects of sin in us. Finally, salvation can only be achieved if God's self-communication is accepted. For Christian faith it is, and completely, by Jesus. The acceptance of God's self-communication, by Jesus or by us, is also always the result of God's freedom-creating power in human acts, 'grace' in Rahner's terminology.

Revelation, as Rahner understands it, is not primarily the revelation of truths but the revelation of God himself. It is an aspect of God's self-communication, that which imparts the personal knowledge of God. This knowledge is personal knowledge, the knowledge of acquaintance, not knowledge of truths about God, not something that can be written down. It is thus not to be identified with scripture, whether Jewish or Christian. It is that which is possessed by the persons—prophets, apostles, Jesus himself—who write or are written about in the scriptures. Rahner, as I have already indicated, sees the history of God's revelation of God as coinciding with the whole of human history. And, as with salvation, revelation proceeds by fits and starts, developing in different ways and to different degrees in every culture and religion. It reaches an unsurpassable completeness only in Jesus.

10.

Because Christian faith in God is faith in the one revealed in the person and life of Jesus it depends on a knowledge of that person and that life. This is as true for those who were intimate with him before his death as it is for us. But for us this knowledge is mediated to us by that original community as it has expanded through two thousand years. And it is complicated by the fact that the original community (and its extension through time and space) was formed by a faith in Jesus' resurrection. So there is no way of getting to know anything (or anything of importance) about Jesus apart from those who believed in his resurrection. Certainly all the writings of the New Testament are written from the point of view of this faith. Modern scientific study of these has helped a great deal to form an objective picture of what Jesus said and did and of the effect this had on his followers. But the project of building up a detailed biography of Jesus is doomed to failure. That does not matter however from the point of view of Christian theology. As theologians we want an accurate picture of the *faith* of Jesus' followers and, if possible, the faith of Jesus himself. Since the authors of the New Testament writings believed that their faith in God was the same as that of Jesus—since they had acquired it through their intimacy with him—they are providing us with first hand information about the nature of that faith. And that is what we really want. Rahner (though not himself a biblical scholar in the strict sense, had studied more works of biblical scholarship than most who are) certainly believed that we are in possession of sufficient knowledge of what the first followers of Jesus believed, and of what Jesus himself believed, to be able to share their faith. He is supported in this conviction both by his philosophical insights into the capacities and deep desires of our human nature, as well as by the history of religion I have sketched above. And he certainly believed that if a person was not in touch with his own humanity, but had a mind full of contemporary illusions or ancient myths, then authentic Christian faith would be virtually impossible.

Rahner felt that one can say something about Jesus' own self-understanding. Jesus certainly saw himself as standing in the historic line of Jewish prophets, but with this difference: he was bringing this line to an end. All other prophets saw themselves as bearers of God's word to Israel, but that word was not seen as God's final word. The prophets saw their words as God's words ('The Lord your God says this' and 'Thus says the Lord'), but still expected God to say more. Jesus, on the other hand, had a message whose very content implied that it was the final one, final because complete and unsurpassable. Rahner sees Jesus' gospel of the kingdom of God as implying God's *self*-communication to the world, not just a message. And not even God could do more than that.

So the first stage of human history was coming to an end; the final stage was beginning. 'Was beginning . . .'? Rahner believes that Jesus did not know, perhaps even was mistaken, about the 'times and seasons' of God's full and irrevocable entry into human history, his 'kingdom'. But he also believes that Jesus saw himself as in some way or other responsible for its inauguration. And that he felt this responsibility because of his experience of God's extraordinary closeness to him. Here is how he puts it:

> Jesus experienced a relationship to God which he experienced as new and unique in comparison with other men, but which he nevertheless considered to be exemplary for other men in their relationship to God . . . Jesus experienced in himself that radical and victorious offer of God to him which did not exist before in this way among 'sinners', and he knows that it is significant, valid and irrevocable for *all* men. According to his own self-understanding he is already before the resurrection the one sent, the one who inaugurates the kingdom of God through what he says and what he does in a way that did not exist before, but now does exist *through* him and *in* him. At least in this sense the pre-resurrection Jesus already knew himself to be the absolute and unsurpassable saviour (1978: 253–254).

Certainly his followers saw him in that light, and even before the resurrection experience. Unless they had his death would not have been the catastrophic disaster it clearly was. And nor would their experience of the resurrection have had the meaning that it did. Since

Christian faith as a whole grows from that experience—in relation to the life and death that preceded it—we will have to deal with it in some detail.

11.

It is taken for granted that specifically Christian faith in God begins with Jesus' followers' experience of his resurrection. Rahner recognizes that resurrection has nothing to do with resuscitation. Nor is he particularly concerned with the 'appearances' of the risen Jesus, or the empty tomb. As with the case of Jesus' virgin birth, we have no way of reaching anything genuinely historical. Nor does that matter. It is the meaning of whatever happened that is important, not the fact that something extraordinary occurred. And in the case of the resurrection no occurrence, however extraordinary, would be sufficient either to produce or to justify what the followers of Jesus came to believe. What then, according to Rahner, did they come to believe? That his death had been 'overcome', so that he was alive with a life that transcended death altogether. But the meaning of this 'new' life was that his claims regarding God's kingdom had been vindicated. Rahner puts it like this:

> *This* Jesus with his *concrete* claim and his history is experienced in the resurrection experience as of permanent validity and as accepted by God. What real claim inseparable from himself . . .? The claim that there is present with him a new and unsurpassable closeness of God which on its part will prevail victoriously and is inseparable from him. He calls this closeness the coming and the arrival of God's kingdom . . . (1978: 279).

He then adds 'By the resurrection, then, Jesus is vindicated as the absolute saviour' (1978: 279). As we have already seen, salvation (for Rahner) is God's self-communication to humanity in a history of sin and death in order to enable us to share the life of God. And he defines the notion of saviour as

> that historical subjectivity in which, first, this process of God's absolute self-communication to the spiritual world as a

> whole exists *irrevocably*; secondly, that process in which this divine self-communication can be recognized unambiguously as irrevocable; and thirdly, that process in which Gods self-communication reaches its climax insofar as this climax must be understood as a moment within the total history of the human race . . . (1978: 194).

To put this (I hope) more simply: faith in the resurrection of Jesus entails the belief that God is fully present in human history in Jesus in order to make us, like Jesus, sharers in a sin- and death-transcending life with God. So much as regards the content of faith in the resurrection; what of its grounds? Rahner rejects both 'mystical visions' and 'sense experience' as possible grounds on philosophical as well as theological grounds. To understand fully what he identifies as the grounds of Christian faith one needs to explain in a little more detail what the attitude of faith consists in. It is an attitude of a person as a whole to the personal presence of God. I say 'as a whole' since the attitude of faith comprises cognitive, volitional and emotive elements. All our powers are involved. The cognitive element can best be understood as the kind of knowledge that one person can come to have of another. It is not theoretical or matter of fact. And this explains the centrality of the volitional element in faith; personal knowledge of a person can only be gained if the persons involved 'open up' to each other, if each wills to know and be known. And finally, such self-transcendence through intimate personal knowledge, and self-donation through receptive affirmation, of the other, answers our deep desire for personal communion and hence is supremely emotionally satisfying, and, when the other concerned is God, is all we could ever hope for. It is for this reason that, in the traditional terminology, Christian faith is held to consist in the three 'theological virtues' of faith (the cognitive), charity (the volitional) and hope (the emotive).

With this conception of faith in mind we can return to the situation of the first followers of Jesus. As a result of their experience of Jesus' resurrection the attitude I have just described was formed in them in relation to God whom they now recognized as personally present to them in the person of Jesus. The foundation of the attitude of faith had been laid by the *metanoia*, the change of heart, brought about in them through their relationship with Jesus before he died. They had been enabled to love him with the gift-love of charity with which he had loved them. They now saw that love of this kind had an absolutely transcendent source. Then came the death that destroyed all their hopes, though it could not destroy the love. It was this love then that gave them eyes to recognize that Jesus was alive through the same transcendent power that had changed their hearts. Now it was their minds that were changed; it was with these changed minds that they now fully understood what had happened to their hearts—and to Jesus.

For Rahner it is of the utmost importance, if one is to avoid a mythological understanding of the resurrection experience, to grasp the unity of the experience his followers had of Jesus before and in his death with their experience of his resurrection. Both are in the last resort an experience of God present in Jesus to answer our deep desire for the fullness of personal community in a death-transcending life. The experience of the resurrection is an experience of sharing it with Jesus, of Jesus sharing it with them. If one asks what actual form this experience took the only truly historical factor one can identify is their experience of one another. It was in their actual community with each other as the ones who had been changed by Jesus that they experienced his 'real presence', his continuing community with them in spite of the fact that he had died. The two disciples who 'spoke' with him on the road to Emmaus and 'broke bread' with him came to know that he was present with them. But an observer who had not known Jesus would have seen only two on the road to Emmaus or at the table in the inn.

The followers of Jesus believed that Jesus was alive because they came to believe after his death that they now shared a common life with him that had come to them from him, a life that transcended both sin and death. Authentic Christian faith is not possible without believing in the possibility of the fulfillment of one's desire for the fullness of personal community in a death-transcending life. Recognising the achievement of the fulfillment of both these desires in the case of Jesus is the form taken by Christian faith in God. The writings of the New Testament document the discovery, first by Jesus and then, through their relationship with him, by his followers, of the existence of a community-creating, death-transcending power at work in their lives. And not only that. Their experience of Jesus eventually led his followers to the conviction that it was not only the power of God but God's personal presence in Jesus, and through him in them, that they had experienced.

12.

This experience, of both Jesus and his followers, of being in the personal presence of God, not in some symbolic 'religious' or mystical way, but in the ordinary sense of the presence of one human person to another, is of course the historical root of the Christian definition of God as the Trinity. And in essence it is very simple. According to the New Testament record that documents what his followers came to believe, Jesus experienced his intimacy with the one whom he called Abba as God's gift to him of all that God is. He had become the 'possessor' of God's (the Father's) own self-expression (Rahner's term for the New Testament 'Word'), his Word. And as a result he, a human person, had become a sharer in and agent of God's own love, his Holy Spirit. It was this recognition of God's presence in Jesus' death-transcending life, and in theirs, that is the heart of the resurrection experience.

As there is no space in this article to give a full account of Rahner's understanding of the doctrine of the Trinity I want to make one point in that regard that I have found very helpful. It is well-known that the terms translated 'person' in Trinitarian formulations do not mean what the word now means to us. There is no suggestion that God is a 'gang of three'. In God there is only one will, one intellect, one subjectivity. But it is less often realized that, as Rahner remarks in a footnote in his book on the Trinity,

> Hence within the Trinity there is no reciprocal 'Thou'. The Son is the Father's self-utterance which should not in its turn be conceived as 'uttering', and the Spirit is the 'gift' which does not give in its turn.' In all the New Testament texts where Jesus addresses the Father 'a *creaturely* starting point for the 'Thou' addressed to the Father' is presupposed. (1970: 76)

This insight is extremely important if one is to avoid mythological interpretations of the Trinity, and also if one is to do justice to the foundations of the doctrine in the experience his followers had of Jesus.

13.

I have noted that the idea of God's self-communication is the key concept in Rahner's theology. And of course it is one that fits the doctrine of the Incarnation very well. The Incarnation can be seen as the supreme expression of God's self-communication to the creation, to Jesus and so to the universe that has become conscious of itself in him and us. Rahner is fully aware of the problems inherent in the notion of God's self-communication to that which is not God, to a spatio-temporal reality in process of evolution and growth. First of all there is the problem of particularity. If it is really *self*-communication in the fullest possible way, successful self-communication that achieves its full acceptance, then it is something that must occur at a particular point in time and space. It is not just the offer and promise that occurs in every human life. This is the real uniqueness of Jesus. His life was the point at which God achieved what was only implicit in creation and only dreamed of by the prophets. That is the substance of Christian faith.

The way in which Rahner applies his conception of God's self-communication to achieve real insight into this most mysterious but fundamental conviction of Christianity is to my mind not only true to an authentic tradition but develops it as well. It involves three essential affirmations. The first is that God's indwelling in Jesus has the same kind of effect on him as it has on us. The uniqueness of the Incarnation and 'hypostatic union' does not lie there. The second affirmation is that faith in the Incarnation entails a quite distinctive conception of our creator. The third, which is closely bound up with the second, is that it is strictly personal reality that provides the best analogy for understanding our relationship with God.

The first affirmation is a consequence of Rahner's determination to avoid mythical conceptions of the Incarnation. The human uniqueness of Jesus does not consist in a difference between him and us, but from his position in history, namely in being the event in which God's self-communication occurs. In Rahner's words, the 'hypostatic union may not be seen so much as something which distinguishes Jesus from us, but as something which must occur once and only once when the world begins to enter upon its final phase'. (1978: 181) And this because 'the intrinsic effect of the hypostatic union for the assumed humanity of the Logos consists precisely and in a real sense *only* in the very thing which is ascribed to all men as their goal and their fulfilment, namely, the immediate vision of God' (1978: 200). Rahner is by no means denying an unusual or extraordinary human holiness to Jesus. He is simply getting rid of any suggestion of 'supernatural' characteristics resulting from God's incarnation in him.

The second affirmation, that the idea of God as creator must be transformed by the doctrine of the Incarnation, is a result of Rahner's view that the notion of creation must be seen as a secondary element within the more fundamental notion of Incarnation. Put differently, the Incarnation is the purpose of creation; creation is for the sake of Incarnation. Rahner's philosophical anthropology has prepared us for this idea. For our created nature comprises a dynamism towards an unlimited good that transcends our own powers to achieve. The Incarnation is God's fulfillment of this deep desire. As such it is 'the unique and *highest* instance of the actualization of the essence of human reality' (1978: 218). But if the doctrine of the Incarnation deepens our understanding of our human nature it does so even more in respect of our understanding of God.

We have already seen that the notions of immanence and transcendence apply equally to the idea of a creator. Although not the universe or a part of it, God is present in every part as its continuing creator. The Incarnation goes a step further: God becomes part of his creation, present in it and to it as one thing to another, as Jesus was present to his followers. The effect of this, on God as it were, is that the creation becomes his own in a new and deeper way. But how this is possible is another matter. How can the infinite creator, that is beyond time and space, become a spatio-temporal reality without ceasing to be the infinite creator. Here is Rahner's answer: 'This brings us to an ontological ultimate which a merely rational ontology would perhaps never suspect. Such an ontology finds it difficult of course to take cognizance of this ultimate, and to insert it as a primal formula right into the primal beginnings and origin of its discourse. The absolute, or, more correctly, the absolute One in the pure freedom of his infinite unrelatedness, which he always preserves, possesses the possibility of himself becoming the other, the finite. He possesses the possibility of *establishing* the other as his own reality by dispossessing *himself*, by giving *himself* away' (1978: 222). The idea is not new. It is already present in Augustine who taught that in the Incarnation God 'assumes by creating' and 'creates by assuming' a human nature. But what could lead us to suppose it true? Rahner offers some help: in the Incarnation God 'creates by emptying himself, and therefore, of course, he himself is in the emptying. He creates the human reality *by the very fact that* he assumes it as his own. He, the Logos (which for Rahner is the Father's self-expression), constitutes the differentiation from himself by the fact that he retains it as his own, and, conversely: because he truly wants to have the other as his own, he constitutes it in its genuine reality. God goes out of himself, he himself, he as the self-giving fullness. Because he can do this, because this is his free and primary possibility, for this reason he is defined in scripture as love' (1978: 222). I think that this quotation gives us a clue to a sense in which this conception of God is not a contradictory one but embodies a deep and essential insight.

In discussing Rahner's philosophy of persons I made the point that it is only through our relationships with other persons that we are enabled to develop as persons. This seems uncontroversial yet it is highly mysterious. For human persons are self-determining. And it is precisely for the development of this capacity that we are dependent on the influence of others in whom it has already been developed. There is not space in this paper to discuss this more fully but both I and Rahner believe we can show that it is only in certain kinds of relationships with others that this is true, namely those in which we are recognized and affirmed as persons and hence infinitely precious. The more I am subject to *this* kind of influence, the more (and not the less) self-determining I become. And the more I am enabled to surrender myself to this influence of the other, the more (and not the less) do I possess myself. It is only by virtue of a self-transcendence in knowing the other and a self-donation in loving them for their own sake, that I come to know and love myself truly. This is the paradox of what I call 'interpersonal causality'.

If all this is true then I think it provides an authentic analogy for what Rahner wants to affirm of God in the Incarnation. If we see all acts of God *ad extra* on the model of this interpersonal causality then I think we see that the expressions used above need not be contradictory but answer to something that, though mysterious, is part of our own experience. Here is what Rahner says:

> Because in the Incarnation the Logos creates the human reality by assuming it, and assumes it by emptying *himself*, for this reason there also applies here, and indeed in the most radical and specific and unique way, the axiom for understanding every relationship between God and creatures, namely that closeness and distance, or being at God's disposal and being autonomous, do not vary for creatures in inverse, but rather in direct proportion. Christ is therefore man in the most radical

> way, and his humanity is the most autonomous and the most free not in spite of, but because it has been assumed, because it has been created as God's self-expression (1978: 226).

One ought to add to this that though a correct phenomenology of intersubjectivity does capture our experience of 'interpersonal causality', it does not explain it. In fact it could be shown that it is only because the transcendent causality of God is at work in the interpersonal transaction that it can achieve the effect of personal growth and community in us. This is of the utmost importance in our understanding of the *metanoia* produced by Jesus in his original followers, and indeed for the way we think of grace and the Church.

14.

I will complete this summary exposition of how Rahner (and I under his influence) tells the Christian story with a brief sketch of his theology of the Church. I have already indicated the novel definition of the Church contained in the Dogmatic Constitution on the Church of the Second Vatican Council *Lumen Gentium*. I have no explicit proof that Rahner was himself the originator of this definition, but it is highly likely, since he was by far the most respected and influential among the *periti* who served the bishops at the Council. But that does not really matter since it corresponds in every detail to Rahner's conception of the nature and purpose of the Church. And this has as its focus and foundation the idea of the Church itself as the *sacrament* of Jesus continuing 'real presence' in the world in order that God be personally present to humanity and humanity be enabled to respond to this presence.

The classical conception of sacrament that Rahner uses includes two elements, that of sign and that of cause: a sacrament is something that really causes what it symbolically signifies. In the case of the Church, in order to be the sign of Jesus', and hence God's incarnate, continuing presence in the world, it must be a historically specific and identifiable reality. Put simply, it must fulfill the function that Jesus' physical body had in identifying his personal presence to his followers in the days before he died. This it does by virtue of its existence as a specific institution since apostolic times. This is provided, for Rahner, by the worldwide episcopate in communion with the bishop of Rome. But his understanding of this needs to be spelt out lest it be misunderstood. In the first place a bishop is identified as the authoritative preacher of Jesus' 'gospel' and the president of the celebration of the rite that expresses Jesus' 'real presence' and 'holy communion' with his followers. So it is the person of the bishop that identifies a local manifestation of the Church. I use these terms carefully. The Church as a worldwide institution is not like a multinational corporation or political state with its principle of unity in its headquarters or head of government. The Church must be seen instead as a 'community of communities', in which each community is everything that all others are, including the community each has with all the others. To use a very humdrum image, the Church is not like a fish (whose principle of unity is its single nervous system centred on its brain), but like a jelly fish whose nature subsists in every part equally. In this understanding of the Church the proper function of the bishop of Rome is not like that of the head of a government or of an organization but the purely symbolic one of identifying the community of communities that constitutes the Church.

As far as the reality signified by the historically identifiable Church is concerned there are two aspects of Rahner's thought that ought to be understood. In the first place the function of the Church is identical with that of Jesus, namely the salvation of humanity. As we have seen, for Rahner this consists in the 'unity of humanity in union with God' to paraphrase the Council's definition. For this to happen God must be present in our world (and the Church is the sign of this presence) and we must recognise this presence and respond to it (and the Church's function in this respect is to be the instrument that brings this recognition and response about). It is with regard to the distinction of this twofold function of the Church that much misunderstanding can occur.

Rahner often uses the term 'universal salvific will' to identify God's intention to save humanity as a whole and every individual. In this he is simply echoing the affirmation of *Lumen Gentium* that 'those also can attain to everlasting salvation . . . who, without blame on their part, have not yet arrived at an explicit knowledge of God, but who strive to lead a good life, thanks to his grace' (1:14). This affirmation occurs at the end of a passage in which the possibility of salvation for (in this order) Roman Catholics in good standing (!), other Christians, Jews, Muslims and believers in other religious traditions is also affirmed. In other words anyone at all can be saved! In what sense then can it be true that, as traditionally expressed, *extra ecclesiam nulla salus*? Only if the distinction outlined above of the two functions of the Church is properly understood. It is the distinction in fact of two necessary conditions for salvation, an objective and a subjective. Objectively it is necessary for God to be present in the human world as in the person of Jesus. And the Church alone is the historical sign of this. No other religion could be this sign since no other religion or spiritual tradition believes this. On the other hand God is present in every person and in all personal relationships revealing his presence and inspiring our response to it. And this is true in every religion and spiritual tradition and in none, even in explicitly atheistic ideologies such as Marxism and secular humanism. It is because of this subjective recognition and response that Rahner speaks of 'anonymous Christians'. It does not at all imply a lack of authenticity or holiness in non-Christians, or the possession of authenticity or holiness in Roman Catholics for that matter. It simply would not make sense for, say, Jewish or Muslim believers, to speak of anonymous Jews or Muslims, since they do not believe in an objective (incarnate) presence of God in the world as Christians do.

With this rather sketchy account of Rahner's theology of the Church I conclude this already overlong paper. I have tried to give a summary and clear account of Rahner's telling of the Christian story and hope that the reader will have caught something of the flavour of his thought. That is really all I can hope for, since there is no shortcut to a deep understanding of Rahner. Years of study are needed. I have spent such years but still can't say whether or not I have achieved this. But I can say how much I value what he has given me.[1]

(2007)

---

1. For the purposes of this essay I list the following writings of Rahner, and of myself:
K Rahner, *Hominisation: The Evolutionary Origin of Man as a Theological Problem* (Burns and Oates, 1965a); *The Theology of Death* (Burns and Oates, 1965b); *The Church and Sacraments* (Burns and Oates, 1966); *The Christian of the Future* (Burns and Oates, 1967); *The Trinity* (Burns and Oates, 1970); *Foundations of Christian Faith* (Darton, Longman and Todd, 1978); *The Love of Jesus and the Love of Neighbour* (St Paul Publications, 1983); *The Practice of Faith* (SCM Press, 1985).
A Shutte, 'What Makes Us Persons?', in *Modern Theology*, 1 (1984): 67–79; 'How Jesus Saves Us', in *Journal of Theology for Southern Africa*, 55 (1986): 3–14; 'A New Argument for the Existence of God', in *Modern Theology*, 3 (1987a): 157–177; 'Community, Apartheid and the Metaphysics of Humanity in Genesis 1-11', in *Philosophy and Theology*, 2 (1987b): 57–75; *The Mystery of Humanity* (Snailpress, 1993).

Chapter Twenty-Nine

Evolution and Emergence: A Paradigm Shift for Theology

It is an extraordinary thing that an idea that in Darwin's time (and to Darwin himself) appeared so alien to and indeed destructive of Christianity should now prove so fruitful for the purpose of finding an expression of Christian faith appropriate for a scientific and secular age. The idea of evolution and the emergence of new forms of being—not simply in the biological sphere but in the cosmos as a whole and in human history itself—has in fact provided Christian theology with a new paradigm within which to conceptualise such basic elements of faith as the notion of creation, the doctrine of God's incarnation in Jesus, the indwelling in us of the Holy Spirit, and the function of the Church in the world. My aim in this article is to outline the steps taken that have made this possible, and to provide a sketch of the theology that results. In my recent work I have relied on many thinkers in this project, especially on the work of Karl Rahner and his 'Christology within an evolutionary view of the world', but also visionaries such as Teilhard de Chardin and, in more recent times, Brian Swimme.

The opposition to Darwin's ideas when they first appeared, particularly that of public figures such as the Bishop of Oxford, has become so notorious that any sympathy with them from those who felt them to be compatible with Christian faith has been largely overlooked. Yet from the very first this was forthcoming, in spite of public opinion. One must remember that at the time Christian orthodoxy was almost universally held to imply what is now seen to be a seriously mistaken view of biblical inerrancy, as well as being bound up with the soundness of the design argument as advanced by Paley and others. Hence any acceptance of evolutionary ideas had somehow to be fitted in to the notion of design as well as a revision of one's attitude to scripture. One even finds Darwin himself writing, in a letter to Asa Gray the Harvard botanist, 'With respect to Design, I feel more inclined to show a white flag than to fire my usual long-range shot . . . If anything is designed, certainly man must be' (in Clark, R. *The Survival of Charles Darwin*. Weidenfeld and Nicholson, 1984: 121). And in the *Origin* itself: 'There is a grandeur in this view of life, with its several powers, having been originally breathed into a few forms or into one.' To which, in the second edition, he added 'by the Creator' (Clark 1984: 150).

Very soon after the publication of Darwin's 'dangerous idea' attempts began to be made to see in evolution God's *method* of creation, or at least as God-directed, whether by intervention or not. And some thinkers, such as Alfred Wallace in particular, made a distinction between the evolutionary origin of the human body and the immediate creation by God of the human soul. A letter from Sir Charles Lyell, the famous geologist, to Darwin is very revealing in both these respects:

> 'I reminded him' (Alfred Wallace) 'that as to the origin of man's intellectual and moral nature I had allowed in my first edition that its introduction was a real innovation, interrupting the uniform course of the causation previously at work on the earth. I was therefore not opposed to his idea that the Supreme Intelligence might possibly direct variation in a way analogous to that in which even the limited powers of man might guide it in selection, as in the case of the breeder and horticulturalist. In other words I feel that progressive development or evolution cannot be entirely explained by natural selection. I rather hail Wallace's suggestion that there may be a Supreme Will and Power which may not abdicate its function of interference, but may guide the forces and laws of Nature' (Clark 1984: 134).

It would be some time before Christian theology was able to detach itself from the argument from design, and even longer before it felt able to abandon the idea of an intervention in world process by God in the case of the creation of the human soul, let alone the Incarnation. But the compatibility of the evolution of new species and Christian faith was an idea that only strengthened with the passage of time. This is exemplified by the following passage from a sermon given to the University by Charles Gore, later Bishop of Oxford, in 1894.

'Objection to the idea of evolution on the grounds of the argument from design, has been, in the main, removed. In part it has been through the theologians abandoning false claims and learning, if somewhat unwillingly, that they have no 'Bible revelation' in matters of science; in part it has been through its becoming continually more apparent that the limits of scientific explanation of nature are soon reached; that the ultimate causes, forces, conditions of nature are as unexplained as ever, or rather postulate as ever for their explanation a Divine mind. Thus if one 'argument from design' was destroyed another was only brought into prominence. No account which science can give, by discovery or conjecture of the method of creation, can ever weaken the argument which lies from the universality of law, order and beauty in the universe to the universality of mind. The mind of man looks forth into nature and finds nowhere unintelligible chance, but everywhere an order, a system, a law, a beauty, which corresponds, as greater to less, to his own rational and spiritual intuitions, methods and expectations. Universal order, intelligibility, beauty, mean that something akin to the human spirit, something of which the human spirit is an offshoot and a reflection, is in the universe before it is in man' (Clark 1984: 235).

In this passage we find already a clear appreciation of the limits of science and the biblical writings, as well as of the original forms of the argument from design. And, more importantly, we also find an albeit somewhat tentative appreciation of two ideas that have since become quite central to the theological annexure of the evolutionary idea. The first is that of the unity and solidarity of a world-process in which humanity (and hence our distinctive mental capacities) is by no means an exception but an integral part. And secondly, it is this mental or spiritual aspect of evolution—rather than a mechanistic regularity or order—that is the clearest indication of a world-transcendent source. These ideas are so important to the story I am telling that I want briefly to indicate their origins in nineteenth century European thought, not indeed scientific or theological thought but philosophy. Of course the argument from design was itself philosophical rather than scientific. And its popularity in a scientific culture had an immediate theological effect. It gave rise to the idea of a 'natural religion' as opposed to a 'revealed' one like Christianity, a religion that was supported by, in fact based on, the discoveries of science. The fact that the scientific world view at that time was a thoroughly materialistic and deterministic one tended to be overlooked.

But not by Kant! He saw his whole philosophical endeavour as an attempt to justify our faith in human freedom, the immortality of the soul and, ultimately, the existence of God, all of which beliefs seemed threatened by the mechanistic Newtonian world-view. He did this by what he himself called his 'Copernican revolution'. For just as Copernicus had shown that the Sun and not Earth was the centre of our cosmic system, so Kant argued that the order science discovered in the world was the order of our minds rather than that of things in nature. Science itself was the creation of the knowing, choosing human subjectivity of the scientist and not something impressed by an objective nature on a passive human mind. Not that the truths of science were illusory, but they were partial, aspectual, provisional insights into the much richer and still not completely understood reality of the world. The importance for our purposes of this 'subjective turn' of Kant's is not so much its improved understanding of science as its focus on the scientist, and in general on the human person, as the knowing, choosing subject who creates and judges science, and who therefore transcends scientific study because always presupposed by it. In doing so Kant revealed both the inherent limitation of any actual or possible science, and at the same time a transcendent aspect of human nature that was the source of science, as well as morality and art—and religion. It was thus humanity itself, or at least this aspect of human nature, that came to provide grounds for a rational faith in human freedom, the immortality of the soul, and the existence of God.

Unfortunately so strong was the hold that the deterministic, mechanistic Newtonian world-view had on the eighteenth century mind that Kant was only able to carry through his 'Copernican revolution' by virtue of a thoroughgoing dualism of body and mind. By virtue of our rational powers of intellect and will we transcend the determinisms of nature, of which as bodily beings we are an inextricable part. Philosophy in the modern period developed in two mutually interacting traditions, an empiricist cast of thought that was born from the influence of the natural, and especially the physical sciences, and a rationalist that emanated from the complex phenomenon of secularization. The empiricist tradition was materialist, stressing the causal links discovered by the different sciences that bound humanity to the determinisms of both nature and society. Rationalist thinkers such as Descartes and Kant, to name only the most influential, influenced by secularization's focus on humanity's capacity for self-determination as the central fact about human nature and the most important value for human life, stressed our transcendence of all such dependencies. It was only in the early nineteenth century, at about the time that Darwin's own ideas were beginning to take their epoch-making shape, that a philosopher overcame this sterile opposition of two half-truths in a synthetic vision in which the post-modern age was born.

It was Hegel who managed to combine the other-dependence of empiricist materialism with the self-determination of rationalistic dualism in a comprehensive view of humanity, both as individuals and as a species, as being essentially in a state of becoming through a process of transformation and transcendence. Hegel's conception of humanity as Spirit (the capital is necessary to denote its difference from the common idea of spirit that opposes it to matter) was a genuine novelty in European philosophy, and perhaps the philosophical expression of what could be called the 'spirit' of the age. It is so easy to read back into it many things that science—in its discoveries of emergence in world-process—and theology—in recent theories of *creation continua*—have since developed, that one must be careful to identify the novelty precisely. I think it consists in the idea of reality, whether human or cosmic, as a process of self-realization through transformation and transcendence. Whether this happens in a single cell or in a person, or in a transition from inorganic to organic being, or from consciousness to human self-consciousness, the structure of the dynamism is the same: there is a finality involved, a finality of self-realization through self-transcendence. Although it is most manifest in human life, where it takes many paradoxical forms, it is present in the simplest form of physical being. At all events it presents a world-view that is evolutionary in a very deep and comprehensive sense, going well beyond both what the special sciences could authorise and Christian orthodoxy would allow.

Perhaps the most important aspect of Hegel's thought as far as theology is concerned is the fact that he applied his evolutionary conception to *humanity*, to the lives of human individuals and also to human history itself, and did so with great thoroughness and in great detail. Here, in the human sphere, he is concerned with the evolution of culture and consciousness and forms of human community. His account culminates in a description of the evolution of art, religion and philosophy, as the most developed forms of Spirit in which humanity progressively attempts to realise its capacity for self-consciousness and self-determination. Although Hegel is concerned to describe accurately the history he is not afraid to judge the forms that human culture takes, negatively as well as positively. But like many nineteenth century thinkers he is convinced of the fact of progress. And for him Christianity is the highest because the most human religion. Its only lack is the fact that it still holds its truth in mythological form, believing stories of God's interventions in history, in revelations and miracles and sacred writings fixed for all time. As a consequence, in his *Lectures on the Philosophy of Religion,* he undertakes a radical project of demythologization, translating all the central doctrines of Christianity into the language of his philosophy of Spirit. In this he was following Kant's pioneering work of demythologization, in his *Religion Within the Limits of Reason Alone.*

Hegel thus applied the evolutionary idea not only to the history of religion, tracing a development through all the forms of religion then known to him, but also to the history of a particular religion, namely Christianity, giving it a formulation he felt was more adequate to the age in which he lived. This was at a time when scholars in many different fields were studying the past, using the methods of science on humanity itself. And there was no human product that received more critical attention than the Christian scriptures.

I think I have said enough to identify what amounted to a revolution in thinking, a revolution that brought the 'modern' period of European history to an end. Darwin's thinking was simply part of it. John Dewey, speaking at the celebration of the centenary of Darwin's birth at Columbia University in 1909, summed up his influence as follows: 'In laying hands upon the sacred ark of absolute permanency, in treating the forms that had been regarded as types of fixity and perfection as originating and passing away, the 'Origin of Species' introduced a mode of thinking that in the end was bound to transform the logic of knowledge, and hence the treatment of morals, politics and religion.' (Clark 1984: 254) This is a judgment with which Teilhard de Chardin would have whole-heartedly agreed: 'Is evolution a theory, a system or an hypothesis? It is much more: it is a general condition to which all theories, all hypotheses, all systems must bow and which they must satisfy henceforward if they are to be thinkable and true' (1959: 219). Teilhard's work was originally viewed with suspicion by Church authorities; it is now no longer. And it is time for us to turn to consider how theology has shaped itself to the new evolutionary paradigm, and how it might with profit continue to do so.

1.

In the intellectual development whereby the notion of evolution has become central to the expression of Christian faith in a scientific and secular culture there are a number of salient themes. First is that of the position of humanity in the universe, both as regards the nature of human persons and the direction of human history. Various traditional dualisms had to be overcome: that of humanity and the rest of nature, and the dualism of matter and spirit that is bound up with that. Then there is the dualism of body and mind or body and soul in human individuals. Secondly there is the question of God and his relationship to the universe, the idea of creation as *creation continua*, the creation of really new forms of being, especially that of life from matter, human consciousness from life, and what is traditionally called grace in human hearts and minds. Finally there is the sphere of history, a history seen by theology as a dialogue between humanity and its god. As far as humanity is concerned, history is seen as involving an evolution of culture and consciousness, and therefore of religion too, an evolution that for theology culminates in the person and teaching of Jesus. With regard to God there are new ways of understanding God's 'special actions' within the universe in human history, what is traditionally called 'the history of salvation'. These attempt to avoid the notion of 'intervention' by God in the course of history, as well as any appeal to the 'supernatural', whether in the form of miracle or authoritative inspiration or revelation.

These themes characterise especially the now well-developed dialogue between theology and the natural sciences, where the evolutionary world-view and its satellite themes occupy centre-stage. A particularly impressive example of this dialogue is the nearly twenty-year long series of seminars organised by the Vatican Observatory and the Centre for Theology and the Natural Sciences at Berkeley, which has just culminated in the publication of its sixth and final 'capstone' volume of papers by participants. The writers were drawn from the ranks of highly respected scientists, philosophers and theologians, and met regularly to discuss and revise their contributions at Castelgandolfo and in California. The series as a whole bore the general title 'Scientific Perspectives on Divine Action'.[1]

As can be imagined the scholars involved were from many different backgrounds and with very different outlooks. Yet in the course of the meetings, and due to the method of discussion and revision employed, a remarkable consensus emerged. Keith Ward, in his article in the capstone volume that ended the series, describes this as follows: 'there is a sort of metaphysical view that has arisen out of this series of discussions between scientists and theologians. It puts in place a background world-view for a restatement of religious doctrines that is probably as important as Aristotle was for the Christian church in the thirteenth century.'

> The scientific understanding of a universe of intelligible law and emergent creativity changes the perspective within which one sees divine action. God will not be seen as an interfering designer correcting a partly incomplete mechanism. God will be more like a universe-environing field of Spirit, setting the parameters of nature, guiding its emergent development, and ensuring the eventual fulfilment of the divine intention for its existence (Russell et al, 2008: 298).

In this, the final volume, the acronym NIODA is used to identify this consensus. It stands for 'Non-interventionist Objective Divine Action' in world process and applies both to God's creative causality in nature and also to his 'special' activity in human and 'salvation' history. This way of understanding God's action in the world is so important for the way we express Christian faith in a scientific and secular culture that I will quote William Stoeger's account of it at some length. Stoeger, incidentally, is not only a scientist (an astronomer), but a philosopher and theologian as well, and has been one of the editors—and a moving spirit—of this project from the beginning.

'Certain events or sequences of events initiated by secondary causal agents' (Stoeger is employing the traditional distinction between the primary causality of God as creator whereby God is the ultimate cause of all that happens in the universe, and the secondary

---

1. R Russell, *et al* (eds) *Scientific Perspectives on Divine Action* (Vatican Observatory, 2008).

causality of things in the universe whereby the integrity of nature is maintained.) '(either those which are freely and consciously chosen, or those which are not) are turning points within creation, or within history, and thus are specially revelatory of God's immanent creative presence. As such, these are in deeper harmony with God's intended purposes and with the essential structures and relationships already established with creation itself. These events or sequences of events would indeed be 'God's special salvific acts,' even though they were not direct acts of God (that is, not without the intermediary of a secondary cause). Nor would they lack a sufficient cause within the manifold of dynamisms and potentialities of creation or of history, presupposing the universal primary creative action of God. They would nonetheless, be special, salvific and revelatory, precisely because they are clear expressions of what God intends, and/or fulfil God's purposes and intentions in a particularly unambiguous or exemplary fashion' (2008: 245).

This way of conceiving God's special salvific acts in terms of God's overall creative action has definite advantages, Stoeger believes, both from the point of view of science and of theology. 'It connects directly with the richly differentiated, transcendently immanent presence and action of the creator God within creation and with God's radically kenotic, deeply effective but hidden availability within nature. Furthermore, it emphasizes that what is fundamental is no so much God's action, or actions, but rather God's ongoing relationship with creation. Again, the divine creative relationship is highly differentiated with respect to each entity and system within the universe—and God's action flows from the character of that relationship' (2008: 245).

As far as science is concerned, and the world-view that is the result of science, this is to my mind an essential way of conceiving God's action in the world. It is also a new way, and a new way that the development of science has itself suggested. Stoeger himself is in no doubt about this 'Thus, we can also say, in a way we could not have before the advent of the natural sciences, that God's universal creative action, though unique, is also realized in a highly differentiated and evolving way throughout nature. This evolutionary, emergent and unfinished character of creation revealed by the sciences serves to emphasize the continuing character of God's action through the regularities, processes and relationships God sustains' (2008: 230).

2.

The evolutionary character of the scientific world-view is perhaps not sufficiently stressed in the rather general picture I have been painting. I now propose to deal with that directly, and first philosophically in its implications and fruitfulness for 'natural theology' and then, in some detail, with its place in theology as such. The classical treatment of the evolutionary origin of humanity as a theological issue is Karl Rahner's 1958 monograph *Hominisation*. Rahner's early work, *Spirit in the World* and *Hearers of the Word* in particular, had provided a new philosophical foundation, derived from the history I have recapitulated above, for the traditional Christian view of humanity and its place in the world.

For Rahner, as for Kant and Hegel, human beings have a dimension that transcends anything the sciences can know since it is what produces and judges the sciences. It is what makes us self-aware, self-determining subjects of thought and action, and is the source not only of science, but of morality, art, religion and, in general, culture. It is what makes us persons in the technical sense, spiritual as well as material beings. To say that we are spiritual is to draw attention to the peculiar internal relation human beings have to themselves (self-awareness and self-determination) that is not merely some part of us related to another part, but of ourselves as a whole in relation to the whole of ourselves. This is contrasted with our materiality which refers to the equally constitutive relationship in which we stand to all that is other than ourselves, the whole universe in fact, personal and impersonal. As spiritual beings we transcend the whole of the impersonal universe in the sense that it does not explain our existence and cannot fulfill those desires that we have precisely as spiritual beings. It must however be pointed out that we are unable to exercise, develop or fulfill our spiritual capacities except through our relationship to the rest of the universe, both personal and impersonal, and in dependence on it.

This insight into our human nature does not, in Rahner's view, depend on faith but on philosophical reflection on experience. But unless one recognizes this character of our human nature it is not possible to understand adequately the essentials of Christian faith. And what is more it makes possible the integration of our understanding of humanity into an evolutionary view of the world. The well-founded theories of contemporary science have enabled us to understand that the universe is an evolutionary process in which, over time, progressively more complex forms of being come into being through a real transformation of what preceded them. Humanity is the most complex (in its materiality) and the most simple (in its spirituality) being known to us. As such we contain in a transformed unity all the preceding forms of being discovered by the sciences. Though these are part of us we cannot be reduced to them but transcend them in the way Rahner makes clear. In addition we are able to contain the universe as such in our minds and endow it with meaning and value in our decisions and our acts. Thus the universe as a whole is most properly understood as a plurality of human persons. It is the object of our thought and choice, and its impersonal aspects constitute the milieu in which a plurality of persons can exist and a medium in which interpersonal transactions can bring about our development and fulfillment. Put simply, there is more of reality in a person than a fundamental particle or physical force.

Again it must be stressed that such a conception of humanity and the world is a purely philosophical one and owes nothing to Christian faith. Nevertheless it provides a way of understanding the Christian conception of our god as our creator that is consonant with our contemporary scientific and secular culture. We experience our transcendent subjectivity in all our cognitive and volitional activity. And at the same time, according to Rahner, we experience our openness to and inclination towards something absolutely transcendent that is immanent in our activity. I say 'something' because it is not any specific object of knowledge or desire; nor is it simply we ourselves as the knowing, acting subjects. It is however inherent in our conscious free activity as the condition that makes it possible, not merely as a 'logical' condition but as a reality that is essentially mysterious.

There is an unlimitedness to human consciousness and desire that indicates an unlimited reality and value as its source, an absolutely transcendent reality and value that is nevertheless immanent in our experience of ourselves as knowing, choosing subjects. There is thus philosophical space that a Christian god can come to occupy.

A reflection on our capacity for free choice will make this clearer. When we deliberately affirm something as true or choose something as good our act transcends all the causal networks the universe contains and the sciences are able to discover. Not that the laws of nature break down in us, or the social influences that have formed us cease to operate. Indeed they are absolutely necessary if we are to act at all. But they are not sufficient. If they were we would not be free. And what holds for the free action must also hold for the capacity to act freely that is part of normal human nature as outlined above. It follows that causal networks of the universe (such as are necessary to produce human beings from pre-human nature), though necessary are themselves insufficient to produce beings like us with the capacity for free action. There must therefore be another kind of causality at work, within the evolutionary process though beyond the reach of science, that is absolutely transcendent of the universe though immanent in its processes to bring us into being.

The production of beings with the capacity for free acts such as ourselves is only the clearest case of a feature that is universal in the evolutionary process uncovered by modern science. This is a process in which really new forms of being are continually coming into existence through a transformation of what preceded them. The most dramatic examples, apart from the emergence of humanity, are those of consciousness from preconscious being, of living from non-living, and of the universe itself from an initial singularity. In general cosmic evolution is from the simple and dispersed to the complex and centred. And at every stage the new form of being is not simply the product of what previously existed. Though necessary, physical things and forces are insufficient to produce biological organisms. Something more is required, a causality that transcends the cosmic process our science can investigate though immanent in it.

Rahner's philosophical anthropology thus not only provides one with a conception of humanity that is thoroughly at home in an evolutionary world-view. It also brings to light a more general feature of a world-view such as this. Emergence of new kinds of being through a transformation of the kinds of being that preceded them is only possible by virtue of the operation of a different kind of causality altogether, one that is incommensurable with the causes science can deal with. Rahner's anthropology amounts to a new form of an argument for the existence and action in the world of a cause that would satisfy the classical Christian definition of a creator, namely one that that is transcendent of the universe but is immanent in all that it is and does. The evolutionary world-view is a perfect exemplification of this. And Rahner's account also satisfies the legitimate requirements of the traditional doctrine of God's 'immediate creation of the human soul' without lapsing into any dualism of body and mind.

There is a final part of Rahner's philosophical anthropology which is of the utmost importance for understanding Christian faith in terms in an evolutionary world-view and that is his treatment of the personal development of individuals. If evolution continues in humanity it is because it is borne by human individuals themselves, in whom there is either development or decline. For human beings, though transcending impersonal reality, are nevertheless dependent on it for all we are and do. There is no thought without images, no images without sensations, no sensations without sense organs sensitive to a spatio-temporal environment in which alone we can exist, express ourselves and communicate with others. This is what is known as our historicity. As transcendent beings we are able to develop an inner life, to live by meanings and values. But we can only do this in a process that unfolds in time and in a milieu that identifies us in space. We develop ourselves only in dependence on what is other than us. And, most importantly, through our relations with other persons, in a social and cultural milieu that humanity itself has constructed. Historicity is a feature of the life of individuals and of humanity as a whole.

For beings such as we are our relations with other persons are crucial for the exercise, development and fulfilment of our distinctively personal capacities of self-consciousness and self-determination. And a philosophical phenomenology of intersubjectivity shows that certain definite kinds of relationship with others are necessary for this. It reveals the startling fact that the more we are influenced by other persons in whom these capacities are already developed, the more self-determining we are enabled to be. Apart from such influence we are unable to grow as persons. This can appear to contradict the fact that the capacity in question is that for self-determination, for action that is free. But careful analysis of experience proves the contrary: the more I am influenced by the other in a certain way, the more the act is my own.

This is in fact what our philosophical anthropology should lead us to expect. For we saw there that the existence of beings with a capacity for self-determination was only possible as the effect of an absolutely transcendent cause immanent in the evolutionary process. And in our experience of ourselves as knowing, choosing subjects we are conscious of an apprehension of reality that is absolute and of a desire for something of absolute value. This experience is however not objective; the transcendent source of our knowing and valuing is only implicit in our experience of ourselves. Here however, in the relationships with others in which we exercise develop and fulfill our capacities for self-knowledge and self-affirmation, we actually experience in an objective way the power and presence of an absolutely transcendent personal reality immanent in the very relationships themselves. It is precisely this that explains the paradoxical 'interpersonal causality' whereby the more we are subject to the influence of the other, the more self-determining we become. If the influence exercised on us was simply that of a finite cause other than us, the more it caused us to act, the less the act would be our own. But the opposite is the case. We are thus bound to recognise that within the relationships in which my capacity for self-determination is developed there is a truly transcendent personal cause at work, whose influence is incommensurable with that of finite causes, personal or impersonal.

This understanding of the necessary conditions for the exercise, development and fulfilment of human persons thus provides the basis for a 'natural theology', a new natural theology moreover that is consonant with a scientific and secular world-view and closer to the reality of religious faith than traditional arguments for the existence of God. It also provides, in my view, a fruitful approach to the problem of death.

In the sketch of the history of religion that I will presently be providing I make the point that however differently different religious traditions conceive the nature of the predicament from which their gods are understood to be able to save us, it is always characterised by two elements: conflict between human beings and death. The account just given of the interpersonal relationships required for personal growth provides a theoretical solution to the first of these, a solution that can only be realised through power from a fully transcendent source. And it is only power of this kind that can provide an answer to the problem of death. If my account of the necessary conditions for personal growth is accurate, and these conditions exist, then they also are able to answer the problem posed by death.

If it is true that human persons are transcendent in the sense that the causes science is able to identify are insufficient to bring us into being, then it follows that those same causes are insufficient to make us cease to be. But, more positively, the dynamism of personal growth through the influence of the other, is one of self-gift from and so to the other. Within the circumstances of ordinary life it is always possible to fool oneself as to whether this has been achieved; a habitual fear and self-centredness can always provide an impediment. Death however confronts one with an unavoidable choice. For human beings death means the limit of human power to control. But the experience of personal growth through the gift of the other can help us to recognise the same feature in death. Self-assertion is futile; self-surrender to a power we have learnt to trust robs death of its threat. Instead it becomes the climax of a life in which we have only ourselves by giving ourselves away.

3.

Seeing creation in terms of emergence, rather than as the act of starting the universe or even as the activity of conservation that keeps it going, though a purely philosophical development, thus provides a firmer foundation for theology proper to build on. On this basis I want now to summarise the aspects of the theory of evolution and emergence which have direct relevance for Christian theology as such.

The first of these is the idea of the unity and integrity of world process such that any metaphysical dualism is avoided. And so is materialism, since the unitary process culminates in the mind and will of human beings. Each individual recapitulates in the womb the whole evolutionary process that has led to humanity, and then continues it in a specifically human way in their own life. Humanity thus appears as a microcosm of the universe as a whole, containing all other levels of reality within itself; it is a paradigm of reality and not just one species amongst others. At the same time the universe itself appears as our true home, the only place, in spite of its imperfections and incompleteness, in which we can be real. Whatever the theological notion of 'salvation' means it cannot mean our being saved 'out of' the world. There is no other place! The evolutionary world-view suggests a better alternative in a further transformation of the human world (and thus the universe), in the line of those transformations that have brought humanity into being and still continue, as we shall see, in human history to this day. In a perspective such as this, the struggle to 'make the world a better place', to overcome dehumanising poverty and injustice and to take good care of the natural environment, can make better theological sense.

The second aspect of evolutionary theory of direct relevance to theology is the notion of energy it embodies, and in particular the idea that the basic energy of the universe is a 'form-producing' energy (to borrow Brian Swimme's felicitous expression[2]) whereby every kind of being manifests over time a capacity for self-transcendence, and always in the direction of greater complexity with the increasing 'centredness' that that entails. The notion that evolution has a direction (in spite of, or perhaps even because of the annihilations and extinctions that have occurred at regular intervals during its 14 billion year history), a direction defined by the production of truly new kinds of being through a transformation and transcendence of what has gone before, is perhaps the single most important feature of the theory as far as theology is concerned. Not only does it offer a new model for the idea of creation, as we have already noted; it also helps one to see the Incarnation in a new way, as well as the ideas of salvation and grace and the notion of the Church—as I presently hope to show.

Extending the notion of evolution to humanity itself, to human history, is a third aspect one must take into account. This must not be confused with a facile idea of progress; even if the newest science is usually the best, the same cannot be said of morality. But evolution, at every level of reality, is never simply progress. It involves experiment, trial and error, though always in the end, new being through transformation and transcendence. In human history evolution takes the form of transformations of culture and consciousness and the communities in which individuals develop. The direction taken by these transformations in the human sphere is similar to that in the evolution of living beings, and indeed to that of the cosmos as a whole. It is an evolution from simplicity and homogeneity towards diversity and complexity. In human culture Eric Voegelin calls this the movement from compactness to differentiation. In primal societies politics and religion, philosophy and theology, economics and spirituality are not distinguished but form an integrated largely unconscious whole. Then technology supersedes magic, philosophy replaces myth, theology is distinguished from philosophy, eventually religion is seen as a distinct sphere of human life and contrasted with secularity. Finally the history of each of theses spheres of life

2. B Swimme, *The Universe Story* (HarperCollins, 1992).

comes to be written. This evolution of culture, consciousness and community takes place within the sphere of religion itself, as in all the other spheres of human life. We will examine this in more detail presently. And then within Christianity there is an evolution in the development of doctrine, spirituality and liturgy.

A final, but possibly the most important, aspect of an evolutionary world-view is the idea of the necessity of a causal factor in world-process that is incommensurable with any cause discoverable by the sciences. This notion of incommensurability is of the utmost importance for dealing in a theological way with Christian faith. It arises, as we have seen, through an insight into our experience of our capacity for self-determination, and is given a more comprehensive and concrete character on our actual experience of personal growth in relationships with other persons. The fact that this experience is something universal available to humanity and not exceptional should not blind us to its essentially mysterious character. If my account is accurate then it is indeed the case that we have real experience of something absolutely transcendent, and therefore incommensurable with human persons, in our ordinary interpersonal relations.

Rahner corroborates this insight and its importance in a theological way in his treatment of the notion of creatureliness and our experience of this. Being a creature in this context entails a unique relationship to our transcendent creator, a relationship that is traditionally expressed by the notion of incommensurability. The notion of the incommensurability of creature and creator is central to classical theism and taken for granted by Aquinas. One cannot add God and the universe and make two. This is not because either is unreal, or that God and the universe are identical, but because there is no common measure in terms of which they could be added to or subtracted from one another The reality of each is too different. An analogy would be that of a poet composing a poem about himself. One cannot say there are two poets, the one composing and the one in the poem. But to say there is only one is misleading because the poem already exists in the poet's mind. Rahner makes use of this idea in his discussion of our creatureliness. The following quotation serves the purpose of making the connection with the idea of 'interpersonal causality' outlined above.[3]

3. See K Rahner, *Foundations of Christian Faith* (Darton, Longman and Todd, 1978).

The radical dependence and the genuine reality of the existent coming from God vary in direct and not in inverse proportion. In our human experience it is the case that the more something is dependent on us, the less it is different from us, and the less it possesses its own reality and autonomy. The radical dependence of the effect on the cause and the independence and autonomy of the effect vary in inverse proportion.

> But when we reflect upon the real transcendental relationship between God and a creature, then it is clear that here genuine reality and radical dependence are simply just two sides of one and the same reality, and therefore they vary in direct and not inverse proportion. We and the existents of our world really and truly are and are different from God not in spite of, but because we are established in being by God and not by anyone else. (1978: 79).

The best example of this apparently contradictory, but in reality paradoxical, relation is that of the human capacity for self-determination. In our discussion of Rahner's philosophical anthropology it was pointed out that only an infinite cause could be sufficient to bring beings with the capacity for freedom into existence, albeit through the causal mechanisms of evolution. It follows that even the exercise, development and fulfillment of our capacity for self-determination is the effect of the creative causality of God. Human freedom means freedom from total determination by worldly causes, not freedom from God. It is precisely this paradoxical truth that my analysis of interpersonal causality is intended to substantiate.

Christian theology grows from the reflection of his first followers on their experience of Jesus. The fruits of this reflection are documented in the writings of the New Testament. We are now in a position to appreciate these against the background of an evolutionary view of the world and the evolution of religious thought, in the history of Israel in particular.

4.

Religion is as old as humanity and is the expression of a deep desire natural to humanity for a comprehensive and enduring fulfilment to all our most basic capacities and needs, especially those beyond our own powers. The gods of all religions are seen as sources of power transcending our own that can do this. Thus all religions see life as a predicament, the general form of which is that we are conscious of deep desires that only power transcending our own is able to fulfil. The history of religion offers many different accounts of this predicament and correspondingly different conceptions of the gods that are able to overcome it. Two elements however stand out as present in all traditions: the desire to overcome sickness and death, and the desire to overcome human conflict of every kind.

Although the gods of the different religions are always seen as having powers that transcend human power, the way these powers are understood depends on the view held of human nature and its capacities, its needs and powers. There is always an intrinsic connection between the conception of our god and the conception of humanity itself. This connection is illustrated in the case of Israel by the idea that humanity is the 'image' of Yahweh. For the historian of ideas it is also true that Yahweh is the 'image' of humanity. And as human culture evolves and conceptions of human nature change, so too do conceptions of our gods. There seems to be a measure of agreement among historians that during what came to be called the Axial period (roughly 800 to 300BC) in all the major centres of civilization, a similar development in outlook took place, a development that one can call (following Voegelin) 'the discovery of transcendence'.[4] All cultures of the time were religious so one could call this a development in religion. However it occurred in Greece as well where it took the form of a rejection of the Greek gods in the name of an absolutely transcendent element in humanity itself as well as an absolutely transcendent sphere that was its source. Plato, for instance, saw the human soul as possessed of a transcendence of anything material, and identified what he called the Form of the Good as the transcendent source of all reality, the gods included.

Be that as it may, in the history of Israel, especially in the time of the later prophets such as Second Isaiah and Ezekiel, it was a development in religion. Yahweh, originally a tribal god among other tribal gods, came to be seen as the god above all gods, and eventually as the only god, transcending not only human powers but all powers absolutely, of whatever spiritual beings the universe contained. The

4. K Voegelin, *Order and History* Volume I (Louisiana University Press, 1969).

final step was to see that Yahweh was not part of the universe at all but its creator. This absolute transcendence of a god was a novelty in the history of religion. And, as the history of religion would lead one to expect, it was connected in the thinking of Irael's prophets and sages to a similar, though derived, transcendence in humanity itself as Yahweh's image. The universe, though necessary for human existence and fulfilment, was neither sufficient to produce or fulfil beings like us who had capacities, and thus needs and desires that only an absolutely transcendent being could fulfil. Hence the endless hostility of the authors of the Old Testament writings towards the 'gods of the nations' who were not to be treated as gods at all since they were powerless to fulfil the transcendent needs of beings such as we.

This conception of humanity and its god gave a special character to the understanding of the human predicament in the later thought of Israel's prophets and sages, an understanding that is spelled out in mythical form in the first eleven chapters of the book of Genesis. These stories, especially those of Adam and Eve in the garden and the Tower of Babel, are stories of idolatry. The human predicament is depicted as a state of conflict within the human family, the consequence of which is death. The cause of conflict is sin. And sin is simply idolatry. Idolatry is self-worship, the desire to be like our transcendent god without dependence on it. And this is almost inevitable for us since we have a godlike capacity for transcendence and creativity, but one that can only be developed and fulfilled by our transcendent creator. The solution developed in the history of Israel to this predicament lay in Yahweh himself taking control of human history, overcoming human disunity by transforming the hearts and minds of his people so that they would accept and engage with him as their saviour and their king. Then they would be a community of love and peace, a universal community that would last forever.

This then is the background of the historic event documented by the writings of the New Testament. In summary: the disciples' experience of Jesus and his effect in their lives, culminating in the mysterious experience of meeting with him after his death and of his continuing presence amongst them, led them to believe that God himself was present in Jesus and in them in such a way that they shared in his own sin-and death-transcending life. This vision and spirit had come to them from Jesus and so they called him 'saviour'.

This interpersonal interaction with Jesus is the event from which all Christian theology derives. It is this which, in our scientific and secular culture, we need to understand in terms of the evolutionary view of the world.

5.

Traditionally this foundational event is called, in the case of Jesus, the Incarnation and, in the case of his disciples, Salvation or Redemption. And traditionally it is understood as an intervention by God in human history for the purpose of our salvation from a situation more or less like what I have just sketched above. *Cur Deus homo?* theologians from Anselm to Aquinas have asked. And the answer given to this question was invariably 'To save us from sin and the effects of sin'. No sin, no Incarnation, no need! In an evolutionary perspective however everything looks different. We have learnt to see creation as a continuing process, a process that produces humanity and continues in human history as an evolution of consciousness, culture and community. From the standpoint of Jesus and his first followers this can now be seen in the history of Israel culminating in them. God is creating a new consciousness in humanity, a new insight into human nature and into God himself that is to permeate our culture and its institutions so that a new community of humanity will result. In this perspective human history is essentially a history of revelation and a history of salvation. And what is more, the mysterious secret finally revealed and realised in his followers' relationship with Jesus, is that this will be a community with God himself, God present in our minds and hearts and in our lives. As Karl Rahner would put it, the whole of human history is a history of God's self-communication to us. And it reaches an unsurpassable climax in the life of Jesus. Subsequent history is to be the spelling out of the implications of this vision and the implementation of this spirit universally. Evolution has now a new direction, the construction on this foundation of a hospitable home for humanity where they can live as a loving family with God.

I want now to show how this basic outlook affects the way we understand the central doctrines that have developed in the history of the Church to explain the nature of Christian faith. I will use the work of Karl Rahner to do this since he has explicitly situated his theology within an evolutionary framework. In particular he sees human evolution as recapitulating that of the cosmos: it is the universe itself that continues to evolve in us, in our thoughts and actions. 'The history of nature and of spirit form an intrinsic and stratified unity in which the history of nature develops towards man, continues on in him as *his* history, is preserved and surpassed in him, and therefore reaches its own goal with and in the history of man's spirit.' (Rahner 1978: 187) Rahner sees this evolution as God's creative achievement and as a moment within that self-communication of God that culminates in the Incarnation and its effects in us: 'Now according to Christian teaching, this self-transcendence of the cosmos in man towards its own totality and towards its ground does not really and fully reach its ultimate fulfilment until the cosmos is not only something established in existence by its ground, is not only something created, but also receives the immediate self-communication of its own ground in the spiritual creatures which are its goal and its high point. This immediate self-communication of God to spiritual creatures takes place in what we call 'grace' while this self-communication is still in its historical process, and 'glory' when it reaches fulfilment. Not only does God create something different from himself, but he also gives himself to this other. The world receives God, the infinite and the ineffable mystery, in such a way that he himself becomes its innermost life. The always unique self-possession of the cosmos, which is concentrated in each individual spiritual person in its transcendence towards the absolute ground of its reality, takes place by the fact that the absolute ground itself becomes immediately interior to what is grounded by it.' (1978: 190)

In this evolutionary understanding of Christianity God (as the one Jesus called Abba) has a quite distinctive character and relationship to us. In the first place it is God who is now recognized as the source of our existence and the one whom we experience in our experience of ourselves as knowing, choosing subjects involved with other persons in a milieu of culture and of nature. And it is God whom we experience especially in those relationships with others in which we exercise, develop and fulfill those capacities that make us subjects, and, in particular, our desire for the fullness of personal community and death-transcending life. For Rahner nobody is without this experience, and it is in this sense that he uses the term 'anonymous Christian'. Of course experience is not knowledge, and primal cultures had only inadequate ideas of God, as are expressed in their religion. But for Rahner the whole of human history can be seen as an evolution towards the true understanding of the power that moves history towards its goal through the insights and freedom of humanity. And this is because he believes that human history is the history of *God's self-communication* to humanity. The notion of God's self-communication to humanity is the fundamental conception in Rahner's theology. It is this idea that defines both salvation and revelation for him.

The salvation of humanity consists in the creation of 'the unity of humanity in union with God', to paraphrase the expression used by the Second Vatican Council. For Rahner the way to this is God's self-communication to us throughout human history, but finally and fully in the life of Jesus. For a union between God and humanity to exist it must be achieved in our human world, the world God created for this purpose. It cannot take place anywhere else, for human beings cannot be real anywhere else. We are 'evolution become conscious of itself'. However transformed, it is this universe that is our eternal home. And it has been created by God with the purpose of making it a home in which God can be with us. We don't go to God; God comes to us. This is the import of Rahner's idea of God's self-communication. And so the Incarnation (the complete and therefore unsurpassable form of God's self-communication) is seen as the purpose of creation, and salvation as the purpose of the Incarnation. One must of course add that the notion of salvation is only appropriate because of sin; it is God's continuing creation and self-communication in the process of overcoming sin and the effects of sin in us. Finally, salvation can only be achieved if God's self-communication is accepted. For Christian faith it is, and completely, by Jesus. The acceptance of God's self-communication, by Jesus or by us, is also always the result of God's freedom-creating power in human acts, 'grace' in Rahner's terminology.

Revelation, as Rahner understands it, is not primarily the revelation of truths but the revelation of God himself. It is an aspect of God's self-communication, that which imparts the personal knowledge of God. This knowledge is personal knowledge, the knowledge of acquaintance, not knowledge of truths about God, not something that can be written down. It is thus not to be identified with scripture, whether Jewish or Christian. It is that which is possessed by the persons—prophets, apostles, Jesus himself—who write or are written about in the scriptures. Rahner, as I have already indicated, sees the history of God's revelation of God as coinciding with the whole of human history. And, as with salvation, revelation proceeds by fits and starts, developing in different ways and to different degrees in every culture and religion. It reaches an unsurpassable completeness only in Jesus.

Because Christian faith in God is faith in the one revealed in the person and life of Jesus it depends on a knowledge of that person and that life. This is as true for those who were intimate with him before his death as it is for us. But for us this knowledge is mediated to us by that original community as it has expanded through two thousand years. And it is complicated by the fact that the original community (and its extension through time and space) was formed by a faith in Jesus' resurrection. So there is no way of getting to know anything (or anything of importance) about Jesus apart from those who believed in his resurrection. Certainly all the writings of the New Testament are written from the point of view of this faith. Modern scientific study of these has helped a great deal to form an objective picture of what Jesus said and did and of the effect this had on his followers. But the project of building up a detailed biography of Jesus is doomed to failure. That does not matter however from the point of view of Christian theology. As theologians we want an accurate picture of the *faith* of Jesus' followers and, if possible, the faith of Jesus himself. Since the authors of the New Testament writings believed that their faith in God was the same as that of Jesus—since they had acquired it through their intimacy with him—they are providing us with first hand information about the nature of that faith. And that is what we really want. Rahner (though not himself a biblical scholar in the strict sense, had studied more works of biblical scholarship than most who are) certainly believed that we are in possession of sufficient knowledge of what the first followers of Jesus believed, and of what Jesus himself believed, to be able to share their faith. He is supported in this conviction both by the philosophical insights into the capacities and deep desires of our human nature that I have outlined, as well as by the history of religion I have sketched above. And he certainly believed that if a person was not in touch with his own humanity, but had a mind full of contemporary illusions or ancient myths, then authentic Christian faith would be virtually impossible.

Rahner felt that one can say something about Jesus' own self-understanding. Jesus certainly saw himself as standing in the historic line of Jewish prophets, but with this difference: he was bringing this line to an end. All other prophets saw themselves as bearers of God's word to Israel, but that word was not seen as God's final word. The prophets saw their words as God's words ('The Lord your God says this' and 'Thus says the Lord'), but still expected God to say more. Jesus, on the other hand, had a message whose very content implied that it was the final one, final because complete and unsurpassable. Rahner sees Jesus' gospel of the kingdom of God as implying God's *self*-communication to the world, not just a message. And not even God could do more than that.

So the first stage of human history was coming to an end; the final stage was beginning. 'Was beginning . . .?' Rahner believes that Jesus did not know, perhaps even was mistaken, about the 'times and seasons' of God's full and irrevocable entry into human history, his 'kingdom'. But he also believes that Jesus saw himself as in some way or other responsible for its inauguration. And that he felt this responsibility because of his experience of God's extraordinary closeness to him. Here is how he puts it:

> Jesus experienced a relationship to God which he experienced as new and unique in comparison with other men, but which he nevertheless considered to be exemplary for other men in their relationship to God . . . Jesus experienced in himself that radical and victorious offer of God to him which did not exist before in this way among 'sinners', and he knows that it is significant, valid and irrevocable for *all* men. According to his own self-understanding he is already before the resurrection the one sent, the one who inaugurates the kingdom of God through what he says and what he does in a way that did not exist before, but now does exist *through* him and *in* him. At least in this sense the pre-resurrection Jesus already knew himself to be the absolute and unsurpassable saviour. (1978: 253–254)

Certainly his followers saw him in that light, and even before the resurrection experience of his being with them although he had died. Unless they had his death would not have been the catastrophic disaster it clearly was. And nor would their experience of the resurrection have had the meaning that it did.

What the followers of Jesus came to see, and what later theology has tried ever since to find appropriate words for, was that the immanence of the transcendent god of Israel in historical events, and especially in the words and acts of the prophets, had reached an unsurpassable climax in Jesus and his relationship with them. In this experience they saw God as uniting Jesus to himself by taking his human nature into himself in such a way that the incommensurability of creator and creature found full expression in Jesus' character and life, and in the influence he had on his disciples. As they came to put it, they experienced Jesus as being 'without sin', in virtue of the unity between God's Spirit and his own. God's self-communication had always provided the ultimate environment of humanity; never before had it been fully accepted.

An evolutionary world-view is a scientific and secular one. It is therefore important that Christianity avoids the appearance of mythical thinking. Too often the figure of Jesus has been presented in this way, as a kind of 'superman' (*ubermensch)* or a mere 'humanoid' apparition of God. There were indeed monophysitist tendencies in Christianity from the start. In view of the universal human tendency towards idolatry outlined above this should not surprise us. The defence of Jesus' genuine humanity is still necessary. And this is one of the main aims of Rahner's 'Christology within an evolutionary view of the world'. He stresses that the 'hypostatic union may not be seen so much as something which distinguishes Jesus from us, but as something which must occur once and only once when the world begins to enter upon its final phase' (1978: 181). And this because 'the intrinsic effect of the hypostatic union for the assumed humanity of the Logos consists precisely and in real sense *only* in the very thing which is ascribed to all men as their goal and their fulfilment, namely the immediate vision of God' (1978: 200). In trinitarian terms, it is the same presence of the Father's Word and Spirit in Jesus and in his followers that enables them to participate in God's sin- and death-transcendent life.

6.

It remains true that for Christian faith God's presence in Jesus has a completeness that cannot be surpassed, since it is God *himself* who is present. But according to the same faith God has always been present in human history though not fully experienced as such. Nor can it be thought that human history, and the evolution of culture and community that implies, is now at an end. Too often religions, and Christianity in particular, attempt to fix their faith on some past event and the earliest expression of its meaning. This is the idolatry of fundamentalism. Instead, in order to do justice to the evolutionary understanding of reality, an authentic faith can only exist in changing forms of culture and community. Such changing forms are always created and carried by a small minority of believers. And it is only in the nineteenth century that the idea of 'the development of doctrine' becomes fully conscious. It is a genuine fruit of human evolution nonetheless, as Newman saw when he observed that 'to live is to change and to live perfectly is to have changed often'. In this light it is not fanciful to see the phenomenon of secularization, in spite of all its imperfections, as a fruit of that unity of humanity and God identified in the Incarnation. Charles Taylor, does in fact see it in this way when he describes it in *A Secular Age* (Harvard, 2007) as the completion of the Axial discovery of transcendence (2007: 774).

So human evolution is not over with the Incarnation. For Christian faith it is at a new beginning. If the Incarnation is the ultimate revelation of God's saving presence in human history, it is not something that is now over and done with. To believe in the resurrection of Jesus is to believe in his continuing 'real presence' in the world. And that means that God's Incarnation continues, though now in the sacramental mode we call the Church, which is a communion of Jesus with his followers.

Christian faith is personal knowledge of a person, given and received in a relationship between persons. For this reason it cannot be exhaustively or finally expressed in any form of words. For the same saving relationship to be achieved in different times and places, different words must of necessity be used for its expression. This of course is the ongoing work of theology as *fides quaerens intellectum*. And if we are to take the notion of an evolution in human history seriously we are bound to look for a development in theology as well. If there is an increase in our knowledge of the world and of ourselves, surely there can be an increase in our understanding of our faith as well.

A word of caution: the newest science is the truest; the same is not true of philosophy, or of any of the other forms of knowledge that constitute wisdom. This more comprehensive, deeper understanding is always the achievement of particular individuals. And it cannot be communicated to others in the way that the knowledge of the sciences can. Nevertheless I think that the achievements of science as well as philosophy enable a deeper, fuller understanding—in our post-modern setting, beyond pre-modern superstition and modern materialism—of the event on which Christian faith is based.

The account given above of the necessary conditions for the exercise, growth and fulfilment of our capacity for self-determination, an account that provides evidence for the presence and influence within the intersubjective relations of human persons of a strictly transcendent yet personal power, does to my mind help one to understand better the relationship between Jesus and his disciples that constituted both their salvation and a revelation of God. There in an extreme form we have the 'interpersonal causality' that reveals the presence of the transcendent in our experience of personal growth: the gift of self from and so to the other. In this connection it is worth remarking that the consonance we pointed out between the self-offering dynamism involved in personal growth and the living of our death as the final gift of self to God, is exhibited perfectly in the disciples' experience of Jesus' resurrection. This is at one and the same time an experience of union with him and an insight into the meaning of his life and death.

It can be reasonably asked of Christians who accept the evolutionary view what form an evolution of Christianity might be expected to take. There is no simple answer to this question. The traditional answer: missionary activity and conversion, no longer seems appropriate. We have to look for an answer to the new social and cultural environment in which any such evolution must take place.

Keith Ward, in his courageous and perceptive work *A Vision to Pursue* (London: SCM, 1991) argues for a critical engagement on the part of Christians with their own tradition, the purpose of which is to renew it. Renewal, as Ward understands it, is something radical in which a real transformation takes place, so that what emerges is something really new though comprising all the essential ingredients of the old. Nor is it only Christians who must engage in this creative criticism; it is a necessity for all religious traditions, a necessity produced by the evolution of consciousness, culture and community of which I have spoken. As always, renewal of a tradition is the work of a small minority of the faithful. Ward however believes that 'within each tradition there are many who stand within the tradition, but think that they can, and should, revise some of its central ideas to take account of advances in scientific knowledge, scriptural and historical scholarship, or changes in moral and philosophical outlook' (1991: 194).

In our post-modern context we are confronted with a plurality of cultural and religious traditions, and new ones are beginning all the time. Insight into evolution should lead us to expect this. And we should also recognise that not all traditions of this kind are equally true or good, not all constitute an evolutionary advance. At the moment this global plurality of cultures and religions is a theatre of conflict if not a war-zone. This is often depicted by religious traditions as at root a conflict between the old and good and the new and bad: 'They see the basic modern religious conflict as one between an ancient and irreformable truth, embodied in one cultural framework, and destructive forces of secularism and materialism, which must be resisted by a return to the old absolute value' (1991: 206). This is a mistake: 'The true conflict is between a form of Enlightenment thinking which has become, self-defeatingly, trapped in a dogmatic system of materialism and a form of religious faith which is open to new insights and repentant of old mistakes. It is not the opposition of one dogmatism to another, as the fundamentalists suppose. It is the endeavour to open up the Enlightenment to its spiritual basis and goal, in the relation of free finite spirits to the unconditioned freedom of the supreme creative Spirit underlying all things. This does necessitate a criticism of all traditions; but only in order that they may move to a wider and deeper grasp of what is implicit within them. It does necessitate a conversation of traditions with one another; but only in order that each may learn its limitations by learning the differing visions found elsewhere' (1991: 207).

This suggests that the way forward, the direction to be chosen, involves developing a conversation between religious traditions and perhaps particularly between those traditions that have lasted, the biblical religions of the Middle East and the Eastern religions of India and China. But a condition of health of such a conversation will be its ability to recognise and express itself in terms of the scientific and secular culture that is here to stay. Indeed I would go so far as to say that it is only a 'natural theology' based on the insights into our human nature provided by this culture that can provide both a standard for judging the truth and value of any religion and also a basis for genuine dialogue between them. I hope I have done enough in this paper to show that a Christian faith expressed in terms of an evolutionary world-view has nothing to fear from such a conversation.

(2009)

Chapter Thirty

On Augustine Shutte's Turn to Symbol

Patrick Giddy

A New Focus on Spirituality

In this concluding chapter I am going to introduce what may seem a tangential line of thought in the theology of Augustine Shutte. I base this on his last notebook entries and on his religious poetry—which had circulated among friends and was published after his death with the title, *The Way Home* (Shutte 2017). I begin with an extract from his poem entitled, simply, 'God'. The critical self-reflection shown here points the way to a more personal appropriation of his faith, beyond theology and toward symbol.

God

God, my god, has been real for me
in the pages I have written or read.
In my journals, as well as in my prayers,
I conversed with him.
In books and articles I have described him
as though with intimate knowledge.
I have even formulated arguments
to prove that he was real
and not just a neurotic fantasy
or mere wish fulfillment.

Over long years I have laboured to create
a conception that was absolutely true,
and ransacked my mind and the minds of others
for arguments that proved its truth
until I was satisfied that I possessed it.

I did not realise I had created an idol—
no infantile idol, no doll in beads,
but a dangerous image, a mirage
that turned me from the reality that made me real
to a fantasy made by me, but yet holding me
a prisoner in my thoughts.

Now that I have stopped writing
and talking to others about him
he has stopped being real for me.
Now that the props have been removed
of my life's play—the prestige of priest or prophet,
the support of partners in my work-
the stage is empty but for me.
I stand, like Hamlet, with a question:
Is God real? It is the emptiness itself
that puts the question, a question
that I myself now am.

The author's relation to the whole Christian tradition and culture comes through in another poem, a reflection on the cathedral, then mosque, then museum, Haghia Sophia in Istanbul. I will include this later. What is apparent from his notebook entries, as we shall see, is that he is thrown back on himself precisely because of having to confront the shortcomings in the received formulations of the faith—and to construct fresh conceptualizations of the religion.

What are these shortcomings, as he sees them? In his 'autobiographical introduction' to the collection—Chapter One above—Shutte remarks of his essay on ecumenism that he affirms there 'the uniqueness of God's presence in Jesus, and thus in the church, in a way that I no longer would'. For any reader, this is intriguing and justifies the incursion proposed in this chapter.

He explains that his changed view is based on his understanding of personal presence. 'Personal presence is a relational concept, depending on both members of that relationship. It is from our side that there is a difference between God's presence in Jesus and God's presence in us. From God's side, as it were, there is no difference.'

This 'no difference' is what he now sees as non-orthodox. He bases his understanding on his philosophical anthropology, outlining the intersubjective nature of being human, and growing as a person, key to how, in his interpretation, Jesus saves us.

In the spirit of the growth of understanding found in the pages of these theology papers, I offer some insights building on Shutte's writings. In the first place, we can note the consonance of the central interpretative idea of 'presence' in his analysis, with that of Jesuit theologian Roger Haight. Haight also sees a problem, in popular Christianity, of what he terms an 'imaginative fixation on Jesus' being God' (2005, 29, footnote). Jesus, he says elsewhere, 'cannot be conceived as essentially different from other human beings' (2019, 196). Here, he says, it is helpful to adopt the interpretative notion of the 'presence' of God in Jesus. Summing up, Haight writes: 'God's enhanced presence to Jesus also means that Jesus is both saved and savior, the receiver of revelation and the revealer, not on the basis of his own power, but through the power of God as Presence within him and us' (Haight 2019, 197). The language of orthodoxy has, in Haight's term, to be 'revised'. And given the structural problems associated with any such revision, unpacked below, this point is big with implications for the way any Christian sees the critical element of their membership of the church.

Wrong direction in theological tradition

First, however, I want to indicate Shutte's intent, more spiritual than theological, in what he takes as his dissent from orthodoxy. In a section in his notebooks he entitles, 'The History of God', he refers to the universal human experience of both freedom and dependence—in all ages and cultures. How to give this dual experience a religious conceptualization? For the tradition at issue here, there is an understanding of God as our transcendent creator and for this reason, immanent in all we are and do. But, he comments, such an understanding has been rare, at least as personally appropriated. He goes on, addressing his thought directly to his listener, namely God.

> In the New Testament writings, we find a unique, and uniquely authentic (so I believe), expression of this understanding. And it is derived from the experience of Jesus' disciples, which is formed by and focused on their experience of him.

But also prevalent has been a mistaken way of understanding this.

> The earliest, most enduring and dangerous of these was to come to see you as related to Jesus in a completely different

way from the way you are related to us. In some way this was natural since the insight into you and your presence in us originated in and was revealed by him. In this sense he was and remains unique. But soon this uniqueness was understood in terms of nature: his nature was different from ours and the same as yours. Not that he was not human but that he was also divine; he had two natures!

One can see how easily this misconception developed. After all Jesus had revealed how completely you were present in every dimension of our lives, so that, apart from our sinfulness, the distinction between what was divine and what was human in our lives was very fine, and difficult to make. It is easy to see how this unity between the two in Jesus, since he was the origin of the insight, was seen as a unity of natures, of your nature and of ours. And since he clearly knew he wasn't you he must be, as well as being a human person like us, also be a divine person like you, different from you but with the same nature, your Son.

This misunderstanding took at least two hundred years to find its full formulation in the doctrine of the Trinity. And it took another couple of hundred years to get its classic definition by Church authorities. But the effect of this development was to give the Church (and the world of the time) the impression that Jesus was radically different from us in that he alone shared your nature. And that fact that he was now seen as a divine person was clearly far more important than that he was human and so just like us. His difference from rather than his similarity to us was the crucial thing for Christians to believe. And this had terrible effects on Christian spirituality, and indeed on the development and behaviour of the Church and its officials. The name given to this was monophysitism, which means 'one nature' and the one nature that came to be attributed to Jesus was of course your own.

So from this time on our faith and spirituality became schizophrenic. There was Jesus our god, a remote metaphysical figure, and there was Jesus the man who suffered for us on our behalf and so averted his divine anger at our sin. But the original experience and insight and inspiration that Jesus had and communicated to his disciples now was wholly obliterated. The sense that the followers of Jesus were, like him, also animated by your Word and Spirit, led to reverence

> and worship of those who clearly lived by this divine power, Mary in particular but all the saints were regarded in this way. There was also the general sense of identity and community with Jesus and us in the celebration of the eucharist. These things kept the original faith alive for many people. But as far as theologians were concerned, there were few and far between whose thinking was true to the original revelation. And they were often dismissed as heretics by the orthodox.

This analysis could be unpacked in a number of ways. The practical upshot of these developments has been that of disempowering ordinary believers from full, intelligent, and responsible participation in the spiritual life communicated through Jesus. This amounts to a structural problem in the development of theology. I want to indicate something of this problem—finally through one of Shutte's reflections in poetry.

Structures of orthodoxy

I can begin with a number of opinions similar to that of Augustine Shutte. James Mackey, for example, has argued that the Roman Catholic Church has an image of itself as 'franchised' in the business of the Christian religion. The metaphor refers to a commercial culture, centred on the idea (in contrast to the feudal economy) of the equality of all players. But here the clerical class has no competitors. What we have here is 'an ecclesiology that characterizes the superstructure model of grace above and beyond nature and of revelation above and beyond history.' The upshot of this is the claim of some within the church to have 'the privilege and responsibility to make this grace and truth known and available to all nations and all ages . . .' (Mackey 2006, 20). This overrides the freedom of scholars to suggest new formulations of the Christian faith. Joseph Moingt, a French Jesuit, similarly, argues that reform is needed so that discussion, debate and maturing of thought may take place among people (*cf* Moingt 2010). Jean-Pol Gallez has summarized this idea in his talk to the CCBF (*Conférence catholique des baptisés francophones*).

Gallez argues that 'the problem is not of ordaining women or not, of allowing priests to marry or not but of foreseeing a new way of living-together within the Church—a new co-citizenship—far from any clerical logic.'

He quotes Moingt, who writes that what is needed is not bolstering the number of priests in the church, but 'restoring the equality at its base, by giving back to the faithful the right of speaking up that they enjoyed long ago, and by letting it spread all over, so that the Christians may take responsibilities, and feel rightly in charge of their Church and of its survival in the world.'

Gallez explains:

> Because of its early collusion with the secular powers the Church got used to functioning within a domination-type of relationship which fails to honour the evangelical paradox of exercising power without domination or inequality. The distinction between the laity and clergy emerged and developed along the centuries, and it restricted the right of proclaiming the Gospel to the clergy. As long as the Church and the society functioned together within the framework of the worldly power, the communication between then worked pretty well. In a world which was almost totally Christian, all could hear its message. But, in a western democratized society which has left religion behind, the way authority is practiced in the Church is felt as non-egalitarian, and the Word cannot any longer be proclaimed to the world because the religious model which bears it has run out of steam (Gallez 2017: 9; my translation).

Finally, Karl Rahner, making a similar point about orthodoxy, points to the misfit of the traditional formulations of the faith, say, of the Atonement, and contemporary folk who testify to a feeling of 'metaphysical overload' in respect of these (Rahner 1983, 61).

Thus, there is a structural, institutional or ecclesiastical side to orthodoxy and to change and development. To get an idea of how Augustine Shutte approached this, here is his poem on his visit to Istanbul, in particular to the Haghia Sophia. This reflection is more poignant today as the president of Turkey has resolved to turn the site once again into a mosque. The poem, in contrast, celebrates how tradition—in this case, orthodox Islam—can be 'let go' in favour of a plural, humanist, world.

Haghia Sophia

It is colossal, even now dwarfing all its surrounds,
a dinosaur, survivor of many extinctions, and still alive.

It was built as a church, but by an emperor to be the centre of an empire
that would eclipse Rome. And for a thousand years it was.
He who commissioned it declared himself greater than Solomon
when he saw the work complete. An image of heaven within,
it seemed to reach heaven indeed without—as did the tower of Babel,
or the towers that bore the American dream. But empires rise and fall.
And so do buildings, their domes and altars, their concrete shells
and skeletons of steel. A new empire was born
when Sultan Mehmet rode his horse into the most sacred space
in Christendom. His workmen covered every human face with plaster.
So the wise maiden and her child (as well as their friends) disappeared
till kind Ataturk reminded Christians and Muslims that they were
God's sons and daughters, and that their sibling rivalry
had damaged their favourite toy. So Haghia Sophia,
first a church and then a mosque, became in the end a museum
to hold the history of Europe within its walls and domes.
Its human faces (the wise mother and her child) reappeared
now face to face with scrolls in Arabic from the Koran.
And still, in the East End where once the high altar stood,
the niche remains to point the way to Mecca.

Inside a church one is as if in heaven
peopled by the familiar—trusting and trusted—
figures of one's faith; one feels at home.
Real heaven is not another place
but this world transformed, made beautiful
by God. And Jesus said the time will come
when we will worship God
neither in Samaria nor in Jerusalem
(or Rome or Mecca), neither there nor here,
for God is spirit, not here or there
but everywhere in everything
as that which gives it life and beauty.
So this great space, Haghia Sophia,

an image of heaven, is only an image,
less real than the road that leads there
or you who have just come in.
This is a place that tells the truth:
God is not in this place.

Clarification by contrast—a contemporary example

In an earlier discussion of Shutte's theology, published in the *Stellenbosch Theological Journal* (Giddy, 2020), I took, as a foil for understanding his interpretation of Jesus in the Christian faith, the thesis of scripture scholar Bart Ehrman. In his popular book, *How Jesus Became God* (2014), Ehrman argues that a properly scholarly unpacking of the early development of the Church's understanding of Jesus, that is to say as 'uniquely divine', reveals this development to be unjustified and undermines the central reason for Christian faith. Ehrman's approach illustrates well the problem with 'orthodoxy' as it has developed (incorrectly, in the author's view). This is because Ehrman concludes that it is no longer reasonable to hold with the Christian faith. This is clearly not Shutte's view.

Ehrman's argument can be formulated as a syllogism.

Premise 1: Either Jesus was 'uniquely divine', or he was not.
Premise 2: The former position is the central belief of the Christian religion.
Premise 3: If the latter position is true, the central belief of the Christian religion is false.
Premise 4: But the idea of the divinity of Jesus can be shown to be based on very weak grounds.
Conclusion: The central belief of Christianity is false.

The major part of his book is concerned with showing the reasonableness of Premise 4, that the grounds for thinking Jesus is divine are very weak. But it is the first premise, we can now see, that is problematic. This 'uniquely divine' characterization of Jesus amounts to the idea that he shares God's spirit in a way we do not and cannot. To deny this, seems to put oneself outside the frame of Christianity.

Ehrman gives a series of arguments for doubting the truth of the 'uniquely divine' status of Jesus. For example, the notion that Jesus was divine, he argues, was written into the text by people 'who already 'knew' that Jesus had been exalted to heaven.' (Ehrman 2014: 206)

Again, the formulation of Jesus' divinity at the Council of Nicaea was pushed through by the emperor Constantine in the interests of unity in the Empire. The ultimate explanation for taking Jesus as divine, he argues, has to do with the Roman cultural background to the writing of the early texts. For the Romans, there were many gradations of god, Jesus could at first have been thought of unproblematically as a bit god-like. There was 'a kind of pyramid of power, grandeur, and deity' (2014: 40). The problem arose with the notion, after the fourth century CE, of the generally unbridgeable chasm between being god-like and being human-like (2014: 43). Jesus has, now, to be one or the other.

There is much that can be disputed in these points. But even if the grounds for doubting the validity of taking Jesus as divine are sound, Ehrman's conclusion does not necessarily follow, namely that the Christian faith is thereby fatally undermined. We can, with Ehrman, trace how the followers formulated their understanding of the place Jesus had in their lives. But there is a significant difference between exactly what one believes, 'belief that', and the total attitude of the person, of intellect, will, and feeling, 'belief in', that is at issue in religion. Religious faith entails a commitment that has a cognitional dimension but also an emotional element. And this would seem the decisive element—at least this is the import of Augustine Shutte's poems.

Let us suppose that religion is a response to a natural human need, and a (often unrecognized) desire. The god of any religion will be understood as meeting that need and will take its character from how that need is perceived. In a desert the god's main characteristic might be 'bringer of the rain'. Now if we can identify a human need that is not simply cultural but natural, a need that human persons have by nature but cannot of their own fulfil, then we have a basis for judging the various religions. Let us suppose, further, that the difficulties of understanding one's deepest wants, and of living one's life in accordance with them, so as to grow more integrated, and hence generous with oneself, is that need. We suppose, in other words, we have identified an existential impasse. Then the religion cannot be *based* on one's understanding, simply, in other words, 'belief that'. If the 'belief that' is shown to be false (the god does not bring rain, in any meaningful sense of this), it is not necessarily the case that the religion should be dropped by any reasonable person. It might be that one's understanding simply needs further growth. Understanding the limits of one's understanding is clearly part of the religious faith. One was mistaken about the central need giving rise to the religion, a need *by nature* and therefore, in this tradition, created by the god. It does not mean such a central need does not exist. It does mean the religious understanding requires development. This development becomes, in this light, central to the faith. But how is it to proceed?

A secular approach to Christian faith

We have here a clue to what Shutte has described in his notebooks as the 'terrible effects' of taking Jesus to be simply a divine person ('monophysitism'). The natural need to grow as a person, we can suggest, can be met by the beneficial influence of another person, for whom your blocks do not apply, and who shares their self-understanding. For Christians, this salvific intersubjective transaction is identified with the person of Jesus. But we can now see how the mistaken turn in orthodoxy will cause this insight to be blocked.

The further problem has to do with the plural nature of contemporary culture. Orthodoxy now appears as a kind of sectarianism. For orthodoxy, God's presence in Jesus is, as we have seen, taken as of a different kind to his presence in anyone else. What the church signifies to humankind would seem to be a measure of exclusion. But the notion of 'presence' is ambiguous—giving us a way out of such an unhelpful sectarian approach. Shutte writes that, 'from our side,' as it were, God's presence in Jesus is historically definitive. But God is present in us too, and in all persons.

The new kind of understanding—which we can perhaps think of as a revised orthodoxy—is now summarised in this notebook entry:

> In the absolute distinction between creator and creature it is appropriate to see God alone (Father, Word and Spirit) on the one side and Jesus and me and you on the other. We, with Jesus, depend on, cling to and move towards God. In the New Testament and in Eastern Christianity, this is the basic pattern: prayer to the Father, with and through the Son, and in the Holy Spirit. It is never prayer to, or life towards three persons each of whom are equally God.

The broad Christian tradition, then, needs a discerning eye; there are elements of truth alongside other elements which block a true Christian spirituality. This point places one's theological discussion within the context of a self-consciously critical membership of the Church.

How then does Jesus save us? In the *Stellenbosch Theological Journal* article referred to above, I introduced at this point Shutte's original (so far as I am aware) way of understanding this, having to do with an impasse in any person's personal growth towards self-understanding and self-donation—and hence in the conditions for personal community. It is a fully secular way of understanding salvation through Jesus. It is linked to the intersubjective conditions pertaining to any person's being and acting.

Now, taking my cue from Shutte's self-critical judgment on his own theology—a theology amounting in effect to an idol—I turn to an image that, to me, does the same work. The impasse spoken of in Shutte's analysis of the human condition—the sense of disempowerment—may very well be symbolized, and summed up, in our anxiety about our own death. In the following poem Shutte speaks of his awareness of his coming death, for some time he had been aware of the incurable nature of the cancer that had been diagnosed in him. He is on a voyage around Cape Horn, and finds hope, mysteriously, in a person he encounters in the remote South American town.

Ushuaia—El fin del mundo

I believe death is a mystery, as mysterious as life itself.
We must not pretend we know its meaning;
the encephalograph's straight line means nothing.
My voyage south, down the coast of Patagonia,
gave me at least a symbol of the meaning
death gives to life—and life to death.
The albatross that flies too far from land dies in the sea.

Cape Horn is Earth's southernmost point
before Antarctica's ground zero.
As we approached it at night by sea,
(temperature minus ten, wind hurricane force four)
I saw in the dark my own death approaching.

Antarctica, not Cape Horn, is the true end of the world–
real death, no symbol. But the barrenness of sea and land,
and the darkness of our southward course,
and especially the cold,
faced me with death, my death, my loss of self.

In some agony I turned,
not away but inward.
I entered death
and there found beauty waiting.
Ahead, in Ushuaia's single street, still slept the simple soul
destined to give death a face for me.
At dawn Ushuaia's sunny snow-strewn slopes and curving shores,
as with loving arms, opened to receive me.
Its young priest was glad to welcome me to his domain.

His domain? His was a world-wide Order,
a world-wide web of *agape* that made the world his home.
Warsaw, Buenos Aires, Ushuaia—
here in his little church he showed me his new altar-piece:
Jesus, alive and strong, was smashing through
a looking-glass (in which I stood reflected)
bringing life in death to life—in me.

Seeing Jesus in this way as a model for God's action in the world and symbol for us of our own participation, links in with a secular culture.

Conclusion

By way of conclusion, I choose the following very personal poem, directed at God, with its declaration of need and also its indication of hope. The negative and the positive cadences found in the original psalm are cast afresh in this personal appropriation of the prayer.

My psalm 22

My God, my God, why have you forsaken me?
You are far from my plea and the cry of my distress.
O my God, I call by day and you give me no reply;
I call by night and I find no peace.

Yet you, O God, are goodness itself.
It was you in whom Jesus put his trust.
Trusted in you even on the cross
and through his death you gave him life
eternal life with you.

But I am not Jesus, not a good man.
People think nothing of me, think little of my faith.
'If his faith is real, why is he such a failure?
His religion is only a sign of his weakness.'

But I know it was you who gave me life.
And it was you who all my life has helped me to grow
blessed me with the love of friends
lit the fire of faith within my heart
and kept it alive in spite of doubt and fear.

For I do doubt. Those who write me off
have authority behind them, and common sense.
Sometimes I feel quite alone, an outsider
to the multitude of true believers
and cast off by those on whom I depend.

Do not leave me quite alone my God:
All my courage and my strength
And what faith I have, comes from you.

If you give me something of the insight
the knowledge of you, your own true Word
you gave to Jesus, something of the inspiration
of your Spirit you gave to him,
then I can hope to be a true son of yours.

As a second conclusion, I want to turn again to how symbols operate in any person's imaginative and effective life of faith. These would operate alongside the orthodox Christian symbols of cross, resurrection, and so on. They are nonetheless the matter of any person's orientation towards the authentic virtue of hope. In this poem, the image of hope in Shutte's imaginative life draws on another Christian poet influential in Shutte's intellectual world. Hope is found in the spontaneous optimism of the child. The context of the poem is self-explanatory.

Radiation

I once met TS Eliot.
Suited and tied, he stood amidst the glass-stained shadows
of St Stephen's church and handed me an English Hymnal
and a Book of Common Prayer.

In the sun outside the hospital
I peer through the hedge at the school
and the playing-fields where my children played.
Though in London or Liechtenstein, they are there
on the far side of the hedge, and I smile.

It is as with the Eucharist, where one is part
of an unnumbered multitude. And kneels
beside one's dear dead ones, and feels at home.
I heard the children's voices from the field
beside the hospital and thought they spoke of me.

I know they know about my visits to this place,
and sometimes when I am alone—though not alone–
in the dark chamber with its radiance,
radiance of creation to heal or to destroy,
I feel close to everyone I ever knew
and, of course, to them.

Bibliography

Shutte, A

1970 'Salvation as *Oop Gesprek*', in *New Blackfriars*, 51: 572–577.

1971 'The Human Meaning of Religion. An Enquiry into the Possibility of the Translation of Christian Faith into Secular Language with Special Reference to Kant and Hegel.' MA Thesis, University of Stellenbosch.

1976 'Religious Laws: The Christian Problem', in *Journal of Theology for Southern Africa*, 15:39–48.

1979 'Indwelling, Intersubjectivity, and God', in *Scottish Journal of Theology*, 32: 201–216.

1982 'A Philosophy of the Human Person for Contemporary Theology', in *Journal of Theology for Southern Africa*, 41:70–77.

1982 'Spirituality and Intersubjectivity. A Philosophical Understanding of the Relation between the Spiritual Nature of Persons and Basic Structures of Intersubjectivity'. Ph.D. thesis, University of Stellenbosch.

1984 'Seeing Life as the Creation of Character', in *New Blackfriars*, 65:180–184.

1984 'What Makes Us Persons?', in *Modern Theology*, 1:67–179.

1986 'How Jesus Saves Us', in *Journal of Theology for Southern Africa*, 55:3–14.

1987 'A New Argument for the Existence of God', in *Modern Theology*, 3: 157–177.

1987 'Community, Apartheid and the Metaphysics of Humanity in Genesis 1–11', in *Philosophy and Theology*, 2:57–75.

1992 'The Possibility of Faith Today', in *Journal of Theology for Southern Africa*, 80:14–23.

1993 *The Mystery of Humanity.* Cape Town: Snailpress.

1993 *Philosophy for Africa*. Cape Town: University of Cape Town Press

1996 'The Great Story' (in nine chapters), *Trefoil Magazine.*

1998 'Euthenasia and the Theology of Death', in *Journal of Theology for Southern Africa*, 102:61–69.

2001 *Ubuntu. An Ethic for a New South Africa*. Pietermaritzburg: Cluster Publications.

2006 'Evil and the Christian Response', in C du Toit (editor) *Can Nature be Evil or Evil Natural?* Pretoria: UNISA Research Institute for Theology and Religion: 39–70.

2006 (editor) *The Quest for Humanity in Science and Religion: The South African Experience.* Pietermaritzburg: Cluster Publications.

2008 'Telling the Christian Story—by Karl Rahner and me', in *Scriptura*, 98:156–173.

2010 'Evolution and Emergence. A Paradigm Shift for Theology', in *Philosophy and Theology*, 22:235–264.

2017 *The Way Home. Poems for the Human Spirit*, edited by A Neale-Shutte *et al* Cape Town: Kirkwood Press.

No date. Notebooks. Unpublished.

Other References

Aquinas. 1963- *Summa Theologiae.* 60 Volumes. Latin text with English translations and notes by members of the English Province of the Dominican Fathers. London: Blackfriars.

Aquinas. 1995. *On Evil* (translated by J Oesterle) Notre Dame: University of Notre Dame Press.

Aquinas. 1975. *Summa Contra Gentiles*. London: University of Notre Dame Press.

Altizer, T. 1966. *The Gospel of Christian Atheism.* London: Westminster.

Augustine. 2003. *City of God.* Penguin Classics.

Augustine. 1961. *Confessions*. Penguin Classics.

Bettenson, H. 1956. *The Early Christian Fathers.* Oxford: Oxford University Press.

Blondel, M. 1893. *L'Action*. Paris: Alcun.

Brink, H. *et al* 1952–8. *Theologische Woordenboek*. Roermond: JJ Roman en Zonen.

Casel, O. [1932] 1962. *The Mystery of Christian Worship*. London: Darton, Longman and Todd.

Clark R. 1984. *The Survival of Charles Darwin: A Biography of a Man and an Idea* London: Weidenfeld and Nicholson.

Cullmann, O. 1959. *Early Christian Worship*. London: SCM

Davies, B. 1993. *An Introduction to the Philosophy of Religion*. London: Oxford.

De Klerk, WA, Degenaar, JJ, and Versfeld, M. 1969. *Beweging Uitwaarts*, Cape Town: John Malherbe.

Didache. 1987. In *Early Christian Writings*. Edited by A Louth, translated by M Staniforth. Penguin Classics.

Dix, Dom G. 1945. *The Shape of the Liturgy*. London: Dacre Press.

Ehrman, B. 2014. *How Jesus Became God*. New York: HarperOne.

Eliade, M. 1958. *Patterns in Comparative Religion*. London: Sheed and Ward.

Eliade, M. 1960. *Myths, Dreams and Mysteries*. London: Harvill Press.

Ellis, G. 1993. *Before the Beginning*. London: Boyars/Bowerdean.

Flannery, A. (editor) 1975. *The Documents of Vatican II*. New York: Pillar Books.

Gallagher, K. 1972. 'Self and Other: the Radical A Priori', in *International Philosophical Quarterly*, 12: 5–18.

Gallez, J-P. 2017. 'Réfonder l'Eglise: l'appel de J. Moingt à tous les baptisés.' Talk to CCBF. [Online]. Available: http://www.baptises.fr/sites/default/files/document/ccbf-21.10.17-jp_gallez

Galtier, P. 1939. *L'Unité de Christ: Être, Personne, Conscience*. Paris: Chez Beauchesne.

Giddy, P. 2020. 'Christian Faith and Unorthodox Belief', in *Stellenbosch Theological Journal*, 6: 275–293.

Gilson, E. 1957. *The Christian Philosophy of St Thomas Aquinas*. London: Gollancz.

Haight, R. 2005. *The Future of Christology*. New York: Continuum.

Haight, R. 2019. *Faith and Evolution. A Grace-filled Naturalism*. New York: Orbis Books.

Hegel, GWF. 1970. *Early Theological Writings*. Chicago: University of Chicago Press.

Hegel, GWF. 1962. *Lectures on the Philosophy of Religion*. 3 Volumes. New York: The Humanities Press.

Heron, J. 1970. 'The Phenomenology of Social Encounter: The Gaze', in *Philosophy and Phenomenological Research*, 10: 243–264.

Hick, J. 1970. *Evil and the God of Love*. London: Collins.

Hick, J. 1982. *God Has Many Names*. New Ed. Westminster: John Knox Press.

Johann, R. 1954. *The Meaning of Love*. New York: Paulist.

Jung, K. [1938] 1960. *Psychology and Religion*. New Haven: Yale University Press.

Jung, K. 1964. *Man and his Symbols*. London: Picador.

Jungmann, J. 1951. *Mass of the Roman Rite*. New York: Benziger Brothers.

Kant, I. 2008. *Religion Within the Limits of Reason Alone*. Torchbooks.

Keller, H. 1936. *The Story of My Life*. Doubleday.

Kellogg, W. and Kellogg, L. 1933. *The Ape and the Child*, New York: McGraw-Hill.

Langer, S. [1942] 1984. *Philosophy in a New Key*. Cambridge, Ma.: Harvard University Press.

Lash, N. 1968. *His Presence in the World*. London: Sheed and Ward.

Lawrence, DH. 1931. *Apropos of Lady Chatterley's Lover*. London: Penguin

Léon-Dufour, X. 1982. 'Mystery', in Léon-Dufour (ed.) *Dictionary of Biblical Theology*. London: Geoffrey Chapman.

Lewis, CS. 1947. *Miracles*. London: Bles.

Mackey, J. 2006. *Christianity and Creation*. New York: Continuum.

Macmurray, J. 1957. *The Self as Agent*. London: Faber.

Macmurray, J. 1961. *Persons in Relation*. London: Faber.

McCabe, H. [1964] 2010. *The New Creation*. London: Continuum.

McCabe, H. [1968] 2003. *Law, Love and Language*. London: Continuum.

McQuarrie, J. 1970. *God-Talk*. London: SCM.

Meissner W. 1966. *Foundations for a Psychology of Grace*. New York: Paulist Press.

Merleau-Ponty, M. 1964. *Signs*. Evanston, Ill: Northwestern University Press.

Moingt, J. 2010. *Croire Comme Même*. Paris: Editions Poche.

Moltmann, J. 1967. *Theology of Hope: on the ground and implications of a Christian eschatology*. London: SCM.

Moore, S. 1968. *No Exit*. London: Darton, Longman and Todd.

Moore, S. 1985. *Let This Mind Be in You*. London: Darton, Longman and Todd.

Nedoncelle, M. 1942. *La Réciprocité des Consciences*. Paris: Aubier.

Nedoncelle, M. 1968. *Love and the Person*. New York: Sheed and Ward.

Ott, L. 1952. *Fundamentals of Catholic Dogma*. Cork: Mercier.

Pieper, J. 1968. *Death and Immortality*. London: Faber.

Plato. 1994. *Gorgias*. London: Oxford University Press.

Powers, J. 1974. *Eucharistic Theology.* New York: Seabury.

Rahner, H. 1963. *Greek Myths and Christian Mysteries*. Biblo-Moser.

Rahner, K. 1963. '*Theos* in the New Testament', in Rahner, *Theological Investigations I* (edited by C Ernst) London: Darton, Longman and Todd: 79–148.

Rahner K. 1965. *Hominisation: The Evolutionary Origin of Man as a Theological Problem*. London: Burns and Oates.

Rahner K. 1965. *The Theology of Death* London: Burns and Oates.

Rahner, K . 1966. *The Church and Sacraments.* London: Burns and Oates.

Rahner, K. 1966. 'On the Theology of the Incarnation', in Rahner, *Theological Investigations.* Volume IV. Baltimore: Helicon Press: 105–120.

Rahner, K. 1966. 'Theology of the Symbol', in Rahner, *Theological Investigation.* Volume IV. Baltimore: Helicon Press: 221–252.

Rahner, K. 1966. 'The Word and the Eucharist', in Rahner, *Theological Investigations.* Volume IV. Baltimore: Helicon Press: 253–286.

Rahner, K. 1967. 'Reflections on the Unity of the Love of Neighbour and the Love of God', in Rahner, *Theological Investigations.* Volume VI. London: Darton, Longman and Todd: 231–249.

Rahner, K. 1967. *The Christian of the Future.* London: Burns and Oates.

Rahner, K. 1968. *Spirit in the World.* London: Herder and Herder.

Rahner, K. 1969. *Hearers of the Word.* London: Sheed and Ward.

Rahner, K. 1970. *The Trinity.* London: Burns and Oates.

Rahner, K. 1978. *Foundations of Christian Faith.* London: Darton, Longman and Todd.

Rahner, K. 1983. *The Love of Jesus and the Love of Neighbour.* London: St Paul Publications.

Rahner, K. 1985. *The Practice of Faith.* London: SCM Press.

Robinson, J. 1963. *Honest to God.* London: SCM.

Russell, RJ., N. Murphy, and W. Stoeger (eds.) 2008. *Scientific Perspectives on Divine Action. Twenty Years of Challenge and Progress*. Vatican City State: Vatican Observatory Publications.

Sartre, J-P. 1969. *Being and Nothingness.* London: Routledge.

Sartre, J-P. 1970. *Existentialism and Humanism.* London: Methuen.

Schillebeecx, E. 1963. *Christ, the Sacrament of Encounter with God.* New York: Sheed and Ward.

Schillebeecx, E. 1952. *De Sacramentele Heilseconomie. Theologische bezinning op S.Thomas' sacramentenleer in het licht van de traditie en van de hedendaagse sacramentsproblematiek*. Antwerp: Nelissen.

Sommerville, JM. 1968. *Total Commitment: Blondel's 'L'Action'*. Washington: Corpus Books.

Stoeger, W. 2008. 'Conceiving Divine Action in a Dynamic Universe', in Russell et al, *Scientific Perspectives on Divine Action*. Vatican City State: Vatican Observatory Publications.

Surin, K. 1986. *Theology and the Problem of Evil*. Oxford: Basil Blackwell.

Swimme, B. 1992. *The Universe Story*. HarperCollins.

Tallon, A. 1979. *Personal Becoming*. The Thomist, 43: 7–177.

Taylor C. 2007. *A Secular Age*. Cambridge: Harvard.

Teilhard de Chardin, P. 1959. *The Phenomenon of Man*. London: Collins.

Teilhard de Chardin, P. 1960. *Le Milieu Divin*. London: Collins.

The Catechism of the Council of Trent. [1566]. Catecheticsonline.com/Trent

Tilley, T. 2002. *The Evils of Theodicy*. Washington, DC: Georgetown University Press.

Tillich, P. [1951] 1973. *Systematic Theology* Vol. I Chicago: University of Chicago Press.

Van den Bussche, H. 1963. *The Lord's Prayer*. London: Sheed and Ward.

Van den Bussche, H. 1967. *The Gospel of the Word*. Chicago: Priory.

Ver Eecke, W. 1975. 'The Look, the Body and the Other', in D Ihde (editor), *Dialogues in Phenomenology*. The Hague: Nijhoff: 222–246.

Voegelin, E. 1969. *Order and History* Vol. I. New York: Louisiana University Press.

Ward, K. 1991. *A Vision to Pursue*. London: SCM

Williams, C. [1942] 1984. *The Forgiveness of Sins*. London: Eerdmans.

Wilson, C. [1956] 2001 *The Outsider*. London: Phoenix.

Printed in the USA
CPSIA information can be obtained
at www.ICGtesting.com
LVHW091811250724
786322LV00002B/181

9 781923 206366